I0877409

REIMAGINING HUMAN RIGHTS

Selected Titles from the Moral Traditions Series
David Cloutier, Andrea Vicini, SJ, and Darlene Weaver, editors

The Vice of Luxury: Economic Excess in a Consumer Age
David Cloutier

Diverse Voices in Modern US Moral Theology
Charles E. Curran

The Structures of Virtue and Vice
Daniel J. Daly

Consumer Ethics in a Global Economy: How Buying Here Causes Injustice There
Daniel K. Finn

Kinship Across Borders: A Christian Ethic of Immigration
Kristin E. Heyer

Keeping Faith with Human Rights
Linda Hogan

Humanity in Crisis: Ethical and Religious Response to Refugees
David Hollenbach, SJ

The Fullness of Free Time: A Theological Account of Leisure and Recreation in the Moral Life
Conor M. Kelly

Reimagining Human Rights: Religion and the Common Good
William O'Neill, SJ

Hope for Common Ground: Mediating the Personal and the Political in a Divided Church
Julie Hanlon Rubio

Love and Christian Ethics: Tradition, Theory, and Society
Frederick V. Simmons, editor

All God's Animals: A Catholic Theological Framework for Animal Ethics
Christopher Steck, SJ

REIMAGINING HUMAN RIGHTS

Religion and the Common Good

WILLIAM R. O'NEILL

GEORGETOWN UNIVERSITY PRESS / WASHINGTON, DC

© 2021 Georgetown University Press. All rights reserved. No part of this book may be reproduced or utilized in any form or by any means, electronic or mechanical, including photocopying and recording, or by any information storage and retrieval system, without permission in writing from the publisher.

The publisher is not responsible for third-party websites or their content. URL links were active at time of publication.

Library of Congress Cataloging-in-Publication Data

Names: O'Neill, William R., author.
Title: Reimagining human rights : religion and the common good / William R. O'Neill, S.J.
Other titles: Moral traditions series.
Description: Washington, DC : Georgetown University Press, 2021. | Series: Moral traditions | Includes bibliographical references and index.
Identifiers: LCCN 2020006439 | ISBN 9781647120344 (hardcover) | ISBN 9781647120351 (paperback) | ISBN 9781647120368 (ebook)
Subjects: LCSH: Human rights—Moral and ethical aspects. | Human rights. | Social justice. | Common good.
Classification: LCC JC571 .O54 2021 | DDC 323.01—dc23
LC record available at https://lccn.loc.gov/2020006439

∞ This book is printed on acid-free paper meeting the requirements of the American National Standard for Permanence in Paper for Printed Library Materials.

22 21 9 8 7 6 5 4 3 2 First printing

Printed in the United States of America

Cover design by Jeremy John Parker

CONTENTS

PREFACE

In 1995 I served as a visiting professor of social ethics at the Jesuit School of Theology (Hekima) in Nairobi, Kenya. The Beijing Conference on Women's Rights had recently concluded, and a number of seminars and workshops in the city were offered to discuss the plan of action and its implications.[1] One session offered a lively political theater in which young women from the neighboring parish of Kangemi recalled the daily burdens of gender discrimination amid extreme poverty. In the subsequent discussion session I found myself grouped with these young women and several Kenyan professional women. We quickly realized that speaking in English would exclude the women from Kangemi. Yet once we shifted to Kiswahili, something remarkable occurred: they took over the conversation. They spoke of rights, specifically rights not to be treated as chattel in domestic affairs. But it was not merely what they said that so impressed me; it was their saying it. Their rights talk was a performance, giving voice to their story as testimony. They were insisting on their place at the table, their "right to have rights," in Hannah Arendt's terms.

This book is, in many ways, an homage to their wisdom; an homage, too, to the victims I saw testifying in the South African Truth Commission and to the many victims of the Rwandan genocide whom I came to know in my research in Rwanda. For several years in the mid-1970s I cared for young Hutu refugees in Tanzania, victims of ethnic cleansing; now I heard the tales of atrocity of Tutsi victims. As a teenager I visited the concentration camp at Dachau, writing, as many did, "Never again" in the visitors' book of comments. At the Kigali Genocide Memorial in Rwanda, where over 250,000 victims of genocide, including children, were buried, I wrote "Never again" again. What did it mean to write that? This book is a humble, first response.

I wish to express my gratitude to the University of San Francisco's Lane Center and Prof. Erin Brigham, for offering me the Lo Schiavo Chair in support of my research in 2018–19; and to the Loyola House Jesuit Community in Nairobi, where I completed my writing. Three faculty seminars at the US Holocaust Memorial (in 2009, 2016, and 2018) provided invaluable background for my study of religion and genocide. I am indebted to Al Bertrand and Elizabeth Crowley Webber of Georgetown University Press editorial staff, Caroline Crossman, marketing coordinator, the Moral Traditions series editors, and the external reviewers for their support and encouragement throughout. I wish to thank Ann Baker in particular for her careful copyediting, which contributed so much to the book. Above all I remain grateful to my friends and colleagues who accompanied me and the refugees, prisoners, and victims of atrocity, whose wisdom and courage inspired this work.

NOTE

1. See United Nations Women, "Beijing Declaration and Platform for Action."

Introduction

> Even now they have not found the mouth with which to tell of their suffering.
>
> —Chinua Achebe, *Things Fall Apart*

In the new millennium, all the world is a market—a complex, globalized network of economic, social, and cultural interdependence. Yet the millennial promise of the global household (*oikoumenē*) remains elusive. Over half a century of solemn declarations decrying genocide and crimes against humanity has not spared us further atrocities. Walter Benjamin's *Angelus Novus*, the "angel of history," still presides over "wreckage upon wreckage."[1] And even here we prove ourselves Babel's worthy children, differing not only over what we say is just or unjust but over the very meaning of our differences.

Will we speak of human rights, and if so, which rights? Or is such talk mere "rhetorical nonsense"—"nonsense on stilts," as Bentham famously put it?[2] Such "nonsense," though, remains a stubborn inheritance. Indeed, the popular use of *rights* seems undeterred by the lack of a clear foundation. When young women of Kangemi in Nairobi, Kenya, invoke a right against domestic abuse, insisting on their rightful "place" in society, they are not, after all, entering the theoretical lists. Rather, they are making sense of human rights precisely as rhetoric, that is, speech aimed at persuasion and conviction.[3] As Bertolt Brecht might say, rights before ethics.[4]

Still, ethics has a place in clarifying the grammar of rights. The long, contentious history of rights belies any genealogical *hubris* in favoring a single rhetorical use. Even "self-evident" rights have a history. Yet for many scholarly critics and partisans alike, one use predominates: natural, subjective rights will always be the stepchild of Enlightenment rationalism, the cultural legacy of the liberal bourgeoise protecting, in Jürgen Habermas's words, "a neutral sphere of personal [self-interested] choice."[5] For Jack Donnelly such rights are a modern invention, emerging only with the bourgeois revolution of the seventeenth and eighteenth centuries.[6] So, too, for critics. Apologists for a divine "right order" dismiss natural rights as the coin of a disenchanted realm, while communitarian, postmodern, and postcolonial theorists echo Karl Marx's critique of "the supposed rights of man," none of which "go beyond the egoistic man . . . ; that is, an individual separated from the community, withdrawn into himself, wholly preoccupied with his private interest and acting in accordance with his private caprice."[7]

Still, the *cris d'coeur* against genocide, apartheid, ethnic cleansing—these are not mere tokens of private interest or private caprice. In the wake of the Shoah, for the many who have suffered and endured, human rights are a stay against atrocity, against forgetting—giving voice to what the preamble to the United Nations' Universal Declaration of Human Rights calls "barbarous acts which have outraged the conscience of [hu]mankind."[8] Neither can the popular resistance of the civil rights movement in the United States or South Africa's anti-apartheid struggle be understood simply as an apology for secular, bourgeois liberalism. Belief in the biblical "*imago dei* (image of God)," says Archbishop Desmond Tutu, "fired our own struggle against apartheid."[9]

Recent studies trace the origins of subjective natural rights to late twelfth-century canonical jurisprudence, so that the modern, individualistic notion appears already as a translation.[10] Rights have not descended from Kant's empyrean, nor even from the "semantic revolution" Michel Villay discerned in Ockham's nominalist epistemology. Antedating the "more egotistical impulses of early modern capitalism," our rights rhetoric, says Brian Tierney, "grew from good seed," and there is the prospect that it will "continue to bring forth fruit."[11] In embracing basic human rights, Tierney argues, we preserve not only "what is best in our tradition" but allow for new fruit to be born in the working of tradition—what Jacques Derrida, following Benjamin, calls the "growth of the original."[12] It is this growth I wish to explore as it comes to fruition in victims' stories, including testimony given at the South African Truth and Reconciliation Commission (TRC).

We have learned much from liberal jurisprudence in parsing claim-rights, immunities, privileges, passive and active rights, and so on; to its theorists I am indebted. But the use of rights by victims and their advocates—in "telling the story," in the words of Lukas Baba Sikwepere, who was blinded in a brutal police attack and later tortured in Cape Town—invites us to imagine otherwise. Rights are not merely powers or properties of sovereign selves "squatting outside the world"; nor, in the first instance, do rights comprise a legal regime or the juridification of rhetoric.[13] Rather, in testimony rights become a grammar of dissent, a mouth to tell of suffering; rights exist under the sign of their negation: at once general, when, as in genocide or apartheid, the victims are legion but always, ineluctably particular.

What would theory look like if, reversing the hermeneutical flow, we began with "telling the story"? Regnant liberal theory and rival communitarian and postmodern critiques bequeath us a series of oppositions or, more precisely, antinomies: we must, it seems, opt for the politics of rights or of the common good, a "thin" formal or "thick" narrative justification, a sacred or secular rhetoric. But neither liberalism nor its critics, I will argue, adequately account for the "growth of the original"—what victims of atrocity and their advocates *do* with rights.[14] Theory, like ethics, comes next: modern hermeneutic theory draws upon rhetoric (in elaborating the "concrete universality" of Aristotelian *phronēsis*), and I will follow suit, arguing in the following chapters for a rhetorical rapprochement of each of the foregoing antimonies.[15]

Chapter 1 offers a reconstructive interpretation of rights as observed in the testimony by victims of the Rwandan genocide and South Africa's apartheid regime, illumining the novelty of such use against our inherited theoretical background. Victims' testimony belies a simple opposition of the politics of individual rights in liberal theory and the politics of the common good in narrative tradition—rival rhetorics that leave little place for a narrative of rights, whether in the TRC or, as we shall see, in the tradition of modern Catholic social teaching. In the Human Rights Committee of the TRC stories speak *as* testimony, elucidating, in Edward Said's words, what the dominant powers have "silenced or rendered unpronounceable."[16] Here, then, is the first, indispensable role of rights: "coming here and telling you the story." In anamnestic solidarity with history's victims, rights reveal what has been silenced: history, in Benjamin's words, as remembrance.[17]

Just so, in revealing transgression, memory speaks *as* command, binding *us* here and now. As testimony in the TRC is woven into collective memory, the critical (deconstructive) role of rights becomes a clearing within which new stories can be told (the constructive hermeneutic role). Yet the cri de coeur of "never again" is never fully redeemed. The legal instantiation of a rights regime, such as that within the International Criminal Court, remains partial, incremental, and itself subject to critique. Still, there is the fitting measure to be taken of retribution, reparation, and redress for victims (the reconstructive role). Such a threefold hermeneutic of rights in the play of *recognizing, redeeming,* and *redressing* claims may well seem odd, if not perverse, to a Western ear accustomed to the "strident language of rights" dividing "mine" and "thine"—but it is far from rhetorical nonsense.[18]

In chapter 2 I take up the criticism that such persuasion is necessarily "local and ethnocentric," as in Richard Rorty's words, bound to "the tradition of a particular community, the consensus of a particular culture."[19] For critics like Rorty the thin, liberal metanarrative of rights is empty. But so, too, as liberal theorists like John Rawls and Habermas might retort, thick communitarian narratives of virtue, as in the religious legitimation of apartheid, are blind. Thinking of rights as narrative grammar, though, offers a via media. Testimony is not so much talk about rights (in formal jurisprudence) as it is the talk that rights makes possible. Telling the story from below is marked not by abstract right but by communicative virtues: virtues that sustain a sense of anamnestic solidarity across differing narratives, so that the Weberian choice of ethical systems is itself ethically encumbered. Here dignity appears in local garb performed in the telling; we need not keep our metaphysics warm by recurring to the abstract ideal of an unencumbered, prediscursive subject.

Our interpretation, then, has something to teach critic and partisan alike. Whether and in what sense the lesson is religious is the topic of chapter 3. Assessing the surplus of religious, and specifically Christian, meaning in rights rhetoric, I contend that religious belief figures in public reasoning not only by narratively embodying claim-rights but by transforming the communicative virtues that are analyzed in chapter 2. What William James would call the cash value of these remarks is evident in both the ethical and the religious implications of taking the victims' side in social-ethical discourse—what liberation theology and modern Catholic social teaching call the "option for the poor."[20]

In chapter 4 I look to the fruits of my inquiry by revisiting the themes of the previous chapters. What can we learn from the threefold hermeneutic of rights (chapter 1) as narrative grammar (chapter 2) displayed in both sacred and secular rhetoric (chapter 3)? For Archbishop Tutu the lesson is restorative—rights figuring in "the healing of breaches, the redressing of imbalances, the restoration of broken relationships."[21] This is the learning I want to underscore in offering a critical assessment of the place of basic rights in justice theory generally and in three issues of applied ethics in particular. I first look to the rapprochement of the politics of rights and of the common good in a restorative critique of race and mass incarceration in the United States; then I extend my critique internationally to the politics of immigration and refugee policy. Finally, I consider the religious integration of what Pope Francis recently called the "cry of the poor" and the "cry of the earth" in a "new humanism" of intergenerational responsibility and duties to the nonhuman world. Just as we need not plump down for either the politics of rights or of the common good, nor choose between a thin secular morality of abstract rights or a thick narrative of ethics, so we need not oppose the cry of the earth to the cry of the poor. Here, where rights rhetoric lives on in transforming itself, we may reappropriate the original—grown and enriched in translation, as a mouth to tell of suffering, yes, but also of terrible beauty.[22]

NOTES

Epigraph: Achebe, *Things Fall Apart*, 162. Achebe's title is drawn from William Butler Yeats's poem "The Second Coming."

1. Walter Benjamin, "Theses on the Philosophy of History," in Benjamin, *Illuminations*, 257–58.
2. Jeremy Bentham, "Anarchical Fallacies," in Bentham, *Works*, 523.
3. Chaïm Perelman, *The Realm of Rhetoric*, 5, 14, 17–18. Rhetoric is "not limited to formally correct inferences" but rather, in Chaïm Perelman's words, it distinguishes "discourse that aims at persuasion and conviction" (5).
4. A play on Bertolt Brecht's quip in *The Threepenny Opera*: "*Erst kommt das Fressen Dann kommt die Moral*" ("Grub first, then ethics").
5. Habermas, *Theory and Practice*, 84; see also Habermas, *Between Facts and Norms*, 28–45, 100–105.
6. Donnelly, *Universal Human Rights*, 86–88.
7. Wolterstorff, "Modern Protestant Developments in Human Rights," 156; Karl Marx, "On the Jewish Question," in Marx, *The Marx-Engels Reader*, 43.
8. UN, Universal Declaration of Human Rights, UNGA Res. 217A (III), 3(1)UN GAOR Res. 71, U.N. Doc. A/810 (1948).
9. Tutu, "The First Word," 5.
10. Tierney, *The Idea of Natural Rights*, 13–89; Tierney, "Natural Law and Natural Rights"; Tierney, "Church Law and Alternative Structures." See also Brett, *Liberty, Right and Nature*.
11. Tierney, *The Idea of Natural Rights*, 347. See Glendon, *A World Made New*.
12. Tierney, *The Idea of Natural Rights*, 347; Derrida, "Des Tours de Babel." Commenting on Walter Benjamin's "The Task of the Translator," Derrida writes, "The translation will truly be a moment in the growth of the original, which will complete itself *in* enlarging itself" (188, italics in the original).
13. Marx, *The Marx-Engels Reader*, 43. On rhetoric, see Freeman, *Human Rights*.
14. See Sandel, "Introduction," 4, 6, 10. For women's critical role in producing "local knowledge" of rights, see Sunder, "Keeping Faith," and Grabe, *Women's Human Rights*.
15. See Gadamer, *Truth and Method*, 19–30.
16. Said, "Nationalism, Human Rights, and Interpretation," 45–46.
17. Walter Benjamin, "Theses on the Philosophy of History," in Benjamin, *Illuminations*, 253–64. See Lenhardt, "Anamnestic Solidarity," and Pensky, "Solidarity with the Past and the Work of Translation."
18. Glendon, *Rights Talk*, x.
19. Rorty, "The Priority of Democracy to Philosophy," 259.
20. James, *Pragmatism*, 31–32.
21. Tutu, *No Future without Forgiveness*, 51.
22. I refer to Yeats's "Easter, 1916" in Yeats, *Collected Poems*, 250–52.

CHAPTER ONE

Interpreting Rights

When sufferings become unendurable the cries are no longer heard. The cries, too, fall like rain in summer.

—Bertolt Brecht

The killings began on the evening of Easter Wednesday, April 6, 1994, and continued for three months. By the end over eight hundred thousand Tutsis as well as Hutus who opposed the genocide were massacred. Between that second week of April and the third week of May it is estimated that the daily rate of killing was at least five times that of the Nazi death camps. Three-quarters of the Rwandese Tutsi population fell victim to the genocide; the elderly, children, the infirm—none were spared. Nor was there haven. The churches, formerly offering sanctuary, were the first places attacked.[1] In their environs "more Rwandese citizens died . . . than anywhere else."[2] The horror was unmitigated but not inexplicable, for the killing was due less to atavistic enmity than to a racist mythology nurtured in the colonial period and abetted by Belgian and later French realpolitik.[3] Although favoring elite interests, the totalizing myth of Hutu supremacy divested the imagined "other" of moral standing so that the massacres by the Interahamwe (the militia) seemed banal.[4] In a perverse inversion of Emmanuel Lévinas's dictum, neighbor refused to see the neighbor's face upon which was inscribed the command "Thou shalt not kill."[5] So, too, members of the United Nations Security Council refused to acknowledge the Rwandan killings as genocide lest they incur legal obligations under the Convention on the Prevention and Punishment of the Crime of Genocide to which they were signatories. At the behest of the United States, United Nations peacekeeping troops in Rwanda (UNIMIR) were summarily withdrawn, along with all foreign nationals.[6] Others were left to die.

Yet mere wretchedness, Albert Camus reminds us, is not tragedy.[7] Whether we see these cruelest months as morally tragic or merely an unimportant failure of realpolitik depends upon evoking what was effaced: bringing to word the transgressed command. And *recognizing* the nature, force, and scope of victims' claims, as I noted in the introduction, is the first, indispensable critical or deconstructive role of rights.[8] Yet memory speaks, I will argue, as command in the solidarity of remembrance, through what Benjamin calls anamnestic solidarity: the constructive role of rights.[9] Here the interpretative burden shifts to identifying correlative duties and duty-bearers in *redeeming* claim-rights. Finally, the deconstructive and constructive uses combine in a hermeneutic of reconstructive *redress*. For the denial of rights leaves moral traces, such as in victims' claims to repentance or reparation. As we shall see, these distinct yet finally inseparable uses of rights configure not only the legal/juridical and ethical but also the religious interpretation of rights. Indeed, our differences regarding the fit of these terms explain, in part, why social reconciliation remains such a vexed issue. Desmond Tutu's pleas for "confession, forgiveness and reconciliation in the lives of nations" meet with his fellow Nobel laureate Wole Soyinka's objection, that justice is ill served by "discharging the guilty without evidence of mitigation—or remorse."[10]

How, then, can the exigent demands of individual rights be reconciled with "the healing of breaches, the redressing of imbalances, the restoration of broken relationships"?[11] Must we choose between the "politics of [individual] rights" and the "politics of the common good" in restorative justice?[12] Or is Tutu's appeal to *Ubuntu*—the fusing of liberal justice and communitarian solidarity—merely a religious bricolage of incommensurable warrants and backings? As will be shown, any rapprochement must take seriously the genealogy of our differences. For it is only against the inherited theoretical background that the originality of Tutu's translation appears. Let me first, then, offer a brief genealogy of our rival rhetorics and then elaborate the threefold use of rights at play in "telling the story." I conclude with a brief response to several salient criticisms of rights rhetoric.

I. A GENEALOGY OF DIFFERENCE

Natural rights, it seems, are the currency of modernity—the coin of a disenchanted realm. The "ultimate and most sublime values have retreated from public life," wrote Max Weber, while our fragmented values (a demystified polytheism) succeed to the "grandiose moral fervor of Christian ethics."[13] With the eclipse of the religiously inspired ideal of the common good, the liberties of the moderns reign supreme.[14] Grotius's modern heirs speak not of the divine finality of natural law (the *jus naturale* of the medievals) but of the natural, inalienable, and sacred rights of man.[15] So it is for partisans and critics alike: the Western effective history of rights begins with what Jürgen Habermas calls the "positivization" (*Positivierung*) of the classical *jus naturale* of modernity. Civic virtue gives way to "a neutral sphere of personal choice" in which, as Mandeville put it, private vice makes public virtue.[16]

Recent historiography, as noted in the introduction, belies the secular myth of origins. In his magisterial treatise Brian Tierney contends that the origins of subjective natural rights in late twelfth-century canonical jurisprudence betrayed little of the "atomic individualism" of the "more egotistical impulses of early modern capitalism." The use of rights was not "necessarily opposed to the communitarian values of traditional societies. Nor was the idea dependent on any particular version of Western philosophy; rather, it coexisted with a variety of philosophies, including the religiously oriented systems of the medieval era and the secularized doctrines of the Enlightenment."[17] Indeed, as we shall see, the originality of Tutu's translation of rights in the South African TRC—one not beholden to the antinomies of modern liberal theory—rests in part on recovering the communitarian values of traditional societies, including the religiously oriented ideal of Ubuntu as expressed in victims' narrative testimony.[18] Yet the history of rights is also a history of forgetting. The secularized doctrines of the Enlightenment set the stage for our (post)modern rhetorical rivalries: variations wrung from the modern strain of natural rights and the neo-Hegelian or Aristotelian ethical riposte.[19]

The Liberal Metanarrative

While for Aquinas natural law (*lex naturalis*) preserves "happiness and its parts for the body politic," for modern social-contract theorists, influenced as they are by nominalist legal theory, social obligation is incurred voluntaristically.[20] Divested of its inner teleology, nature, one might say, has ceased to tell a moral tale. For there is, says Hobbes, "no such *Finis Ultimus,* (utmost ayme,) nor *Summum Bonum,* (greatest Good)." Augustine's *cor inquietum* is now but "a continuall progresse of the desire, from one object to another"—the natural *bonum commune* of "the old Morall Philosophers" becomes the war "of every man against every man."[21] In this nominalist vein Hobbes opposes liberty as the "RIGHT OF NATURE" (*Jus Naturale*) "to use his own power, as he will himselfe, for the preservation of his own Nature" to the "LAW OF NATURE, (*Lex Naturalis*)," which "determineth, and bindeth."[22] For, stripped of Grotius's natural sociability, it is "the foresight of their own preservation" that leads men "who naturally love Liberty, and Dominion over others" to submit to "that restraint upon themselves, (in which wee see them live in Common-wealths)."[23] Society is itself a grand artifice, "an Artificiall

Person" created by our mundane fiat.[24] And hence the irony: to attain our mortal ends we must sacrifice our natural right of liberty to the ordained order of Hobbes's "Mortall God," Leviathan.[25]

Locke's state of nature is, by contrast, a relatively peaceable kingdom. Deferring to the "judicious Hooker," Locke grounds nature's civility of mores in our natural equality, from which springs "the obligation to mutual love." Yet the "law of nature" regulating our natural "state of liberty" turns less on Aquinas's (or Richard Hooker's) bonum commune than on the domain of individual, prepolitical rights.[26] For Locke, writes Louis Dupré, "the existence of individual rights precedes that of the community, which previously had been considered the concrete source of right."[27] Private property (even in one's "own person") becomes the regnant metaphor of rights, the preservation and protection of which underwrite the social contract.

Rousseau, too, appeals to the doctrine of a social contract. Yet where Hobbes's *pactum subjectionis* resolves the will of all into the will of one, Rousseau depicts the social bond (*lien social*) as the will's self-limitation; indeed, it is only "with civil society" that we acquire "moral freedom, which alone makes man the master of himself." Pace Hobbes, freedom is found not in slavery to the appetites but in "obedience to a law one prescribes to oneself."[28] Sovereignty arises through a "reciprocal commitment" so that in contracting, "as it were, with himself," each person "finds himself doubly committed, first as a member of the sovereign body in relation to individuals [*souverain*], and secondly as a member of the state [*état*] in relation to the sovereign."[29] Thus it is that the "extravagant shepherd" of Rousseau's *Confessions* justifies the sovereignty of the general will (*volonté général*), at once harking back to the natural rights championed by Locke yet anticipating the Romantic historicization of law as the "general will" of the *Volk*.[30]

Purifying Rousseau's doctrine of the general will, Kant regards the formal generality, or "universal voice," of will as entirely sui generis: the will's transcendental freedom is the "*ratio essendi*" of the moral law. Freedom of the will (*die Willkür*) is internally limited by practical reason itself, the autonomous "self-legislation" of *der Wille*.[31] Expressed in synthetic a priori judgments in the corpus of *Naturrecht*, the categorical imperative abstracts entirely from the realm of prudential experience, formulable in hypothetical imperatives. The original contract, whereby "all (*omnes et singuli*) the people give up their external freedom in order to take it back again immediately as members of a commonwealth, that is, the people regarded as the state (*universi*)," is "a mere idea of reason."[32] Civic virtue, for Kant, is no longer the natural fruition of prudence (Aristotelian phronēsis); rather, it is a rein upon it as the "subjective principle of self-love."[33] The boundaries between morality, as in subjective rights, and [prudential] "self-love" have become "distinct and sharp."[34]

Many variations are worked on this theme of subjective rights as powers or properties of sovereign selves abstracted from the ensemble of natural social relations. Indeed, in modern liberal theory individual rights constitute the ground of mutual obligation, which, A. P. d'Entrèves observes, "would not otherwise exist by the law of nature."[35] Yet recent historiography questions the notion of rights as a grand metanarrative displacing "local, customary or traditional moralities and all forms of transcendental faiths."[36] So, too, do critical racial theorists reveal the inherent moral myopia of racial bias that, in Cornel West's words, "permeated the writings of the major figures of the Enlightenment" (a criticism I shall return to in the final chapter).[37] Indeed, "the dominant discourse of the egoistic, bourgeois self," as the decolonial theorist Upendra Baxi writes, precludes "any intercultural, multicivilizational discourse on the genealogy of human rights."[38] Criticism of the hegemony of modern liberal rights discourse abounds; but the liberal heritage in Anglo-American political philosophy has yet to cede the stage.

In *A Theory of Justice*, for instance, John Rawls recurs to the heuristic device of a social contract in which mutually disinterested agents select the principles of justice under a "veil of ignorance."[39] Fairness is achieved by bracketing agents' knowledge of each other's particular cultural roles, economic status, natural and acquired abilities, and particular desires, goals, and so on—everything that would be "naturally" encompassed within the Aristotelian virtue of civic friendship (*philia*).[40] In Rawls's thought experiment, self-interested choice, under the veil of ignorance, is tantamount to fairness or impartiality once the veil is lifted.[41] Reflecting modernity's skepticism regarding a comprehensive conception of the common good, perfectly prudential agents, says Rawls, would prefer an increment of liberty (immunity from interference) to that of any other social good.[42] In *A Theory of Justice* Rawls claimed that such recognition obtains *sub specie aeternitatis* so that our natural rights are "established independently from social conventions and legal norms."[43] Rawls's defense of liberty in *Political Liberalism*, however, is indebted less to the formal dictates of Kantian morality than to the aims of "the public political culture of a democratic society," such as that seen in "the political institutions of a constitutional regime and the public traditions of their interpretation."[44] Yet if the justification of rights defers to the latent wisdom of democratic public traditions, their interpretation is still beholden to the abstract formalism of Kantian *Moralität*.[45]

Since *we* can no longer appeal to the ethical ideal of a common good as a common end (the very raison d'être of law, human and divine, for Aquinas and indeed for Tutu), our negative rights prevail.[46] Lexical priority is accorded to the familiar liberties "normally protected" in the constitutions of liberal regimes, namely, the claims to "freedom of thought and liberty of conscience; the political liberties and freedom of association, as well as the freedoms specified by the liberty and integrity of the person; and finally, the rights and liberties covered by the rule of law."[47] Rawls's revised theory, though more modest in import, thus commends itself precisely as a resolution of the distinctively modern problem of establishing fair conditions of coexistence for citizens with differing, even incommensurable conceptions of the (common) good.[48] Indeed, the plurality of narrative traditions implies that political reason will be *common* (i.e., shared and public) only if we abstract it from any comprehensive doctrine of the *good*—including a fortiori any religious doctrine. In public reasoning our conception of justice, writes Rawls, "should be, as far as possible, independent of the opposing and conflicting philosophical and religious doctrines that citizens affirm."[49] Religious belief—even the ineluctably social ideal of Ubuntu—is consigned to the sphere of our private or nonpublic reasoning; at best it secures an overlapping consensus, as in Rawls's Kantian constructivism. But religious belief per se remains in the vestibule of public reason, falling under the "veil of ignorance." Our rights talk is disenchanted.[50]

Communitarian Narratives

Even as the banner of rights was raised, however, the modern doctrine itself was called into doubt.[51] The "rights of man," writes Burke, are a "monstrous fiction" spawning anarchy—"false ideas and vain expectations" bringing ruin in their wake.[52] Rights are an "entailed inheritance" resting in the "prejudice" or "latent wisdom" of Englishmen, for we have "given to our frame of polity the image of a relation in blood."[53] Bentham, too, regards rights as "the child of [positive] law." For "from real law come real rights," writes Bentham, "but from imaginary laws, from 'law of nature,' come imaginary rights." "Natural rights" are but "simple nonsense" and "natural and imprescriptible rights, rhetorical nonsense, nonsense upon stilts."[54] For Bentham, as for Burke, natural rights are a dubious progeny, exciting "a spirit of resistance to all laws—a spirit of insurrection against all governments."[55] Still others deplore the want of such a spirit; for Marx the modern doctrine of rights merely enshrines the proprietary interests of the bourgeoisie: "None of the supposed rights of man . . . go beyond the egoistic man, man as he is, as a member of civil society; that is, an individual separated from the community, withdrawn into himself, wholly preoccupied with his private interest and acting in accordance with his private caprice."[56]

No less enamored of such "fictions," Alasdair MacIntyre dismisses the doctrine of "natural or human rights" in our own day as one "with belief in witches and unicorns." For MacIntyre the abstract, rationalist tenor of the politics of individual rights belies its "highly specific and local character." Far from being a bastion against Burkean prejudice, the modern doctrine of individual rights presumes "a socially established set of rules" that "only come into existence at particular historical periods under particular social circumstances."[57] Recalling the Romantic critique of the empty formalism of Kantian morality, such communitarian theorists demur: the self is not "essentially unencumbered."[58] Rather, it is constituted in the ensemble of social relations, that is, the distinctive mores of Hegelian ethics (*Sittlichkeit*), albeit bereft of "Reason's cunning."[59] Knit together by shared history and sentiments, we are embedded within a particular political community and endowed by birthright with a distinctive cultural heritage. Even our cherished liberty "has a pedigree."[60] Not only, say his critics, is Rawls's agent deprived of sufficiently determinate motives for rational choice under the veil of ignorance; the formal constraints of choice, including the veil itself, also depend for their justification upon a richer conception of the good.[61] Rawls's belated gambit of reasoning from within a certain political tradition redeems the incoherence of the original theory, but at the price of adequacy and the putative sublimation of particular social conventions and legal norms. In depicting rights as properties of subjects' abstract identities (what Seyla Benhabib terms the "generalized other"), Rawls has not bracketed agents' cultural horizon so much as tacitly assumed the cultural horizon of the postmodern liberal bourgeoisie.[62]

For Richard Rorty such historicization of liberal theory is the fitting denouement of Rawls's thought experiment. Philosophy holds a mirror, not to nature or natural rights but to our cultural mores, characterizing, in Rawls's words, "a democratic society under modern conditions."[63] To the "thoroughly enlightened" postmodernist, the "natural, inalienable, and sacred rights" of the individual are a supreme fiction. Rorty's "post-modernist bourgeois liberalism" is "one in which no trace of divinity remain[s], either in the form of a divinized world or a divinized self," that is, a self endowed with "objective moral values" or human rights.[64] In Rorty's agnostic piety, rights are redeemed not as self-evident or sacred verities but as "local and ethnocentric" customs—"the tradition of a particular community, the consensus of a particular culture."[65] Rights talk, like edifying discourse generally, is "relative to the group to which we think it is necessary to justify ourselves—to the body of shared belief which determines the reference of the word 'we.'" For Rorty, as for Burke and Bentham, rights are the progeny of positive law—our "latent wisdom" and prejudices. We can no longer, in T. S. Eliot's words, keep "our metaphysics warm."[66] Far from serving as a universal ideal language or a neutral metanarrative in adjudicating cultural narratives, for these postmodern critics the discourse of human rights is revealed to be but one of many *petits récits,* the cultural legacy of the Western bourgeoisie.[67]

Still other variations are worked on the theme of the common good. If postmodern communitarian interpretations hark back to premodern mores or Burkean prejudice, characteristically modern critiques inspired by Bentham and Marx preserve universality at the expense of subjective rights. In its various permutations, utilitarianism defines the common good as the maximum total or average utility, where utility is measured by an impartial aggregation of individual welfare (interests or preferences). The common good thus represents a "benevolent reduction," says Bernard Williams, of "all interests, ideals, aspirations and desires" of disparate agents to the representative preferences, differing only in degree, of a common ascriptive subject, be it R. M. Hare's critically informed "archangel" or a thoroughly rational egoist.[68] As Rawls notes, utilitarianism characteristically adopts "for society as a whole the principle of rational choice" for a single agent.[69] In the utilitarian calculus individual liberties bear only a contingent relationship to the common good: liberty rights are bereft of intrinsic value and may, in consequence, be sacrificed if the sums so dictate.

Where utilitarianism assimilates social choice to individual choice writ large, Hegel's or Marx's conceptions of the common good subordinate the individual to the social good. The common good is not so much an aggregative, welfarist construction as it is a suprapersonal good that is mediated historically: either the state's ethical substance (Hegel) or the collective good of the proletariat as a universal class (Marx).[70] In both instances discrete, subjective preferences and interests derive their moral standing from implicit reference to a superordinate objective good that is only dimly perceived by the individual agent in civil society. Here the methodological individualism characterizing the utilitarian calculus is displaced by a historically mediated collectivism. Yet, as in utilitarianism, the totalizing rhetoric of the common good trumps the individual's negative rights to choose as she sees fit.

A Religious Rapprochement? Roman Catholic Social Teaching

In each of the foregoing variations, whether communitarian, utilitarian, or Marxist, the politics of the common good supersedes the politics of human rights. Yet the genealogy of rights, I argue, is not fixed by liberal interpretations, nor is the antimony bequeathed us in modernity exhaustive. Religiously integrated rights rhetoric preserves a certain rapprochement, which will be considered in greater detail in chapter 3. Still, questions remain as to whether we can pour the new wine of rights into the old wineskins of our distinctive faith traditions. The Roman Catholic Church's belated rapprochement with liberal modernity is illustrative.

From its inception with Leo XIII's epochal encyclical *Rerum novarum* in 1891, modern Roman Catholic social teaching has defended a rich, religiously inspired doctrine of the common good (the metaphysically laden common good of the medieval schoolmen). Only later would the modern rhetoric of human rights be grafted onto the tradition, most notably in John XXIII's *Pacem in terris* (1963) and the Conciliar texts *Gaudium et spes* and *Dignitatis humanae* (1965).[71] In a characteristically irenic turn, Pope John resolves the seeming antinomy of rights and the common good by stipulative fiat. *Pacem in terris* glosses the premodern teleology of *Mater et magistra* (depicting the common good as "the sum total of those conditions of social living, whereby [we] are enabled to achieve [our] own integral perfection") in deontological terms of human rights: "It is agreed that in our time the common good is chiefly guaranteed when personal rights and duties are maintained."[72]

Limited internally by the like dignity or intrinsic worth of others, liberty is positively oriented to the good of moral community as, in Jacques Maritain's words, "a whole composed of wholes": neither an artifice of interest, as in liberal contractarian thought, nor the "local and ethnocentric" hypostasis of communitarian mores.[73] We realize the limited good of moral community in which all share singly, not en masse, only when the "inviolable rights of the human person," including both socioeconomic rights and civil political liberties, are protected in what John Courtney Murray defines as "public order."[74] Establishing "true religion," or imposing distinctively religious duties, falls outside the state's proper province for the common good—now "chiefly guaranteed," says Pope John, in the set of basic institutional arrangements supporting a rights regime.[75]

The turn to rights, as we shall see in the next chapter, recalls the latent wisdom of the tradition, most notably the Thomistic critique of the Spanish *imperium* of Francisco de Vitoria and Bartolomé de Las Casas in the sixteenth century. Still, the Church's modern embrace of rights was momentous. After all, Pope Gregory XVI (1831–46) had railed against modern liberties and proscribed religious liberty as a "crazed absurdity" (*deliramentum*).[76] Strains of antimodernism persisted in the pontificates of Leo XIII (1878–1903) and his successors, Pius X and Pius XI, even as their social encyclicals betrayed an emerging acceptance of natural or human socioeconomic rights. Only with the triumph of liberal democracies and the rise of state communism did

Pius XII (1939–58), in J. Bryan Hehir's words, take "the first steps to bring the church's teaching on political-civil rights in line with the socio-economic teaching" of his predecessors' encyclicals.[77] Félicité de Lamennais, Frédéric Ozanam, and Wilhelm Emmanuel von Ketteler were vindicated, as natural rights were grafted onto the traditional stock of natural law. Finally, with the pontificate of Pope John XXIII (1958–63), the full range of civil, political, and socioeconomic rights recognized in the Universal Declaration was incorporated into magisterial teaching in *Pacem in terris* and two years later fully affirmed in the Conciliar Declaration *Dignitatis humanae.* Popes became ardent defenders of human rights and, in the vanguard of ecclesial reform, local Church leaders and organizations gave practical witness to the Church's teaching in the arenas of health care, education, and social welfare.

As the postconciliar reception of the Council reveals, however, controversies persist. Though lauded for his care for the environment, support of migrants and refugees, and similar modern concerns, Pope Francis incurs the enmity of powerful prelates for relaxing the Church's strictures on sexuality and marriage. For many the Church's social teaching remains our "best kept secret."[78] At issue, though, are more than vagaries of doctrinal emphasis; the controversies betray deeper methodological differences in mediating the tradition.[79] For the Church in a modern, religiously pluralist world, natural rights or human rights are a negotiable currency, redeemed in polities that are marked by differing, even incommensurable comprehensive doctrines of the good.[80] Yet if the deontology of rights prevails in its social teaching, the Church's teaching on sexuality remains, in part, beholden to a premodern, perfectionist teleology—a comprehensive doctrine of the common good in which personal dignity is realized within an organically stratified social order and complementary gender roles.[81] Sexual ethics, moreover, remains tethered to the finality or perfection of the individual act, such that certain acts by their very nature contravene their finality (*telos*) and hence are deemed intrinsically evil (*intrinsece malum*). Any deliberate interference in the natural, procreative finality of intercourse is thus proscribed, whether it be masturbation, artificial contraception, or same-sex relations. Deriving from our embodied animal nature (i.e., our "natural" inclinations to procreate and rear children), such act-centered teleological prohibitions were enshrined in tradition long before the personalist "turn" to rights.[82]

Differing methodological warrants figure, then, in the Church's politics, for example, by invoking religious liberty to denounce same-sex marriage.[83] (Chapter 3 is devoted to the political role of the Church and other distinctive faith traditions in a discursive interpretation of the common good.) The burden of my argument now is merely to show that in adopting rights rhetoric the Church has not so much resolved as deferred our antimony. For we must still choose between rival rhetorics: the consensual politics of rights typified by religious liberty over a teleology of intrinsic evil grounded in a particular comprehensive doctrine of the good. Indeed, Pope John Paul II's gambit in *Splendor veritatis* to redefine intrinsic evil by using the rhetoric of rights merely underscores the tension; in naming slavery, unjust labor conditions, and the like as intrinsically evil, John Paul preserves the category but effectively alters its content.[84] No previous pope had deemed slavery or unjust labor conditions as "intrinsically evil."[85] Laudable as the pope's appeal to the new wine of rights might be, it gives us little reason to preserve the old wine of teleological prohibitions. The antinomy remains.

Other faith traditions, too, must come to terms with reconciling their thick comprehensive doctrines of the good with the thin rhetoric of rights. For liberal theorists like Rawls, the radical plurality of such conceptions in modern democratic regimes implies that our political reason will be "shared and public" only if we methodically abstract it from any comprehensive doctrine of the (common) good.[86] Conversely, for communitarian critics precisely this narratively embodied common good determines the reference of the word "we." For critic and partisan alike, then, we are faced with a Hobson's choice: whether to choose natural rights—the abstract, formal currency of rational natural law redeemed in a neutral sphere of personal self-interested choice—or the common good, the coin of our particular realms pegged to our "thick," narratively dependent (*sittlich*) traditions.

II. THE RHETORIC OF RIGHTS

In one memorable diatribe, Bentham dismisses natural rights as "rhetorical nonsense" and imprescriptible natural rights as "nonsense upon stilts."[87] And yet, so I will argue, it is precisely their rhetorical sense (as subjective claims aiming "at persuasion and conviction") that makes rights a "mouth to tell of suffering."[88] What, then, shall we say of human rights? Or, more precisely, what does the use (in Wittgenstein's terms, "the grammar") of rights, such as found in the TRC, tell us of their meaning?[89] For it is just here that the originality of Tutu's translation appears: a translation that completes itself *in* enlarging itself—precisely by overcoming the limits (*aporiae*) of our rival rhetorics.[90] Let me offer the following theses in elaborating the threefold hermeneutic of human rights in recognizing, redeeming, and redressing claims: (1) Human rights are warranted subjective claims. (2) Basic human rights are specified by the internal goods shown forth in the rhetorical practice of claim-making.

Together these theses underscore the critical or deconstructive hermeneutic function of rights in *recognizing* basic claims, as in victims' testimony. (3) Basic human rights (negative and positive) in turn specify a corresponding set of negative and positive duties. (4) In *redeeming* basic claim-rights and fulfilling correlative duties, the narrative embodiment (schematization) of rights resolves the putative antinomy of "the politics of rights" and "the politics of the common good."[91] Just as theses 1 and 2 allow us to elucidate what the dominant powers have "silenced or rendered unpronounceable," so do theses 3 and 4 govern the constructive use of rights in the working of tradition.[92] Finally: (5) The interplay of the critical and constructive uses of rights underwrites the reconstructive work of *redress* in anamnestic solidarity, such as in reparation, restitution, and so on. In the next sections I will first explore the narrative use of rights and then make my case for the respective theses.

(i) The Critical or Deconstructive Use of Rights: Imagining Evil

Hannah Arendt once remarked that to "describe the concentration camps *sine ira* [without outrage] is not to be 'objective' but to condone them."[93] Similar sentiments are voiced in the International Panel commissioned by the Organization of African Unity (OAU) to investigate the Rwandan genocide:

> Our experiences in Rwanda—the witnesses to whom we listened and the memorial sites we visited—often left us emotionally drained.... The nature of these events demands a human, intensely personal response.... Readers have a right to expect us to be objective and to root our observations and conclusions in the facts of the case and we have striven rigorously to do so. But they must not expect us to be dispassionate.[94]

In the wake of the Shoah the developing corpus juris of international human rights law provides the rudimentary rhetoric of such a response. We speak "where language halts," of atrocities and crimes against humanity.[95] The term "genocide," itself of modern coinage, is such an evaluative description, invoking national, racial, and religious groups' natural right to exist.[96] Such law, of course, remains comparatively weak and the powers of enforcement are often wanting, as the unfolding tragedies of the Democratic Republic of Congo and South Sudan amply attest.[97] Yet the rhetoric of rights remains a lingua franca, giving voice to our "internationalized conscience" in the testimony of victims.[98]

So it is that truth commissions, war crimes tribunals, the testimony of international and indigenous nongovernmental agencies (NGOs), and indigenous modes of reconciliation provide a narrative documentation of rights abuses—the rupture, estrangement, and social anomie—apart from which talk of *re*-conciliation remains otiose.[99] We must have words to speak of rape and torture; of Tutsi children "murdered in their homes, hospitals or schools, drowned, burned alive"; of parents who "threw their children into the [river] to spare them death with a machete" as "in the words of one survivor, 'a last gesture of love.'"[100] In the cries of victims—in their "*J'accuse*"—what one Rwandese survivor called "the fire inside" finds voice. Before "so much death, so much grief, so many families wiped out," rights talk loses the formally abstract, individualistic patina it has acquired in Western liberal theory.[101] Here rights recall the horror of the Shoah, the "barbarous acts" that, says the Universal Declaration of Human Rights, "outraged the conscience of [hu]mankind." Yet Arendt's ira is never simply given. Indeed, acts of genocide and mass atrocity are barbarous *because* they deny the "first word of the face . . . 'Thou shalt not kill.'" Like torture, such acts reduce the victim to a state where, in Elaine Scarry's words, "the created world of thought and feeling, all the psychological and mental content that constitutes both one's self and one's world, and that gives rise to and in turn is made possible by language, ceases to exist."[102] To be reduced to cries and screams, to be denied even the mark of Cain's humanity: this is the "unmaking" of the victims' world, the effacing of memory.

Such unmaking, of course, may be the burden of long-standing oppression as much as it is of torture.[103] Archbishop Tutu, chair of the TRC, speaks eloquently of the consequences of apartheid's heritage in Southern Africa, "where blacks have had their noses rubbed in the dust by white racism, depersonalizing them to the extent that they have—blasphemy of blasphemies—come to doubt the reality of their own personhood and humanity. They have often come to believe that the denigration of their humanity by those who oppress them is the truth about themselves."[104] Apartheid, says Tutu, "systematically stripped Coloureds, Indians and especially blacks of their rights and denuded their humanity."[105] The "system conspired to undermine your sense of worth," treating "us as if we were things. We had a struggle song, '*Senzenina?—Isono sethu bubumnyama*' ('What have we done?—Our sin is that we are black')."[106]

Against the backdrop of such blasphemy, victims' testimony becomes a mouth to tell of suffering. The TRC was charged by the Promotion of National Unity and Reconciliation Act of 1995 to promote "unity and reconciliation by providing for the investigation and full disclosure of gross violations of human rights committed in the past." Pragmatic considerations, to be sure, impinged upon the practicable mandate of transitional justice, restricting the juridical or "quasi-juridical" critique of apartheid to the "gross violations of human rights" that occurred between March 1, 1960, and May 10, 1994.[107] Of the three committees of the commission, the first to begin hearings was, fittingly, the Human Rights Violations Committee, which focused primarily upon the victims of apartheid. Through two years of public testimony, that committee sought to establish victims' identities and ultimate fates as well as those responsible for the atrocities.[108] A victor's justice was not meted out, for despite considerable opposition, members of the ruling National Party who suffered rights violations at the hands of the cadres of the PAC (Pan African Congress) or the ANC (African National Congress) were invited to testify as well.[109] "Principles of the Geneva Convention" were applied "equally to both the former state and the liberation movements."[110]

In the TRC "our nation," writes Tutu, "sought to rehabilitate and affirm the dignity and humanity of those who were cruelly silenced for so long, turned into anonymous, marginalised victims."[111] Here testimony evokes what had been systemically effaced: "Now through the Truth and Reconciliation Commission," writes Tutu, victims "would be empowered to tell their stories, allowed to remember and in this public recounting their individuality and inalienable humanity would be acknowledged."[112] Lukas Baba Sikwepere testified, "I feel what—what has brought my sight back, my eyesight back is to come back here and tell the story. But I feel what has been making me sick all the time is the fact that I couldn't tell my story. But now I—it feels like I got my sight back by coming here and telling you the story."[113] Telling the story is at once a part of Sikwepere's story and what is woven into collective memory. So, too, the converse: in Jean Baudrillard's words, "forgetting the extermination is part of the extermination itself."[114]

In East London, Nomonde Calata, wife of Fort Calata, a member of the "Cradock Four," testified,

> During the time when the [Eastern Province] *Herald* was being delivered, I looked at the headlines. And one of my children said: "mother, look here, the car belonging to my father is burnt." At that moment I was trembling because I was afraid of what might have happened to my husband . . . Nyami [Goniwe, widow of another of the Cradock Four] was always supportive, I was still twenty at the time and I couldn't handle this. So I was taken to Nyami's place and when I got there Nyami was crying terribly.[115]

"At this point in her evidence," says Tutu, "Mrs. Calata broke down, uttering a piercing wail which in many ways was the defining sound that characterized the Truth and Reconciliation Commission—as a place where people could come to cry, to open their hearts, to expose the anguish that had remained locked up for so long, unacknowledged, ignored and denied."[116]

Recounting the testimony of Mrs. Calata, Afrikaner journalist Antjie Krog writes,

> The academics say pain destroys language and this brings about an immediate reversion to a pre-linguistic state—and to witness that cry was to witness the destruction of language . . . was to realize that to remember the past of this country is to be thrown back into a time before language. And to get that memory, to fix it in words, to capture it with the precise image, is to be present at the birth of language itself. But more practically, this particular memory at last captured in words can no longer haunt you, push you around, bewilder you, because you have taken control of it—you can move it wherever you want to. So maybe this is what the Commission is all about—finding words for that cry of Nomonde Calata.[117]

No word, of course, redeems the unspeakable. "When an act of violence or an offense has been committed," says Primo Levi, "it is forever irreparable."[118] But in victims' bearing witness, the breach, the rupture no longer appears as mere wretchedness. It acquires the quality of tragedy: at once general, as in genocide or apartheid when the victims are legion, but always, ineluctably particular: the cry of Nomonde Calata. Haltingly, in the telling of victims' stories, in narrating the gross violations of human rights suffered, we speak the transgressed command: history as remembrance, history as anamnestic solidarity.[119]

Sikwepere's testimony shows that he *is* a victim of apartheid, not a terrorist or criminal as depicted in apartheid media. For countless victims like Sikwepere and Calata, rights became a "pedagogy of seeing" or imagining evil.[120] As Pumla Gobodo-Madikizela, a psychologist serving on the Human Rights Committee, observes, the narrative testimony of victims affirms this: "You are right, you were damaged, it was wrong."[121] Our descriptions of the killings—and of the "psychic subhumanization" preceding them[122]—thus not only express their enormity but elicit our outrage.[123] "Silence," writes legal theorist Martha Minow, is thus "an unacceptable offense, a shocking implication that the perpetrators in fact succeeded."[124]

A Brief Excursus on Testimony

In the wake of the Shoah, "our generation invented a new literature, that of testimony," wrote Elie Wiesel. The new literature, of course, has antecedents in classical treatments of rhetoric, but bearing "testimony for the future" emerges as a distinctive response to genocide and mass atrocity, and I follow Wiesel's interpretation here.[125] The "new literature" of testimony has itself inspired a vast literature of interpretation and critique, and a comprehensive analysis would exceed the scope of our inquiry.[126] We must, though, surely acknowledge the limits of both giving and verifying testimony.[127] Truth commissions and tribunals restrict who can testify and the conditions under which testimony is formally admissible.[128] Not all suffering is brought to word—in South Africa the TRC addressed only gross violations of human rights that occurred over a limited period of time; in Rwanda the *gacaca* process (lower-level, popular tribunals) betrayed irregularities and bias.[129] Neither does a formal decision procedure assure veracity: forensic documentation and multiple attestations of other witnesses or even of perpetrators must suffice.[130] Yet culled from many sources the "new literature" weaves a greater story inscribed in collective memory—the obscenity of the Shoah, the horrors of apartheid, and the Tutsi genocide: these are attested.[131]

Still, further questions remain. For the very notion of testimony itself is contested in postmodern criticism, as in Jacques Derrida's assertion that "if the testimonial is by law irreducible to the fictional, there is no testimony that does not structurally imply in itself the possibility of fiction, simulacra, dissimulation, lie and perjury—that is to say, the possibility of literature, of the innocent or perverse literature that innocently plays at perverting all of these distinctions."[132] For Derrida the structural *aporiae* of testimony embedded in European jurisprudence preclude a strict division of law (aspiring to objective, ostensible proof) and literature. Indeed, says Derrida, in *Adieu to Emmanuel Lévinas,* "in the operation of justice one can no longer distinguish between fidelity to oath and the perjury of false witness, and even before this, between betrayal and betrayal, always more than one betrayal."[133]

And yet, we must ask, betrayal of what? For just as testimony in the new literature does not seek to reproduce a singular punctual event, neither is the aim of testimony simply identification. In the victim-centered testimony of the TRC, the "truth of wounded memories" is not that of oath-taking at a criminal trial.[134] Indeed, in his deconstruction of oath-taking as haunted by the possibility of literature, Derrida risks obscuring the *différance* at play in the "new literature"—what he himself later acknowledges as the "trace" of the "forgotten wound" that persists in testimony.[135] For here it is precisely the trace, the *object* of testimony, that belies form; in bearing witness to the enormity of the Shoah we, in Wiesel's words, write "not with words but against words."[136]

"This inside me . . . fights my tongue," says one witness to the Human Rights Committee of the TRC. "It is . . . unshareable. It destroys . . . words"—even in its speaking.[137] Here we face the limits of language and hence of knowledge.[138] Words betray words. If language first communicates communicability, testimony communicates what in the deepest sense cannot be communicated—the interstices, the silences, the cries—in Wiesel's words, "the impossibility of communication."[139] And is that not what testimony *says*? That, in Wiesel's words, the "past belongs to the dead and the survivor does not recognize himself in the words linking him to them"?

Yet the saying is far from negligible; silence remains an "unacceptable offense." "Scream as loud as you want; no one will hear you," torture victims in apartheid jails were often told by tormentors who were confident that knowledge of the crimes would never go beyond the cell walls. "The defeat of the apartheid regime," writes Charles Villa-Vicencio, "offers the opportunity for the suppressed anguish of these victims to be heard. 'Now there is a chance for the whole world to hear the victims scream,' Marlene Bosset of the Cape Town-based Trauma Centre for Victims of Violence and Torture told The South African Conference on Truth and Reconciliation organized by the Justice in Transition Project."[140] *Cries* that are heard: this is testimony, whether victims' diaries, personal narratives, or even silent memorials. In Rwanda I entered church after church filled with the bodies of those who had sought sanctuary. In some, skulls were piled one upon another; on one skull a simple flower had been placed, a piercing reminder of the command that had been so transgressed. Even when the cry is directly embodied, as in the young Mozambiquan refugee mother collapsing in exhaustion with two infants at her breast at a camp in Malawi, this is "unshareable. It destroys . . . words." But I will never forget.

We can never find suitable words for Nomonde Calata's cry. But the words we have, our flawed and stubborn words, gesture to her cry; they claim us, *disclosing* the wordless one who cries.[141] Here truth appears, less as the cognitive content of propositions that figure in oath-taking than as disclosedness (*aleitheia*). At their best this is what rights *do*. Their hermeneutical function (the illocutionary force of telling the story) claims us; the response, the hearing, is not identification, for we can never fully share, as Wiesel and Levi remind us, except in anamnestic solidarity—in cries that are *heard*.[142] A story becomes testimony, then, when it embodies and discloses what "fights my tongue": the silence, the gaps, but always the claim, the face's command, evoking a primordial sense of responsibility. Mere description of the camps, Arendt reminds us, will not suffice.[143]

In the sections that follow I will explore the rudiments of response—the nature and force of claims, the duties borne by the hearers or recipients, and the justificatory grounds for their redemption. As I argued in the introduction, rights are a stay against atrocity, against forgetting. But rights are not the story; what is said by victims will always be greater than the grammar of its saying. Rights are only a mouth to tell of suffering, of beauty under the sign of its negation.

The First Thesis: What We Say, Rights as Warranted Claims

Recounting their torture or the torture of their loved ones to the TRC's Human Rights Violations Committee, Lukas Baba Sikwepere and Nomonde Calata give voice to "barbarous acts which have outraged the conscience of [hu]mankind."[144] So, too, for the women raped and tortured in Rwanda, whose ordeal the introduction to the OAU Report decries as "outrages against humanity." Their claims in the TRC and the OAU Report are morally (and legally) exigent; their violation, unlike that of mere Hohfeldian privileges, warrants our outrage.[145] For if the "basic norms of human rights" imply the acknowledgment of victims' humanity, so also they reaffirm "the utter wrongness of its violation."[146]

Human rights thus fall under the general rubric of subjective claim-rights—rights, in Alan Gewirth's words, that imply "a correlative duty of some other person or persons to act or to refrain from acting in ways required" by the claimant's possessing "that to which he has a right," such as Sikwepere's claim to security.[147] In legal parlance, Sikwepere's claim-right obtains *in rem* and imposes a general duty of forbearance.[148] Explicating such claim-rights, we may say Sikwepere has a right to X (the object or substance of the claim, e.g., security), which he may legitimately enjoy, assert, or enforce against potential recipients or respondents.[149]

Claim-rights, of course, may be contested, as in the hearings of the Human Rights Violations Committee of the TRC or the International Criminal Tribunal for Rwanda (ICTR) held in Arusha, Tanzania. The accused may deny their complicity or claim they were obeying positive law (e.g., apartheid statutes). In the latter instance the issue turns on rival claims or, more precisely, on the reasons for believing a claim to be justified. That in the hearings of the TRC or the ICTR *human* rights are, in Ronald Dworkin's felicitous term, "trumps," attests to their presumptive, reason-giving force.[150] By virtue of their paramount or supreme importance, human rights bear a certain threshold weight against other claims, even if they are not necessarily indefeasible.[151]

To say, then, that Sikwepere or Calata have a claim-right is not merely to say that they have an interest in others acting thus or that they benefit from others so acting, though they may.[152] Their right to freedom from torture or intimidation serves rather as a warranted claim, so that it is rightly demanded, if not trumped by still more exigent claims. In the TRC or the ICTR we appeal to such subjective rights—in Henry Shue's words, "the rational basis for a justified demand"—to vindicate or verify prescriptive claims that others *ought* not to deprive Sikwepere or Calata of their basic security.[153] Though claim-rights may express our interests or benefits due, it is as commonly recognized warrants in our practical rhetoric—what Aristotle calls "reasoned speech"—that our interests acquire the sense of rights.[154]

Sikwepere's or Calata's subjective claims are, in this sense, objectively obliging. That is, justified or warranted subjective *claims* generate obligations so that a claim-*right* imposes a correlative (objective) duty upon its recipients, all things considered. And since it is not merely the case that the recipient ought to do (or refrain from doing) A—say, in accordance with a general precept of natural law—but that she ought to do (or refrain from doing) A because of Sikwepere's or Calata's warranted claim, we may say that their subjective claim-right constitutes an entitlement, legitimately enjoyed, asserted, or enforced.[155] We rightly condemn "entitlement failures" in victims' testimony, and, as I will show, such failures constitute appropriate grounds of redress.[156] Just how a subjective right [*jus subjectivum*] provides the rational basis for a justified demand [*jus objectivum*] is the burden of the next chapter.

As noted earlier, subjective claim-rights, though reason-giving, are not indefeasible. Not all human rights, legal or moral, enjoy equal priority; claim-rights may trump other claim-rights. Thus, freedom of speech, such as to incite hate crimes, may be overridden by others' security right not to be intimidated. In making sense of rights as warrants in persuasive speech we must assess their relative weight or force. Rights may be trumps, but trumps make sense only in the context of a game in which there are other cards and trumps of differing value.[157] Only in the context of a coherent rhetorical *practice* of claim-making, that is, can rights be rightly demanded.[158] We may say rights such as freedom of speech warrant corresponding duties—generally and for the most part—even if on occasion other warrants like security rights prevail.[159]

The Second Thesis: What We Show, Basic Human Rights

In the preceding section I argued that rights serve as warrants of subjective claims or entitlements in the practice of claim-making, as in testimony. What distinguishes subjective claim-rights from other inherent properties or powers is precisely their logical force in carrying conviction as a matter "not of fact, but of right."[160] And yet, as is the case in the narratives of apartheid and Hutu supremacy, our practices may be distorted, even systematically so. In the TRC and the ICTR the rhetoric of *human* rights reveals such distortions (the critical, deconstructive role of rights) and demands their redress (both the constructive and the reconstructive role of rights). But here's the rub: can we speak meaningfully, in the words of the Universal Declaration of Human Rights, of "a common standard of achievement for all peoples and all nations," where human nature is the ascriptive basis of subjective rights?[161]

For Burke, like Bentham, rights are the progeny of positive law. For MacIntyre, too, the politics of individual rights belie the law's "highly specific and local character," while for Rorty human rights remain the "local and ethnocentric" idiom of the postmodern, liberal bourgeoisie.[162] Now, were natural or human rights merely the stepchild of Enlightenment rationalism or normative properties of sovereign selves, justified as self-evident verities—in Marx's words, the rights of individuals "separated from the community"—such criticism might well hit the mark.[163] Yet in fixing the sense or meaning of human rights as the highly specific liberal-philosophic use of rights, MacIntyre emulates the very emotivists he criticizes.[164] That is, his critique of the liberal translation of rights neglects both the predecessor culture of late medieval canonical jurisprudence and the embodiment of human rights in modern international law, such as in the hearings of the TRC or the ICTR.[165]

As Brian Tierney contends, the origins of subjective natural rights betrayed little of the abstract formalism, atomistic individualism, or religious disenchantment of modern liberalism. Neither must we assume that such practices are "socially local," for both canon and international law expressly set a "common standard of achievement" for states and peoples alike.[166] But, MacIntyre might demur, the systematic extension of rights rhetoric in modern international law remains elusive inasmuch as the workings of legal tradition betray quite differing conceptions of the ends and goods internal to the practice. Is not the ideal of a common standard, such as the Universal Declaration of Human Rights, gainsaid by the subsequent elaboration of seemingly incommensurable generations of rights? If regnant liberal theory cedes pride of place to negative claims or immunities, as in the International Covenant on Civil and Political Rights and the Optional Protocol, non-Western usage favors positive second-generation economic, social, and cultural rights, as in the International Covenant on Economic, Social and Cultural Rights or even third-generation rights of peoples to self-determination and development. The various covenants, conventions, and declarations elaborated in international law offer a veritable bouillabaisse of putative rights yet fail to establish their relative priority, such as whether one's negative right to property (Article 17 of the Universal Declaration) is trumped by another's right to basic subsistence (Article 25).

Here I believe our rhetorical construal of rights is illuminating. As we saw in the preceding section, the practice of rights exhibits the internal goods of recognizing both the meaning and the potential validity of rights claims. So, too, in recognizing *human* rights as warrants we implicitly recognize the subject (claimant/respondent) as worthy of respect. In the Human Rights Violations Committee of the TRC, victims' testimony, such as Sikwepere's "*telling* you the story," implicitly affirms "the dignity and humanity of those who were cruelly silenced for so long."[167] Aiming precisely at degrading the victim, torture, as described in part 1, denies not only his voice or his claim but also his very capacity to make a world as agent. Thus, writes Tutu, the deliberations of the TRC sought to restore "the civic and human dignity" of those "who for so long had been consigned to the edges of society as voiceless and anonymous."[168] Sikwepere's narration before the Human Rights Committee of the TRC (the story/telling) displays his dignity: "I feel what—what has brought my sight back, my eyesight back is to come back here and tell the story."[169]

His testimony, we might say, exhibits, in a performative or illocutionary fashion, "the value and dignity of human life."[170] As R. J. Vincent observes,

> Not only are [human] rights an important part of the language of morals, but they have, too, a unique role within that language. It is to denote a particular moral attitude. The demeanour of someone claiming his or her rights is not that of begging or pleading, and the response if the claim is met is not one of gratitude. Equally, if the claim is not met, the response is not one of disappointment but of indignation. This is because rights are insisted on as part of one's status as a person. They are not favours done by the holders of power to those beholden to it.[171]

Human rights, that is, express our moral self-knowledge as "dignified objects of respect, both in [our] own eyes and in the view of others."[172] Conversely, where such respect is denied, as in the Hutu or apartheid supremacist narratives, "the appropriate reaction *is* indignation," for at issue is not merely this or that subjective end but our very status as moral agents (what Tutu, following traditional African belief, terms Ubuntu).[173] Such a view of human rights is supported, I believe, in the rights rhetoric of such advocates as Tutu, Julius Nyerere, Adolfo Pérez Esquivel, and others. Their rhetoric testifies that they will no longer passively acquiesce in servitude. As Paulin Hountondji of

Benin remarks, it is here, pace Rorty, that the discursive reference of the word "we" is extended in its concrete universality:

> What varies, not only from one culture to another, . . . but also within one culture from one period to another and from one class or social group to another, are the forms of this indignation, the modes of expression of this universal demand for respect and, consequently, the details of the rights considered to be essential and inalienable. But in no society is awareness of dignity truly absent, perhaps because in no society, alas, has this dignity ever been fully respected.[174]

The principal instruments of international positive law (the international "Bill of Rights") presume as much. The initial clause of the preamble to the UN's Universal Declaration of Human Rights (1948) solemnly recognizes "the inherent dignity" and "equal and inalienable rights of all members of the human family."[175] The question of justification (the backing) will occupy us in the next chapter; the burden of our argument thus far is more modest: the sense of rights in victims' testimony is mediated through the rhetorical practice of urging, pressing, or rightly claiming.[176] Indeed, human rights practice exhibits the internal, discursive goods of recognizing not only the object and force (nature) of claim-rights but "the individuality and inalienable humanity" of the subject (claimant/respondent) of such claims.[177] And yet, as Hountondji remarks, dignity appears in local garb, so that to respect Sikwepere qua concrete other is necessarily to respect his story—to recognize his particular point of view in redeeming his "equal and inalienable claims."[178] As I will show, respect for agential autonomy (in this limited, discursive sense) bids us recognize the concrete "modes of [its] expression," so that redeeming claim-rights precludes a simple antinomy of Moralität (equal respect) and Sittlichkeit (mutual recognition or solidarity).[179]

Rawls's thought experiment, for instance, illumines the latent wisdom displayed in the very design of the original position.[180] Rights are not finally conjured of the contracting parties' disinterested rationality in a feat of conceptual legerdemain.[181] Attaining and sustaining a rational consensus as a discursive finality presumes, rather, that Rawls's parties adopt a practical attitude of respect. Each regards the other as a worthy interlocutor, equally entitled to representation (mutual recognition). In his later writings Rawls explicitly introduces the "model conception of the person" to remedy what he acknowledges as the "very misleading" error in *A Theory of Justice* of viewing a theory of justice "as part of the theory of rational choice."[182] Rather than conflating Hobbesian and Kantian interpretations of rational natural law, Rawls invokes a Kantian conception of citizens who deliberate "as representatives of free and equal persons."[183] The rhetoric of claim-making in the contracting parties' deliberation and, implicitly, the parties' forgoing merely strategic interaction thus show forth their status *as* moral persons constituting, implicitly, a universal audience.[184]

And so it is, curiously, for MacIntyre himself. In responding to the bête noire of ethical relativism, MacIntyre argues that the potential rapprochement of rival traditions depends upon reflective recognition of good reasons internal to them precisely as extended arguments—a variation, as he himself notes, upon the Kantian material formulation of respect for persons.[185] Moreover, MacIntyre regards the virtue of justice as a "necessary component of *any practice* with internal goods and standards of excellence . . . in the light of which we have to characterize ourselves and others, whatever our private moral standpoint, or our societies' particular codes may be."[186] Justice, accordingly, denominates a family of well-ordered, reflective practices across traditions; and if, as MacIntyre acknowledges, "a morality of virtues requires as its counterpart a conception of moral law," one wonders if a (basic) rights-based interpretation of justice might not "characterize ourselves and others" in our "handing on" (*traditio*) of argument, a practice that is neither "highly specific" nor "socially local."[187]

It is precisely the relation between what is tacitly shown in human rights practice—our latent wisdom—and what is said (the particular claim) that determines the ethical substance of basic rights. In recognizing the *subject/claimant* as worthy of respect we specify the *force* and *object* of rights, in Hountondji's words, "considered to be essential and inalienable." For in ascribing worth, rather than mere price, to subjects/claimants as rationally autonomous agents, we implicitly valorize (recognize as warranted) the prerequisites of their exercising agency—or, in Rawls's terms, the "adequate development and full exercise" of their "moral power" of rational autonomy: civil liberties, of course, but no less security and subsistence.[188]

The Derivation of Basic Human Rights: A Rawlsian Excursus

Liberty, for instance, is not only instrumental in realizing determinate conceptions of the good (a "general, all-purpose means") but constitutive of Rawls's agents' fully "exercising their capacity to form, to revise, and to pursue a conception of the good, and to deliberate in accordance with it."[189] Rationally autonomous choice is itself constrained for Rawls, when liberties of speech or assembly are systematically suppressed, so that "limits on freedom are at bottom limits on our reason: on its development and education, its knowledge and information, and on the scope of the actions in which it can be expressed."[190] If, moreover, in the exercise of deliberative reason we regard the capacity for a conception of the good "not as a means to but [as] an essential part of a determinate conception of the good," basic liberties, such as those of conscience or association, would be no less constitutive of such a determinate conception.[191] Only thus would it be reasonable.[192]

What Rawls calls our "supremely regulative, highest-order interest" in adequately developing and fully exercising our capacity for rationally autonomous choice thus extends to the conditions (or capabilities) constitutive of its development and exercise—not only negative civil-political liberties but basic security and subsistence.[193] Torture and intimidation under apartheid, we saw, systemically suppressed agents' very capacity to conceive "ends and purposes worthy of . . . devoted pursuit."[194] But so too does the denial of basic subsistence. As recent studies by Amartya Sen and Martha Nussbaum attest, severe deprivation distorts rational choice: "The poor and deprived frequently adjust their expectations and aspirations to the low level of life they have known. Thus they may not demand more education, better health care. . . . they may not even *know* what it is to feel healthy."[195]

In *Political Liberalism* Rawls concedes that the first principle according priority to liberties may "easily be preceded by a lexically prior principle requiring that citizens' basic needs be met, at least insofar as their being met is necessary for citizens to understand and to be able fruitfully to exercise those rights and liberties." Certainly, concludes Rawls, "any such principle must be assumed in applying the first principle." Though Rawls chooses not to "pursue these . . . matters here," the concession is hardly negligible.[196] For if, in Rawls's words, one of the "characteristic marks of a natural rights theory" is that it "assigns rights to persons by principles of equal justice," and if they are given "a special weight," subsistence claims, no less than negative liberties, would enjoy priority.[197] In *The Law of Peoples,* conversely, rights derive their force *as* law, not from the Kantian conception of persons but in a nominalist vein, from the collective will of *peoples.* "Decent peoples," says Rawls, will recognize subsistence even as they relegate liberties of democratic participation and freedom of expression to "liberal aspirations."[198] Yet how the "natural rights" of reasonably autonomous persons can be reconciled with the voluntaristic construction of peoples' rights remains a puzzle.

Inasmuch, however, as we adopt the Kantian conception of persons in modeling reasonable autonomy we exhibit our self-knowledge (as moral persons worthy of equal respect) by according lexical priority to basic civil liberties, welfare, and security.[199] Such rights, we may say, are basic inasmuch as they are implied (a) in recognizing the *subject/claimant* of human rights practice and, hence (b) in redeeming any human rights claim, including, a fortiori, any other basic rights claim.[200] Henry Shue arrives at a similar conclusion by looking to the instrumental relationship of basic rights to rights in general: "Enjoyment of [basic rights] is essential to the enjoyment of all other rights."[201] What Rawls terms the "fair value of liberty" is imperiled if persons' basic positive claims to adequate nutrition or security are denied.[202] No less, one's basic security is threatened if, as in pregenocidal Rwanda or apartheid South Africa, liberties of effective participation are systemically suppressed.[203] So, too, does the robust exercise of civil-political liberties prove integral to forestalling famine.[204] Failure to recognize these basic rights, conversely, betrays the very *practice* of human rights.[205]

(ii) The Constructive Use of Rights: Never Again

In the preceding sections I argued that our rights do not descend from Kant's noumenal realm or the abstract metanarrative of Rawls's thought experiment. Neither are they of merely local or ethnocentric provenance, merely one of innumerable local narratives or petits récits.[206] For the rhetoric of basic human rights figures not only in the discursive constitution of social goods, as in the objects of prudential choice in the Rawlsian contract, but in the constitutive goods or prerequisites of practical discourse itself: civil liberties, welfare, and security. The systemic denial or deprivation of these goods rightly demands our outrage, Arendt's ira.

So rights become a pedagogy for seeing or imagining evil. Getting the memory right, fixing it in words, is the first hermeneutic use of rights in anamnestic solidarity—finding words for Calata's cry. History, Benjamin reminds us, is not an exact science exhausted by historicist explanation; rather, it is remembrance.[207] "There is a secret agreement between past generations and the present one" that binds us, says Benjamin, in anamnestic solidarity.[208] Yet "the slain," objects Max Horkheimer, "are really slain" and the "injustice, the horror, the sufferings of the past . . . irreparable." For Benjamin, though, it is the very irrevocability of the "injustice, the horror, the sufferings of the past" that *we* remember in testimony.[209]

Now the import of anamnestic solidarity is only adumbrated by Benjamin.[210] Subsequent interpretations by Christian Lenhardt, Helmut Peukert, Johann-Baptist Metz, and others touch on the paradox of such solidarity for a materialist historiography: if history is to be redeemed it must cease to be history, cease to remember, for history bears the mark of Cain.[211] No future generation can call itself happy if its happiness rests on the unrequited suffering of the past. For Habermas such memory congeals in collective guilt, the irreparable debt of memory borne in the German *Historikerstreit*.[212] Yet a prior question concerns us here: How, we may ask, can the memory of suffering generate solidarity? Mere wretchedness, after all, is not tragedy; indeed, for Horkheimer the suffering of those who perished has no part in the future.

For Benjamin outrage, not guilt, is the temporal index of memory; his redemptive criticism rests in the weak messianism of a materialist theodicy.[213] It *is* the irreparable suffering *we* remember—a world of suffering and passion, wreckage upon wreckage still (we will return to the question of theodicy in chapter 3). In anamnestic solidarity the *disaparecidos* appear and what the dominant powers have silenced is pronounced; pace Horkheimer this critical interpretation (bringing to word the transgressed command) is already an exercise of anamnestic solidarity. Forgetting the extermination, conversely, *is* part of the extermination.

But how does memory speak? For Horkheimer the slain cannot claim us; their rights claims pass with the interests or benefits that funded them. And yet it is not the pastness of the past that speaks in memory, but rather its presence. Rights "get that memory, . . . fix it in words," and the words command. Arendt's moral outrage is not added to brute empirical descriptions of the camps; it is the very condition of our seeing or interpreting them aright. Not the pastness of the past, but its presence, claims us; neither is remembering what the Universal Declaration of Human Rights calls "barbarous acts which have outraged the conscience" of humanity merely useful, such as in forestalling future genocide. Rather, the logic of remembrance (*anamnesis*) is self-implicating: *we* cannot get the memory right sine ira. *Our* history bears the mark of Cain, and so we say, as we must, "never again" again and again.

We return, then, to narrative. For anamnestic solidarity encompasses the slain, yes, but also those who, like Nomonde Calata, cherish their memory and, no less, victims, like Lukas Baba Sikwepere, who suffer and endure. Torture, atrocity, rape: these, too, as Levi reminds us, are "forever irreparable"; *this* is memory's burden.[214] To think of rights hermeneutically, then, is to extend anamnestic solidarity to all of history's victims—and, no less, to remember the Molochs, the systematic distortions that make victims necessary. Still, we must say more. For the effaced appear in memory as command—the grammar of anamnesis binding us, here and now.

The narrative disclosure of gross violations of human rights committed in the past is thus Janus-faced. The critical deconstructive role of rights in disclosing the "injustice, the horror, the sufferings of the past" sets the stage for the work of narrative reconstruction, the forging of a shared or collective memory.[215] José Zalaquett recalls that though in the aftermath of the Augusto Pinochet regime in Chile members of the Truth Commission failed to agree on a common narrative history of the coup, all concurred in denouncing "the human rights violations committed by the military regime."[216] Such a measure of narrative truth transcending merely local and ethnocentric mores is a sine qua non of subsequent reconciliation, since

> society cannot simply black out a chapter of its history; it cannot deny the facts of its past, however differently these may be interpreted. Inevitably, the void would be filled with lies or with conflicting, confusing versions of the past. A nation's unity depends on a shared identity, which in turn depends largely on a shared memory. The truth also brings a measure of healthy social catharsis and helps to prevent the past from reoccurring.[217]

Zalaquett's wisdom is reflected in the central place accorded victims' testimony in the TRC. The telling of stories is, to be sure, no panacea; many stories remained untold. Nor is the "disclosedness" of truth tantamount to reconciliation (although it is an integral element of it).[218] Still, when the TRC submitted its five-volume report on October 29, 1998, the years of anguished testimony had forged a remarkable narrative linking the stories of over twenty-three thousand victims like Sikwepere and Calata into what Charles Villa-Vicencio describes as "the greater story that unites."[219] Displayed here, I believe, is the dual hermeneutical role of rights in fostering a passionate critique of supremacist narrative, be it of apartheid or Hutu power, and in constructing a "shared memory" in anamnestic solidarity.[220] Through victims' testimony the TRC revealed the systematic distortions and evasions of apartheid; no mitigating redescription of apartheid would henceforth serve. But the disclosure of atrocity is a clearing for new stories to be told—in Minow's words, "a new national narrative."[221]

In the "uniquely public testimony" of the TRC, memory speaks; speaks, indeed, in Wiesel's words, "for the future."[222] Testifying of being tortured at the age of sixteen, says Mzukisi Mdidimba, has "taken it off my heart": "When I have told stories of my life before, afterward I am crying, crying, crying, and felt it was not finished. This time, I know what they've done to me will be among these people and all over the country. I have some sort of crying, but also joy inside."[223] What Wole Soyinka calls "the burden of memory" is borne in such testimony.[224] Wounded memory—"trauma's *lived* memory," in Pumla Gobodo-Madikizela's words—speaks "among these people and all over the country."[225]

It is thus rights rhetoric that fixes the memory in words: in narrating genocide or apartheid, rights reveal the complex, causal nexus, letting us, in W. D. Auden's words, "unearth the whole offence."[226] To remember the Rwandan genocide or South Africa's apartheid is to comprehend the constellation of their causes, the preceding acts of which they are the denouement, that is, the systemic denial of victims' mutually implicative claim-rights and the impunity accorded their executioners under a supremacist regime.[227] Such comprehension of the systemic causes of evil—such remembrance—imposes a primordial responsibility for the victim that we may parse in terms of the duties correlative to basic rights. Such duties extend a fortiori to the successor regime in Rwanda and its complicity in abetting massive human rights violations in the Democratic Republic of the Congo (DRC).[228] As I will show, cognate duties comprise not only forbearance, as in philosophical liberalism, but also structural protection against further deprivation and fitting provision of the ethical substance of rights.[229] Typically such institutional embodiment entails appropriate constitutional provisions in (re)establishing the rule of law and civic deliberation (restorative justice).[230] Yet perhaps no less significant is the promise of traditional forms of mediation or other analogous practices of restorative justice in civil society.[231] The promise, to be sure, as in *gacaca* in Rwanda, is not always fully redeemed.[232]

In either event, the shared memory of victims' testimony must be inscribed within a greater story that is "conducive to human rights and democratic processes."[233] The "real reparation we want," says Albie Sachs, "lies with the constitution, the vote, with dignity, land, jobs and education."[234] In establishing the TRC the "National Unity and Reconciliation Act" of the Interim Constitution looked to "a future founded on the recognition of human rights." And in a characteristically African inflection of rights, Tutu links the final success of the TRC's "narrative project" with fitting redress of the vast economic "disparities between the rich, mainly the whites, and the poor, mainly the blacks."[235] For "the huge gap between the haves and the have-nots, which was largely created and maintained by racism and apartheid, poses the greatest threat to reconciliation and stability in our country."[236]

The Third Thesis: Correlative Duties

A word, then, about duties. As I argued earlier, recognizing Sikwepere's and Calata's basic claim-right to security, precisely as warranted, obliges others *not* to deprive them of the good they rightly claim. Such a right obtains *in rem* inasmuch as it imposes a general duty of noninterference.[237] All agents must *forbear* from depriving others of the substance of such basic claims. As in apartheid or genocide, the systemic denial of basic security, subsistence, or civil liberties is morally tragic, rightfully meriting our ira, indignation. Basic human rights, whether negative or positive, specify negative duties of forbearance or, in Shue's words, "duties to avoid depriving" persons of security, subsistence, and (basic) civil-political liberties. Thus, in general we may say, if I have a justified human rights claim to X, then others ought not to deprive me of X.

For Robert Nozick, liberties that impose such negative duties "fill up the space of rights."[238] Under the banner of negative freedom, some heirs of the regnant liberal tradition relegate positive delimitations of liberty, such as claim-rights to adequate nutrition, to an inferior sphere, if they do not dismiss them altogether as mere rhetorical license. Such positive rights, avers Maurice Cranston, were "unknown to Locke and the natural rights theorists of the eighteenth century." Including them in the Universal Declaration of Human Rights has the unhappy effect of "pushing all human rights out of the clear realm of the morally compelling into the twilight world of utopian aspiration."[239] In a similar vein, Joel Feinberg argues that only passive negative rights (not to be done to) merit the title of categorically exceptionless human rights.[240] For while negative rights enjoin duties of forbearance, an entitlement to "be given certain essentials—food, shelter, security, education" imposes positive obligations that "cannot be guaranteed categorically and universally."[241]

Yet one wonders whether passive negative rights can be guaranteed categorically and universally if the duties corresponding to such rights are solely negative. In defending the primacy of negative liberty in his celebrated essay "Two Concepts of Liberty," Isaiah Berlin concedes that merely enjoying liberty to choose will not suffice, since if "in a totalitarian state I betray my friend under threat of torture, perhaps even if I act from fear of losing my job, I can reasonably say that I did not act freely."[242] That other Black South Africans did not suffer Sikwepere's or Calata's fate does not, then, suffice to show that their claim-*right* was recognized as morally compelling. As Shue argues, even a passive negative right such as freedom from torture presumes—precisely because it obliges categorically—institutional safeguards or social guarantees against typical major threats.[243]

Precisely as warranted, my subjective claim-rights are limited internally by the like claims of others, including positive claims (e.g., to protection), so that merely exercising negative toleration while at the same time ignoring typical major threats (e.g., those posed by apartheid to civil-political liberty) will not suffice.[244] Rights permit us not only to name atrocity, to speak the unspeakable, but also to prevent or redress systemic entitlement failures: such positive claims constitute the ethical substance of the pledge "Never again!" The

OAU report rightly condemns UNIMIR's failure to protect vulnerable Tutsis, both prior to and in the course of the tragically preventable genocide.[245]

Recognizing basic civil-political liberties (e.g., freedoms of speech, assembly, religion) *as* rights (and hence bearing a certain moral threshold weight) thus implies appropriate institutional protection. For where such protection regularly fails, whether by denying liberty immediately, or mediately through the implied threat of torture, we can hardly speak of rights as trumps. A coherent *practice* of claim-making (of redeeming rights) implies, we may say, that if I have a justified basic human rights claim to X, then others bear not only a negative duty not to deprive me of X but likewise a positive duty to protect me from systemic deprivation of X, which is typically satisfied by securing appropriate institutional guarantees. One observes here the asymmetry of rights and positive duties inasmuch as the *same* right may generate differing positive duties in local rights regimes, for example, through common or statute law. As we shall see later, recognizing universal claim-rights implies, no less, recognizing the concrete, culturally specific modes of their redemption.

Effectively transposing the negative/positive distinction from rights to duties (with the respondent bearing the correlative obligation) fails, however, to account for the passive, positive character of certain rights claims, such as to be provided with the substance or object of one's claim-right. Gewirth argues that positive duties not only serve to guarantee negative rights; they may extend to providing social goods like child nutrition when agents are incapable, or rendered incapable, of satisfying such claims themselves.[246] Positive rights, of course, may be secured through recognizing negative duties not to deprive others of the good in question (e.g., nutrition). Yet given our criticism of preserving the fair value of liberty in the preceding section, recognizing positive claims to the provision of basic social goods seems entirely apt. Since claim-rights serve to specify my entitlement to the actual enjoyment of a social good such as freedom of speech, my right of freedom of speech implies my justified expectation that the conditions presumed for its fulfillment be satisfied. I cannot reasonably say that others ought to respect my freedom of speech—believing that my freedom of speech implies my freedom from torture—but that others have no reason to honor such security claims.[247]

Must we not say, then, that the justificatory (rhetorical) force of my claim that others ought to respect my freedom of speech implies a family of mutually implicative claims and correlative duties? If I have a justified basic human rights claim (either negative or positive) to X, then others ought to (1) *forbear* from depriving me of X, (2) *protect* me from systemic deprivation of X through fitting structural guarantees, and (3) *provide* me with X when I am unable or rendered unable to obtain it myself.[248] A child's right to nutrition, for instance, would be denied not only in withholding nutrition but also in denying the appropriate means of obtaining it, such as in guaranteeing women's basic human rights to equitable employment, land tenure and inheritance, education, and so forth.

Our making sense of rights, after all, reflects the latent wisdom embodied not only in the International Bill of Rights but in emerging international law.[249] Article 22 of the Universal Declaration recognizes the indispensable character of positive rights and, as Mary Ann Glendon notes, "connects them to traditional protections of the individual." Indeed, says Glendon, the Declaration presumes "that one set of values could not long endure without the other . . . a better standard of living cannot be accomplished without larger freedom" just as "freedom is threatened by dehumanizing conditions."[250]

The African (Banjul) Charter on Human and Peoples' Rights adopted by the OAU in 1981, moreover, resembles the Inter-American regime (the American Convention on Human Rights, adopted in 1978) in its recognition of social, cultural, and economic rights as well as civil and political liberties.[251] Elaborating African usage, Julius Nyerere argues eloquently that "those who control a (person's) livelihood control a (person); his freedom is illusory and his equal humanity is denied when he depends upon others for the right to work and to eat."[252] Such rights, says Nyerere, are not the fruit of noblesse oblige; rather, they are grounded in the "equality and human dignity of all those involved. For human dignity involves equality and freedom, and relations of mutual respect among men (and women)."

The Fourth Thesis: The Narrative Embodiment of Rights

Our preceding remarks do not, of course, offer a knockdown justification of rights discourse; yet they illumine the sense or meaning, in Wittgenstein's terms the "grammar," of basic human rights in our varied local narratives. Human rights preserve what we might call the banality of goodness or the intrinsic worth or value of persons that Rawls acknowledges as "beyond all price."[253] Accorded lexical priority over less exigent claims, including other human rights claims such as the right to property, basic rights define the moral minima of respect presumed in any reasonable conception of flourishing—what Shue calls the "morality of the depths."[254]

Mere impartial regard of the good, or even *de facto* unanimity in conceptions of the good, will not, then, suffice; for our narratives may be distorted if agents' basic rights are suppressed. Indeed, narratives may be systematically distorted if the denial of basic rights is integral to or characteristic of the narrative itself, as in the narrative legitimation of racial discrimination within apartheid or patriarchal bias. Systematic distortion occurs in a particularly pernicious form when, as in Tutu's words, the indoctrination of victims is such that they come to regard themselves with "self-hatred and self-disgust."[255] In recounting the historic inequities borne by women, for instance, Onora O'Neill remarks, "It is well established that the most deprived often acquiesce in their lot—this is the traditional problem of the 'happy slave.' More specifically, it is well known that preferences adapt to realities, even to the grim realities. So too do beliefs."[256]

Precisely by disclosing systematic distortion, by illumining the *morally* tragic character of such suffering, even when not fully recognized by victims themselves, the rhetoric of basic rights permits us to redress the problem of false consciousness in appraising agents' attitudes and beliefs.[257] Yet the rhetoric of basic rights is not imposed, as if it were a final metavocabulary on Nomonde Calata's story; rather, it is expressed as the grammar of her testimony. "Happy slaves" may, of course, be the masters' appellation; slaves themselves may adopt other subversive rhetorical strategies. The gravamen of our criticism is rather that even in the masters' narrative, slaves cannot *reasonably* declare themselves happy or free: the internal grammar of basic rights forbids such moral solecism.

For Nyerere, as for Tutu, the rhetorical practice of human rights in our concrete narrative traditions preserves the mutual recognition of agents as worthy of respect, thereby permitting us to speak of *moral* solidarity. Where, conversely, these claim-rights are denied, as in supremacist or discriminatory narratives, the *common good* of discourse is itself imperiled—our narratives belie their rhetorical character as reasoned speech.[258] And yet rights and narrative are not opposed. If basic rights claims configure our comprehensive conceptions of the good, so too does the latter determine our circumstantial assignment of correlative duties (the respondent or recipient of rights claims) in redeeming rights claims. Recognizing universal validity claims implies recognizing the concrete, culturally specific modes of their redemption.[259] Basic rights, that is, are neither a *petit* nor a *gran récit*; rather, they are a "depth grammar" at play in and across our varied narrative traditions.[260] Such *claim*-rights specify the discursive goods of reasoned speech, that is, our saying, but always, already in what is said—the concrete rhetorical practice of Ubuntu in the TRC, which Dirk Louw calls "restorative communication."[261]

The grammar of rights (in Wittgenstein's terms, our describing the sense or meaning of basic rights) thus reveals the grammatical (normative) role of rights in the critique and construction of narrative. For what is *said* in our particular narratives, that is, the practical locutions or judgments, is tacitly governed by the grammar of our *saying*, what Wittgenstein describes as "the scaffolding of our thoughts."[262] To imagine a well-formed narrative is thus to "imagine a form of life" (*Lebensform*) configured by the ethical substance of basic human rights, if not also their explicit invocation.[263]

Like rules of Wittgensteinian language games, such basic rights admit of differing interpretations—in Hountondji's words, the "modes of expression"—so that the universal maxim of *respect* for the concrete other bids us *recognize* its particular narrative embodiment, whether Hutu or Tutsi, Xhosa, Zulu, or Afrikaner.[264] Yet what is said in our varied narratives must be consistent with what is shown in the narration of free and equal moral persons: a well-formed narrative both expressing (regulatively) and preserving (constitutively) our discursive autonomy. That is, our particular narratives must embody—or, in Kantian terms, must schematize—the suasive force of basic rights, for example, in Sikwepere's or Calata's right to freedom of speech, security, or adequate nutrition. (In Kant's Second Critique the synthetic role of a schema is played by the type of pure, practical judgments, i.e., a realm or kingdom of ends. By analogy, the ideal of a well-formed narrative schematizes the grammar of rights by specifying correlative duties and hence generating particular, properly circumstantial action-descriptions.[265])

Rights, after all, are not a mélange of discrete normative claims abstracted from the ensemble of social relations, as in Marx's critique of classical liberalism. Rather, basic rights and correlative duties hang together grammatically and configure a coherent rhetorical practice. Redeeming a basic right, whether negative or positive, invariably presumes recognizing a set of mutually implicative warrants or cognate claims, such as liberty rights implying other no-less-basic claim-rights to security and subsistence. In a similar vein, the duties correlative to such basic rights enjoin more than mere forbearance. Rights cannot, then, be simply subsumed under a rubric of deontological side-constraints on sovereign selves' behavior.[266] Positive duties of protection in particular depend for their fulfillment upon our distinctive cultural systems (legal, institutional, etc.). Subsistence rights, for instance, imply not only provision of culturally appropriate food; they also imply the culturally fitting means of protecting the most vulnerable, typically women and children, against deprivation by providing employment opportunities, extension of land tenure and credit, security against sexual assault, liberties of effective participation, and so forth.

Such positive duties, as the Universal Declaration recognizes, introduce a teleological, or in Sen's terms a consequentialist, motif.[267] For teleological or properly consequential considerations impinge upon the differential assignment of duties. In each case we must ask which set of societal institutional arrangements will best preserve, protect, and provide for the enjoyment of security, subsistence, and basic civil-political liberties. The latter, which include liberties of effective participation, privilege local wisdom in the design and implementation of policy.[268] The (deontological) politics of rights thus turns on the discursive politics of the common good.

We do not, after all, speak a grammar but grammatically, so that we must look to the fitting institutional embodiment (narrative schematization) of a rights regime. And speaking grammatically in our varied schematizations constitutes an irreducible common good, a good incrementally realized in implementing a rights regime and realized only in common.[269] (As we shall see in chapter 4, such narrative schematization extends to future generations.)

Taking the Victims' Side

We observed in sections (i) and (ii), then, the disclosive or hermeneutical function of rights, that is, the deconstructive critique of systematic distortion and the constructive "irruption of the poor in history"—in Gustavo Gutiérrez's telling phrase, their construction as historical subjects: "Our time bears the imprint of the new presence of those who in fact used to be "absent" from our society. . . . By 'absent' I mean: of little or no importance, and without the opportunity to give expression themselves to their suffering, their comraderies, their plans, their hopes."[270]

It is this irruption that the TRC documents in the testimony of Sikwepere, Calata, and the myriad of those deemed "'nonpersons' . . . who are not considered to be human beings with full rights."[271] In anamnestic solidarity we remember the effaced: those denied voice, speak. So it is in our discursive rendering of the common good: we speak of a primordial responsibility for victims. Our moral entitlement to equal respect or consideration justifies preferential treatment for those whose basic rights are most threatened or denied—in Camus's phrase, our taking "the victim's side."[272] If equal respect implies not identical treatment but recognition of the *concrete* other, so one may distinguish legitimately between indiscriminate regard for moral persons and discriminate response to their differing situations.[273] Aquinas's observation that a stranger in dire straits merits greater attention than one's own less needy father pertains a fortiori to equals: the fulfillment of equal basic rights in materially dissimilar conditions justifies a discriminate response.[274]

Such a discriminate response is expressed in the graduated moral urgency of differing human rights, that is, the lexical priority of agents' basic rights over other less exigent claims (e.g., property rights) and in the differing material specification of duties presumed for the same human rights.[275] A regime of rights may thus embody a legislative or juridical preference for the least favored in society or those bearing the historic burden of discrimination, for example, disabled children or poor women and their families; and differential material entitlements correspond to the differing interpersonal prerequisites of agency, such as the greater nutritional needs of pregnant women.[276]

If, moreover, as Rawls avers, we regard ourselves as all equally worthy of being represented, then the claims of those denied such recognition, often through systemic suppression of their basic rights, become (and remain) morally imperious.[277] Seeing the victims' point of view, as in Sikwepere's epistemic or hermeneutical privilege, emerges as a touchstone of the legitimacy of our prevailing institutional arrangements; only thus can we offer an equitable assessment of our legal enactments, juridical decisions, or economic policies. At issue is not merely a fair, consensual arrangement of inequalities like Rawls's difference principle; rather, it is the fairness or impartiality of the consensus itself, that is, the persons' equitable representation in their common social institutions.

Consensus, as we have seen, may well be illusory if agents' moral powers are repressed in passive acquiescence in servitude or suppressed in systematically denying their point of view in gendered hierarchies. The epistemic or hermeneutical privilege of the most vulnerable rests, then, not in canonizing a particular point of view but rather in revealing the partiality of such illusory or coerced consensus such as in the systematic distortions of apartheid or gender bias. Merely including the vulnerable—always and invariably we must think of women, children, and the disabled—in existing institutional arrangements or ameliorating their economic status will not suffice. Only if the rights of the most vulnerable, including a fortiori their *participatory* rights as narrative agents, are duly recognized can we arrive at true (valid) judgments of fairness in the design and implementation of policy—hence their properly epistemic privilege.[278] Precisely this privilege, as seen in reflections on testimony, guards against a facile identification with those who suffer systemic deprivation. As Gutiérrez reminds us, seeing the victims' point of view is always asymptotic; only a proper epistemic humility on the part of the privileged will disclose the genuine creativity of their rights talk.

The common good itself thus bids us ask, in the spirit of Ubuntu: In light of the "wreckage," in Benjamin's words, to which every civilization is heir, who are the most vulnerable in our midst? What policies will *best* protect their basic rights, all things considered? How can those whose basic rights are systemically imperiled be restored to full and equal citizenship? The answers, of course, are never given simply or once for all. Indeed, a consequentially sensitive account of rights needed for realizing the common good (the *telos* or finality of embodying a rights regime) invariably admits of degree. In this respect the common good (of a well-formed narrative) remains a regulative ideal, more or less realized in any given polity: the restorative imperative runs throughout our public reasoning. Critically, the construction of such well-formed narratives tempers our mundane conception of happiness (the finality/telos of Sittlichkeit): no generation can call itself happy that does not remember.

But, just so, our well-formed narratives, precisely in schematizing rights, comprise a family of language-games that, as such, are not rigidly limited but open-textured.[279] Rights are not a moral Esperanto displacing our native tongues or the differing rhetorics (values, ideals, etc.) of our comprehensive conceptions of the common good.[280] Albie Sachs speaks of "building national unity and encouraging the development of a common patriotism, while fully recognizing the linguistic and cultural diversity of the country."[281] In recognizing this family resemblance in diverse linguistic and cultural traditions, we foster national and global unity as a limited, political common good schematized in the corpus of international human rights law.

We may say, then: (1) reasoned political speech depends on our native tongues (grammar without language is empty); yet, precisely *as* reasoned, (2) political speech exhibits a common narrative telos (language without grammar is blind). As I argued previously, a narrative is well-formed precisely inasmuch as it preserves the constitutive goods of reasoned speech. To deny Sikwepere's or Calata's telling of their story, or the kindred conditions of their tellings, conversely betrays the common good of discourse in our varied narrative and legal traditions—a narrative project that, as Holocaust historian Saul Friedlander reminds us, must always resist the temptations of closure.[282] The critical and constructive hermeneutic uses of rights disclose the inevitable lacunae of our *legal* regimes.

Yet here we enter contested terrain. For critics like Charles Beitz and Joseph Raz, following Rawls, the proper subject of rights theory is the *political* (practical/juridical) role of human rights in the "law of peoples." International politics and jurisprudence, not moral critique, set the stage. Conversely, for "naturalist," "traditional," or "orthodox" theorists like Gewirth and James Griffin, human rights are a species of *moral* claim-rights to be justified accordingly.[283] Moral and political conceptions, however, are not rigidly defined, and theories trespass on one another. As I shall show in chapter 2, both conceptions presume the rhetorical (suasive) force of rights; and it is to the mediating role of rhetoric we now turn. For rights talk is less talk *about* rights (political or moral) than it is the talk—the reasoned speech—those rights make possible (e.g., victims' testimony). Law itself, the Universal Declaration reminds us, bears witness to "barbarous acts which have outraged the conscience" of humanity. Human rights begin not with lawyers or moralists but with victims.

Yet rights are not merely a grammar of dissent. Indeed, human rights law plays a privileged role, not only in recognizing but in redeeming rights and redressing their violations, even if law remains an imperfect paradise. The legal schematization of rights proceeds incrementally, resisting closure. The grammar of rights is never simply "mirrored" in law; it is *spoken* (narrated) under the rubrics of a well-formed narrative.[284] As in the TRC, rights are never fully redeemed; our flawed words fall short of the ideal. The schematization of rights implies even as it transcends established jurisprudence: a critical *ethos* of rights must be nourished in the vigilant mobilization of NGOs (national and transnational), churches, mosques, and the like.[285]

So it is: the threefold hermeneutic of rights rhetoric applies to moral and political conceptions alike, as in both Rawls's restrictive account of human rights in *The Law of Peoples* and in the priority of "permissive" civil liberties in Habermas's discourse ethics.[286] Not only failures of compliance, then, but institutional lacunae, such as the unduly restrictive scope of international law regarding refugee policy, must be addressed. Taking the victims' side becomes an abstract formulary if they have no voice, no mouth to tell of suffering. Yet mass atrocity, rape, and forced displacement in the DRC or South Sudan remain forgotten tragedies, cries that "fall like rain in summer."

(iii) The Reconstructive Use of Rights: Specific Redress for Victims

In schematizing rights we must thus consider the "effective history" of human rights law, both the progressive disclosure of systemic rights violations (the critical or deconstructive role of rights) and the fitting institutional guarantees against their recurrence (the constructive role of rights).[287] In anamnestic solidarity the faces of the *desaparecidos* must appear; the systemic violation of their rights must be redressed. Indeed, the third hermeneutical role of appropriate specific redress for victims presumes both the discovery of truth and a restitution (or establishment) of the rule of law. To speak of social reconciliation through a general amnesty, while effacing the victim or abetting further victimization, is to fall prey to the semantic hubris Jeremiah decried: "falsely saying, 'peace, peace,' when there is no peace" (Jer. 6:14). As the Rwandan theologian Augustin Karekezi, SJ, observes,

> In the light of all that happened, it is clear why the survivors and victims of this genocide express moral indignation at calls for reconciliation *which ignore the issue of justice*. Some even claim that focusing on truth and justice will only serve to open old wounds and make reconciliation impossible. Such a position ignores the fact that the wounds

> will bleed for years. It is not by our looking in the other direction that the victims will be healed. Those who talk of a "general amnesty" speak from the privileged position of neutral outsiders who ignore the reality of those who must live with the consequences of what has been done to them—above all, the widows and orphans.[288]

Although subject itself to criticism, the conditional amnesty process overseen by the Amnesty Committee of the TRC required that those applying for amnesty had to confess their complicity in gross human rights violations. In the amnesty hearings, perhaps for the first time, victims learned the fate of loved ones—how a spouse was tortured, where a son was buried. Such public admission of guilt, in concert with the discovery of truth and the institution of the rule of law, belied the generation of any counternarrative that tacitly legitimated the evasions and systematic distortions of apartheid.[289] "No one in South Africa," says Tutu, "would ever again be able to say, 'I did not know' and hope to be believed."[290] In a similar vein, international tribunals, such as those in Arusha or the Hague or adaptations of traditional forms of mediation, serve to interrupt the culture of impunity, of killing without consequence, that culminates in further violation.[291]

Finally, specific redress of evil must honor, insofar as is feasible, not only the legitimate claims of retributive justice but likewise victims' claims to restitution and reparation. Within practical limits, the Reparations and Rehabilitation Committee of the TRC strove to offer a limited compensation to the victims of apartheid. To be sure, the sway of restorative justice is necessarily limited. Neither the critical naming of evil nor constructive, systemic redress are eo ipso therapeutic; in some circumstances testimony may even retraumatize victims.[292] So, too, some victims, having suffered grievously, like Steve Biko's family, opposed the TRC's granting of amnesty.[293] Leading beneficiaries of apartheid—the judiciary, businesspeople, journalists—never fully confessed their complicity; and the most notorious ministers of the apartheid regime, P. W. Botha and others, refused to testify.[294] Limited, too, were the scope and resources devoted to reparations and rehabilitation. Many victims of apartheid lacked legal title to compensation, and reparations, already modest, were deferred while perpetrators received amnesty.[295]

The Fifth Thesis: Critical and Constructive Hermeneutics at Play in Redress

We saw in section (i) that rights rhetoric, as in the South African TRC, expresses victims' indignation—their ira—at both personal and social deprivation. Individual victims are named and the history of their victimization is chronicled, yet in the context of a moral indictment of apartheid precisely as a systematic transgression of the common good. The abstract, individualist tenor of liberal rights theory thus gives way to an internal deconstructive critique of apartheid narrative. As elucidated in section (ii), the negative duties of forbearance, that others refrain from depriving agents of their basic negative and positive rights, fund the critical interpretation of narratives and limit the range of narrative descriptions or redescriptions. The Rwandan killings are perforce genocide; politically motivated rape is just that; apartheid, as Tutu argues, is necessarily depicted as intrinsically evil. So, too, do positive duties of protection reveal the systemic nature of deprivation—the complex, causal factors such as repression of civil liberties—that typically precede atrocities or genocide. In unmasking systemic transgressions, such duties reveal the vulnerability of particular social groups, like those of Tutsis in pregenocidal Rwanda.[296] The very notion of a well-formed narrative thus becomes a critical type or schema in identifying what Habermas terms "systematic distortions" of our civic discourse, the effacing of the other.[297]

Yet if rights bring to word the transgressed command, enjoining a primordial responsibility for the victim, so they also disclose the victim's truth—what Judge Ismael Mahomed of the TRC named the "truth of wounded memories."[298] What Sikwepere says is, in part, the disclosedness (*aleitheia*) of what Tutu calls his "God-given personhood and humanity." As narrative grammar, basic rights temper what we say (rights as side-constraints) even as they function constitutively in our preserving and protecting our moral self-knowledge *as narrating agents*.[299] Grammar never simply constrains our practical speech or rhetoric; it is not finally one thing to speak and another to speak grammatically.

Just as those most vulnerable deserve protection in the design of society's basic institutions, so systemic failures of forbearance or protection in the denial of basic rights warrant repentance, reparation, and restitution. Limited as it was, the Reparations and Rehabilitation Committee of the TRC, for instance, recognized the specific entitlements of victims in the name of just recompense and not mere indiscriminate aid. Innocent suffering, of course, imposes its own obligations; but suffering due to the denial of rights must itself be parsed in terms of rights lest the specificity of offense be merely ignored or suppressed.

The critical role of human rights in discovery of truth and the constructive role of rights in establishing the rule of law thus culminate in the reconstructive role of specifying ancillary claim-rights: both victims' right to reparation and (as shall be seen in chapter 3) their right to forgive or withhold forgiveness, as well as the correlative duties of redress (e.g., perpetrators' duty to repent, to satisfy the demands of retributive justice, and to make fitting reparation). It is just this narrative embodiment or schematization of both general and specific rights that lets us speak of narrative truth. For as the hearings of the TRC revealed, the world is not tidily arranged into victims and perpetrators. We like our heroes neat, but under torture victims betray comrades; complicity in atrocity is abetted by fear of reprisal. Bystanders are not, for that reason, innocent; indeed, "unearthing the whole offense" displays a range of culpability. Yet if the critical hermeneutic of rights permits us to identify pro tanto both victim and perpetrator, so the constructive hermeneutic of rights precludes our essentializing either victim or perpetrator. Under the rubrics of rights the narrative (legal) construction of identities remains fluid.[300] As Graham Greene once observed, "A writer writes about the victims, and the victims change."[301] Victims can become executioners; some have. We must count the supremacist essentializing of victimhood among the precursors of genocide in both Rwanda and Bosnia.[302] So, too, the successor regime in Rwanda must be held accountable for its complicity in mass atrocity and rape in the DRC.[303]

Merely to remember, then, is no stay against future atrocity—history has taught us that. But to remember morally is to recognize the command of the face, even of one's enemy. And so, under the rubrics of rights we read history, in Benjamin's words, as "the history of the suffering or passion of the world."[304] The universality envisioned in such reading is modest: not "bourgeois civil rights" as the "standard maximalist morality of the West," but the ethical substance of our ira, the grammar of our dissent.[305] The concrete universality of schematizing rights finds expression in irreducibly plural narratives and in the voices, often suppressed in *les gran récits*, of victims weaving narratives anew. Such weaving, we have seen, is perforce incomplete—the passion of the world, alas, is never spent. But neither, then, is their passionate remembrance—the promise of Benjamin's "anamnestic solidarity."

It is just this solidarity, given in the narrative schematization of rights, that the family resemblance of well-formed narratives is revealed. Inscribed within our narration and rendered in accordance with our diverse cultural wisdom, the grammar of rights allows for a limited rapprochement of our discrete cultural narratives, of the Xhosas, the Zulus, the Afrikaners, and others.[306] Even our disagreements regarding narrative history and appropriate legal or juridical redress are thus framed against an anterior consensus—in Zalaquett's words, "a shared memory." And so, too, official public apologies, to paraphrase Minow, both "reflect and help to constitute" a shared memory, for such apologies are, in part, performative locutions: they (re)interpret the past; reaffirm the rule of law ("community norms" as a "moral baseline"); and, implicitly, bind the future behavior of those in whose name the apology occurs. In this latter respect apologies serve as promissory notes of restorative justice, redeemable in both general, institutional safeguards against the offense ever recurring and specific acts of restitution or reparation.[307] In the redress of evil, apologies enact our recognition and remembrance of evil and lack authenticity, where and to the degree these performances are wanting.[308]

Even the most authentic of apologies, however, does not pay the "price of pain."[309] In testimony, words betray words: "This inside me . . . fights my tongue."[310] Perhaps it must be so, this talk of rights where language halts. Our shared memories are fragile; they seldom go all the way down. Indeed, the narrative meaning of a given apology, like that of any institutionalized response such as the TRC, remains open-textured and depends, in part, on the history of its consequences (what Hans-Georg Gadamer calls *Wirkungsgeschichte*).[311] Yet where no such moral membrane, no common moral remembrance or reparation exists, we seem fated to an endless *agon*: "the habit-forming pain, [m]ismanagement and grief: We must suffer them all again."[312]

III. CONCLUSIONS

These five theses show that our rights talk is not only a grammar of dissent against systemic violation, our recognizing or imagining evil. Narratively embodying or schematizing a rights regime exhibits the complex interrelation of our threefold hermeneutic. As in the TRC, the recognition of systemic rights violations comes to fruition through general redress and the constructive implementation of a human rights regime. "Never again," we say, as we must. But so, too, anamnestic solidarity strikes a reconstructive note in specific redress of victims. Indeed, reparation sets the stage for both recognition of and general redress of systemic racism while, as in the case of forced displacement, specific redress of victims secures what Arendt called their very "right to have rights." Together these hermeneutical uses of rights become, in Jean-Marc Éla's words, a "pedagogy of seeing" and of redressing atrocity.

Basic rights configure our narrative traditions, so that Tutu's translation—"truly . . . a moment in the growth of the original"—resolves the seeming antimony between the politics of rights and the common good.[313] Such rhetorical rapprochement, I believe, sheds light not only on the TRC's use of rights but on *our* whole making sense of rights.[314] Indeed, the story or narrative of rights is just that: the progressive inclusion of previously marginalized groups (religious, racial, ethnic minorities, women, the disabled) is less a function of formal inference than of contesting the dominant narrative (the critical hermeneutical role at play in getting the memory right). If for Horkheimer the slain have no part in the imagined future, then anamnestic solidarity bids us imagine otherwise, as memory commands (the constructive hermeneutical role in telling a greater story). Only thus can we imagine the happiness of future generations. Finally, haltingly, we must redress cries that are heard (the reconstructive hermeneutical role). That such redress is perforce limited—that there is no price for pain—that, too, is memory's burden.

Let me then, in conclusion, test my theses against several salient postmodern criticisms: (1) that our "rights talk" is excessively individualistic; (2) that human rights are a product of Western, cultural hegemony; and (3) that the foundationalist backing of rights is illusory.[315]

Individualism

In my first thesis I argued that claim-rights, though ascribed subjectively, are redeemed intersubjectively. Rights establish the intersubjective (objective) validity of subjective claims precisely *as* warrants in the rhetorical *practice* of claim-making.[316] And, like practices generally, the practice of rights realizes internal common goods, such as Sikwepere's or Calata's demand for respect and recognition in the victim-centered testimony of the TRC. Moreover, the grammar of rights, as stated in the second thesis, reveals the mutually implicative character of our basic claims of social, cultural, and economic rights that are recognized, in Hountondji's words, "to be essential and inalienable" in expressing "this universal demand for respect."[317] And, as I argued in the third thesis, duties correlative to such basic claims comprise not only forbearance but systemic social protection and provision.

Individual claim-rights, then, are never simply "the rights of egoistic man," as Marx alleged. Nor is the object of our subjective claims merely "private interest" or "private caprice"—it is not, in Habermas's words, "a neutral sphere of personal [self-interested] choice."[318] Rather, showing forth *our* moral self-knowledge, the rhetoric of rights in the TRC "completes itself in enlarging itself"—the subject/recipient of rights being less the abstract sovereign self of classical liberalism than the discursive culturally embedded "we" of Ubuntu. "*Ubuntu* is an evolving spirit," writes Villa-Vicencio, "existing between memory and an ability to create something new."[319] Tutu describes Ubuntu's ideal of "social harmony" as "the *summum bonum*—the greatest good." Humanity is never resolved into abstract relations of sovereign selves.

Rather, says Tutu, "We belong in a bundle of life. We say, 'a person is a person through other people.' It is not 'I think therefore I am.' It says rather: 'I am human because I belong.' I participate, I share."[320] As incorporated in the Interim Constitution establishing the Truth and Reconciliation Commission, the spirit of Ubuntu permeated its deliberations—deliberations that, in Tutu's words, sought to restore "the civic and human dignity" of those "consigned to the edges of society as voiceless and anonymous."[321]

The threefold hermeneutic of rights, precisely as a rhetorical practice, describes what *we* do; and what we *do*, as we saw in our fourth thesis, is preserve and protect agential capabilities through narrative schematization. It is this narrative embodiment or schematization that, as in the TRC, permits us to distinguish victim, bystander, and perpetrator within the space (*locus*) of rights—my fifth thesis. The next chapter explores the internal relation of discursive (prudential) autonomy and the cognitive and conative virtues exhibited in playing the language game of "reasoned speech." For the moment it suffices to say that the narrative schematization of basic rights embodies the common good so that, in a well-formed narrative, the discrete interests of individuals are not only consistent with, but ordered to, the discursive telos of instantiating a rights regime.[322] Such a discursive teleology illumines the moral grammar of our ethical (sittlich) traditions, including our distinctively religious traditions, and permits a significant if still limited degree of narrative inter-translatability.[323] But this, too, is contested—whence the criticism that the individualism of rights betrays the illicit universalization of Western cultural hegemony.[324]

Cultural Hegemony

Makau Mutua objects to the Universal Declaration's "bias and exclusivity," while postmodern critics like Jean-François Lyotard regard the very "demand for [universal] legitimation" in itself a symptom "of cultural imperialism."[325] The discourse of rights is finally revealed as but one of many local narratives, or petits récits, whose justification rest only in the "pragmatics of their own transmission."[326] And so, says Rorty, the "emergence of the human rights culture" owes "nothing to increased moral knowledge, and everything to hearing sad and sentimental stories."[327]

Rights talk may betray exclusivity and bias—this, after all, was the burden of our critique of the regnant liberal-philosophic politics of rights in part I. And yet, to follow Rorty or MacIntyre, fixing the sense of rights by its postmodernist bourgeois liberal use, such as is seen in the "hyperindividualism" of American rights talk, is tacitly to concede its hegemony—denying the fecundity of non-Western translations—and what Upendra Baxi calls "the power of the emergent, countervailing subaltern discourse" of rights.[328] Might we not rather learn from Tutu's translation? Tutu invokes human rights in a Gramscian vein—venturing, in Edward Said's words, to offer "interpretations of those rights in the same place and with the same language employed by the dominant power," disputing "its hierarchy and methods," elucidating "what it has hidden," and pronouncing "what it has silenced or rendered unpronounceable."[329]

In our critical narrative reconstruction such basic rights do not suppress our native tongues; rather, they provide that Lukas Baba Sikwepere and Nomonde Calata speak—securing thereby the rudiments of democratic political legitimation and hence of critique. Tutu's and Nyerere's rhetoric underwrites our ira while constructively privileging "those who were cruelly silenced for so long" in weaving cultural narratives anew.[330] Liberalism, then, does not exhaust the semantics of rights. Indeed, precisely in failing to complete itself in enlarging itself (i.e., in anamnestic solidarity), liberal rights talk generates what Arendt calls the internal paradoxes of modern rights: that the "right to have rights" is systemically suppressed by bias and exclusivity. We speak, of course, where language halts, even in speaking otherwise; but, just so, the emergence of "countervailing subaltern discourse" represents an indictment of *Western* hubris and barbarism. The UN Declaration (as its preamble attests) is written, says Michael Ignatieff, "in full awareness of Auschwitz and dawning awareness of Kolyma." Without "the Holocaust, then, no Declaration."[331]

Foundationalism

Yet, Ignatieff continues, "Because of the Holocaust, no unconditional faith in the Declaration either." For the Universal Declaration "set out to reestablish the idea of human rights at the precise historical moment" in which a foundation of rights "in natural human attributes" is raised into question—my third and final criticism.[332] In a disenchanted world the sacredness of human nature is illusive; as Ignatieff concedes, the "idea of dignity and human worth" remains "culturally specific and relative."[333] Rorty's agnostic piety, to be sure, leaves little room even for Ignatieff's limited, prudential defense of universal negative rights.[334] We must, rather, forsake our "desperate hope for a noncontingent and powerful ally" in the defense of rights, says Rorty, whether this be "the common core of Platonism, or religious insistence on divine omnipotence, and of Kantian moral philosophy."[335] Metaphysically bereft, we are left with "sad and sentimental stories" of purely "local and ethnocentric" provenance.[336] Curiously, we come full circle here, since for Rorty the criticism of (rights) criticism resolves itself in "bias and exclusivity." There is "no criterion that we have not created in the course of creating a practice; no standard of rationality . . . that is not obedience to our own conventions."[337] To the "enlightened" postmodernist, Enlightenment's final disenchantment is of itself; our "doubts about whether the aims of liberal society were 'objective moral values,' seem merely quaint."[338]

In a similar vein, postcolonial critics decry the abstract formalism and epistemic universality underwriting the rights of deracinated sovereign selves.[339] Drawing upon Michel Foucault, Baxi adopts a "critical attitude" toward the discursive making of subjects—the *poiesis* of subject-construction through cultural and disciplinary regimes. In Baxi's decolonial critique the supposed "rights of man," abstracted from concrete social relations, mask "practices of violent social exclusion" and culminate in the "domination of the non-European peoples and the ruthless unmaking of their lifeworlds."[340] Gayatri Chakravorty Spivak, too, questions the myth of the sovereign bourgeois subject, whose dynamics of representation render the subaltern silent and invisible in "the space of difference."[341]

Yet if Rorty's light-minded aestheticism leaves us only "sad and sentimental stories," post- and decolonial critique tells a different story: of lifeworlds colonized and knowledges subjugated. In privileging alterity such critique offers, I believe, a compelling, deconstructive rhetoric, unsettling not only Rorty's "post-modernist bourgeois liberalism" but, as we shall see, Habermas's "ideal speech" situation as well. Yet by its own logic this story too must be deconstructed, its vocabulary (colonization, subjugation, domination, etc.) interrogated. Rorty might well dismiss such evaluative tropes as mere postmodern pieties ("obedience to our own conventions"). Indeed, as he reminds us, with the radical deconstruction of the subject (Foucault's "death of man"), other petits récits will be told and the Nazis, too, will have their tale. The epistemic critique of foundationalism, after all, is not perspicuously emancipatory. Following Spivak, Drucilla Cornell chastises Derrida for his "almost willed naivete" in failing to address the dynamics of representing those consigned to history's margins.[342]

Why, then, privilege the subaltern? The question turns on the suasive force of rhetoric in telling *this* postcolonial or decolonial story. What funds the tropes for the great decolonial critic Julius Nyerere is the critical or deconstructive use of "*haki za binadamu*": basic claims comprising *uhuru* (liberation); democratic, collective self-representation and self-determination (*kujitegemea*); freedom from systemic deprivation and exploitation; the right "to work and to eat"; and so on. Nyerere's politics of *Ujamaa*, in a communitarian vein gives, in Burke's words, to the "frame of polity the image of a relation in blood," the *jamaa* of extended family. But Ujamaa extends these bonds in concrete universality, not only to citizens of the newly independent Tanzania but to the pan-African decolonial struggle and finally to the solidarity of solidarities comprising our common nature as *binadamu*.[343] We possess rights, not in abstraction from the ensemble of social relations but precisely in virtue of them. Nyerere's rhetoric rests not on the "delusive geometrical accuracy" of self-evident bourgeois rights but on the emancipatory potential of basic rights rhetoric to realize the concrete universality of Ujamaa.[344] Here basic rights are not so much "sutured into the torn cultural fabric of responsibility," in Spivak's words, as inscribed, critically and constructively, in the politics of Ujamaa.[345] Rights are not added to brute descriptions of the world; rather, they figure in how we see, how we refigure our story.

For Nyerere as for Tutu, such basic rights interrupt the dominant, hegemonic discourse. Rights let us imagine otherwise. We need not, then, aspire to Grotius's self-evidence or to the apodictic certitude of Kantian Moralität. For in the TRC, rights speak in victims' stories, not in "grand narratives of legitimation."[346] If it is curious to dismiss Tutu's rhetoric as abstract and formal, it is curiouser and curiouser to say that he has, in MacIntyre's words, "entangled himself in error."[347] Our reading of Tutu's translation, after all, recalls the very rhetorical/juridical origins of modern rights; as Tierney remarks, "Medieval rights theories were not typically derived from . . . metaphysical considerations."[348] Neither does the rhetoric of rights in the Universal Declaration presume (logically or semantically) a particular logocentric foundation. As René Cassin, a member of the original drafting committee, observed, consensus in recognizing the suasive force of dignity and rights (i.e., as *loci communi*) does not presume resolving "the metaphysical controversies, notably the conflict between spiritual, rationalist, and materialist doctrines on the origins of human rights."[349]

Our rhetorical reading of rights is modest; yet where Ignatieff rejects a metaphysically laden conception of dignity, we look rather to its performative (illocutionary) expression, as in Sikwepere's or Calata's demand for respect. If torture destroys language, rights bring to word the transgressed command. Human rights are not a metanarrative; nor are they merely one of many petits récits. Rather, and precisely as narrative grammar, rights figure in the "pragmatics of [narrative] transmission," in displaying the normative consensus or "latent wisdom" always and already at play in our rational (nonstrategic) claim-making. It is not we who have nothing to say to the torturers of the innocent, "of the form 'there is something within you which you are betraying'"; it is the torturer who, in effacing the other, forsakes reasoned speech.[350]

What we say in international human rights law, despite its sometimes severe limitations, attests to our implicit agreement and original consensus regarding the moral priority of "the inherent dignity" and "equal and inalienable rights of all members of the human family," the "commonality among persons that is born with the birth of language."[351] One may, of course, play the skeptic: the burden of my argument thus far is not to show that one must, on pain of logical contradiction, opt into the language game of rights; but rather to elucidate the semantics of such practical claims being true for us in the rhetorical practice of human rights—the working of tradition. As with other linguistic practices, it may be that, in Wittgenstein's words, "I have exhausted the justifications," and having "reached bedrock . . . am inclined to say: 'This is simply what I do.'"[352] Yet saying this is not to acquiesce in rhetorical anomie. As I will show, rights retain their persuasive, reason-giving force even if they are not logically self-evident verities.[353]

NOTES

Epigraph: Brecht, "When Evil-Doing Comes like Falling Rain," in *Bertolt Brecht Poems, 1913–1956*. Quoted in Keane, *Season of Blood*.

1. See Prunier, *The Rwanda Crisis*, 237–68; Africa Rights, *Rwanda*; Human Rights Watch, *Leave None to Tell the Story*, 1–30. See also Gourevitch, *We Wish to Inform You*; Power, *A Problem from Hell*, 337; Guichaoua, *From War to Genocide*.
2. Africa Rights, *Rwanda*, 865.
3. Alain Destexhe observes, "Archaic political divisions were progressively transformed into racial ideologies and repeated outbreaks of violence resulting from the colonial heritage which was absorbed by local elites who then brought it into the political arena. The present generation has internalised the ethnological colonial model." Destexhe, *Rwanda and Genocide in the Twentieth Century*, 47. Cf. Mamdani, *When Victims Become Killers*, 34–39, 41–102; ICTR, "Prosecutor versus Jean-Paul Akayesu"; "Historical Context of the Events in Rwanda in 1994," 47–59.
4. See Stearns, *Dancing in the Glory of Monsters*, 15.
5. See Lévinas, *Ethics and Infinity*, 89. "The first word of the face is 'Thou shalt not kill.' It is an order. There is a commandment in the appearance of the face."
6. As Gérard Prunier concludes, "The symbolic impact of the UN withdrawal was . . . disastrous. The message to the killers was that the international community did not care and that they could go on with their deadly business without fear of intervention or even disapproval." Prunier, *The Rwanda Crisis*, 275–76.
7. Albert Camus writes that "it is the failing of a certain literature to believe that life is tragic because it is wretched." Camus, *Lyrical and Critical Essays*, 201.

8. See Longman and Rutagengwa, "Religion, Memory, and Violence in Rwanda."
9. Benjamin, *Illuminations*, 253–64. Anamnestic solidarity is born as the memory of victims. I will appropriate the term to include victims of injustice, not merely the dead.
10 Archbishop Desmond Tutu, commenting on the Rwandan genocide, as cited in TRC, *South Africa Report*, vol. 5, chap. 9, par. 4. Soyinka, *The Burden of Memory, the Muse of Forgiveness*, 31.
11. Tutu, *No Future without Forgiveness*, 51–52.
12. Sandel, "Introduction," 4, 6, 10.
13. Weber, "Science as a Vocation," 148–55.
14. Constant, "De la liberté des anciens comparée à celle des modernes."
15. National Constituent Assembly of France, *Declaration of the Rights of Man and of the Citizen*, 290–93.
16. Habermas, *Theory and Practice*, 84. See also Habermas, *Between Facts and Norms*, 28–41, 42–45, 100–105; Mandeville, *The Fable of the Bees*.
17. Tierney, *The Idea of Natural Rights*, 347. See also Glendon, *A World Made New*.
18. For an analysis of the genre of testimony, see Eaglestone, "Identification and the Genre of Testimony." See also Beverley, "The Margin at the Center"; Twiss, "Can a Perpetrator Write a Testiminio?"
19. See Ishay, *The History of Human Rights*; Hunt, *Inventing Human Rights*.
20. Aquinas, *Summa Theologiae* I–II, Q. 90, a. 2; Q. 94, a. 2.
21. Hobbes, *Leviathan*, chap. 11, 77, and chap. 13, 96.
22. Hobbes, chap. 14, 99. Hobbes thereby separates what Francisco Suárez merely distinguishes. Cf. Suárez, *A Treatise on the Laws and God*, 5–7.
23. Hobbes, *Leviathan*, chap. 17, 128.
24. Hobbes, *Leviathan*, chap. 16, 123.
25. Hobbes, *Leviathan*, chap. 17, 132.
26. Locke, *The Second Treatise of Government*, 4–6.
27. Dupré, *The Enlightenment*, 160.
28. Rousseau, *The Social Contract*, bk. 1, 65.
29. Rousseau, bk. 1, 62.
30. Barker, introduction to *Social Contract: Essays*, xxx. Rousseau's "slight of mind" is abetted by blurring the logical distinction between being a member of a class (citizens as members of the sovereign body) and being a part of a whole (the general will). Ultimately, writes Barker, "I must reflect that if I am the thousandth part of a tyrant, I am also the whole of a slave. Leviathan is still Leviathan, even when he is corporate" (xxxv).
31. Rousseau, *The Social Contract*, bk. 2, 84. Kant, *Critique of Practical Reason*, 5 (pagination from Prussian Academy edition, vol. 5).
32. Kant, *The Metaphysical Elements of Justice*, 315–16 (pagination from Prussian Academy edition, vol. 6). Accordingly, "We cannot say that a man has sacrificed in the state a part of his inborn external freedom for some particular purpose [i.e., prudential end]; rather, we must say that he has completely abandoned his wild, lawless freedom in order to find his whole freedom again undiminished in a lawful dependency, that is, in a juridical state of society, since this dependency comes from his own legislative Will [*Wille*]."
33. Kant, *Religion within the Limits of Reason Alone*, 31.
34. Kant, *Critique of Practical Reason*, 36.
35. d'Entrèves, *Natural Law*, 57.
36. Gray, *Enlightenment's Wake*, 123.
37. West, *Prophesy Deliverance*, 61.

38. Baxi, *The Future of Human Rights*, 44, 46. Baxi decries the "overt epistemic racism" of modern liberal rights discourse as "consistent with the catastrophic practices of cruelty toward the non-Euro-American Other" (47).
39. Rawls, *A Theory of Justice*, 118–23. Rawls, *Political Liberalism*, 13–14.
40. Rawls, *Political Liberalism*, 24–25, 273, 305. Rawls's perfectly prudential (self-interested) choosers are finally indiscernible, so that the selection of the first principles of justice derives not so much from actual contractual deliberation as from the suitably limited rational choice of a representative individual. In the introduction to the paperback edition of *Political Liberalism*, Rawls introduces an attenuated form of "civic friendship" as discursive reciprocity in the public reasoning of constitutional democratic regimes (li).
41. Rawls, 13–14. Moral or political maxims are represented as the construction of suitably delimited hypothetical (prudential) choice, so that while rational choosers may will "under [universal] moral laws," their subjection is, in Kant's terms, "problematical" rather than "apodictic." For Rawlsian constructivism the *justification* of a political conception of justice is founded upon the very hypothetical imperatives Kant denounced as "vain illusion and splendid misery." The form, if not the modality, of moral judgment is retained (i.e., of justice as fairness), as is Kant's conception of prudence (as rational self-interest)—the onus now is to unite what Kant so assiduously rent asunder. See Kant as quoted in Cassirer, *Rousseau, Kant, Goethe*, 24.
42. The first principle of justice thus provides that "each person has an equal right to a fully adequate scheme of equal basic liberties, which scheme is compatible with a similar scheme for all." The lexically subordinate "difference principle" justifies social and economic inequalities under conditions of "fair equality of opportunity" and only if they redound to the "greatest benefit of the least advantaged members of society." Rawls, *Political Liberalism*, 5–6, 291.
43. Rawls, *A Theory of Justice*, 514, 442–43n30.
44. Rawls, *Political Liberalism*, 13.
45. Rawls, 12.
46. Aquinas, *Summae Theologiae* I–II, Q. 90, a. 2; II–II, Q. 58, arts. 6, 7, 8, 12.
47. Rawls, *Political Liberalism*, 291ff.
48. Rawls's revised *The Law of Peoples*, however, underscores the lexical priority (and interdependence) of basic negative and positive rights for illiberal or hierarchical, albeit "decent," regimes: while "well-ordered" hierarchies may limit certain civil-political liberties such as equal liberty of conscience or democratic suffrage, they must secure for all members of the people basic human rights to life (the means of subsistence and security); to liberty (to freedom from slavery, serfdom, and forced occupation, and to a sufficient measure of liberty of conscience to ensure freedom of religion and thought); to property (personal property); and to formal equality as expressed by the rule of natural justice (that is, similar cases be treated similarly). Rawls, *The Law of Peoples*, 65.
49. Rawls, *Political Liberalism*, 9–10. "In formulating such a conception," concludes Rawls, political liberalism applies the principle of toleration to philosophy itself." As we shall see in chap. 4, Rawls's later writings favor a more "inclusive" interpretation.
50. In his latest writings Rawls revises his earlier strictures, permitting reasonable (religious) comprehensive doctrines to "be introduced in public reason at any time" provided that public reasons, in a reasonable political conception, are duly presented. *Political Liberalism*, li. We will consider the implications of these revisions in chap. 3.

51. John Donne, "An Anatomy of the World," in Donne, *John Donne*, 276, lines 205–18: "And new philosophy," says Donne, "calls all in doubt . . . Prince, subject, father, son, are things forgot, For every man alone thinks he hath got to be a phoenix, and that then can be None of that kind, of which he is, but he."
52. Burke, *Reflections on the Revolution in France*, 45. See also Wilkins, *The Problem of Burke's Political Philosophy*, 59–60, 109–10.
53. Burke, *Reflections on the Revolution in France*, 41–42, 96–97.
54. Bentham, "Anarchical Fallacies," in Bentham, *Works*, 523.
55. Bentham, 501.
56. Marx, *The Marx-Engels Reader*, 43.
57. MacIntyre, *After Virtue*, 67–70.
58. Sandel, *Liberalism and the Limits of Justice*, 54, 94. See Walzer, *Thick and Thin*, 21–25.
59. See Hegel's criticism of Kantian Moralität in Hegel, *Philosophy of Right*, par. 135. In postmodern neo-Hegelian criticism, however, tradition exhibits no ontological telos.
60. Burke, *Reflections on the Revolution in France*, 39. See Sandel, "Introduction," 4, 6, 10; MacIntyre, *After Virtue*, 204–43.
61. See, Taylor, *Sources of the Self*, 88–90.
62. Benhabib, "The Generalized and the Concrete Other," 87.
63. Rawls, "Kantian Constructivism in Moral Theory."
64. Rorty, *Contingency, Irony and Solidarity*, 45.
65. Rorty, "The Priority of Democracy to Philosophy," 259.
66. T. S. Eliot, "Whispers of Immortality," in Eliot, *The Complete Poems and Plays*, 33.
67. Rorty, *Contingency, Irony and Solidarity*, 73.
68. Williams, *Ethics and the Limits of Philosophy*, 86ff.; Hare, *Moral Thinking*.
69. Rawls, *A Theory of Justice*, 21.
70. See Hegel, *Philosophy of Right*, pars. 257–360; Marx, Preface to *A Contribution*, 261–65.
71. See John XXXIII's *Pacem in terris*, nos. 60–66, 139, 143–45; *Gaudium et spes* in O'Brien and Shannon, Catholic Social Thought 172–250, nos. 25ff., 30; Second Vatican Council, *Dignitatis humanae*, nos. 6–7, 551–68; Paul VI, *Populorum progressio*, 251–77, nos. 22–24, 43–75; John Paul II, *Sollicitudo rei socialis*, 422–68, nos. 38–40. See also Hollenbach, *The Common Good and Christian Ethics*; Curran, *Catholic Social Teaching*.
72. John XXIII, *Mater et magistra*, no. 65, and *Pacem in terris*, no. 60. Such a rights-based interpretation permits Pope John to extend the common good globally, in *Pacem in terris* no. 139. See Pope Pius XII, Radio Message, 200; and *Gaudium et spes* in O'Brien and Shannon, *Catholic Social Thought*, no. 26, and in Second Vatican Council, *Dignitatis humanae*, no. 6.
73. Jacques Maritain, "The Person and the Common Good," in Maritain, *The Social and the Political Philosophy of Jacques Maritain*, 85; Rorty, "The Priority of Democracy to Philosophy," 259.
74. See Murray, *We Hold These Truths*, 155–74. See Murray, "Memo to Cardinal Cushing," 81–86.
75. See Second Vatican Council, *Dignitatis humanae*, no. 4. "Positive" correlative duties to preserve and protect agents' basic capabilities (the objects of basic rights) generate structural imperatives, e.g., the state's obligation to guarantee citizens' basic welfare.
76. Pope Gregory XVI, *Mirari vos arbitramur*, no. 2730. Religious liberty figured prominently among Pius IX's "Syllabus of Errors."
77. Hehir, "The Modern Catholic Church and Human Rights," 117.
78. See DeBerri et al., *Catholic Social Teaching*.

79. See Curran, *The Development of Moral Theology* and *Tradition and Church Reform*.
80. See Hollenbach, "A Communitarian Reconstruction of Human Rights."
81. See Rosen, *Dignity*, 47–54. John Paul II's apostolic letter *Mulieris dignitatem* (1988) appeals to equal rights in rejecting the natural subordination of women (e.g., in Leo XIII's *Arcanum divinae sapientiae* [1880]) while maintaining the "specific diversity and personal originality" of the two sexes.
82. Pope John Paul II, *Veritatis splendor*, no. 80, citing the *Pastoral Constitution on the Church in the Modern World, Gaudium et Spes*, 27. Abortion is regarded as intrinsically evil, on both modern deontological and traditional teleological grounds.
83. See USCCB, "Our First Most Cherished Liberty." Consequential arguments are likewise offered to buttress either strain of natural law, e.g., that recognizing same-sex marriage imperils both the natural, heteronormative institution of marriage and the human rights of children.
84. Pope John Paul II, *Veritatis splendor*, no. 80. For a more detailed analysis of John Paul II's gambit, see my "The Bond of Peace."
85. See Noonan, *A Church That Can and Cannot Change*. Noonan writes that "in the development of morals, the honorable possession of one kind of property becomes a hideous affront to humanity" (221). Noonan, "Development in Moral Doctrine," 669.
86. Rawls, *Political Liberalism*, 9–11, 212–54.
87. Bentham, "Anarchical Fallacies," in Bentham, *Works*, 523.
88. Perelman, *The Realm of Rhetoric*, 5, 14, 17–18. For Wittgenstein, "Grammar tells what kind of object anything is." Wittgenstein, *Philosophical Investigations*, pt. 1, 373.
89. In Linda Hogan's words, rights function as "emancipatory politics whose modus operandi is ultimately that of persuasion." Hogan, *Keeping Faith with Human Rights*, 3.
90. See Holkeboer, "Out of the Crooked Timber of Humanity," 149–65.
91. Sandel, "Introduction," 4, 6, 10.
92. Said, "Nationalism, Human Rights, and Interpretation," 45–46.
93. Arendt, "A Reply," 79.
94. OAU, "Rwanda: The Preventable Genocide," par. 7.
95. Rilke, "On Music," in Rilke, *Selected Poems*, 169.
96. Raphaël Lemkin coined the term "genocide" in his *Axis Rule in Occupied Europe*. See Straus, *Fundamentals of Genocide*.
97. Jason Stearns distinguishes three distinct periods beginning in 1996. Stearns, *Dancing in the Glory of Monsters*, 8.
98. Esquivel, "Afterword," 105; UN, preamble to Universal Declaration of Human Rights.
99. See Hayner, *Unspeakable Truths*; and Biggar, *Burying the Past*.
100. Africa Rights, *Rwanda*, 798ff. Women and children were especially vulnerable. "Thousands of Tutsi women were raped . . . [T]he systematic rape was a form of terrorism against the Tutsi community—intended to intimidate, humiliate and degrade the Tutsi women and others affected by her suffering. . . . Some of the girls and women . . . suffered horrific physical tortures before they were raped. . . . Systematic rape was one of the instruments of genocide used to devastating effect by the extremists" (748–50); "A substantial portion of children who have survived massacres and attacks have suffered horrific wounds" (798–99); "Many children witnessed the atrocities and many were displaced or orphaned" (853–61).
101. Testimony of a Rwandese survivor, as cited in Africa Rights, *Rwanda*, 735. See Hatzfeld, *Life Laid Bare*; Kigali Genocide Memorial, *We Survived Genocide in Rwanda*.

102. Scarry, *The Body in Pain*, 30.
103. Pumla Gobodo-Madikizela speaks of the "effacing of pain," citing Eileen Scarry. Gobodo-Madikizela, *A Human Being Died That Night*, 128.
104. Tutu, "The Theology of Liberation in Africa," 163.
105. Tutu, *No Future without Forgiveness*, 20.
106. Tutu, 13, 17.
107. Arthur, "How 'Transitions' Reshaped Human Rights."
108. The commission was charged to "establish as complete a picture as possible—including the antecedents, circumstances, factors and context of [gross human rights] violations as well as the causes, motives and perspectives of persons responsible" (Section 3[1][a], Promotion of National Unity and Reconciliation Act, no. 34 [1995]).
109. See Asmal, Asmal, and Roberts, *Reconciliation through Truth*, 12–27.
110. Villa-Vicencio and Verwoerd, "Constructing a Report," 287. See TRC, *Final Report* (Cape Town, October 28, 1998), IV, secs. 60–81. Villa-Vicencio led the Research Department of the TRC.
111. Tutu, *No Future without Forgiveness*, 32–33.
112. Tutu, 32–33.
113. Testimony of Lukas Baba Sikwepere, at the Human Rights Commission hearing in Heideveld, Cape Town; as reported in Krog, *Country of My Skull*, 31; TRC, *South African Report*, vol. 5, chap. 9, par. 9.
114. Jean Baudrillard, quoted in Young, *The Texture of Memory*, 1; See Minow, *Between Vengeance and Forgiveness*, 118.
115. Fort Calata was a member of the Cradock Four; he, together with Matthew Goniwe, Sparrow Mkhonto, and Sicelo Mhluali, was abducted and murdered by the state police in June 1985. Their "horribly mutilated bodies" were discovered a week later. Yet the full story of what happened, including the perpetrators' identities, was revealed only during the commission's hearings. See Tutu, *No Future without Forgiveness*, 98.
116. Tutu, 114.
117. Krog, *Country of My Skull*, 42–43. Krog served as a journalist reporting on the hearings of the TRC.
118. Levi in Wiesenthal, *The Sunflower*, 191.
119. Jürgen Habermas interprets "Benjamin's concept of 'anamnestic solidarity' with past injustice" in secular terms. See Habermas, *The New Conservatism*, 233.
120. Éla, "Christianity and Liberation in Africa," 143.
121. Pumla Gobodo-Madikizela, as quoted in Minow, *Between Vengeance and Forgiveness*, 61.
122. Ali A. Mazuri argues that "violations of human rights are preceded by the process of psychic subhumanization." See Mazuri, "Human Rights and the Moving Frontier of World Culture," in Alwin, *Philosophical Foundations of Human Rights*, 243.
123. In du Toit's words, "In the particular circumstances of transitional justice in postapartheid South Africa, the conception of truth as acknowledgment embodied in the victims' hearings of the TRC thus represented a political choice for the priority of restoring the civic and human dignity of the victims of gross human rights violations." Du Toit, "The Moral Foundations," 134.
124. Minow, *Between Vengeance and Forgiveness*, 5.
125. Elie Wiesel, "The Holocaust as Literary Inspiration," in Wiesel et al., *Dimensions of the Holocaust*, 9.

126. See Langer, *Holocaust Testimonies*. For an analysis of the genre of testimony, see Eaglestone, "Identification and the Genre of Testimony." See Beverley, "The Margin at the Center."
127. See Stone, "Holocaust Testimony."
128. See Hopgood, *The Endtimes of Human Rights*.
129. See Burnet, "The Injustice of Local Justice."
130. See Twiss, "Can a Perpetrator Write a Testiminio?"
131. As Alvin H. Rosenfeld contends, the new literature is one "of fragments, or partial and provisional forms, no one of which by itself can suffice to express the Holocaust, but the totality of which begins to accomplish and register a powerful effect." Rosenfeld, *A Double Dying*, 33–34.
132. Derrida, *Demeure*, 29.
133. Derrida, *Adieu to Emmanuel Lévinas*, 33–34.
134. Ismael Mahomed, as cited in Tutu, *No Future without Forgiveness*, 33.
135. See Derrida's interpretation of Benjamin's *Zur Kritik der Wewal* in Derrida, "Force of Law," 3–67. Robert Eaglestone deconstructs the rhetorical strategies in which "the 'doubleness' of testimony . . . both repels and attracts identification." See "Identification and the Genre of Testimony," 121.
136. Wiesel, "The Holocaust as Literary Inspiration," 8.
137. Krog, *Country of My Skull*, 26.
138. For Derrida the trace reveals "the limits of the linguistic and the limits of the rhetorical." Derrida and Ferraris, *A Taste for the Secret*, 76.
139. Wiesel, "The Holocaust as Literary Inspiration," 8.
140. Villa-Vicencio, "Telling One Another Stories," 37–38. Villa-Vicencio cites Bosset in *Democracy in Action* 8, no. 5 (August 31, 1994): 16.
141. Wallace Stevens, "The Poems of Our Climate," in *The Palm at the End of the Mind*, 158.
142. In Primo Levi's words, "We, the survivors, are not the true witnesses . . . we are those who by their prevarications or abilities or good luck did not touch bottom. Those who did so, those who saw the Gorgon, have not returned to tell about it." Levi, *The Drowned and the Saved*, 63–64.
143. Reading Derrida and Lévinas in light of the Shoah, Robert Eaglestone, too, rejects a positivist historiography in his *The Holocaust and the Postmodern*.
144. Preamble to Universal Declaration of Human Rights.
145. See Hohfeld, *Fundamental Legal Conceptions*.
146. Minow, *Between Vengeance and Forgiveness*, 146.
147. D. D. Raphael distinguishes subjective rights as "rights of recipience" and "rights of action." See Raphael, "Human Rights," 207–17. Gewirth, *Human Rights*, 2. In contrast to "liberties, powers, and immunities," human rights "are entirely or mainly kinds of claim-rights" (2). See Raz, *The Morality of Freedom*, 166.
148. See Feinberg, *Social Philosophy*, 59–61.
149. See Gewirth, *Human Rights*, 2–12, and *Reason and Morality*, 63–68. As Gewirth observes, the "claim-making may be only implicit or dispositional, a matter of attitude, of how the agent regards himself in relation to other persons" (*Reason and Morality*, 66).
150. See Ronald Dworkin, *Taking Rights Seriously*, xi.
151. See Cranston, *What Are Human Rights?*, 39; and Gewirth, *Human Rights*, 3. R. J. Vincent argues that "a right as a *justified* claim suggests . . . social acceptance of the right as of great importance" (*Human Rights and International Relations*, 9). In Dworkin's words, "We may

define the weight of a right, assuming it is not absolute, as its power to withstand . . . competition. . . . We might, for simplicity, stipulate not to call any political aim a right unless it has a certain threshold weight against collective goals in general; unless, for example, it cannot be defeated by appeal to any of the ordinary routine goals of political administration, but only by a goal of special urgency." Dworkin, *Taking Rights Seriously*, 92.

152. For an elaboration of the interest and benefit theories of rights, see Waldron, *The Right to Private Property*, 62–105.

153. Shue, *Basic Rights*, 13. In Shue's definition, "a moral right" (of which human rights comprise a subset) "provides (1) the rational basis for a justified demand (2) that the actual enjoyment of a substance be (3) socially guaranteed against standard threats." As we shall see in the next chapter, such practical "ought" claims are relativized to the agent's reasons for acting: the validity of one's right's claim that "another ought to do, or forbear from doing, A" depends on the fitting ascription of reasons that vindicate or verify the judgment. That rights qua warrants serve to generate such claims permits us to speak derivatively of rights as claims or "claim-rights." See Gewirth, *The Community of Rights*, 8–20.

154. Aristotle, *Politics*, 1253a9ff: "Nature . . . does nothing without some purpose; and for the purpose of making man a political animal she has endowed him alone among the animals with the power of reasoned speech. . . . Speech . . . serves to indicate what is useful and what is harmful, and so also what is right and what is wrong," 28. We may translate "*logos*" as "argument" in practical discourse. See NE 1094b13, 1095a30, 1104a1, etc. See also Arendt, *The Human Condition*, 175ff.

155. See Donnelly, *Universal Human Rights*, 10–13.

156. See Sen, *Poverty and Famines*, 1–8, 45–51, 154–66; and Drèze and Sen, *Hunger and Public Action*, 9–17, 56–61. See Donnelly, *Universal Human Rights*, 11.

157. See John Langan, "Defining Human Rights: A Revision of the Liberal Tradition," in Langan, *Human Rights in the Americas*, 74.

158. See Wittgenstein's remark that "It is not possible that there should have been only one occasion on which someone obeyed a rule. . . . And hence also 'obeying a rule' is a practice." *Philosophical Investigations*, pt. 1, pars. 199, 202.

159. Properly speaking, neither rights nor duties are "prima facie," as W. D. Ross supposed, for a right/warrant may be trumped without thereby ceasing to be a right. Conversely, a correlative duty to satisfy the claim, e.g., honor hate speech, arises only if the claim *is* indeed warranted/justified. See Melden, *Rights and Persons*, 4–15. That on a given occasion my *claim*-right is overridden implies that, *hic et nunc*, my right/warrant fails to justify my claim to X, i.e., generate a correlative duty to satisfy the claim.

160. Perelman and Olbrechts-Tyteca, *The New Rhetoric*, 31.

161. Preamble to Universal Declaration of Human Rights, 153.

162. See MacIntyre, "Community, Law," 100. See also my rejoinder to MacIntyre in "Rights as Rhetoric: Nonsense on Stilts," in the same volume.

163. Marx, "On the Jewish Question," 43.

164. See MacIntyre, *After Virtue*, 18, 68.

165. That the meaning of human rights is not wholly dependent on a particular modality of justification is apparent in Jeremy Waldron's observation: "At the level of rhetoric, the shift from 'natural rights' to 'human rights' marks a loss of faith in our ability to justify rights on the basis of truth about human *nature*. To call them *human* rights is now to characterize the scope of the claims being made rather than hint at anything about their justification." *Nonsense upon Stilts*, 163.

166. Curiously, nothing in MacIntyre's own Aristotelian definition of practice as a "coherent and complex form of socially established cooperative human activity through which goods internal to that form of activity are realized" precludes our viewing rights thus. None of the examples cited from Aristotle ("flute-playing, or war, or geometry") nor his own illustrations (chess, architecture, enquiries of physics, chemistry, and biology, history, painting, music) are, after all, of a "socially local character" (*After Virtue*, 187).
167. Tutu, *No Future without Forgiveness*, 32–33.
168. Tutu, 87.
169. Testimony of Lukas Baba Sikwepere in Krog, *Country of My Skull*, 31.
170. Tierney, *The Idea of Natural Rights*, 347.
171. Vincent, *Human Rights and International Relations*, 17. See Alexis de Tocqueville's observation: "There is nothing which, generally speaking, elevates and sustains the human spirit more than the idea of rights. There is something great and virile in the idea of right which removes from any request its suppliant character, and places the one who claims it on the same level as the one who grants it." De Tocqueville quoted in Minogue, "Natural Rights, Ideology and the Game of Life," 34.
172. Feinberg, *Social Philosophy*, 58–59.
173. Tutu, *No Future without Forgiveness*, 34–36.
174. Hountondji, "The Master's Voice," 325.
175. UN, Universal Declaration of Human Rights. The *Convention against Torture and Other Cruel, Inhuman or Degrading Treatment or Punishment*, A/Res/39/46, 10 Dec., 1984, recognizes explicitly that "the equal and inalienable rights of all members of the human family . . . derive from the inherent dignity of the human person." See Glendon, *A World Made New*, 173–91.
176. Feinberg, *Social Philosophy*, 58–59.
177. Ignatieff, *Human Rights as Politics and Idolatry*, 18, 57. Tutu, *No Future without Forgiveness*, 32–33. See Dworkin, *Taking Rights Seriously*, 272–73.
178. See Williams, "The Idea of Equality," 236–37; Seyla Benhabib, "The Generalized and the Concrete Other," 88; cf. Mead, *Mind, Self, and Society*, 152–64, 379–89.
179. As noted in the introduction, our rhetorical (nonessentialist) reading of rights allows for multiple uses. We need not assume that every conception of dignity yield an explicit doctrine of rights. Aquinas's conception of dignity, for instance, leaves the question unresolved. See Tierney, "Natural Law and Natural Rights," 389–406.
180. See Burke, *Reflections on the Revolution in France*, 96. I have argued that the practical attitude of respect functions as a "prejudice" in Gadamer's sense, i.e., a prejudgment of our practical understanding, in the design of Rawls's original position (*The Ethics of Our Climate*, 67–75). As such it is disclosed rather than constructed in rational choice. See Gadamer, *Truth and Method*, 265–307. The term "latent wisdom" is Burke's. See Burke, *Reflections on the Revolution in France*, 305–6, 412.
181. See Rawls, *A Theory of Justice*, 513–14.
182. John Rawls, "Justice as Fairness: Political not Metaphysical," in Rawls, *Collected Papers*, 401n20.
183. Rawls, *Political Liberalism*, 290, 370–71. See Habermas, *Justification and Application*, 27–28.
184. See Perelman, *The Realm of Rhetoric*, 14, 17–18. See Perelman and Olbrechts-Tyteca, *The New Rhetoric*, 13–62.
185. MacIntyre, *Three Rival Versions of Moral Inquiry*, 5; see also MacIntyre, *Whose Justice? Which Rationality?*, 349–88.

186. MacIntyre, *After Virtue*, 191–92 (emphasis added).
187. MacIntyre, 200.
188. See Kant, *Groundwork of the Metaphysic of Morals*, 77ff. (pagination is from Prussian Academy edition, vol. 6). Rawls, *Political Liberalism*, 74.
189. Rawls, *Political Liberalism*, 76.
190. Rawls, 222, no. 9; see also 108. Rational autonomy, defined as the capacity to realize ends "worthy of devoted pursuit," thus comprises basic *external* liberties.
191. Rawls, *Political Liberalism*, 314–15.
192. Thus Rawls distinguishes "basic" liberties as those comprising "essential social conditions" for the adequate development and full exercise of the respective moral powers. Rawls, 293.
193. Uniting discrete agential capabilities to the respect due to practically rational agents addresses several potential lacunae in capability theory, such as why discrete capabilities, as developed capacities, *should* be realized and how basic capabilities are themselves internally related. It is in the realization of this "moral power" (to "the essential minimum degree") that we may say "citizens are free." Rawls, 81. Rational autonomy, says Rawls, "rests on persons' intellectual and moral powers" and is exhibited in their "exercising their capacity to form, to revise, and to pursue a conception of the good, and to deliberate in accordance with it" (72).
194. Rawls, 104.
195. See Nussbaum, "Human Capabilities," 91; see Sen, "Gender Inequality and Theories of Justice," 259–73. See O'Neill's criticism of Rawls in "Justice, Capabilities, and Vulnerabilities," 146n7.
196. Rawls, *Political Liberalism*, 7; see also 289–371. Rawls argues that in assigning special priority to equal basic rights, a democratic regime must ensure that "all citizens have sufficient material means to make effective use of those basic rights" (157).
197. Rawls, *A Theory of Justice*, 505–6n30. Rawls concedes that the use of primary goods is "always to be assessed in the light of assumptions about [what Amartya Sen terms] capabilities" (*Political Liberalism*, 183; see also Rawls, *The Law of Peoples*, 13n3). Sen defines a "person's capability" as "the alternative combination of functionings that are feasible for her to achieve. Capability is thus a kind of freedom: the substantive freedom to achieve alternative functioning combinations (or less formally put, the freedom to achieve various lifestyles." Capabilities, thus conceived, specify the constitutive means of developing and exercising our moral powers, whereas an "'index' of primary goods holdings" is "informationally poorer, . . . because of the parametric variation of resources and primary goods vis-à-vis the opportunity to achieve high quality of living." Sen, *Development as Freedom*, 65, 75, 78. See also Sen, "Gender Inequality and Theories of Justice," 263–66. Martha Nussbaum argues in a similar vein, "By measuring who is better off and who worse off in terms of resources, the Rawlsian model neglects a salient fact of life; that individuals vary greatly in their needs for resources and in their abilities to convert resources into valuable functionings." Nussbaum, *Women and Human Development*, 68.
198. Rawls, *The Law of Peoples*, 36, 78–80. See Müller, "Rawls's Relational Conception of Human Rights," 58–76; Finlayson and Freyenhagen, *Habermas and Rawls*.
199. Rawls, *Political Liberalism*, 18n20, 104. The force of the latter interest is apparent in Rawls's concession that, were the parties "moved to protect only . . . material and physical desires," e.g., money and wealth, we might say they "modeled citizens' heteronomy" rather than "their rational autonomy" (76).

200. Basic rights are "inalienable" inasmuch as they derive from the mutual recognition and respect owed to moral agents. As such, we may forgo the *exercise* of a basic right, e.g., security, when risking one's life for another, but not the right itself.
201. Shue, *Basic Rights*, 19; see 18–34.
202. Rawls, *A Theory of Justice*, 176–80, 194–200, 224–27; see also *Political Liberalism*, 324–31.
203. See Shue, *Basic Rights*, 71–78.
204. See Sen, *Development as Freedom*, 160–88. Sen assesses famine in terms of "entitlement failures": failures of agents to enjoy customary or legal claim-rights to food and other prerequisites of nutritional well-being such as access to health care, medical facilities, elementary education, potable water, and sanitary facilities.
205. Shue defines "basic rights" as "everyone's minimum reasonable demands upon the rest of humanity . . . rights are basic . . . only if enjoyment of them is essential to the enjoyment of all other rights" (*Basic Rights*, 19ff.). Interpreting basic rights in terms of the normative *recognition* of human claim-rights, rather than the enjoyment of the object claimed as a right, resolves several lacunae of Shue's otherwise incisive argument: the internal relation between recognizing the subject/claimant as worthy of respect and the object/force of basic rights shows why rights claims are "basic," not only with respect to human rights practice but to practices generally. Saying that enjoyment of basic rights "is essential to the enjoyment of all other rights" does not suffice to show that rights "trump" other prima facie "reasonable demands," e.g., claims of virtue. Indeed, Shue's depiction of basic rights as the "morality of the depths" makes sense only if we tacitly assume the maxim of respect as deciding which narrative conceptions of the (common) good are to count as "reasonable."
206. See Lyotard, *The Postmodern Condition*, 27.
207. See Benjamin, "N [Theoretics of Knowledge]."
208. Benjamin, "Theses on the Philosophy of History," in Benjamin, *Illuminations*, 254.
209. Max Horkheimer, quoted by Walter Benjamin in *The Arcades Project*, 478. See Max Horkheimer, "Thoughts on Religion," in *Critical Theory*, 179–80.
210. For a genealogy of the term, see Max Pensky, "On the Use and Abuse of Memory." See McCarthy, *Ideals and Illusions*, 205–10.
211. See Lenhardt, "Anamnestic Solidarity"; Peukert, *Science, Action and Fundamental Theology*. We will consider Metz's interpretation in chapter 3.
212. See Habermas, "*Vom öffenlichem Gebrauch der Historie*," in *Eine Art Schadensabwicklung*, 141. I am indebted to Max Pensky's critique of Habermas in "On the Use and Abuse of Memory," 368–77.
213. Benjamin, "Theses on the Philosophy of History," 255; see also Pensky, "On the Use and Abuse of Memory," 365.
214. Levi in Wiesenthal, *The Sunflower*, 191.
215. Thus the Promotion of National Unity and Reconciliation Act, no. 34 (1995), charged the TRC to contribute to the building of "a historic bridge between the past of a deeply divided society characterized by strife, conflict, untold suffering and injustice, and a future founded on the recognition of human rights, democracy and peaceful coexistence and development opportunities for all South Africans, irrespective of colour, race, belief or sex." See Villa-Vicencio and Verwoerd, "Constructing a Report," 280.
216. Zalaquett, *Introduction to the English Edition*, xxiv.
217. As André du Toit observes, "The relevant sense of truth is of a more holistic *narrative truth*—that involved in the overall framing of the events and experiences that together

make up the victim's own 'story.'" See du Toit, "The Moral Foundations," 136; Boraine, "Truth and Reconciliation in South Africa," 152; and Zalaquett, "Balancing Ethical Imperatives and Political Constraints," 1433.

218. See Gadamer, *Truth and Method*, 482–85. Martha Minow notes that in response to the relative absence of women's testimony regarding their own suffering, the commissioners "created hearings specifically focused on women's own experiences." She concludes, "The women who testify, indeed everyone who testifies, render vivid and palpable the human faces of suffering and survival." Minow, *Between Vengeance and Forgiveness*, 84. See Tutu, *No Future without Forgiveness*, 184–89.
219. Villa-Vicencio, "Telling One Another Stories," 34.
220. See Asmal, Asmal, and Roberts, *Reconciliation through Truth*, 11. Reconstructing a civic narrative remains a necessary if insufficient condition of legal/ethical reconciliation.
221. Minow, *Between Vengeance and Forgiveness*, 78.
222. Verwoerd, "Continuing the Discussion," 70.
223. Tina Rosenberg, "A Reporter at Large: Recovering from Apartheid," *New Yorker*, November 18, 1996, 92.
224. Soyinka, *The Burden of Memory, the Muse of Forgiveness*.
225. See Judge Ismail Mahomed of the TRC, "Constitutional Court of South Africa, Case no. CCT 117/96 (July 25, 1996), Azanian Peoples Organization (AZAPO) and Others vs. President of the Republic of South Africa and Others," as cited in Tutu, *No Future without Forgiveness*, 29. Gobodo-Madikizela, *A Human Being Died That Night*, 86, 90.
226. W. D. Auden, "September 1, 1939," in Auden, *The Collected Poetry*, 57.
227. See Shriver, *An Ethic for Enemies*, 63–72.
228. See Prunier, *Africa's World War*; Hochschild, *King Leopold's Ghost*. The International Rescue Committee estimates that 5.4 million have died, principally due to disease and malnutrition (https://www.rescue.org/country/democratic-republic-congo#what-caused-the-current-crisis-in-congo accessed 2/28/2019). See *Human Security Report 2009/2010*, which criticizes the ICRC's methodology and offers a lower figure.
229. See Shue, *Basic Rights*, 35–64; Gewirth, *The Community of Rights*, 31–70.
230. Mark Osiel thus speaks of "liberal" or "discursive social solidarity," in deliberative democratic polities. See Osiel, *Mass Atrocity, Collective Memory*, 17. See Crocker, "Truth Commissions, Transitional Justice," 99–121.
231. See the executive summary in OAU, "Rwanda: The Preventable Genocide," par. 51, chap. 24, and recommendations, par. 9. *Gacaca* are "lower-level tribunals that attempt to blend traditional and contemporary mechanisms to expedite the justice process in a way that promotes reconciliation." See Stover and Weinstein, *My Neighbor, My Enemy*.
232. See Burnet, "The Injustice of Local Justice," 173–93. See Clark and Kaufman, *After Genocide*.
233. Minow, *Between Vengeance and Forgiveness*, 57.
234. Albie Sachs, "Human Rights: Good or Bad for South Africa," Harvard Law School Human Rights Program, January 21, 1998, as quoted in Minow, *Between Vengeance and Forgiveness*, 132.
235. Minow, *Between Vengeance and Forgiveness*, 60.
236. Tutu, *No Future without Forgiveness*, 221. See Gobodo-Madikizela, *A Human Being Died That Night*, 126.
237. Vincent, *Human Rights and International Relations*, 9.
238. Nozick, *Anarchy, State, and Utopia*, 238.

239. Cranston, *What Are Human Rights?* 34, 41. Yet compare Locke's remarks in *The Second Treatise of Government*: "Men, being once born, have a right to the Preservation, and consequently to Meat and Drink, and such other things as Nature affords for their Subsistence" (303). See Shue, *Basic Rights*, 188n16; Melden, *Rights and Persons*, 237–42.
240. Feinberg, *Social Philosophy*, 88. For the genealogy of "active" and "passive" rights, see Tuck, *Natural Rights Theories*, 5, passim. For a critique of Tuck's interpretation, see Tierney, *The Idea of Natural Rights*, 217–20.
241. Friedman, "Good Ends, Bad Means," 106.
242. Isaiah Berlin, "Two Concepts of Liberty," in Berlin, *Four Essays on Liberty*, 130n1.
243. Shue, *Basic Rights*, 32–33. "The protection of 'negative rights' requires positive measures, and therefore their actual enjoyment requires positive measures" (39). In Gewirth's terms, Shue proposes that the distinction "negative" and "positive" properly pertains to the nature of the duties borne by the *recipient* of rights' claims rather than the *object* of rights.
244. See Ignatieff, *Human Rights as Politics and Idolatry*, 84.
245. If duties of forbearance were violated in the summary withdrawal of UNIMIR troops, immediate duties of protection were violated when increasingly palpable "standard threats" were ignored. See Power, *A Problem from Hell*, 329–89.
246. Gewirth, *The Community of Rights*, 33–38.
247. See Hart, "Are There Any Natural Rights?"
248. Shue speaks of "duties to aid the deprived" rather than of provision, but a child's right to nutrition, for example, is not consequent upon deprivation (either of the right or the substance of the right). As we shall see, in the former case, i.e., where agents are systemically deprived of their rights, an ancillary set of duties is generated: not only of aid but of reparation, restitution, and so forth. See Shue, *Basic Rights*, 51–55.
249. See Ignatieff, *Human Rights as Politics and Idolatry*, 90.
250. Glendon, *A World Made New*, 187; see also 202, 238.
251. The Charter is distinctive, however, in recognizing the rights of "peoples" or "solidarity rights": for example, the rights of peoples to existence and self-determination; to dispose freely of "their wealth and natural resources"; to economic, social, and cultural development, including "equal enjoyment of the common heritage of (hu)mankind"; and so forth. H. O. W. Okoth-Ogendo concludes that the OAU Charter's raison d'être rested not only in the need for an effective structure "at the regional level for the institutional coordination, supervision, or implementation of efforts" to be directed toward "the promotion and protection of human rights," but even more in "the need to develop a scheme of human rights norms and principles founded on the historical traditions and values of African civilizations rather than simply [to] reproduce and try to administer the norms and principles derived from the historical experiences of Europe and the Americas." Okoth-Ogendo, "Human and Peoples' Rights," 76.
252. Nyerere, "Kanisa na Maisha ya Watu," in *Man and Development*, 97–98. My adaptation of the English translation, in light of the *Kiswahili* text, can be found in "The Church's Role in Society," 121. See also Nyerere's *Freedom and Unity, Freedom and Socialism, Freedom and Development*, and *Ujamaa*.
253. Rawls, *A Theory of Justice*, 513. Significantly, in his lectures on Kant, Rawls explicates the various formulae of the categorical imperative by interpreting the formal, canonical constraint of impartiality in terms of treating "humanity" as an end, understood as reason's "pure, practical interest" in realizing agents' characteristic "moral powers." Rawls's own

departure from Hobbesian instrumental rationality thus tacitly introduces the Kantian conception of moral powers and correlative interests. Rawls, *Lectures on the History of Moral Philosophy*, 181–216.

254. See Gewirth, *Human Rights*, 41–78; Donnelly, *Universal Human Rights*, 62–65; Rawls, *Political Liberalism*, 58–66. See the refined understanding of needs, capabilities, and functionings as defining the moral minima of agency in the analyses of Sen, "Gender Inequality and Theories of Justice," 259–73; Nussbaum, "Human Capabilities," 259–73; and Nussbaum, "Emotions and Women's Capabilities," 364–98. See also Sen, "Well-Being, Agency and Freedom." Basic rights, says Shue, "specify the line beneath which no one is to be allowed to sink. This is part of the reason that basic rights are tied as closely to self-respect as Feinberg indicates legal claim-rights are" (*Basic Rights*, 18). Basic rights are thus consistent with multiple comprehensive conceptions of the good, including theories of justice that incorporate other "justicizing" criteria once basic rights are fulfilled. See Vlastos, "Justice and Equality," 31–72.

255. Tutu, "The Theology of Liberation in Africa," 167.

256. O'Neill, "Justice, Capabilities, and Vulnerabilities," 142. See Nussbaum, *Women and Human Development*, 111–66.

257. As Bernard Williams observes, the more extreme the degradation, the more likely it is that its victims "do *not* see themselves differently from the way they are seen by the exploiters; either they do not see themselves as anything at all, or they acquiesce passively in the role for which they have been cast" ("The Idea of Equality," 236–37). So, too, Isaiah Berlin observes, the "triumph of despotism is to force the slaves to declare themselves free" (Berlin, *Four Essays on Liberty*, 165).

258. See Dupré, "The Common Good and the Open Society," 689–92, 705–12, and *Marx's Social Critique of Culture*, 1–57. I have developed my critique in greater detail in *The Ethics of Our Climate*, 62–78, 119–23.

259. See Cahill, "Embodying God's Image," 55–77.

260. Wittgenstein, *Philosophical Investigations*, pt. 1, pars. 497, 664.

261. Louw, "The African Concept of *Ubuntu* and Restorative Justice," 169.

262. Wittgenstein, *Philosophical Investigations*, pt. 1, par. 373.

263. See Wittgenstein, *On Certainty*, pars. 110, 204, 559.

264. Glendon writes of the Universal Declaration: "The Declaration's architects expected that its fertile principles could be brought to life in a legitimate variety of ways. . . . As Jacques Maritain put it, many different kinds of music could be played on the document's thirty strings" (*A World Made New*, 230). See Maritain, "Introduction," in *Human Rights*, i–ix, at viii.

265. See Kant, *Critique of Practical Reason*, 68–71. Kant describes the schema of a concept as "a rule for the synthesis of the imagination," i.e., a rule linking concepts a posteriori or a priori to perception (Kant, *Critique of Pure Reason*, 135, B 81). The ideal of a well-formed narrative extends the Kantian ideal of a kingdom of ends diachronically (as inscribed in a narrative tradition) and synchronically (as intersubjectively rather than monologically realized). Construed thus, the kingdom of ends is not a type for the abstract, ahistorical subject; rather, it is historicized, concretely, in social narrative.

266. Nozick, *Anarchy, State, and Utopia*, 28–33.

267. See Sen, *On Ethics and Economics*, 76; see also 47–51, 70–78; and Sen, *Resources, Values and Development*, 314.

268. Shue, *Basic Rights*, 71.

269. I am indebted to my colleague William Rehg, SJ, for his illuminating analysis of an irreducibly common good in "Solidarity and the Common Good."
270. Gutiérrez, *A Theology of Liberation*, xx.
271. Gutiérrez, xxix.
272. Camus, *The Plague*, 230. In the present context the term "victim" is an evaluative moral description referring to those suffering deprivation of their basic rights; as such, it is reducible neither to class membership nor to a particular psychological state. Neither can we assume that victims suffer passively; indeed, to speak of victims' rights is to underscore their agency. I have developed this analysis in "No Amnesty for Sorrow."
273. See Outka, *Agape*, 20. See Dworkin, *Taking Rights Seriously*, 227.
274. Aquinas, *Summae Theologiae* II–II, Q. 31, a. 3.
275. See John Paul II, *Sollicitudo rei socialis*, nos. 42–43; see Eagleson and Scharper, *Puebla and Beyond*.
276. See Drèze and Sen, *Hunger and Public Action*, 37–42.
277. Rawls, "Fairness to Goodness," 539.
278. Our "Aristotelian constructivism" corresponds to what Rawls terms "imperfect procedural justice," where "there is an independent criterion for the correct outcome" (respect for the basic rights of the poor) even if no impeccable decision procedure ensures their satisfaction. Rawls, *A Theory of Justice*, 74. For an analysis of the role of basic human rights in social reconciliation, see my "Imagining Otherwise."
279. Wittgenstein, *Philosophical Investigations*, pt. 1, pars. 68, 179.
280. See Walzer, *Thick and Thin*, 7, 4.
281. Albie Sachs, "Preparing Ourselves for Freedom," in *Spring Is Rebellious*, 29.
282. Friedlander, "Trauma, Memory, and Transference," 252, 261.
283. See Beitz, *The Idea of Human Rights*; Raz, "Human Rights without Foundations"; Griffin, *On Human Rights*.
284. See Buchanan, *The Heart of Human Rights*, 50–51. Cf. Griffin, *On Human Rights*.
285. Stephen Hopgood distinguishes "local and transnational networks of activists" who seek redress of abuses from the "global structure of laws, courts, norms and organizations" pursuing a rigid, "secular, monotheism" (*The Endtimes of Human Rights*, ix).
286. See Habermas, *Between Facts and Norms*, 107, 123, and *The Postnational Constellation*. In more recent writing Habermas acknowledges the equal status of basic socioeconomic rights in appealing to "the mediating role of the concept of human dignity" ("The Concept of Human Dignity," 468–69). Curiously, Habermas now invokes Kant's conception of "the infinite dignity" of moral persons (474)—a Rawlsian gambit Habermas earlier criticized in *Justification and Application*, 178n12. See Ingram, "Mediating the Theory and Practice of Human Rights."
287. See Gadamer, *Truth and Method*, 300–307.
288. Karekezi, "In Memory of the Victims," 5.
289. See Villa-Vicencio, "Truth and Reconciliation," 2.
290. Tutu, *No Future without Forgiveness*, 91.
291. See the executive summary in OAU, *Rwanda*, par. 51, chap. 24, and recommendations, par. 9. See Karekezi, Nshimiyimana, and Mutamba, "Localizing Justice."
292. See Mendeloff, "Trauma and Vengeance."
293. In 1999 amnesty was denied since the perpetrators failed to demonstrate their political motivation in torturing and murdering Biko.
294. See Mamdani, "Reconciliation without Justice."

295. In Timothy Garton Ash's words, "the amnestied killer immediately walk[ed] free" while decisions regarding reparation were still to be adjudicated. (Ash, "True Confessions," *New York Review of Books*, July 17, 1997, quoted in Minow, *Between Vengeance and Forgiveness*, 61.
296. Carney, *Rwanda before the Genocide.*
297. See Habermas, "The Hermeneutic Claim to Universality," 181–211. See Ralph Ellison's eloquent depiction of our "national tendency to deny the common humanity shared by my character and those who might happen to read of his experience," in *Invisible Man*, xxvi.
298. Ismael Mahomed, as cited in Tutu, *No Future without Forgiveness*, 33.
299. Nozick, *Anarchy, State, and Utopia*, 28–33.
300. See Gobodo-Madikezela, *A Human Being Died That Night*, 171–72n4.
301. Graham Greene, "Virtue of Disloyalty," in *The Portable Graham Greene*, 609.
302. See Sells, *A Bridge Betrayed.*
303. See Galloy, *Women's Bodies as a Battleground.* For more on the failure of the ICTR and Gacaca courts to address crimes committed by members of the Rwandan Patriotic Front (RPF), see Longman, *Memory and Justice in Post-Genocide Rwanda*, 107–8, 300, 313–39.
304. Benjamin, *Origin of German Tragic Drama*, 166.
305. Walzer, *Thick and Thin*, 46.
306. See Soyinka, *The Burden of Memory, the Muse of Forgiveness*, 3–92 passim.
307. For the role of aesthetic commemoration, see de Gruchy, *Christianity, Art and Transformation*, 171–212.
308. The performative efficacy of apology depends, in turn, on the standing of, respectively, the one apologizing and those to whom apology is due. See Tavuchis, *Mea Culpa.*
309. Levi in Wiesenthal, *The Sunflower*, 191.
310. Krog, *Country of My Skull*, 26.
311. Gadamer, *Truth and Method*, 300–307.
312. Auden, *The Collected Poetry*, 57–58.
313. Derrida, "Des Tours de Babel," 188.
314. See Wittgenstein, *On Certainty*, par. 141.
315. See Cobbah, "African Values and the Human Rights Debate"; and Young, *Justice and the Politics of Difference*, 59.
316. "Obeying a rule," Wittgenstein reminds us, "is a practice" (*Philosophical Investigations*, pt. 1, pars. 199, 202).
317. Hountondji, "The Master's Voice," 325. See Jack Donnelly's right-based criticism of "neoliberal" economic theory in *Universal Human Rights in Theory and Practice*, 67, 231–33.
318. Habermas, *Theory and Practice*, 84.
319. Villa-Vicencio, *Walk with Us and Listen*, 121.
320. Tutu, *No Future without Forgiveness*, 34–35.
321. Tutu, 87.
322. Jeremy Waldron distinguishes individual interests as the subject matter of rights from "communal goods" such as "the good of a shared language"; yet, precisely as rhetoric, rights preserve the common good of agency. "Interests" are not given discretely, but rather in the linguistic medium of practical argument (rhetoric)—which is analyzed in chap. 2 under the rubric of ethical reciprocity. See Waldron, "Nonsense on Stilts?—A Reply," in Waldron, *Nonsense upon Stilts*, 151–209, at 186.

323. For "if language is to be a means of communication," as Wittgenstein famously observed, "there must be agreement not only in definitions but also (queer as they may sound) in judgments." Wittgenstein, *Philosophical Investigations*, pt. 1, par. 242.
324. See Pollis and Schwab, *Human Rights*, 1, 4.
325. Makau Mutua, as quoted in Glendon, *A World Made New*, 224. Mutua's address was given at the Human Rights Policy Conference sponsored by the Belfer Center of the Kennedy School of Government of Harvard University, November 4, 1998. Mutua develops his trenchant critique of liberal, hegemonic rights rhetoric in his *Human Rights*, 10–46. Yet Mutua argues in favor of reimagining human rights for African postcolonial states in "Human Rights in Africa."
326. Lyotard, *The Postmodern Condition*, 27.
327. Rorty, "Human Rights, Rationality and Sentimentality," 78, 71.
328. Glendon, *Rights Talk*, x; see also xii, 171–83. Baxi, *The Future of Human Rights*, 27.
329. Said, "Nationalism, Human Rights, and Interpretation," 45–46. See Gramsci, *Selections from the Prison Notebooks*, 3–23.
330. Tutu, *No Future without Forgiveness*, 32–33. See Ignatieff, *Human Rights as Politics and Idolatry*, 68.
331. Ignatieff, *Human Rights as Politics and Idolatry*, 16, 65, 73, 81.
332. Ignatieff, 79–80.
333. Ignatieff, 164.
334. Ignatieff, 18, 57.
335. Rorty, "Human Rights, Rationality and Sentimentality," 78, 71.
336. Rorty, "The Priority of Democracy to Philosophy," 259.
337. Rorty, *Consequences of Pragmatism*, xlii–xliii.
338. Rorty, *Contingency, Irony and Solidarity*, 45.
339. See Linda Hogan's incisive criticism in *Keeping Faith with Human Rights*, 70–100.
340. Baxi, *Human Rights in a Posthuman World*, 24. Baxi, *The Future of Human Rights*, 24.
341. Spivak, "In Response," 233. See also Spivak, "Righting Wrongs."
342. Cornell, "The Ethical Affirmation of Human Rights," 103–4.
343. Nyerere, "*Kanisa na Maisha ya Watu*," 97–98.
344. Burke, "Speech on Moving His Resolutions," 170; Grotius, *Prolegomena to the Law of War and Peace*, par. 39; See d'Entrèves, *Natural Law*, 55–56; and Wittgenstein, *Philosophical Investigations*, pt. 1, par. 68.
345. Spivak, "Righting Wrongs," 202.
346. Lyotard, *The Postmodern Condition*, xxiii–xxiv.
347. To invoke "the rhetoric of rights," says MacIntyre, is thus "already to have entangled oneself in error" (MacIntyre, "Community, Law," 73).
348. Tierney, *The Idea of Natural Rights*, 5.
349. René Cassin, quoted in Slaughter, *Human Rights, Inc.*, 47.
350. Rorty, *Consequences of Pragmatism*, xlii.
351. See Hollenbach, "A Communitarian Reconstruction of Human Rights," 145. See Krog, *Country of My Skull*, 42–43.
352. Wittgenstein, *Philosophical Investigations*, pt. 1, par. 217.
353. See Melden, *Rights and Persons*, 26–31.

CHAPTER TWO

Justifying Rights

> The ideology of human rights is probably the only one which can be combined with such diverse ideologies as communism, social democracy, religion, technocracy and those ideologies which may be described as national and indigenous. It can also serve as a foothold for those . . . who have tired of the abundance of ideologies, none of which have brought . . . simple human happiness. The defense of human rights is a clear path toward the unification of people in our turbulent world, and a path toward the relief of suffering.
>
> —Andrei Sakharov

In the preceding chapter I argued that the sense of human rights rests precisely in their rhetorical force. In the South African TRC, stories become testimony: "reasoned speech" aiming at persuasion and conviction.[1] Yet if rights are not "nonsense on stilts," we may still wonder if, like Wittgenstein's ladder, they permit us to "see the world aright."[2] For we must still ask whether this "other" rhetoric makes sense *for us*.[3]

Many years ago Ugandan poet Okot p'Bitek warned us against the scholarly hubris of treating African wisdom as a proof text, trimmed to fit Western mythologies, such as the "myth of the 'primitive.'"[4] The question looms large here. For, p'Bitek reminds us, in appropriating the surface grammar of Ubuntu or Ujamaa we risk reinscribing the deep grammar of what Richard Rorty calls "*our* body of shared belief," leaving our justificatory prejudices in place. After all, the "rightness" of Julius Nyerere's or Desmond Tutu's rhetoric is hardly perspicuous. Indeed, to the Western critic, Tutu's fusing of liberal *autonomy* ("a person is always an end, never a means to an end") with communitarian *solidarity* ("social harmony" as "the *summum bonum*") might seem little more than a bricolage of incommensurable backings.[5] As Chinua Achebe says, in quoting W. B. Yeats, "things fall apart."

But can the center hold? For Kantian critics, African traditional wisdom, such as religious belief in Ubuntu, must pass through the crucible of modernity—what Jürgen Habermas calls the "secular sublation (*Aufhebung*) of ontotheology by the philosophy of history."[6] John Rawls looks to the abstract formalism of a generalized other, bracketing the concrete socio-religious bonds of Ubuntu or Ujamaa behind a veil of ignorance. Postmodern critics, of course, demur. For Rorty, our faith in fundamental human rights is merely vain expectation—a supreme, if beneficent fiction, "relative," says Rorty, "to the group to which we think it is necessary to justify ourselves—to the body of shared belief which determines the reference of the word 'we.'"[7] Like all "edifying" discourse, Tutu's or Nyerere's petit récits are finally "local and ethnocentric," the latent wisdom of "a particular community, the consensus of a particular culture."[8] *We* must, it seems, choose between the empty formalism of the Kantian metanarrative of rights (Moralität) or the ethical (sittlich) blindness of incommensurable narrative traditions—reason having lost not only its law but its cunning (Hegel's *List der Vernuft*).[9]

Yet in the TRC's narrative of rights, victims' testimony is neither empty nor blind. African scholars such as Laurent Magesa, Bénézet Bujo, Mercy Amba Oduyoye, Emmanuel Katongole, Agbonkhianmeghe E. Orobator, Anne Nasimiyu-Wasike, Aquiline Tarimo, and Elias O. Opongo, among many, have left us eloquent interpretations of African ethical wisdom (e.g., of Ubuntu underlying testimony at the TRC). To them I can only express my deep indebtedness.[10] Surely p'Bitek is right. African wisdom need not be justified in terms amenable to the Western academy. But the burden of translation—reversing the hermeneutical flow—remains *for us*. If, as Donald Davidson tells us, in interpreting novel meaning we must at the start "assume general agreement on beliefs," it is precisely *these* beliefs—these "conditions of truth that actually obtain (in our opinion)"—that we must now raise into question.[11]

We must, then, interrogate our own prejudices, for in resolving the first antinomy of rights and the common good (the burden of chapter 1) we are caught on the horns of the second and third: that in justifying morality we must opt in a Kantian vein for the rights of a generalized other or, following Hegel, for the concrete "local and ethnocentric" mores of a particular community. The wisdom of concrete universality, or generalized respect for the concrete other within a narrative of rights, finds little rhetorical place here. Neither is there place for the distinctively religious inflections of African wisdom in a public realm where religious tropes and narratives are consigned to the vestibule of public reasoning (our third antinomy, to be taken up in chapter 3). How, then, to proceed? In what would such an interrogation of our justificatory prejudices consist?

I will take a cue from Tutu's rhetorical strategy when writing to B. J. Vorster, then South Africa's prime minister, in May 1976:

> I am writing to you, Sir, as one who is a member of a race that has known what it has meant in frustrations and hurts, in agony and humiliation to be a subject people. The history of your own race speaks eloquently of how utterly impossible it is, when once the desire for freedom and self-determination is awakened in a people, for it to be quenched or to be satisfied with anything less than freedom and self-determination. . . . Blacks . . . now claim an *inalienable right to do things for themselves* in cooperation with their fellow South Africans of all races.[12]

Appealing to Vorster's self-knowledge as a "member of a race that has known what it has meant. . . to be a subject people," Tutu engages in what Rawls calls conjecture, that is, engaging in immanent criticism of opponents' views.[13] So, too, we saw in the reports of the TRC: testimony and apology turned on a body of tacitly shared beliefs epitomized by Ubuntu. But Rorty might object that such strategies beg the question, for the *crux interpretum* arises just when bodies of belief are *not* shared—when we cannot say to the torturers of the innocent, "There is something within you which you are betraying."[14] I too will pursue an immanent critique, beginning here with Rorty's objection that "emergence of the human rights culture seems to owe nothing to increased moral knowledge" but "everything to hearing sad and sentimental stories." Other paths, of course, are possible. My gambit is to show that precisely the finite situated character of "what we *do*" in telling the story, in giving testimony, implies our self-knowledge (reflective apperception of "what *we* do"). It is on this latent wisdom—parsed in the communicative virtues of recognition and respect—that our spade is turned. Here we reach bedrock.

So let us begin, in a Chekhovian vein, not with a grand metanarrative but with the play of seemingly incommensurable "sad and sentimental" petits récits. In his poignant tale *Things Fall Apart,* Achebe recounts the passing of ancestral ways in the Igbo village of Umuofia. With the introduction of Christianity, mere anarchy was loosed upon the villagers' world: the white man "put a knife on the things that held us together," laments elder Obierika, "and we have fallen apart." So great, indeed, was the sense of anomie that the villagers of Umuofia could not even find "the mouth with which to tell of their suffering."[15] Achebe's own petit récit, of course, does not merely describe their world's unmaking; by subtly evoking "the suffering or passion of the world," Achebe summons the reader to become a mouth to decry the white man's hubris.[16]

But whence our ira? Our (post)modern reading, after all, poses a criticism of such criticism itself.[17] For if our ethical attitudes toward life are finally irreconcilable, as Max Weber believes, our criticism of Achebe's missionary, Mr. Smith, is no less arbitrary than his misreading of Umuofia's customs. Neither our modern tolerance of differing convictions nor our predecessors' passionate intensity wins the palm. Finally, says Weber, one "has to decide which is God for him and which is the devil."[18] A strong relativism precludes the attempt to justify a universal (nonrelative) rule of tolerance: to object that the choice offered by Mr. Smith is coerced presumes that God and the devil *should* play by the same rules.[19] Is it simply, as Kader Asmal and his coauthors urge, a "brand of playground relativism" to "ignore or suppress the moral distinctions between the battle to preserve apartheid and the battle to abolish it"?[20] Or is insisting that "apartheid was evil . . . a crime against humanity," merely the particular, local, and ethnocentric expression of *our* mores—the tradition of a particular community?[21]

Conjecture implies that we take such questions seriously. In part I in this chapter I consider the hermeneutic role of recognizing ethical difference in interpreting action, that is, the *semantic* content of differing normative validity claims. [22] In part II the implications of extending such recognition to systems of belief—*epistemic* recognition of normative validity claims—are considered. In part III I analyze the conative implications of I and II, arguing that the *meaning* of such *belief* (normative validity claims) reveals the tacit role of respect in our practical rhetoric, of prudence as a virtue, irreducible to the formal operations of technical reason.

In part IV I argue further that the interplay of these communicative virtues denominating agents in their alternating roles of interpreter and claimant gives rise to the ethical reciprocity of discourse vindicating our validity claims. What we do in testimony, that is, is exhibit the internal goods of respect and recognition (semantic/epistemic) in practical deliberation. Recalling Arendt's ira, such ethical reciprocity discloses not only "factual truth—verifiable and documentable," but what Tutu, citing Judge Albie Sachs of the South African Constitutional Court, terms "social truth, the truth of experience that is established through interaction, discussion and debate."[23] In part V I return to the arguments of the previous chapter and show how rights, as the grammar of such saying (social truth), redeem the truth of wounded memories in public reasoning.[24] In part VI I address several potential criticisms by comparing our chastened, pragmatic rendering of Aristotelian/Thomistic prudence with the justificatory discourses of Habermas and Alan Gewirth. As we shall see, our immanent critique or conjecture reveals significant affinities with "conditions of truth," which were once part of our heritage but have been largely eclipsed in modernity. Our learning from Nyerere and Tutu is also a recovery.

I. THE INTERPRETATION OF ETHICS: SEMANTIC RECOGNITION

"Which is God . . . and which is the devil"? In its more refined elaboration, ethical relativism implies that internally coherent systems of belief are practically exclusive of one another. For example, in the absence of a defensible common moral measure, Achebe's protagonist, Okonkwo, defends a cultural practice—ancestor veneration—while Smith opposes the practice in virtue of his cultural system of belief.[25] If we are to make sense of ethical difference we must show, minimally, that Okonkwo's practical judgment that "one ought to do A" is morally incommensurable with or exclusive of Smith's judgment that "one ought not to do A," where the pertinent action-descriptions are semantically coextensive. For, as Bernard Williams observes, "there must be some action, practice, *etc.*, which under some agreed description will be a locus of disagreement between the holders [of the respective systems]. If this condition is not met, it is unclear what room is left for the notion of exclusivity at all, and hence for the problems of relativism."[26]

But ethical relativism typically implies more than the mere practical incompatibility of actions (or brute action-descriptions). At issue are the differing systems of belief that rationalize the actions (in virtue of which the actions are properly understood as a consequence) and the incommensurability of the systems themselves. Thus, Okonkwo adheres to the rites of ancestor veneration, while Smith abjures the practice as demonic. Differences that are truly incommensurable imply practically exclusive systems of belief, invoked, as we shall see, in the rationalization (explanation) and justification of action. If doing A is not entailed or is underdetermined by the system of belief, the differences may turn out to be notional or trivial. We cannot, then, beg the question of interpretation or translation; our understanding of the relatively "other world" of Okonkwo cannot aspire to the methodological abstraction of theoretical reason as if the meaning of cultural behavior were exhausted by empirical description.[27] Neither are such practices merely amenable to the interpreter's caprice, such as Smith's assumption that Okonkwo worships demons. The interpreter must rather seek to understand the patterns of belief expressed in Okonkwo's behavior so that understanding—even and precisely of difference—emerges as a fusion of her intentional horizon with that of Okonkwo (*Horizontverschmelzung*), a knowing of the known.[28]

Cultural difference, of course, may introduce a certain text-like caesura that ruptures the intentional immediacy of ordinary dialogue, as in the interpretation of ancestor veneration.[29] Just as a classical text's meaning transcends the immediate *mens auctoris* (mind of the author), so the meaning of a cultural text or practice is often not reducible to the reader's explicit intentions.[30] In the naming ceremony of her daughter Ezinma, for instance, Ekwefi participates in a social institution or practice that transcends (sublates rather than nullifies) her discrete intentions, uniting her to a vital tradition in which the memory of the ancestors (the living dead) is cherished. Yet in our recourse to the explanatory force of social science in interpreting such traditions, we must still finally recur to the "webs of significance" we have spun.[31] If the meaning of cultural practices is in part determined by reasons for acting, then only intensionally equivalent descriptions (or redescriptions in translation) suffice to signify what Okonkwo or Ekwefi did intentionally in venerating their ancestors.[32]

Our interpretation of differing ethical practices thus exhibits a double hermeneutic: interpreting Okonkwo's behavior implies that we identify imaginatively with his internal reasons (conative attitudes and beliefs).[33] We must come to see the world from Okonkwo's intentional perspective and understand his reasons for acting in view of his interpretation of his circumstances, not merely from the generalization of our own (e.g., what Smith's reasons would be were he in Okonkwo's circumstances).[34] A generalization of Smith's moral bias, though impartial in one sense of the word, falls short of such understanding, just as apartheid's rationalization rested on a systemic misreading of black aspirations.[35]

The event of such a fusion of horizons, moreover, occurs against the backdrop of a still richer affinity, for the interpretation of Okonkwo's reasons presumes an appreciation of his preinterpreted lifeworld, or what Clifford Geertz terms the "collectively created patterns of meaning" which, as "cultural systems," form the repertory of his potential reasons for acting.[36] Our cultural behavior implies the "infinity of what is not said," the cultural patterns of meaning, expressed not only in narratives, proverbs, and titles but, as for Ezinma and Ekwefi, in rite and ritual.[37] In interpreting what *is* said we must thus attend not only to an utterance's explicit propositional content or expression but to its symbolic or semiotic significance.[38] Tutu, for instance, recounts the myriad "daily pinpricks, the little discourtesies, the minute humiliations" that in the mundane experience of apartheid "demeaned our people and had a deeply corrosive effect on their dignity."[39]

Ethical relativism, as a nontrivial, systemic comparison, presupposes our understanding of difference, of the salient attitudes and beliefs that configure our cultural systems. To argue that there is no common rationally defensible measure of moral appraisal across such systems we must first understand or recognize the complex patterns of meaning to which agents implicitly recur in rationalizing (explaining) their actions. For only with such an agreed description of what Okonkwo does can we make sense of our normative differences as a locus of disagreement regarding normative validity claims. We must read or translate cultural texts aright.

Such a *habitus* I term "virtue"—not in the immediate ethical sense of the term but as a characteristic dispositional attitude of one who engages in the practice of cultural interpretation. Only by *understanding* understanding as a historically transmitted pattern of meanings do we avoid the epistemic distortions of imposing our own rationalizations.[40] Cultural texts, like classical texts generally, acquire novel meaning in transmission—indeed, it is thus we speak not only of the pastness of the past but of the past's presence.[41] Yet such texts, though polysemic, are not infinitely malleable. One can, like Achebe's Mr. Smith, misread a cultural text and, as I will argue in the following parts, be justly censured for so doing.[42]

II. THE INTERPRETATION OF ETHICS: EPISTEMIC RECOGNITION

A comparison of ethical judgments presumes, we have seen, that Mr. Smith fittingly interprets the meaning of "what Okonkwo's does" (e.g., venerate his ancestors). But among the reasons typically used to explain cultural practices (e.g., ancestor veneration) is the shared belief that they are justified, that Okonkwo *ought* to venerate his ancestors. What Okonkwo does in Achebe's novel is act, generally and for the most part, in accordance with claims he deems valid—what Weber calls "normative validity claims."[43] We must not only make sense of the semantic content of Okonkwo's claims; for the question of ethical relativism to arise we must make sense of them precisely as normative validity claims rather than, say, merely emotive expressions.

Indeed, for Weber,

> the meaningful content of a social relationship will be called an "order" only if the conduct is, approximately and on the average, oriented to determinable maxims. This order will be called "valid" [*gelten*] only if the de facto orientation to these maxims occurs, among other reasons, *also* because (in some appreciable way) it is regarded by the actor as somehow valid—obligatory or exemplary—for action. Naturally, in

> concrete cases the orientation of an action to an order involves a wide variety of motives. But the circumstance that, along with the other sources [of conformity], the order is also held by at least part of the actors to be exemplary or binding—and thus as one that *ought* to obtain—naturally increases the probability that action will in fact be oriented to it, and often to a very considerable degree.

Such an order, says Weber, "enjoys the prestige of being considered exemplary or binding or, as we shall say, 'legitimate.'"[44]

Making sense of ethical relativism implies, then, that our agreed description of "what Okonkwo does" is semantically rich enough to be regarded by Okonkwo as "exemplary or binding," that is, it satisfies a validity claim. Such norms, of course, obtain no less in the breach (e.g., Okonkwo's slaying of Ikemefuna), so that we distinguish reasons that justify action (epistemic recognition of what Okonkwo believes he ought to do) from those that de facto explain it (semantic recognition). Yet in thus making sense of differing, even incommensurable, normative validity claims—the locus of disagreement—we implicitly extend our locus of agreement. *Our* interpretative inventory must include agreed-on descriptions, not only of exemplary or binding actions but of the putatively incommensurable validity claims under which they fall—and in virtue of which they are "held . . . to be exemplary or binding." We can say that claims "regarded by the actor as somehow valid—obligatory or exemplary—for action" are incommensurable only if we hold constant the meaning of such claims themselves. We must, minimally, recognize the logical form or syntax of claims of the form: "S (Okonkwo or Mr. Smith) ought to do A under the agreed description."[45]

Only thus can we speak of practically incommensurable *validity* claims. For we cannot say reason becomes practical for Okonkwo in one way yet in quite another way for Mr. Smith. (On such an interpretation their confrontation becomes notional rather than real.)[46] What Donald Davidson says of interpreting across Weber's orders applies here in the practical realm: what "justifies the procedure [i.e., the principle of charity in interpreting others' belief] is the fact that disagreement and agreement alike are intelligible only against a background of massive agreement."[47] But how does reason become practical for Mr. Smith or Okonkwo (or us)?

Even granting that reason is chary in her practical office, so that we do not begin by assuming Kantian synthetic a priori judgments, we may say that practically rational agents act in accordance with their purposes or ends—and *ought* to do so if tempted otherwise. We assume, in Weber's words, that Okonkwo's actions are "approximately and on the average, oriented to determinable maxims." We behave irrationally, conversely, when we act so as to defeat our purposes or ends.[48] As Williams observes, "in the practical or deliberative sense" the judgment that one ought to do A is "relativised to the *agent's* set of aims, projects, objectives, etc. (including of course moral and other constraints that [she] may recognize)."[49] "Ought," that is, operates on intentional action descriptions that are satisfied by the agent's reasons for acting or, more precisely, by her best reasons, all things considered.[50]

Understanding Okonkwo's judgment that "he ought to do A" (e.g., venerate his ancestors) implies, then, an understanding of *his* understanding of the "moral and other constraints" (normative validity claims) that vindicate his action. Just as when in part I we saw that Mr. Smith erred in misdescribing Okonkwo's intentional action as "demon worship" (though Okonkwo might well agree that "one ought not to worship demons"), so he errs in merely generalizing his own maxims or normative validity claims. The question of relativism would arise for Mr. Smith only if his judgment were relativized to Okonkwo's "set of aims, projects, objectives, etc. (including of course moral and other constraints that he may recognize)."[51]

Our conclusions thus far are modest. We have, of course, still to resolve the question posed for Mr. Smith: whether our differing "bodies of shared belief," in Rorty's words, are finally incommensurable.[52] Yet posing the question itself is not value-free. For we can say Mr. Smith's and Okonkwo's bodies of shared belief are incommensurable only if our own system of belief is semantically rich enough to interpret their validity claims. We must, that is, recognize both (1) the explanatory force of claims regarded by the actor as valid in generating agreed action descriptions (semantic recognition) and (2) their justificatory force *as* normative validity claims (epistemic recognition). And just as the former bids us interpret Okonkwo's behavior from the perspective of his web of beliefs, so the latter guards against the genealogical hubris of subsuming his cultural horizon within our own (e.g., as in the cultural-anthropological designation of "primitive" religion).[53] Mr. Smith errs in regarding a contemporary's form of life as merely a primitive stage of his own history, thereby consigning Okonkwo, Ezinma, and Ekwefi to perpetual nonage.

III. THE ETHICS OF INTERPRETATION: RESPECT

The interpretative role of the double hermeneutic alluded to earlier—that in understanding what Okonkwo does, one interprets a preinterpreted social world—precludes a simple separation of descriptive and evaluative judgments. Understanding the sense or meaning of Okonkwo's beliefs presumes our imaginative identification with them.[54] Such a practical attitude of sympathetic identification is an evaluative prejudice: a forestructure of the understanding (*Vorverständnis*), although its precise moral meaning is yet to be clarified.

My imaginative identification with Okonkwo's internal reasons, the hermeneutical requirement that I see the world from Okonkwo's perspective and not merely from the generalization of my own, does not, of course, imply my ultimate agreement with specific beliefs.[55] And such identification, as with the victims of mass atrocity, may never be complete. Yet the practical import of recognition (semantic and epistemic) is not morally nugatory. My recognition of the pattern of beliefs of my interlocutor and of the conditions of their potential validity is tantamount to one aspect of the Kantian injunction of respect for persons: each person "is owed an effort at identification" in virtue of her intentions and purposes.[56]

In identifying with the intentional perspective of another, moreover, I implicitly acknowledge her as a practically rational subject.[57] My difference (e.g., regarding belief in sorcery or spirit possession) presumes a logically prior intersubjective recognition. In seeing the world from her perspective, I see it *as* a practically rational subject—one playing the "language game" of practical reasoning.[58] In interpreting Okonkwo's practical judgments under the rubrics of normative validity claims, one implicitly acknowledges him as a subject capable of forming, revising, and rationally pursuing a conception of the good.[59] If actions must fall under some agreed-on description to be a locus of disagreement between the holders of the respective systems, a fortiori, there must be some agreement about the holders themselves.[60] Failing to acknowledge such subjects as practically rational, conversely, puts the very question of *ethical* relativism in question. At issue is no longer the ethical extension of validity claims but rather the epistemic extension of just who counts as a practically rational agent. (The argument here turns on the capacity to act rationally—not the need to satisfy a particular eudaimonistic telos. Disabled children, such as those born with Down syndrome, are fully rational subjects.)

What is implied, then, in our intersubjective recognition of the validity claim that "S (Okonkwo *or* Mr. Smith) ought to do A under the agreed description"?[61] As touched on in the reflections in part II, in the practical or deliberative sense the judgment that one ought to do A is "relativised to the agent's set of aims, projects, objectives, etc. (including of course moral and other constraints that [she] may recognize)."[62] Only thus could we say that "doing A" is implied by Okonkwo's system of belief or that Mr. Smith's and Okonkwo's systems of belief are incommensurable. Disagreement about whether "Okonkwo ought to venerate his ancestors" is intelligible only against a background of agreement as to the logical force of such a prescription.[63] As we saw above, one agreed use of practical reason is prudence. Kant thus distinguishes the "tacit premise or rule of practical inference" (the "objective law" of hypothetical imperatives) from merely subjective maxims. "Who wills the end," says Kant, "wills (so far as reason has decisive influence on his actions) also the means which are indispensably necessary and in his power."[64]

Conversely, one acts irrationally in failing to adopt the fitting means, thereby frustrating one's aims, projects, and objectives. Yet we cannot simply assume that such aims, projects, or objectives are internally coherent. Like Catullus, it may be that "I hate and I love. And if you ask me how, I do not know: I only feel it, and I'm torn in two."[65] Asking Kant, alas, fails to resolve Catullus's dilemma. Ordered to the "producible ends of pleasure," the semantic indeterminacy of happiness precludes the generation of *prudential* imperatives, leaving us mere *consilia*.[66] Technical imperatives fail to justify actions per se, but only as relative to a "merely possible purpose," so that even an incontinent agent may be said to act rationally.

Clearly we must say more; for though I may hate and I may love, I do neither rationally if I fail to determine which reasons enjoy deliberative priority. The objective determination of action, that is, implies that my intentions are rationally coherent and directed to the performance of the action "judged best on the basis of all available relevant reasons."[67] The conclusion of the apodosis (that I ought to perform A) presumes that no further pertinent reasons tell decisively against my performing A. Pace Hobbes and Hume, then, reason is never merely a "slave of the passions."[68] What prudence requires is that a practically rational agent S (myself or another) act in accordance with her best reasons, all things considered. But such a formal deliberative rule or maxim cannot be derived from a merely instrumental or technical analysis of my reasons, that is, of ends and means.[69] (As for Carl Gustav Hempel, the "requirement of 'total evidence'" is not a postulate of a theory of inductive logic, but rather, in Davidson's words, a "maxim" for its application; so for Davidson, the rule of acting in accordance with my *best* reasons is a maxim of reason's practical application.)[70]

Neither can S's interest in following the rule count as a *further* reason for S acting: this would invite an infinite regress of defining best reasons in terms of themselves. Rather, we must say simply, "This is what *we* do" in acting prudentially: we exhibit our (higher-order) interest in acting in accordance with those interests or with reasons we judge best, all things considered. We follow the maxim blindly, in Wittgenstein's terms; no further reason is necessary. In sum, a practically rational, prudential agent "S" will act in accordance with her best reasons, all things considered, and ought to do so (i.e., follow the formal, prudential maxim) even if tempted otherwise. Let us call actions that fall under the precept "p" (where "p" signifies "S acts in accordance with her best reasons all things considered"). "Ought," then, in its prudential sense, exhibits a higher-order interest "that p." Since we prescribe not only for ourselves but for others, my higher-order interest may be generalized for "p": "ought," that is, remains a logical constant, so that the conative force of "ought" holds for practical judgments generally (whether first-, second-, or third-personal).

Formally, then, the conative propositional attitude in prescriptive judgments of the form "$S_{1,2,3,\ldots n.}$ *ought* to do A" (precisely as relativized to the agent's set of aims, projects, objectives) exhibits an interest that "$S_{1,2,3,\ldots n.}$ do A" under the pertinent description (to act in accordance with $S_{1,2,3,\ldots n.}$'s best reasons/judgment). That is, in the practical or deliberative sense, to prescribe that "$S_{1,2,3,\ldots n.}$ ought to do A" displays a pro attitude or higher-order interest in $S_{1,2,3,\ldots n.}$ acting in accordance with his or her best reason(s), or eo ipso in the "rational action of $S_{1,2,3,\ldots n.}$" or "$S_{1,2,3,\ldots n.}$ acting rationally."[71] Since having a standing interest or habitus in prescribing is logically antecedent to the interpretation (semantic specification) of agents' particular occurrent reasons for acting, we may speak generally of an agent's interest *qua* rationally autonomous, in agents acting rationally.

In playing the language game of practical reason, our prescriptive validity claims thus presume a formally generalized interest in agents acting rationally: that is to say, the reflective valorization—or respect—of agents as practically rational.[72] In prescribing *as* a practically rational, autonomous agent, I show forth my standing interest in or respect for rationally autonomous agency. Such *respect* (as a conative virtue) implies both my *semantic recognition* of $S_{1,2,3,\ldots n.}$'s reasons for acting and my *epistemic recognition* that these are her best reasons, all things considered: this is simply what *I* do—the "*self*-evidence"—not of the Cartesian *res cogitans* but of the player in the game.[73]

To the cognitive virtues of semantic and epistemic recognition we may add, then, a conative virtue (standing disposition or habitus) of respect exhibited in prescription. One aspect of such respect emerged earlier in my discussion of the role played by recognition in interpreting Okonkwo's relatively other world. In Williams's words, respect detached from its transcendental basis signifies (1) that persons "should be regarded from the human point of view," that is, each agent "is owned an effort at identification: that he should not be regarded as the surface to which a certain label can be applied, but one should try to see the world (including the label) from his point of view."[74]

Moreover, since extreme degradation may distort an agent's "consciousness of his own activities," says Williams, "we evidently need something more," thus (2) the precept "that one may not suppress or destroy that consciousness." It is precisely in this sense, says Williams, that we must understand "Kant's celebrated injunction to 'treat each [agent] as an end in himself, and never as a means only.'" Tutu speaks in a similar vein: "Apartheid treats human beings, God's children, as if they were less than this. It manipulates persons and treats them as if they were means to some end. Immanuel Kant declared that a person is always an end, never a means to an end."[75]

Let us say, conversely, that through the "daily pinpricks, the little discourtesies, the minute humiliations" one, like Desmond Tutu's father—this "dignified, educated man"—acts against his own best judgment by responding to insult or being addressed by a white shopkeeper as "*Ja*, boy" in a manner "ingratiating and obsequious." Saying "he ought to behave thus" expresses the shopkeeper's interest in the ritual humiliations of apartheid.[76] But in showing her contempt for *his* aims, projects, or objectives, she is not arguing otherwise or making a practical validity claim—she is not *arguing* at all. As in Lewis Carroll's tale "Achilles and the Tortoise," Achilles must assume the rule of modus ponens even in denying it (since "this is the rule that gives its meaning to 'if'").[77] The shopkeeper, like Achebe's Mr. Smith, cannot reasonably prescribe that Tutu's father should act irrationally or against his own best reasons. Neither can she object that his best reasons *are* revealed in responding to insult in a manner "ingratiating and obsequious."

"Something more," as Williams says, is required. And that something more, I argue, is our interest qua practically rational prescribers in agents acting rationally; or, in Rawls's terms, our highest-order interest(s) in citizens realizing their moral powers *as* practically rational (autonomous) agents. Just as for Kant, whose practically rational agents are self-existent ends (*selbständiger*), so my generalized interest in agents acting rationally is logically antecedent to their contingent (*bewirkender*) ends or particular reasons for acting (e.g., the shopkeeper's interest in apartheid).[78] Yet whereas Kant recurs to a transcendental epistemology in recognizing agents as ends worthy of respect, we turn, rather, to the pragmatic discursive (intersubjective) conditions of practically rational judgment.[79] Worth or dignity is exhibited performatively as we *play* the language game. And all prospective players are worthy of respect. (While Aristotelian eudaimonism presumes a hierarchy of virtue [*aretē*/excellence], the communicative virtues underwrite "the morality of the depths."[80] As I argue in chapter 1, the duties of preserving and protecting the claims of the most vulnerable, for example, Down syndrome children, are morally exigent.)[81]

Our practical rhetoric exhibits what we *do* when, forsaking merely strategic or coercive interaction, we engage in what Aristotle termed reasoned speech (speech characterized by the conative virtue of respect and the cognitive virtues of recognition, both semantic and epistemic).[82] We need not, then, proceed *more geometrico*; indeed, my argument shows that other-regarding aspects of what Rawls calls "reasonable autonomy" are implied by "rational autonomy" or prudential judgment. The maxim to act in accordance with one's best judgment is one I impose upon myself when playing the language game of practical prescription. What *I* do in prescribing is exhibit my *self*-knowledge as a practically rational (autonomous) agent, as one who practices the communicative virtues. It is just this self-knowledge as a rationally autonomous agent that informs *my* intentions; my best reasons, that is, must be consistent with the self-knowledge (*autos*) exhibited in prescribing them (*nomos*). But what does this mean concretely? How do the communicative virtues shape what we do when our intentions conflict, as in complex pluralist polities like our own?

IV. ETHICAL RECIPROCITY

Interpretation, I have argued in parts I and II, is agent-relative in the sense that interpreting and redeeming practical validity claims implies sympathetic identification with one's interlocutor as a practically rational agent. In part III I argued further that my interest in agents acting autonomously (i.e., with agential respect) supervenes upon recognizing others' status as practically rational agents.[83] The practical attitude of respect supervening upon such recognition, moreover, pertains reciprocally to the interpretations of each agent, so that we may fittingly speak of mutual recognition and respect as characteristic *communicative* virtues. Yet the generalized attitude of respect is not tantamount to respect for a "generalized other."[84] What Kierkegaard says of love as embracing "everyone in particular but no one in partiality" pertains no less to the attitude of mutual respect.[85] Inasmuch as the virtue of respect presumes my sympathetic identification with the particular attitudes and beliefs of my interlocutors, I respect not the abstract identity of a generalized other but the specific identity of Okonkwo, Obierika, and Ezinma.[86]

Dignity, one might say, is always clothed in local garb, so that I respect Okonkwo, Obierika, and Ezinma as agent-authors only if I respect the narrative agency expressed in their particular webs of signification: their narratives, stories, and ceremonies—what Iris Marion Young terms their "rhetorical dimensions of communication."[87] Just as intersubjective recognition implies a sympathetic identification with the cultural perspective of one's interlocutor, so one's respect for agents as cultural artificers implies respect for the semantic (and semiotic) richness of their cultural expressions—in Seyla Benhabib's words, the "heterogeneity of their identity."[88] We must recognize the wisdom of their relatively other world.[89] Consonant with our hermeneutical analysis, then, the ideal of respect is not so much a supreme moral principle that subsumes the particular under a given universal (in Kant's terms, in a "determinative judgment") as it is a universal disclosed to "reflective judgment" in the ultimate particularity of *praxis,* that is, in semantic/epistemic recognition.[90]

In the interplay of the communicative virtues, respect is thus fittingly generalized, but always in recognition of the concrete other. The universal "continues to determine itself through the particular" so that I cannot merely generalize my own maxims as if these, in Kant's terms, were the deliverances of pure reason alone. If each is owed an effort at identification, then universal norms, as Habermas avers, cannot be inferred monologically, as if in an introspective thought experiment. Both monogamy and polygamy, for instance, may be *willed* consistently as universal maxims.[91] Rather, norms governing our mutual interaction must be vindicated in discursive procedures of reciprocal role-taking. Internally constrained by the equal respect due rationally autonomous agents, the deliberative generation of ethical norms rests in de facto consensus, recalling Habermas's principle of discourse ethics: "Only those norms can claim to be valid that meet (or could meet) with the approval of all affected in their capacity *as participants in practical discourse.*"[92]

Conversely, I forsake the language game of reasoned speech and behave heteronomously if, like Mr. Smith or the white shopkeeper, I revert to a merely strategic or technical use of rhetoric.[93] Like Mr. Smith, I tread "roughly on the people's faith" if I fail to recognize (1) Okonkwo's reasons for acting in virtue of (2) his normative validity claims.[94]

And yet reciprocal role-taking will not of itself suffice. For mere de facto approval of participants may be itself systemically distorted, whether due to vast disparities of power (e.g., when corporate entities are accorded the status of legal persons) or extreme degradation (e.g., in face of systemic violence, famine, or displacement). Moreover, preferences and beliefs adapt to "grim realities" so that, in Tutu's words, victims come to regard themselves with "self-hatred and self-disgust."[95] Here, too, generalized respect for concrete others requires "something more": (3) reciprocal role-taking constrained (regulatively) and informed (constitutively) by basic rights.

Habermas, to be sure, criticizes Rawls's "shifting of normative premises from the procedure to the concept of the person" in order to present "an unprotected flank to the familiar neo-Aristotelian objections."[96] Yet it is precisely these "familiar neo-Aristotelian objections," that is, Rawls's dependence upon a normative concept of the person embedded in narrative tradition, that Habermas himself must finally acknowledge. Just as for Rawls, our attaining impartial consensus in discourse ethics presumes a "normative concept of the person," that is, Habermas's tacit "prejudice" of equal respect for all.[97] The latter prejudice may, of course, be interpreted and applied in as-yet-unforeseen circumstances; but it cannot pace Habermas be radically problematized in discourse.[98] Problematization "can never be so profound" as to bracket Arendt's ira.[99] As seen in victims' testimony, the performative attitude of respect functions constitutively in determining our self-knowledge *as* discursive agents (our ticket of admission to rational, reflective discourses).[100] When, in Tutu's words, "blacks have had their noses rubbed in the dust by white racism, depersonalizing them to the extent that they have—blasphemy of blasphemies—come to doubt the reality of their own personhood and humanity," what warrants our moral outrage is not primarily a failure of impartiality but rather that they take this to be the "truth about themselves."[101]

While Habermas offers an intersubjective interpretation of the canonical, formal formulation of Kant's categorical imperative (abstract universality), *ethical* reciprocity gives us a pragmatic, intersubjective rendering of the complete determination by linking universality to respect for autonomous agents in anamnestic solidarity.[102] In adopting the performative attitude of respect in rational discourses we thus take a step in resolving the Rousseauean antinomy of private (moral) and public (ethical) autonomy, but at the price of forsaking a purely formal, abstract interpretation of impartiality. How does this play out? How do the communicative virtues we discussed in parts I through III ground our interpretation of rights?

Here we join the arguments of chapter 1. For *generalized respect* for the concrete other—the reflective valorization of agency—implies valorizing the basic conditions or capabilities of its exercise. *Epistemic recognition* of these prerequisites of agency, in turn, generates basic claim-rights and correlative duties. *Semantic recognition* provides for the fitting embodiment (schematization) of such claim-rights and correlative duties in "telling the story." In the Human Rights Violations Committee of the TRC, Lukas Baba Sikwepere's testimony thus implicitly affirms "the dignity and humanity of those who were cruelly silenced for so long" and gives voice to victims' latent wisdom.[103]

Such wisdom is crucial. Were it not for the emphasis on victims' rights, the formal, procedural reciprocity of the criminal justice system would never have recognized "the truth of wounded memories." Vast disparities of power, a heritage of deprivation, and the "grim realities" of repression, as postcolonial critique reminds us, would continue to distort social truth and systematically distort consensus. Yet under the banner of the Human Rights

Committee, stories like those of Nomonde Calata and Sikwepere speak *as* testimony, "getting the memory" and "fixing in words" what was silenced or rendered unpronounceable. Here, we may say, testimony evokes what was systemically effaced. "Now through the Truth and Reconciliation Commission," writes Tutu, victims "would be empowered to tell their stories, allowed to remember, and in this public recounting their individuality and inalienable humanity would be acknowledged."[104]

The latent wisdom of rights, then, redeems our "effort at identification" by preserving the ethical reciprocity at play in discourse. Generating consensual norms (what is said in discourse), including nonbasic rights, implies not only reciprocal role-taking but also recognition of basic rights implied in the saying, in the testifying. Only thus does reciprocity become ethical. Exhibited in the mutual recognition and revision of validity claims, ethical reciprocity, to be sure, does not suffice to guarantee a right reading—practical wisdom does not bequeath us such an impeccable decision-procedure. Rights can be contested; and rights rhetoric can be elaborated discursively when new rights or new claimants are recognized, such as those of transgendered or disabled persons. But discourse ethics is thicker than Habermas assumes; it proceeds, "always, already," under the sign of basic rights. We need not, in Habermas's words, "step outside" the hermeneutical circle, for it is already bounded, implicitly, by a kingdom of ends.

V. THE GRAMMAR OF RIGHTS

In a sense we have now come full circle. My initial conjecture into making sense of relativism in parts I–III revealed the finite, situated character of what we *do* in prescribing or playing the practical language game. For what is said in prescriptive judgments of the form "$S_{1,2,3,\ldots n.}$ *ought* to do A" exhibits what *we* do in saying or prescribing: a logic of self-implication in the affinity of knower (prescriber) and known (what is prescribed). In part III we saw how redeeming practical validity claims expresses our formally generalized interest in agents acting rationally, that is to say, our respect for agents as practically rational (autonomous). In part IV I argued further that the "prejudice" of respect, in concert with other communicative virtues, generates the interpretative context of ethical or rights-based reciprocity. Ethical relativism, then, ceases, to be an option *for us*.

We need not appeal to transcendental necessity. Neither need we accept the sharp antinomy of prudence (rational autonomy) in *recognizing* the "concrete other" or of morality in *respecting* the "generalized other" (in the formal principle of universalization) that persists in the Kantian legacy of Rawls and Habermas. Rather, prudence, in exhibiting our virtuous self-knowledge, enjoins a *generalized respect* for concrete others in *recognizing* the good of "everyone in particular but no one in partiality." Still, a puzzle remains: if we overcome the antinomy of prudence (Hegelian "narrative") and morality (Kantian "metanarrative"), what place (*locus/topos*) remains for rights?

For Kant's heirs rights are abstracted from concrete social relations as a formal metanarrative, while critics like Rorty assimilate human rights rhetoric to the "local and ethnocentric" narrative of the postmodern liberal bourgeoisie. But Sikwepere's or Calata's testimony is neither "local and ethnocentric" nor does the implied "universal audience" of testifying displace our native tongues. Rather, we nod to Wittgenstein in interpreting rights as the grammar of testifying. Just as grammatical rules systematically configure well-formed narratives, so too does the grammar of rights configure our telling the story—personal testimony, yes, but also the greater stories in which collective memory speaks. Schematized in narrative through the allocation of duties (forbearance, provision, and protection), rights become *loci communes* of persuasion and conviction—suasive warrants moving us to act.[105] Like the grammar of a well-formed story, rights hang together—it is never a question of following rules *seriatim*, redeeming one right at a time. Neither do such rules give us an algorithmic decision procedure. Rights may conflict here and now and the schema of correlative duties may vary according to place and circumstance. The manner by which basic rights—to nutritional well-being, to women's effective participation—are fittingly realized will differ in Tabora, Tanzania, and West Oakland, California.

We do not speak a grammar (as narrative or metanarrative), but grammatically. As we saw in chapter 1, in their critical or deconstructive hermeneutic role, rights illumine systematic distortions of prevailing consensual norms so that we rightly decry apartheid, in Wole Soyinka's words, as a fundamental "denial of humanity."[106] For Calata, rights "get that memory, . . . fix it in words, . . . capture it with the precise image." But rights are also a clearing for new stories to be told.[107] The hermeneutic function of rights is thus not merely regulative, but constitutive; rights likewise play a constructive and reconstructive role in weaving or reweaving our differing narrative histories, such as in the telling of women's stories. Mercy Amba Oduyoye thus decries the "sociocultural norms" that "demand submissive and subordinate behavior of women": "Now we have come to realize that a theology appropriate for Europe is not necessarily appropriate for Africa. Similarly, the theology deemed appropriate for African men is not always appropriate for women. An Akan proverb says *Nea oda ne gya na onim senea ehyehye fa* ('It is the person sleeping by the fire who knows the intensity of the heat')."[108]

As Oduyoye's remarks attest, the regulative and constitutive uses of autonomy underwrite the threefold hermeneutic of rights in identifying and redressing systematic distortion. The concrete universality that is proper to ethics is attained not in methodological abstraction from our native tongues but in speaking—in the configuring and refiguring what is handed down in well-formed narratives. But, just so, our well-formed narratives, precisely in schematizing rights, comprise a family of narratives that as such are not rigidly limited but open-textured.[109] Universality remains concrete in anamnestic solidarity.

Our sense of justice is thus thickened (or schematized) in narrative; but precisely as narrative tradition—as a vital traditio, a handing on—it is not reified as a suprapersonal, total organism to which agential rights are subordinate. It is, moreover, this thickened sense of justice that permits us to resolve, at least in part, a conundrum: how so-called first- and second-generation rights are reconciled with third-generation collective rights such as the right to development or indigenous claims to land, language, or culture. Respecting Sikwepere's or Calata's "telling the story" implies a recognition of and respect for the (sittlich) systems, the vital traditions by which their stories are handed on (e.g., the spirit of Ubuntu informing their testimony).

Human rights, that is, are ascribed subjectively but enjoyed, asserted, and enforced collectively (e.g., the goods enjoyed in common of land, language, or culture). Moreover, correlative duties fall not only on individual recipients but also on mediating social institutions and structures so that we can speak of the systemic schematization of a rights regime as a *common* good. But if rights are enjoyed collectively, so too are rights threatened or denied collectively (e.g., in systemic bias due to race, ethnicity, gender, disability, indigenous status). The critical hermeneutical role of rights discloses such systemic vulnerabilities (e.g., of indigenous people), while the constructive and reconstructive roles of rights seek systemic redress (e.g., in generating ancillary or special group rights or rights to fitting reparation). (There may be, of course, other special group rights ascribed on the basis of membership. My argument here is that membership is critical not only to enjoying basic *human* rights but to asserting and enforcing them. Spivak's "strategic essentialism" comes into play: women's rights are human rights.)

A Brief Codicil on the History of Rights: Las Casas and Tutu

In the preceding part we saw how concrete universality that is proper to prudence (*phronēsis/prudentia*) is exhibited in the narrative embodiment or schematization of rights as narrative grammar. Rights are storied and they come to us as preinterpreted—unfolding within, even as they contest cultural systems in which they are inscribed. Neither is this adventitious; the interpretation of rights and a fortiori correlative duties presumes the effective participation of those most affected. For this very reason, then, we must take the historicity (or what Ignacio Ellacuría calls the "*historicizacion*") of rights seriously.[110] Indeed, the moral logic of rights rests less in formal axiomatic inference than in the rhetorical working of tradition: formerly excluded groups—slaves, women, indigenous people—speak, elucidating, as in Said's words, "what [the dominant tradition] has hidden."[111]

This speaking "will truly be a moment in the growth of the original" that completes itself "in enlarging itself." Novelty arises not so much in the form of a semantic revolution as it does in reimagining what has been "handed on" in the face of new repression (or better, new recognition of old repression), for example, the rights of disabled, gay, lesbian, bisexual, or transgendered persons. In defending the natural rights of indigenous people in the American Indies against the fulminations of Juan de Sepulveda, neither Francisco de Vitoria nor Bartolemé de las Casas merely cited Aquinas on the *jus naturale*. In grafting "quite consciously, a juridical doctrine of natural rights onto Aquinas teaching on natural law," Las Casas followed Vitoria in using "Aristotle's own teaching . . . to subvert the assertion that all barbarian peoples were slaves by nature."[112] "The impression that texts are being wrenched from their original meaning typically arises," writes Brian Tierney, "not because Las Casas misunderstood his sources, but because he was deploying them in a new context that their original authors could not have foreseen."[113] This is just how a tradition lives on in transforming itself: it is Tutu's achievement in transforming the bourgeois, hegemonic rhetoric of rights into a counterhegemonic critique.

Yet if the universality of rights is not that of a fixed ahistorical ideal, neither is it infinitely malleable; a certain "family resemblance" must be preserved. (As shall be seen in the final chapter, family resemblance may become systematically distorted, e.g., when racial or ethnic bias conspires to deny persons' "right to have rights.") I have argued that such resemblance rests in the interplay of the communicative virtues that are instantiated in modern and premodern ethical systems.[114] The family resemblance of well-formed narratives is not, then, merely adventitious—not merely the overlap of reiterative particularities, in Walzer's words—but rests in anamnestic solidarity.[115] Indeed, our hermeneutical gambit confirms Tierney's conclusion that the "one necessary basis for a theory of human rights is a belief in the value and dignity of human life."[116] The sense of our rights rhetoric implies only that certain basic goods be protected (semantic recognition), that they be protected *as* subjective claim-rights and not merely as, say, duties owed to God (epistemic recognition), and that they inhere as *subjective* claim-rights owed to moral subjects as worthy of respect. But our practical performative construal of dignity does not presume a secular ontology "within the limits of Reason alone." Las Casas's theological defense of the natural rights of indigenous people in the American Indies, no less than Tutu's or Nyerere's appeal to the *imago Dei,* fully satisfy these criteria. No theological reduction is required.

VI. ARISTOTELIAN CONSTRUCTIVISM: AUTONOMY AND SOLIDARITY

As intimated earlier, our immanent critique or conjecture reveals certain affinities with the "conditions of truth" that were once part of the Aristotelian/Thomistic repertory. Our learning from Nyerere and Tutu is *for us* a recovery. Our arguments trace the formal lineaments of the Aristotelian/Thomistic interpretation of prudence—although as good postmoderns we no longer seek to "keep our metaphysics warm."[117] Kant, indeed, dispelled our metaphysical illusions and left us with a truncated notion of prudence as rational self-interest in which there is little rhetorical "place" for Ujamaa or Ubuntu. But our Aristotelian constructivism invites us to imagine otherwise. Let us briefly, then, consider Kant's objections and the variations on his critique worked by two contemporary theorists, Habermas and Gewirth.

In sharply distinguishing prudence (rational self-love) from morality, Kant dismisses Aristotle's eudaimonistic reasoning as "vain illusion." Civic virtue is no longer the natural fruition of prudence (Aristotelian phronēsis) but rather a rein upon it as the "subjective principle of self-love."[118] Harking back to the technical reduction of prudence in Hobbes and Hume, Kant's critique colors subsequent interpretations of eudaimonism, even when his empirical psychology is rejected.[119] Eudaimonism remains self-regarding, and onerously so, from a moral point of view.[120] But this, alas, is a serious misreading of Aristotle and his medieval interpreter, Aquinas, who both distinguish prudence from mere technical reasoning (*technē*). For while technē pursues contingent ends in the making of things (*poiēsis*), phronesis/prudentia aims at the *ultimate* particular: the virtuous praxis in the making of a self.

For Aristotle and Aquinas, not only is *eudaimonia* tempered by the virtue of "particular justice"; it has as its natural harmonic the ideal fruition of the common good in the formation of the just polis (the *koinōnia teleios/communitas perfecta*). "General justice" is "complete virtue in the fullest sense" for Aristotle precisely because it tends to produce or conserve the happiness (and the constituents of the happiness) of a political association to which are subordinated all domestic and merely individual goods.[121] In Aquinas's words, moral perfection presumes the "communitas perfecta": the "common good is the end or purpose of individual persons living in the community." General justice or "*justitia legalis*" is ceded primacy over all the moral virtues inasmuch as it directs them to the "common good," which "surpasses the individual good of one person."[122] Indeed, it is only when regarded in light of "general justice" as "complete virtue in the fullest sense" that the Aristotelian virtues (*aretai*) satisfy the formal definition of eudaimonia as "final" and "self-sufficient." Phronēsis/prudentia thus legislates for the common good, that is, the whole or most complete realization of eudaimonia of which individual flourishing is a "part." Prudence (phronēsis) implies a common perception of "sublimity" and a common "seeking what is right" (*sunesis*), even as the sublimity of the perfect community (koinōnia teleios) is expressed in the blessedness (eudaimonia) of its members—in the sublimity of the perfect community all share singly, not en masse.[123]

Chapter 1 recalled the early modern eclipse of the ethical ideal of phronēsis/prudentia, due in part to skepticism regarding Aristotle's metaphysical teleology. Such skepticism is abetted, though, by a further misreading. Kant conflates the logical force or syntax of eudaimonia with its interpretation, mistaking deliberation for its object. In his treatment of technical imperatives Kant identifies the logical *force* of prescription with formal consistency so that the modal conclusion, "S ought to do A (where A is the necessary means)" is entailed by S willing the end. In prudential imperatives the "maxim of self-love" specifies the end as pleasure—and hence explains our empirical motivation (rational self-love). The making of a self is left to Moralität.

Were it "only as easy to find a determinate concept of happiness," says Kant, "the imperatives of prudence would agree entirely with those of skill and would be equally analytic."[124] However, since the producible ends of pleasure remain indeterminate, there is "no imperative possible which in the strictest sense could command us to do what will make us happy." Yet the inference is consequent upon the synthetic (semantical) indeterminacy of Kant's conception of happiness: the imperative of prudence has not ceased to be, in Kant's own terms, "an analytic practical proposition." As H. J. Paton remarks, the formal principle "remains analytic however many synthetic propositions may be required in order to determine theoretically the means to our happiness."[125] Kant confuses the logical syntax of the "maxim of prudence" that "good *is to be done*," with its putative object of rational self-love.[126] Is it surprising, then, that for Kant the "maxim of self-love [prudence] merely advises; the law of morality commands"?

Kant's heirs follow suit in separating morality and prudence. Habermas criticizes Rawls for presenting an "unprotected flank to the familiar neo-Aristotelian objections"—a *phronetic* thickening in Rawls's later work that blurs the distinction of morality (Moralität) and ethics (Sittlichkeit). Seeking to preserve the distinction, Habermas himself differentiates three semantically distinct senses of "ought" in the pragmatic (strategic), the ethical (hermeneutical), and the moral (formal-procedural) employments of practical reason.[127] Yet, curiously, Habermas precisely here departs from Kant, who appeals to a common logical syntax of practical judgments.[128] For if "$S_{1,2,3,\dots n.}$ ought to do A" under the relevant description, then it is the case that "S ought to do A" whether the judgment is analytical or synthetic a priori. In varying the sense of "ought," conversely, such distinct employments generate separate value spheres, reinscribing the problematic of Weberian relativism.[129]

Curiouser and curiouser, as Alice might say, Habermas himself appears to recognize the limits of such a syntactical gambit in his revised interpretation of the discourse principle ("D" in *Faktizität und Geltung*). Ranging now over *all* valid (*gültig*) action norms, whether these be pragmatic, ethical-political, or moral, the discourse principle, says Habermas, "reflects those symmetrical relations of recognition built into communicatively structured forms of life in general."[130] Yet is this not to concede that practically rational "ought" judgments are, eo ipso, governed by the "symmetrical respect that everyone should accord the integrity of all other persons" (the differentia of *moral* judgments in Habermas's earlier critique)?[131]

Gewirth, too, distinguishes prudential and moral senses of ought, if only to derive the latter from the former by appealing to the "dialectically necessary" prerequisites of exercising "prospective, purposive agency."[132] In our informed, rational (prudential) choice, Gewirth argues, we implicitly regard freedom and well-being, the necessary conditions for our pursuit of purposes, as necessary goods. Recalling the first formulation of the categorical imperative (in its regulative construal), formal considerations are introduced as sufficient reason for generalizing the initial ascription of rights claims: the nonmoral prudential "ought" acquires moral (universal) import, since to "avoid self-contradiction" one must admit that the generic rights presumed for the exercise of one's prospective, purposive agency must be accorded all prospective, purposive agents. One must, then, "refrain from interfering with (one's) recipients' freedom and well-being" and act in accordance with their "generic rights" as well as one's own.[133]

The "canonical form" in which Gewirth's reasoning is expressed is the "precept addressed to every agent: Act in accord with the generic rights of your recipients as well as of yourself."[134] Termed the Principle of Generic

Consistency, the precept combines "the formal consideration of consistency" with the "material consideration of rights to the generic features or goods of action" as specified by the agent's freedom and well-being. For Gewirth these generic features, viewed as the "most general and proximate necessary conditions" of purposive activity, offer "objective, ineluctable contents for testing the truth or correctness of moral judgments." The generic features of action are not "correspondence correlates" of moral judgments; rather, they establish, through "the normative structure of action, certain requirements for moral judgments" and thus serve as "necessary premises from which moral judgments logically follow."[135]

Must prospective, purposive agents reason thus? Teasing thick communitarian conclusions from such thin self-regarding premises seems, after all, a bit like pulling real rabbits from an imaginary hat—a slight of mind. As observed earlier, circumstances may constrain preferences such that an agent may will certain ends like mere subsistence without *necessarily* acknowledging the full import of freedom and well-being. That is, the contingent value imputed to agency may finally be too thin to generate Gewirth's full panoply of rights. Even more problematic is the normative extension of Gewirth's Principle of Generic Consistency. For even if we concede that agents necessarily value the generic goods of agency, we need not assume that they regard freedom and well-being as *generically* good or valuable. The obligation of a prospective, purposive agent to desire a state of affairs in which *her* freedom and well-being are universally respected does not eo ipso suffice to justify her honoring the like claims of others or their honoring hers. *Singular* prescriptions may be properly attributed to every agent and universally distributed without thereby implying the universal prescription that humanity in one's own person (qua prospective, purposive agent) be respected. As Kant himself recognizes, such a universalization of prudence results not in a universal teleology wherein "universal happiness" is a "type of the morally good" but rather in an intermonadic universe of competing subjective ends, "the extreme opposite of harmony, the most arrant conflict."[136]

Autonomous agents might thus advance certain claims as prospective, purposive agents without assuming that the fact of autonomous agency (the *quaestio facti* of autonomy) suffices for their justification. In Gewirth's construal, indeed, one's putative rights claims derive their force from the various purposes one pursues (reflecting what Rawls would call one's higher-order interests) rather than from the regulative ideal of autonomous agents as ends in themselves.[137] In Kantian terms, autonomous agency has a price rather than a dignity.

It is precisely the latter that our Aristotelian constructivism seeks to show; that in distinguishing rational from merely strategic uses of rhetoric our reasoned speech presumes just such intersubjective recognition and respect. Divested of its metaphysical basis (the *telei* of natural kinds), prudence gives the deliberative maxim: act in accordance with best reasons, all things considered. Our maxim, like Aristotle's first principle, is tautological and conveys no novel information. But it is not *unsinnig* (nonsensical), for *obeying* the maxim blindly reveals what *I* do: that I exhibit my self-knowledge as autonomous precisely in exhibiting the conative virtue of respect, generalized for practically rational agents. Such *respect,* as we saw, implies both my *semantic recognition* of $S_{1,2,3,\ldots n.}$'s reasons for acting as well as my *epistemic recognition* that these are her best reasons, all things considered: This is simply what *I* do, the "*self*-evidence" of the player in the game.[138] And just as phronēsis/prudentia prescribes objectively for subjective fulfillment in the koinōnia teleios/communitas perfecta, so too is our maxim of application generalized for "$S_{1,2,3,\ldots n.}$" in prescribing within a community of rights. Freedom and well-being are *generically* valued precisely as constitutive goods of agency, as goods inscribed in our narrative traditions as the grammar of rights (anamnestic solidarity).

The interplay of the communicative virtues thus reveals the affinity of knower (what *I* do in prescribing) and the known (the domain of rationally autonomous agents). Autonomy is exhibited in solidarity so that my self-knowledge *as* autonomous is not that of the transcendental ego in synthetic a priori judgments, but rather the pragmatic "we" of ethical reciprocity. Practical reasoning is ab ovo what *we* do. This is the lesson of Ubuntu and Ujamaa. In Tutu's words, "We belong in a bundle of life. We say, 'a person is a person through other people.' It is not 'I think therefore I am.' It says rather: 'I am human because I belong.' I participate, I share."[139]

VII. CONCLUSIONS

Ours, to be sure, is far from a knock-down argument. Indeed, we may fail to recognize the maxim in prescribing, so that "ought" locutions merely coerce, chide, and cajole. Reason then ceases to be *practical*: "ought" ceases to function as a logical constant across persons.[140] (If the sense or meaning of "ought" varies across persons, it ceases to be the case that "S ought to do A" if and only if S ought to do A.) Practical reason, as Aristotle knew, is parsimonious; its motives are seldom apodictic. Yet "what we do" in prescribing—in playing the practical language game—suffices to show the "conditions of truth that obtain" and fund a "general agreement on beliefs," that is, on the relevance of Nyerere's and Tutu's rhetoric *for us*.[141] There are good reasons, then, for *our* "faith in rights," for the reasons given in the testimonies of Sikwepere, Calata, and the countless victims who suffered and endure. Here "spades are turned," not upon an ineluctable, transcendental "foundation" but on the modest bedrock of our lives: what Tutu calls "holy ground."[142]

NOTES

Epigraph: Sakharov, as quoted in Weston, "Human Rights," 28.

1. See Perelman, *The Realm of Rhetoric,* 14, 17–18.
2. Wittgenstein, *Tractatus Logico-Philosophicus,* 6.54.
3. I have in mind here those of us, African and non-African, schooled in the Western academy.
4. p'Bitek, *African Religions in Western Scholarship.*
5. Tutu, *Hope and Suffering,* 160, and *No Future without Forgiveness,* 34–35.
6. Habermas, "To Seek to Salvage an Unconditional Meaning without God Is a Futile Undertaking," in Habermas, *Justification and Application,* 136.
7. Burke, *Reflections on the Revolution in France,* 59–60, 109–10.
8. Rorty, "The Priority of Democracy to Philosophy," 259.
9. In a thoroughly disenchanted world, says Rorty, "nothing counts as justification except by reference to what we already accept. . . . There is no way to get outside our beliefs and our language so as to find some other test than coherence" (*Philosophy and the Mirror of Nature,* 178).
10. Orobator, *Practicing Reconciliation, Doing Justice*; Opongo, "Between Violence, Reconciliation Rituals and Justice"; Nasimiyu-Wasike, "The Missing Voices of Women"; Bujo, *The Ethical Dimension of Community*; Ilesanmi, "Civil-Political Rights or Social Economic Rights for Africa?"; Ilesanmi, "Human Rights Discourse in Modern Africa"; Oduyoye, "Feminist Theology in an African Perspective"; Oduyoye, "Christian Feminism and African Culture"; Mveng, "Impoverishment and Liberation"; Hinga, "Jesus Christ and the Liberation of Women in Africa"; Okure, "The Will to Arise"; Magesa, "Christ the Liberator and Africa Today"; Éla, *Le Cri de l'homme africain*; Éla, "*La Foi des pauvres en acte*"; Éla, "Christianity and Liberation in Africa."
11. As Davidson observes, "Since knowledge of beliefs comes only with the ability to interpret words, the only possibility at the start is to assume general agreement on beliefs. We get a first approximation to a finished theory by assigning to sentences of a speaker conditions of truth that actually obtain (in our opinion) just when the speaker holds those sentences true. The guiding policy is to do this as far as possible, subject to considerations of simplicity, hunches about the effects of social conditioning, and of course, our common-sense, or scientific, knowledge of explicable error." Donald Davidson, "On the Very Idea of a Conceptual Scheme," in Davidson, *Inquiries into Truth and Interpretation,* 196.
12. Tutu, *The Rainbow People of God,* 7–9 (emphasis added).
13. Rawls, "The Idea of Public Reason Revisited," in Rawls, *The Law of Peoples,* 155–56.
14. Rorty, *Consequences of Pragmatism,* xlii.
15. Achebe, *Things Fall Apart,* 162.
16. Benjamin, *Origin of German Tragic Drama,* 166.

17. Hilary Putnam argues that if evaluative norms are relativized to local cultures, then norms of interpretation are no less ethnocentric: "Other cultures become, so to speak, logical constructions out of the procedures and practices of American culture" (232). Putnam, "Why Reason Can't Be Naturalized." Such criticism would seem to tell against Lyotard's condemning "cultural imperialism": as relativized to our "narrative knowledge," such critique would be limited to "the pragmatics of its own transmission." See Lyotard, *The Postmodern Condition*, 27.
18. Max Weber, "Science as a Vocation," in Weber, *From Max Weber*, 147.
19. See Philip Gourevitch's assessment that "the war about the [Rwandan] genocide was truly a postmodern war: a battle between those who believed that because the realities we inhabit are constructs of our imaginations, they are all equally true or false, valid or invalid, just or unjust, and those who believed that constructs of reality can—in fact, must—be judged as right or wrong, good or bad.... Rwanda demonstrated that the question is a matter of life and death." Gourevitch, *We Wish to Inform You*, 259. Williams, "An Inconsistent Form of Relativism."
20. Asmal, Asmal, and Roberts, *Reconciliation through Truth*, 7, 4–16.
21. Minow, *Between Vengeance and Forgiveness*, 78. Rorty, "The Priority of Democracy to Philosophy," 259.
22. Charles Villa-Vicencio draws upon this Gadamerian motif in his assessment of the "Herculean task of creating a less divided future" in South Africa. Villa-Vicencio, "Telling One Another Stories," 35.
23. Tutu, *No Future without Forgiveness*, 33. See Sachs, untitled essay in "The Task for Civil Society," 106.
24. Tutu, *No Future without Forgiveness*, 33.
25. See Richard Berstein's definition of "relativism" in *Beyond Objectivism and Relativism: Science, Hermeneutics, and Praxis*: Concepts such as "rationality, truth, reality, rights, the good, or norms ... must be understood as relative to a specific conceptual scheme, theoretical framework, paradigm, form of life, society, or culture.... For the relativist, there is no substantive overarching framework or a single metalanguage by which we can rationally adjudicate or univocally evaluate competing claims of alternative paradigms" (8).
26. Williams, "The Truth in Relativism," in *Moral Luck*, 132–42.
27. See Clifford Geertz's assertion that our understanding of culture is not "an experimental science in search of law but an interpretative one in search of meaning." Geertz, "Thick Description," in *The Interpretation of Cultures*, 5.
28. See Hans-Georg Gadamer, "On the Problem of Self-Understanding," in Gadamer, *Philosophical Hermeneutics*, 45. In the "working of tradition," says Gadamer, "this process of fusion is continually going on, for there old and new are always combining into something of living value." Gadamer, *Truth and Method*, 306. In part V we will consider the role of rights rhetoric in revealing potential distortions of such a *Horizontverschmelzung*.
29. For a criticism of the applicability of "worship" or "veneration" to traditional practices, see Bediako, *Christianity in Africa*, 216–33.
30. See Paul Ricoeur, "The Model of the Text," in Ricoeur, *Hermeneutics and the Human Sciences*.
31. Geertz, *The Interpretation of Cultures*, 5.
32. See Habermas, *The Theory of Communicative Action*, 1:273ff., 2:153ff. "Intensional" expressions designate a set of functions, such as "Okonkwo believed or intended," which can be satisfied only by preserving Okonkwo's sense or meaning. In the familiar example,

while it is true that Oedipus intended to slay the haughty stranger and similarly true that the stranger was his father the king, one cannot say that Oedipus intended the latter, although the statements are extensionally equivalent. Similarly, one cannot, as Mr. Smith, *understand* Okonkwo's ancestor veneration without recognizing the meaning imputed by Okonkwo. See Kneale and Kneale, *The Development of Logic*, 609.

33. See Giddens, *New Rules of Sociological Method*, 158. Giddens argues that "sociology, unlike natural science, deals with a pre-interpreted world where the creation and reproduction of meaning-frames is a very condition of that which it seeks to analyze, namely human social conduct: this is why there is a double hermeneutic in the social sciences." See Gadamer, *Truth and Method*, 291–300.
34. See Bernard Williams, "Ought and Moral Obligation," in Williams, *Moral Luck*, 120–21.
35. See J. L. Mackie's distinction of differing "stages" of universalization, the first of which rules out "as irrelevant mere numerical as opposed to generic difference, the difference between one individual and another simply as such." Mackie, *Ethics*, 83. See Piet Meyer's assertion that Afrikanerdom was threatened by "Russian and Chinese communism, Indian imperialism, Eastern Middle Eastern and North African Mohammedanism, West European liberalism, American capitalistic sentimentalism, and fervent anti-white Bantu animism in Africa." Quoted in Asmal, Asmal, and Roberts, *Reconciliation through Truth*, 90. Meyer was appointed chair of the South African Broadcasting Corporation in 1959. See Gobodo-Madikizela, *A Human Being Died That Night*, 61–62.
36. Geertz, *Islam Observed*, 19.
37. See Gadamer, *Truth and Method*, 438–56. See Bernard Lonergan, "Unity and Plurality," in Lonergan, *A Third Collection*, 243.
38. See Kristeva, *Revolution in Poetic Language*, 124–47.
39. Tutu, *No Future without Forgiveness*, 14.
40. See Bujo, *African Theology in Its Social Context*, 15–28.
41. See T. S. Eliot, "Tradition and the Individual Talent," in Eliot, *Criticism*, 525.
42. The skeptic must show, in a Wittgensteinian vein, what an understanding of misunderstanding would *mean*. See Wittgenstein, *On Certainty*, pars. 156ff.
43. For Weber cultural norms are "legitimate" inasmuch as they are fittingly predicated of a given domain of agents, e.g., the villagers of Umuofia (*Einverständnisgeltung*).
44. Weber, *Economy and Society*, 31; see Habermas, *The Theory of Communicative Action*, 1:189ff.
45. See Ian Hacking, "Language, Truth and Reason," in Hacking, *Rationality and Relativism*, 48–66. For further criticism see Bohman, "Two Versions of the Linguistic Turn."
46. Williams, "The Truth in Relativism," in *Moral Luck*, 132–42. Whether confrontations are real or notional is itself relative: the human rights movement, for instance, may render initially notional options, e.g., recognition of the full equality of women, as real confrontations demanding redress. Similarly, in accordance with Tarski's "Convention T," we cannot say it is true for Okwonkwo that "he ought to venerate his ancestors" but not true for us that he ought to venerate his ancestors. Such epistemological relativism belies the possibility of "real" ethical confrontation.
47. Donald Davidson, "Radical Interpretation," in Davidson, *Inquiries into Truth and Interpretation*, 137. See also "Thought and Talk" in the same volume, 155–70. Interpreting validity claims entails an extensive application of the principle of charity: the reader assumes the (potential) truth of the other's claims against the backdrop of his/her "patterns of belief" and interprets the sense or meaning of her claim accordingly. The phrase

"principle of charity" is derived from Neil Wilson's "Substances without Substrata." Willard Quine applies the principle to logical constants in *Word and Object*. For a critical application of the principle, see Lukes, "Relativism in Its Place."

48. See Philippa Foot, "Morality as a System of Hypothetical Imperatives," in Foot, *Virtues and Vices*, 161ff.
49. Williams, *Moral Luck*, 120 (emphasis added).
50. See Donald Davidson, "Actions, Reasons, and Causes" and "Intending," in Davidson, *Essays on Actions and Events*, 3–19, 83–102, respectively. Donald Davidson, "How Is Weakness of the Will Possible," in Davidson, *Essays on Actions and Events*, 41; see also Davidson, "Reply to Essays I–X," 206.
51. Williams, *Moral Luck*, 120.
52. Rorty, "The Priority of Democracy to Philosophy," 259.
53. See Mveng, "Black African Art as Cosmic Liturgy," 139. See Mulago, "Vital Participation," 139; Magesa, *African Religion*, 25, 23; Oduyoye, "The Value of African Religious Beliefs"; Bujo, *African Theology in Its Social Context*, 17–37.
54. See W. V. Quine, "Two Dogmas of Empiricism," in Quine, *From a Logical Point of View*. For a criticism of Quine's failure to question the fact/value dichotomy, see Putnam, "Pragmatism and Moral Objectivity."
55. See Davidson, *Inquiries into Truth and Interpretation*, 196. The *hermeneutical* requirement that I see the world from another's perspective need not imply that I sympathize, morally or emotively, with his or her beliefs. On the contrary, identifying beliefs held as true is a condition of moral appraisal: the evasions and distortions of apartheid are rightly condemned.
56. Bernard Williams, "The Idea of Equality," in Williams, *Problems of the Self*, 236–37. See Williams, "Saint-Just's Illusion," in Williams, *Making Sense of Humanity*, 135–50. Such effort, of course, holds only insofar as we are making sense of relativism. Its ethical implications must still be shown.
57. As Gadamer observes, "The mere presence of the other before whom we stand helps us to break up our own bias and narrowness, even before he opens his mouth to make a reply. That which becomes a dialogical experience for us here is not limited to the sphere of arguments and counter-arguments the exchange and unification of which may be the end meaning of every confrontation. Rather . . . there is something else in this experience, namely, a potentiality for being other [*Anderssein*] that lies beyond every coming to agreement [*Verständigung*] about what is common." Gadamer, "Text and Interpretation," 26. See Bernasconi, "You Don't Know What I'm Talking About."
58. *Ex hypothesi*, a third "angelic" party might interpret Okonkwo's and Mr. Smith's judgments yet refrain from playing the language game of practical reasoning: in such a case neither Okonkwo's nor Mr. Smith's systems of belief would represent what Williams terms a "real option." Yet it is only with such real, not merely notional, options that genuine appraisals of relativism occur. See Williams, *Moral Luck*, 182–85.
59. As Lukes elaborates, in applying the principle of charity, "The necessary model of the agent appears to require at least that those whose beliefs are to be identified are in general behaviourally rational in their actions and that they are, in general, sensitive to deductive argument and inductive evidence (though the degree to which these propensities are developed will depend on situations and opportunities). It will also involve the assumption that they have at least two fundamental cognitive interests: in explaining, predicting and controlling their environment, and in achieving mutual understanding." Lukes, "Relativism in Its Place," 265.

60. Williams, *Moral Luck*, 179.
61. See Hacking, *Rationality and Relativism*, 48–66. For further criticism, see Bohman, "Two Versions of the Linguistic Turn."
62. Williams, *Moral Luck*, 120. The mere formal coherence of empirically ascertainable preferences will not, then, suffice; for though preference A (a desire for heroin) may imply preference B (the necessary means of obtaining it), one may indeed prefer C (even if it is not acted upon), as in the case of Harry Frankfurt's *unwilling* addict. The coherence of one's *reasons* (and hence the interpretation of one's best reasons) is finally relative to one's life plan, so that the consequential assessment of systems theory cannot be uncritically applied to action. See Harry C. Frankfurt, "Freedom of the Will and the Concept of a Person," in Frankfurt, *The Importance of What We Care About*, 11–25.
63. Davidson, *Inquiries into Truth and Interpretation*, 137.
64. Kant, *Groundwork of the Metaphysic of Morals*, 417 (nos. 44–45); see Beck, *A Commentary on Kant's Critique of Practical Reason*, 85.
65. Catullus, *The Poems of Catullus*, 197.
66 See Kant, *Groundwork of the Metaphysic of Morals*, 418 (no. 37), and *Critique of Practical Reason*, 36.
67. Donald Davidson, "How Is Weakness of the Will Possible," in Davidson, *Essays on Actions and Events*, 41; and Davidson, "Reply to Essays I–X," 206. Amended thus, the formal principle (logical syntax) of hypothetical imperatives implies that a rational agent will act in accordance with her best reasons and "ought" to do so even if tempted otherwise. Hypothetical imperatives govern intentions, so that the logical nexus between intentions and "acting in accordance with best reasons" is provided by the tacit condition, "so far as reason has decisive influence on actions." See O'Neill, *The Ethics of Our Climate*, 85–88.
68. Hume, "A Treatise of Human Nature," sections 3, 5.
69. Significantly, Kant's conception of technical, hypothetical imperatives is thus underdetermined, while the conception of prudential, hypothetical imperatives is overdetermined, inasmuch as Kant assumes one's "total" or comprehensive end must be satisfied materially in terms of rational self-love or "greatest well-being." But this is to import a dubious empirical psychology into what, on Kant's own terms, remains a formal (if not analytical) requirement.
70. Davidson, "Reply to Essays I–X," 206. For Davidson, Hempel's requirement of total evidence is a maxim for applying inductive logic: Hempel's requirement resolves the ambiguity of consistent true premises yielding incompatible conclusions. See C. G. Hempel, "Inductive Inconsistencies," 439–69.
71. One's actions, conversely, would be heteronomous if, say, through rashness or incontinence one acts intentionally, albeit not from her best reasons, all things considered. Cf. Davidson, "Reply to Essays I–X."
72. Since the sense or meaning of "ought" is logically constant (i.e., if "I ought to do A" then it is the case [i.e., for $S_{1,2,3,\ldots n}$.] that I ought to do A), the interest expressed is formally generalized for the domain of $S_{1,2,3,\ldots n}$. And since each practically rational subject (S) exhibits such interest, we may describe her rational action as autonomous: the maxim (*nomos*) is one the I (*autos*) imposes.
73. Wittgenstein, *Philosophical Investigations*, pt. 1, par. 217.
74. There is, says Williams, "certainly a distinction . . . between regarding a man's life, actions or character from an aesthetic or technical point of view, and regarding them from a pont

of view which is concerned primarily with what it is *for him* to live that life and do those actions in that character." *Moral Luck*, 237.

75. Tutu, *Hope and Suffering*, 160.
76. See Davidson, *Essays on Actions and Events*, 21–42.
77. Carroll, *The Complete Works*, 1104–8; Hare, "Rawls' Theory of Justice," 88.
78. Kant, *Groundwork of the Metaphysic of Morals*, 427–29.
79. Kant, 436–37. In offering an intersubjective (discursive) and pragmatic account of what Kant describes as the "fact of pure reason," i.e., the practically rational sense of "ought" (*Sollen*), my analysis recalls Habermas's discourse ethics; cf. Habermas, *Moral Consciousness and Communicative Action*. However, my interpretation differs in several salient respects: Habermas proceeds from a general theory of communicative speech acts, while I analyze a particular class of locutions, i.e., practically rational judgments. Habermas, moreover, proposes a formal, procedural conception of justice and draws upon a discursive reformulation of Kant's "formal" formula of the categorical imperative. My analysis, conversely, is grounded in a substantive conception of respect for rationally autonomous agents and derives from a discursive reconstruction of the "material" and "complete" formulae (formulae by no means coextensive with, or necessarily entailed by, the formal formulation).
80. Shue, *Basic Rights*, 18. Neither Aristotelian *aretai* (virtues) nor maximizing self-interest in contractarian bargaining under Humean circumstances of justice (Rawls) are presumed. Rather, as understood here, rational agency comprises the *capacity* to act for a reason (intentionally), and for reasons one holds "best," even when such "rationalization" of action is implicit or imputed. Such basic rationality is implied in giving and receiving care: one is never simply a means, but always an end, worthy of equal respect and consideration. Persons' "moral powers" are thus relativized to what Martha Nussbaum calls "Aristotelian, not Kantian" dignity. In Nussbaum's words, "bodily need, including the need for care, is a feature of our rationality and our sociability; it is one aspect of our dignity, then, rather than something to be contrasted with it." Nussbaum, "Beyond the Social Contract," 450.
81. Nicholas Wolterstorff extends the moral domain to all those divinely endowed with dignity; see his *Justice*, 323–61. Our interpretation offers a via media that incorporates both pragmatic and theological backing.
82. See Wittgenstein, *Philosophical Investigations*, pt. 1, par. 217. Here the Kantian "fact of pure reason" is relativized pragmatically as "what I (we) do" in playing the practical language game. Aristotle, *Politics*, 1253a9ff.
83. See Kant, *Groundwork of the Metaphysic of Morals*, 424. See Feinberg, *Social Philosophy*, 90.
84. See George Herbert Mead's interpretation of the "formal" formulation, in his *Mind, Self, and Society*, 152–64, 379–89. Cf. Benhabib, "The Generalized and the Concrete Other," 87.
85. Kierkegaard, *Works of Love*, 10.
86. In Benhabib's words, we "recognize the dignity of the generalized other through an acknowledgment of the moral identity of the concrete other" ("The Generalized and the Concrete Other," 92).
87. Young defines the rhetorical dimensions of communication in terms of "the evocative terms, metaphors, dramatic elements of the speaking, by which a speaker addresses himself or herself to this particular audience." See "The Ideal of Impartiality and the Civic Public" in Young, *Justice and the Politics of Difference*, 71.

88. Benhabib, "The Generalized and the Concrete Other," 88.
89. Seyla Benhabib argues in an analogous fashion for procedural rules or presuppositions "of argumentative speech": "the moral ideal that we ought to *respect* each other as beings whose standpoint is worthy of equal consideration (the principle of universal moral respect)" and that we ought "to treat each other as concrete human beings whose capacity to express this standpoint we ought to enhance by creating, whenever possible, social practices embodying the discursive ideal (the principle of egalitarian reciprocity)" (*Situating the Self*, 30–31). In attending to agential goods I have sought to show the internal relation of these moral ideals or virtues.
90. Concurring with Hegel, Gadamer observes that practical "judgment is really always both. The universal under which the particular is subsumed continues to determine itself through the particular." Gadamer, *Reason in the Age of Science*, 135.
91. The example is Stephan Körner's in *Kant*, 40–41.
92. Habermas, *Moral Consciousness and Communicative Action*, 66 (emphasis in the original).
93. Chaïm Perelman's "new rhetoric" signifies not a stylistic, productive art but the art of redeeming practical validity claims in argument. Gadamer writes in a similar vein of Plato's dialectical foundation of rhetoric: "The task is to master the faculty of speaking in such an effectively persuasive way that the arguments brought forward are always appropriate to the specific receptivity of the souls to which they are directed." First, one must accordingly have "a grasp of the truth (i.e., the ideas)," and second, "one must have a profound knowledge of the souls of those one wishes to persuade." Such an understanding of rational rhetoric must be distinguished from the modern view of rhetoric as "perfectly manipulated information." Gadamer, "On the Scope and Function of Hermeneutical Reflection," in Gadamer, *Philosophical Hermeneutics*, 21–25.
94. Achebe, *Things Fall Apart*, 169ff.
95. Tutu, "The Theology of Liberation in Africa," 167.
96. Habermas, *Justification and Application*, 178n12.
97. Criticism of "systematic distortions" presumes "the symmetrical respect that everyone should accord the integrity of all other persons" (Habermas, *Justification and Application*, 6).
98. Habermas, *Moral Consciousness and Communicative Action*, 108–9. In Habermas's words, "Within the horizon of the lifeworld, practical judgments derive both their concreteness and their power to motivate action from their inner connection to unquestioningly accepted ideas of the good life, in short, from their connection to ethical life and its institutions. Under these conditions, problematization can never be so profound as to risk all the assets of the existing ethical substance. But the abstractive achievements required by the moral point of view do precisely that." In *Justification and Application* Habermas writes, "in modern societies, moral norms must detach themselves from the concrete contents of the plurality of attitudes toward life that now manifest themselves; they are grounded solely in an abstract social identity that is henceforth circumscribed only by the status of membership in some society, not in this or that particular society" (47).
99. As William Rehg astutely observes, "By defining solidarity in terms of the relations of mutual recognition that preserve the identity of a form of life, Habermas does not always adequately distinguish specifically *moral* solidarities from the more substantive, prereflective lifeworld solidarities that do not extend beyond this or that particular group." Rehg, *Insight and Solidarity*, 110.
100. See Habermas, "A Review of Gadamer's *Truth and Method*," 358.

101. Tutu, "The Theology of Liberation in Africa," 163.
102. Our understanding of ethical reciprocity thus integrates Seyla Benhabib's communicative norms of equity and complementary reciprocity. In Benhabib's words, "each is entitled to expect and to assume from the other forms of behavior through which the other feels recognized and confirmed as a concrete, individual being with specific needs, talents and capacities" ("The Generalized and the Concrete Other," 92, 87).
103. Tutu, *No Future without Forgiveness*, 32–33.
104. Tutu, 32–33.
105. See Aquinas's argument in *Summa Theologiae* I–II, Q. 56, a. 3, where he describes virtue as "a habit by which we perform well. Now a habit is ordered to a good act in two ways. In one way, insofar as by such habit [one] acquires the facility to do a good act; for example, through the *habit of grammar* [one] has an aptitude to speak correctly. But the habit of grammar does not make [one] always speak correctly, for one who is competent in grammar can commit a barbarism or a solecism.... In another way, habit not only induces an aptitude to act well, but also its right use; for example, justice not only gives [one] readiness of will to do what is just, but also makes him act justly" (emphasis added).
106. Soyinka, *The Burden of Memory, the Muse of Forgiveness*, 70ff.
107. In accordance with the principle of charity we may hold the epistemic *validity* of claim-rights constant and solve for meaning/semantic recognition, i.e., how rights claims are best redeemed here and now.
108. Oduyoye, *Daughters of Anowa*, 164, and "Christian Feminism and African Culture," 442.
109. Wittgenstein, *Philosophical Investigations*, pt. 1, pars. 68, 179.
110. See Tarimo and O'Neill, "What San Salvador Says to Nairobi."
111. Said, "Nationalism, Human Rights, and Interpretation," 45–46.
112. Tierney, *The Idea of Natural Rights*, 276.
113. Tierney, 278, 280.
114. Wolterstorff, "Modern Protestant Developments in Human Rights," 156.
115. For Walzer's appeal to "reiterative universalism," see "Nation and Universe," 509–56.
116. Tierney, *The Idea of Natural Rights*, 347.
117. Whereas in Rawls's "Kantian constructivism" the constitutive operations of reason govern impartial choice, our Aristotelian constructivism derives rights from the play of communicative virtues.
118. Kant, *Religion within the Limits of Reason Alone*, 31.
119. See Wolterstorff, *Justice in Love*, 5–10.
120. "All material practical principles," writes Kant, "are, as such, of one and the same kind, and belong under the general principle of self-love or one's own happiness." In his *Critique of Practical Reason*, prudence generates singular imperatives, devoted to one's own selfish interests, while in *Groundwork* he sharply delineates the "practically good... which determines the will by concepts of reason" from "the pleasant... which influences the will, not as a principle of reason valid for everyone, but solely through the medium of sensation by purely subjective causes valid only for the sense of this person or that." Kant, *Critique of Practical Reason*, 22, 73; *Groundwork of the Metaphysic of Morals*, 413.
121 Aristotle, *Nicomachean Ethics*, 1129b6–1130b8.
122. Aquinas, *Summa Theologiae* I–II, Q. 58, arts. 6, 12. See also *De Reg. Princ.* I, 15 for Aquinas's commentary on Aristotle's *Politics* in I, 1252b27; III, 1280b5; and VII, 1324a5ff., 1325b31. Aquinas, *Political Writings*, 40.

123. Aristotle, *Politics* III, 1280b32–1281a10. The Aristotelian conception of the "perfect community" reflects its finality and sufficiency for human flourishing. See Aristotle, *Nicomachean Ethics,* 1094b7–b10, 1129b15, 1143a1ff., 1160a9; *Politics,* I, 1252a1–1253a38. For Gadamer's interpretation of the relation of phronēsis and *sunesis* in Aristotle's *Nicomachean Ethics,* see *Truth and Method,* 322–24.
124. Kant, *Groundwork of the Metaphysic of Morals,* 417–18.
125. Paton, *The Categorical Imperative,* 126.
126. In making a distinction between technical and prudential imperatives, Kant errs, writes Lewis White Beck, for in "'what concerns the will' both are analytical . . . ; in what concerns the understanding, i.e., the cognitive context in the choice of particular means to the end in view, both are synthetic." Beck, *A Commentary on Kant's Critique of Practical Reason,* 86n26.
127. Jürgen Habermas, "On the Pragmatic, the Ethical, and the Moral Employments of Practical Reason," in Habermas, *Justification and Application,* 1–17.
128. Kant, *Groundwork of the Metaphysic of Morals,* 413.
129. See Habermas's analysis of "Occidental rationalism" in *The Theory of Communicative Action,* 157–85.
130. Habermas, *Between Facts and Norms,* 107–8.
131. Habermas, *Justification and Application,* 6.
132. Gewirth, *Reason and Morality,* 171.
133. Gewirth, 171.
134. Gewirth, 135.
135. Gewirth, 176.
136. Kant, *Critique of Practical Reason,* 28.
137. See Rawls, "Kantian Constructivism in Moral Theory," 525–26, and "Social Unity and Primary Goods," 164–65.
138. Wittgenstein, *Philosophical Investigations,* pt. 1, par. 217.
139. Tutu, *No Future without Forgiveness,* 34–35.
140. Those beholden to Kant might object that in prescribing prudently we acknowledge the maxim's prescriptive force for each agent *seriatim* but deny that it holds generally, so that rationality remains disinterested. Yet in this case ought judgments do not so much prescribe as range over a congeries of discrete interests: each agent has a higher-order interest in acting accordance with her best reasons/judgment but no corresponding higher-order interest in your acting with your best reasons/judgment. Here, too, the sense of ought varies according to person.
141. Davidson, *Inquiries into Truth and Interpretation,* 196.
142. Thus Tutu recalls "the story of the victims, the survivors who were made to suffer so grievously, yet despite this are ready to forgive. This magnanimity, this nobility of spirit, is quite breathtakingly unbelievable. I have often felt I should say, 'Let us take off our shoes,' because at this moment we were standing on holy ground." Tutu in Weisenthal, *The Sunflower,* 267.

CHAPTER THREE

Rights and Religion

Before I was a civil rights leader, I answered a call, and when God speaks, who can but prophesy.

—Martin Luther King Jr.

Modernity, in Max Weber's words, is "disenchanted." Yet the proceedings of the South African Truth and Reconciliation Commission were hardly "godless and prophetless"; nor have the "ultimate and most sublime values" retreated from public life.[1] Religion is a stubborn inheritance. But what is the role of religious narratives in complex pluralist societies? Should religion disturb our undogmatic slumbers?[2] Under the spell of modernity's disenchantment, the antinomies recur, albeit in a religious guise. We must, it seems, plump down for either the thin, quintessentially secular "politics of [universal] rights" or the thick, tradition-dependent "politics of the common good."[3]

Such disputes reflect the Kantian belief that modern human rights discourse must be independent of the ethical substance of particular traditions, including a fortiori religious traditions.[4] In light of the preceding chapter's reconstructive critique, however, we may question whether rights are merely a secular creed—in Eli Wiesel's words, "a world-wide secular religion."[5] For an antinomy of sacred or secular warrants/backing neglects religiously integrated/schematized rights rhetoric, such as that of the TRC (as I argue in part I). In assessing the implications of such rhetoric (part II), I seek to show how well-formed religious narratives not only provide ultimate backing for the virtue of respect but also motivate our compliance with a rights regime and enrich our moral "imaginary" in applying rights in the public realm. And yet there remains a surplus of religious meaning in the call to prophecy, forgiveness, and martyrdom (part III).

I. THE ETHICS OF PUBLIC DISCOURSE

For Weber the retreat of the "ultimate and most sublime" notions of the good in modernity left in its wake our differing, even irreconcilable ends. "The intrusion of reflection into life histories and cultural traditions," writes Jürgen Habermas in a Weberian vein, "has fostered individualism in personal life projects and a pluralism of collective forms of life."[6] Far from being historically adventitious, the radical pluralism of our religious, philosophical, and moral doctrines is, in John Rawls's words, "a permanent feature" of our democratic, political culture.[7] For Kant's liberal heirs the plurality of such traditions implies that political reason will be *common* or shared and public only if we abstract it from any comprehensive doctrine of the *good*.[8]

Our conception of justice, writes Rawls, "should be, as far as possible, independent of the opposing and conflicting philosophical and religious doctrines that citizens affirm."[9] Under the veil of ignorance Rawls's Kantian constructivism confines nonpublic religious belief to the vestibule of such an inquiry; while Habermas's more comprehensive liberalism divests "higher or deeper" doctrines of "any logical force on their own."[10] For Habermas, the "secular sublation (*Aufhebung*) of ontotheology by the philosophy of history" demystifies the public sphere.[11] For Robert Audi, only a purely "secular rationale" suffices for citizens' motivations in advocating or supporting public policy.[12] For Richard Rorty, "post-modernist bourgeois liberalism" abjures every "trace of divinity," either "in the form of a divinized world or a divinized self."[13]

Still, what Weber once called the "grandiose fever" of religious ethics is hardly spent.[14] For Michael Sandel or Jeffrey Stout, Rawls's gambit of assimilating religious belief to a set of "self-imposed" (or "self-authenticating") preferences belies its meaning *as* religious,[15] or in Paul Tillich's words, a matter of "ultimate concern."[16] For critics of a communitarian stripe, like Alasdair MacIntyre or Michael Walzer, our very conception of justice derives from the fragmented substance of our differing ethical traditions or our "higher" or "deeper" religious doctrines. For MacIntyre the thinness of liberal tolerance is finally vacuous; our universal rights talk, in Bentham's words, mere "rhetorical nonsense."[17] Inspired by MacIntyre's retrieval of Aristotelian virtue (through peregrinations from Saint Benedict to Thomas Aquinas), Stanley Hauerwas's ecclesial ethics denies any "universal ethic grounded in human nature per se."[18] So, too, in John Milbank's radical orthodoxy: only a "remnant Christendom" (the church as *societas perfecta*) can redeem the antinomic, social atomism of modernity.[19] Still other, less sectarian critics seek a distinctively religious interpretation of rights. For Michael Perry the very idea of human rights is "ineliminably religious," while, in a similar vein, Max Stackhouse grounds human rights in "transcendent moral laws."[20]

The issue is thus joined. Is the most reasonable doctrine a thin public morality (e.g., a moral Esperanto of rights) or, as Walzer urges, must we concede that "morality is thick from the beginning, culturally integrated" in particular narrative traditions?[21] May we discern yet a third possibility, a via media neither thick nor thin? This, I will argue, is the heritage of the TRC, the American civil rights movement, and modern Roman Catholic social teaching.

Religious Schematization: The TRC

The "idea of natural rights," Tierney reminds us, was not originally "dependent on any particular version of Western philosophy"; rather, "it coexisted with a variety of philosophies, including the religiously oriented systems of the medieval era and the secularized doctrines of the Enlightenment."[22] As the most recent Parliament of Religions attests, religiously oriented systems of the modern era, like their medieval forebears, have succeeded in culturally integrating a grammar of human rights.[23] So it must be, for as I argue in chapter 2, there is no "teleological suspension of the ethical"; our narrative traditions are not, as Rorty avers, hermetically (hermeneutically) closed.[24] Religious traditions, just like narrative traditions generally, remain subject to internal, grammatical critique, such as in apartheid's legitimation by the Dutch Reformed Church (DRC).[25]

Far from being inimical to religion, though, such immanent critique appeals to what Tutu calls "theological and religious insights and perspectives."[26] The influential Dutch Reformed pastor C. F. Beyers Naudé introduced a *status confessionis* condemning apartheid in 1965, while at the behest of the Alliance of Black Reformed Christians in South Africa the World Alliance of Reformed Churches (WARC) followed suit. The ecumenical Kairos Document of 1985 and the Belhar Confession of the Dutch Reformed Mission Church (DRMC) formally adopted a year later both denounced the "state theology" of apartheid.[27] "The unbanning of political organizations and the release of Nelson Mandela and other political prisoners in 1990," writes Charles Villa-Vicencio, "resulted in a different kind of church response to the apartheid state. This response included the statement of the Rustenburg Conference held in November 1990, which brought together the most representative gathering of churches ever assembled in South Africa. The statement included a confession of guilt for the sins of apartheid."[28]

Without such national and international ecumenical solidarity, writes John de Gruchy, "it is highly unlikely that the resilience and hope of those who suffered so greatly in prison, under house arrest, and in many other ways, could have been sustained."[29] In December 1992 Mandela himself acknowledged the role the "confessing" churches played in opposing apartheid and urged them to act "as a midwife to the birth of our democracy."[30] The maieutic role of the churches appears not only in the religiously integrated critique of apartheid but (re)constructively, in the "narrative project" of the TRC. "From the beginning," says Antjie Krog, Tutu "unambiguously mantled the commission in Christian language."[31] The TRC was supported by major religious groups, and religious symbolism (tropes, rituals, etc.) permeated the hearings. The commission, said Tutu, "accepted my call for prayer at the beginning and end of our meetings, and at midday when I asked for a pause for recollection and prayer." Religious motifs of reconciliation and forgiveness were sounded in the Human Rights Violations Committee, when "we agreed that when victims and survivors came to our victim-oriented hearing to testify about their often heart-rending experiences, we would have a solemn atmosphere with prayers, hymns and ritual candle lighting to commemorate those who had died in the struggle."[32]

Not only does Tutu's Ubuntu theology ground his rhetoric of rights and critique of apartheid as "heresy"; the TRC itself becomes a rite of public reasoning—the *locus/topos* of rights "on holy ground."[33] Rights rhetoric is framed or schematized in Christian narrative. At the very first meeting of the Human Rights Violations Committee (December 16, 1995) Tutu announced, "We will be engaging in what should be a corporate nationwide process of healing through contrition, confession and forgiveness."[34] Of such supposedly "nonpublic" religious reasons, Tutu writes, "very few people objected to the heavy spiritual Christian emphasis on the Commission."[35]

Still, as André du Toit, executive secretary of the TRC, remarked, there is no simple fit between "the influence of religious style and symbolism" and "political and human rights concerns."[36] How are we to reconcile rights ("the morality of the depths") with the "higher" *telei* of Christian narrative—contrition, confession, and forgiveness, or what Albie Sachs calls a victim's "right to forgive" (and hence to withhold forgiveness)—with a Christian duty to forgive? As we shall see, forgiveness remains a complex, tensive symbol inasmuch as a "Christian duty to forgive" is *morally* supererogatory.[37] Yet, as Tutu urges, even mere legal coexistence may finally depend on it: there is no future without forgiveness. But just how are we to reconcile these disparate legal, ethical, and religious senses of reconciliation?

Religious reasons need not, as du Toit fears, "supplant political and human rights concerns."[38] As will be seen in greater detail in part III, the distinctively Christian *duties of redress*—love of enemies, forgiveness, and so on—presume the juridical protection of a victim's *right* to forgive or withhold forgiveness. The Christian disciple "justices"—"acts justly," in the prophet Micah's words (6:8)—even as justice bears the mark of "loving tenderly." But love of the disciple who "walks humbly with her God" is never less than just. Still, the churches must walk humbly here, for their martyrs' heroism does not absolve them from complicity with the martyr-makers in Rwanda or abetting the systematic distortions of apartheid or Hutu supremacy. Indeed, the Roman Catholic Church was deeply implicated in the Tutsi genocide—a failure all the more tragic since the developing body of its social teaching should have spurred it to act.[39] Yet Church authorities were silent, even complicit, in supporting the supremacist ideology that culminated in genocide.[40] Priests and sisters numbered among the *génocidaires*. In March of 2017 Pope Francis acknowledged the "sins and failings of the Church" that had so "disfigured the face" of Catholicism and pleaded for a "purification of memory."[41]

II. RE-ENCHANTING THE PUBLIC SPHERE

One might, of course, still dismiss Tutu's appeal to restorative justice or the Catholic Church's belated turn to rights as "merely quaint."[42] But there is, I believe, a rich vein to be mined in Tutu's and Pope John XXXIII's teachings.[43] Let me elaborate. Pace Bentham, I argued in chapter 1 that the sense of rights rests precisely in their suasive, rhetorical force. Lukas Baba Sikwepere's or Nomonde Calata's rights warrant their claim that others respect their basic security. Human rights, in turn, show forth our faith in what the Universal Declaration of Human Rights calls the "dignity and worth of the human person," while basic human rights preserve the conditions or capabilities of practically rational discursive agency.[44] In ascribing worth rather than mere price to persons as agents, we implicitly valorize the prerequisites of their exercising agency—not only our negative civil liberties but the positive basic rights to security and subsistence upheld by the Catholic encyclical tradition.[45]

Exhibiting the banality of goodness rather than "the ultimate and most sublime values" of our comprehensive religious doctrines, basic human rights comprise the grammar of our practically rational rhetoric—what the Conciliar text *Dignitatis humanae* calls "worthy persuasion" in and across our varied narrative traditions.[46] Rights—neither a thin abstract metanarrative, as in Rawls's Kantian constructivism, nor a culturally determined thick narrative, as in MacIntyre's neo-Aristotelian critique—rather configure our narrative (sittlich) traditions, as in the critique of apartheid, and permit us to speak of their limited moral (moralisch) family resemblance.[47] And so our well-formed narratives constitute a family of language-games not rigidly limited but open-textured.[48]

Now it is just this open-textured family resemblance that permits us to speak of a common civic good as the end or discursive telos of political reasoning in complex, pluralist polities. Such shared political reason aims not at optimal preference satisfaction (whether through maximizing utility or impartial liberal constraints) but, as for Tutu or Pope John, the properly circumstantial instantiation of a basic rights regime.[49] As grammar vanishes into speech, so the logic of rights is expressed in what is concrete and particular, for instance, the religiously inspired practice of the TRC. The grammar of rights, that is, must be narratively schematized, as in the TRC or Rev. Martin Luther King Jr.'s "Letter from Birmingham City Jail." For only as embodied or schematized in our narratives is the complex interplay of rights and correlative duties exhibited as coherent (integral and comprehensive) rhetorical practice.[50] As in any natural language, the relation of grammar and narrative remains vital—our sense of civil rights is not fixed *in abstracto* but forged in the narrative history of their application, such as in the hearings of the TRC or in the American civil rights movement.

In his most recent writing Rawls concedes as much. Inspired by King's legacy and the writings of John Courtney Murray, Rawls relaxes the strictures of his earlier "method of avoidance."[51] His revised or "wide view" of public reason now permits reasonable comprehensive religious doctrines to "be introduced in public reason at any time," provided that public reasons, in accordance with the duty of civility, are duly presented.[52] Thus, while "the wide view of public political culture" permits us, in Rawls's words, to introduce "the familiar story of the Good Samaritan," his "proviso" bids us "justify our proposal in terms of proper political values."[53]

Yet what such justification implies is hardly perspicuous. In his illuminating criticism Jeffrey Stout objects to Rawls's contractarian ideal of a "free-standing political conception" upon which "reasonable" citizens must concur.[54] Neither "declaration" (of our own reasonable comprehensive doctrine) nor "conjecture" (engaging in immanent criticism of opponents' religious views) presume such a "free-standing" conception.[55] For Rawls our reasoning in common is thus still beholden to the abstract formalism of Kantian constructivism and narrative-independent common (public) reasons.

In Aristotelian constructivism, conversely, the grammar of rights rhetoric is concretely embodied (schematized) in narrative. We need not trim King's or Tutu's rhetoric of religious reference. Indeed, as we shall see, the family resemblance of well-formed narratives is rich enough to permit declaration and conjecture in public reasoning. Consider, then, the implications of taking up Rawls's wager. What might citizens of a religiously pluralist constitutional regime learn in introducing "the familiar story of the Good Samaritan" in their public political reasoning?

Justification of Respect: *Agapē*

In the preceding chapter we saw that the interplay of the communicative virtues (1) provides backing or justification for a rights regime in the maxim of *respect* (i.e., generalized respect for the concrete other), just as (2) basic human rights are *recognized* as warrants (fixing motivation in public reasoning) and (3) fittingly *interpreted* (embodied/schematized) in narrative tradition. Belief in "the value and dignity of human life," in Tierney's words, runs through the "universal heritage" of human rights and is concretely specified in multiple religious and secular traditions. Yet what of the maxim of respect itself—once, that is, we emulate Hans-Georg Gadamer and forsake a purely transcendental *Letzbegründung*?

For Rorty, who interprets Gadamer in a relativist vein, the "faith . . . in the dignity and worth of the human person" affirmed in the Universal Declaration of Human Rights is metaphysically bereft. For Rorty's "light-minded aestheticism," the "emergence of the human rights culture" owes "nothing to increased moral knowledge" and "everything to hearing sad and sentimental stories."[56] And yet our "sentimental education" is perforce disenchanted: just as in Rawls's earlier exclusivist view of public reason, Rorty assumes the rationalist critique of religion even as he abjures the logocentric mystifications of rationalism itself.[57] Ironically, for the celebrated ironist, Rorty's "detheoreticized politics" (his comprehensive "post-modern bourgeois liberalism") pays its debt to the *siècle des lumières* precisely as "the enlightenment [is] driven away."[58]

One may, of course, treat the parable of the Good Samaritan as a "sad and sentimental story"—but only if we neglect its *narrative* import. For the exemplary story is prefaced by the lawyer's question, "Teacher, what must I do to inherit eternal life?" (Luke 10:25). Jesus' reading of the law is just that: a divine *command* of love (*agapē*).[59] The parable of the Good Samaritan extends the bonds of obligation universally, even to one's professed enemy: "Do this," says Jesus, "and you will live" (Luke 10:28). Christianly one *must* take the victim's side, must privilege, for example, Nomonde Calata's testimony in the TRC. Other religious traditions say no less in adumbrating their distinctive paths toward the relief of suffering. Yet the "must" of the Gospel parable, like other such narratives, exercises not only suasive, motivational but also logical force. Our faith in fundamental human rights, that is, may itself be religiously inspired.[60] In King's words, recalling the prophet Amos, "When God speaks who can but prophesy?"[61]

Religious attitudes and beliefs thus provide what Rawls calls "grounding reasons" since "the roots of democratic citizens' allegiance to their political conceptions lie in their respective comprehensive doctrines."[62] Indeed, for Rawls's political (noncomprehensive) liberalism, the very stability of a rights regime rests on the "overlapping consensus" of such reasonable, comprehensive doctrines—a consensus that is not simply given but is exhibited and revised in public reasoning.[63] Yet Rawls fails to explicate the logical force of such a genetic account—how, that is, citizens' public political reasons are grounded in their differing nonpublic comprehensive doctrines.

For Habermas the justification of public reasons must be entirely immanent: inasmuch as "the critique of reason is its own work," there is "neither a higher nor a deeper reality to which we could appeal."[64] The "rational sublation of theology and its essential contents" renders distinctively religious grounding reasons, if not religion itself, otiose.[65] For Rorty, conversely, grounding reasons are themselves illusory. In Rorty's postmodernist bourgeois liberalism, "no trace of divinity" remains, either in the form of a divinized world or a divinized self, whose subjective claim-rights are objectively vindicated.[66] Curiously, Habermas and Rorty alike betray the Enlightenment prejudice that we are entitled to hold a universal morality of rights only *if* (a) it admits of rational justification that is independent of (b) "religious conceptions of transcendent powers or states and their relation to human beings."[67] In the spirit of Kantian Moralität, Habermas affirms (a) as grounds for "methodological atheism" with respect to (b), while Rorty denies that (a) can be satisfied, so that religious conceptions (b) are but "local and ethnocentric" mores.[68]

Our rhetorical gambit, however, permits us to affirm (a) while recognizing the logical force of (b) as "higher or deeper" doctrines comprising our overlapping consensus. In the preceding chapter I argued that our reasoned speech, aiming at persuasion and conviction, exhibits communicative virtues of respect and recognition (semantic and epistemic). These, in turn, underwrite the family resemblance of reasonable narrative traditions in the schematization of basic human rights claims. Neither thick nor thin, the "depth grammar" of basic rights configures our narration (our Aristotelian constructivism). Yet our discursive rendering of Kant's "fact of pure reason"—the finite, intersubjective redemption of practical validity claims—remains modest. The "self-evidence" of rights claims lies not in the apodicticity of Kantian Moralität but in the *self*-knowledge of the player in the game.

Habermas, indeed, offers just such a pragmatic appeal to the performative contradiction entailed in denying my interlocutor's implicit claim to equality of respect and recognition.[69] Yet precisely in forsaking Karl-Otto Apel's *Letztbegründung,* Habermas implicitly recovers the theological "bedrock" upon which, says Wittgenstein, our "spade is turned": we may say "This is simply what I *do*" when "I have exhausted the [rational] justifications."[70] For what I do in exhibiting faith in dignity need not, as Kant believed, be transcendentally justified, independent of all experience. Yet what is "given" performatively may nonetheless be received as "gift" or divine bestowal.[71] In Tutu's words, "What endows human beings, every single human being without exception, with infinite worth is . . . the fact that each one of us has been created in the image of God. This is something intrinsic. . . . It means that each one of us is a God-carrier, God's viceroy, God's representative. This is why treating anybody as if they were less than this is veritably blasphemous."[72]

Julius Nyerere argues in a similar vein: "We say [we] are created in the image of God. I refuse to imagine a God who is poor, ignorant, superstitious, fearful, oppressed, wretched—which is the lot of the majority of those . . . created in [God's] image."[73] What Tutu and Nyerere do, that is, is exhibit not only their faith in dignity but in the reasons that ground it: belief in the created imago Dei or the primacy of agapē. "What I do" implies my reflective apperception of "This is what *I* do" in believing. Now, such grounding reasons do not so much justify dignity (as if a further transcendental justification were necessary) as explain why no further justification is needed. We are, for Tutu, created in the imago Dei *as* rationally autonomous agents; my exhibiting dignity is "simply what I as a rationally autonomous agent do."[74] Our overlapping consensus, to be sure, need not depend on such grounding reasons; consensus need not go all the way down. The grounding reasons for our common faith in dignity may differ. As the drafters of the Universal Declaration foresaw, Christians, Jews, Muslims, and Buddhists may root their "faith in fundamental human rights, in the dignity and worth of the human person" in their respective narrative traditions.

"Standing on holy ground," the bedrock of my faith, I may thus offer *distinctive* grounding reasons for my faith in dignity even if the sense or meaning of dignity itself is not, in Perry's words, "ineliminably religious." King's faith in the "moral law or the law of God" grounds his conviction that "any law that degrades human personality is unjust"—a conviction not less public or common for its being prophetic.[75] The intelligibility of King's or Tutu's faith bears implicit reference to its "deepest ground"—here, as Wittgenstein says, his "spade is turned."[76] We need not, then, trim King's letter or Tutu's rhetoric of religious reference.[77] Nor need we assume with Audi that only secular reasons suffice for citizens' motivation; like Habermas's methodological atheism, Audi's principle of secular motivation betrays an *ignoratio elenchi*. What is "proved" is not required by public reasoning and may even tacitly enshrine the Enlightenment's prejudice against religious prejudice.[78] Nor is such latent wisdom ethically inconsequential. Invoking religious wisdom precisely as religious guards against investing the state with quasi-idolatrous ultimacy—and surreptitiously sacralizing civic discourse. Habermas turns his spade on the very religious grounding reasons he would deny.[79]

Motivation (Epistemic Recognition)

In response to his critics, Tutu remarked that in the TRC "theological and religious insights and perspectives" informed "much of what we did and how we did it."[80] Such insights and perspectives serve to schematize rights rhetoric in religious narrative (see part I). As in the TRC, rights talk unfolds in schematized application—in the victims' testimony (even religiously inflected testimony) rights make possible. The (semantic/epistemic) recognition of such schematized rights claims enriches our interpretative repertory, illumining the rhetorical "place" (locus/topos) of rights in declaration and conjecture. So, too, does introducing the Gospel parable play a maieutic role by instilling an ethos of rights through the cultivation of character (ēthos). Thus Habermas, in his most recent "post-secular" writings, acknowledges that the "liberal state depends in the long run on mentalities which it is unable to generate from its own resources."[81] In the face of apartheid, the "commitment to reconciliation" of "nearly all the leaders in the black community," writes Tutu, was "due to the influence and witness of the Christian Churches."[82]

"Worthy persuasion," after all, is not merely a function of inference from a freestanding political conception, but of testimony, of "*telling* the story." Grammar without narrative is empty. Yet such "influence and witness" neither supplant nor overdetermine the rhetorical (suasive) force of rights. Narrative without grammar is blind. The parable of the Good Samaritan inspires us not only to do the right deed but to do it for the right reason.[83] For Tutu, as for King and the US bishops, the hortatory (parenetic) force of the parable rests not only in distinctively religious warrants but also in the narrative embodiment of rights. No mere "sad and sentimental story" of pity for the stranger, the parable motivates citizens of faith to *see* the stranger "in all her truth"—the stranger, says Simone Weil, "exactly like me," albeit "stamped with a special mark by affliction."[84]

As will be seen in part III, one may act for the sake of rights even if, as in the narrative testimony of victims, the grammar of rights remains latent.

Indeed, precisely inasmuch as the grammar of rights is internalized in stable dispositions, primary reasons, such as belief that "pass raids" were humiliating or unchristian, suffice. Proper "political justification" can, of course, be given; but neither the rhetorical force nor the validity of the claim depend upon *explicitly* invoking rights, much less on a "free-standing political conception" of justice. Conscience (in the unmediated apperception of "respect") need not make Kantians of us all! Rather, the universal maxim of respect under which the particular is subsumed "continues," in Gadamer's words, "to determine itself through the particular," as in familiar religious motifs, tales, and tropes.[85] It is just this concrete determination, this *epistemic recognition* of the schematized rights claim, that typically moves us to act.[86] "That is what filled some of us with such a passionate commitment to fight for justice and freedom," writes Tutu. "We were inspired not by political motives but by our biblical faith."[87] When Tutu introduces the Gospel parable in condemning apartheid as "vicious, evil, unchristian" because, like the robbers on the way to Jericho, it "artificially and deliberately" induces need, "causing suffering to many people," he is still playing the language game of human rights.

Interpretation (Semantic Recognition)

The parable shows how citizens of faith incorporate the communicative virtues of respect and epistemic recognition in their religiously integrated rights rhetoric. The familiar story (1) grounds Christians' faith in human rights, and (2) motivates them to comply with a properly circumstantial rights regime, recognizing especially the basic claim-rights of the most vulnerable. The "exemplary narrative," writes Wolfgang Schrage, "shows that the *obligation* to love has no limits: love does not reach a boundary beyond which nothing is required."[88] For "love does not follow the dictates of convention and prejudice but dares to ignore them, dares with sovereign freedom to surmount the barriers that separate people. A person who loves can see in anyone a neighbor in need." Not even an enemy (as Samaritans were for Jews) is beyond the pale of agapē.[89]

Here the third virtue follows suit: (3) the parable tutors our imagination in ratifying, revising, and specifying public reasons. In their modern-day "reading of the law" Tutu, King, and the US bishops *ratify* their "commitment to constitutional democracy" and the duty of civility—political virtues, says Rawls, upon which our overlapping consensus depends.[90] Introducing the parable (interpreted thus) manifests their allegiance to what Rawls calls "the democratic ideal of public reason." But manifesting their allegiance is not logically antecedent to or independent of public reasoning—it is just what citizens, including citizens of faith, do in realizing "the democratic ideal." The "family resemblance" or "overlapping consensus" of reasonable, comprehensive doctrines is realized or exhibited performatively in public reasoning. (The grammar of rights is thus neither sacred nor secular per se, but, in Rawls's terms, it is properly political).

In their pastoral letter on the economy, for instance, the US Catholic bishops introduce the Gospel story as an exemplary narrative of the "dual command of love that is at the basis of all Christian morality."[91] Enjoining "mutual care and respect" for the dignity or "sacredness of every person as a creature formed in the image and likeness of God," such neighbor-love in turn is "made real" in redeeming persons' fundamental rights. For such basic rights to security, subsistence, and civil liberties, say the bishops, are "the prerequisites for a dignified life in community"—the moral charter of "public order."

Such satisfaction, moreover, may be implicit, as in King's "Letter from Birmingham City Jail," in which civic and religious narratives are intertwined, or symbolic, as when "young ministers of the gospel and a host of their elders" engaged in nonviolent resistance.[92] Seeing the latent family resemblance aright permits citizens of faith to exercise their religious liberty without undue regimentation of their public reasoning.[93] Explicit recognition of our latent wisdom may, of course, be fitting, such as when contesting a particular grammatical remark (rights claim). But we need not say that "citizens of faith who cite the Gospel parable of the Good Samaritan" *must* "go on to give a public justification for the parable's conclusions in terms of political values."[94] Rawls himself concedes that "proper, political values" may remain inchoate, as in "the Abolitionists and those in the Civil Rights Movement": "The proviso was fulfilled in their cases, however much they emphasized the religious roots of their doctrines because these doctrines supported basic constitutional values—as they themselves asserted—and so supported reasonable conceptions of political justice."[95]

We need not, then, insist upon juridically parsing Tutu's condemnation of apartheid as "veritably blasphemous for it is to spit in the face of God."[96] Satisfying the *ideal* of public reason turns less on explicit "public justification" by citizens of faith than on citizens generally applying the "principle of charity" in semantic recognition of such schematized rights claims. Holding "belief [validity] constant as far as possible," in Donald Davidson's words, permits us to solve "for meaning" in interpreting Tutu's implicit (religiously schematized) claim-rights.[97] Only thus do citizens—and not merely citizens of faith—"go on" to recognize the diverse concrete modes of expressing rights.

We cannot, then, beg the question of interpretation: the benefits of citizens' mutual knowledge of their comprehensive religious doctrines, says Rawls, "bring out a positive ground for introducing such doctrines"—one that is finally irreducible to mere "self-imposed" or "self-authenticating" preferences.[98] Yet neither are such positive grounds restricted merely to ratifying a prevailing public consensus. For, as Rawls acknowledges, "the content of public reason is not fixed." Moral perceptions, after all, must be tutored (e.g., by what King calls the "strong, persistent, and determined action" of the African-American—and African churches).[99] "The Bible," says Tutu, turns out to be "the most subversive, most revolutionary" book imaginable in a situation of injustice and oppression.[100]

As Tutu's words testify, the "ideal of public reason"—the telos of the civic common good—is, at its best, imperfectly realized in our public political culture. Our public reasoning may be incomplete, or distorted, even systematically so.[101] Introducing the Gospel story of the Good Samaritan reminds us how the dictates of convention and prejudice conspire against our heeding what King calls the "deep groans and passionate yearnings of those that have been oppressed."[102] Where political values are distorted, then, the realization of the ideal of public reason, may, in Rawls's words, "*require* that [religious] comprehensive reasons be invoked," that is, reasons distinctively though not uniquely religious.[103] For "the Abolitionists and those in the Civil Rights Movement," the ideal of public reason is fulfilled not by *ratifying* public reasons but by conjecture (immanent critique) in the *revision* of our "freestanding" political conception of justice.

If, then, the hermeneutic virtue of semantic recognition permits citizens to interpret religiously integrated rights rhetoric, so such rhetoric may in turn extend the semantic recognition/interpretation of rights, as for the abolitionists and those in the civil rights movement. Luke's parable, we may say, becomes the "moral squint" through which Christians see (Luke 10:30) and respond compassionately (Luke 10:33) lest, like the priest and the Levite of the tale, "members of the oppressor race," too readily "see and pass by" (Luke 10:32–32).[104] The claims of those suffering the systemic suppression of their basic rights become morally—and religiously—exigent.[105] "Our God is a God who has a bias for the weak," says Tutu, "and we who worship this God, who have to reflect the character of this God, have no option but to have a like special concern for those who are pushed to the edges of society, for those who because they are different seem to be without a voice."[106]

Here the "familiar story of the Good Samaritan" reveals the boundless, universal scope of love precisely in enjoining a moral solidarity with those who suffer: my "neighbor, the masses."[107] Thus the lesson (in public political reasoning) is that our moral entitlement to equal respect or consideration justifies preferential treatment for those whose basic rights are most imperiled—in Camus's phrase, our taking "the victim's side."[108] Recalling the parable in addressing a women's group, Tutu speaks of seeing apartheid's victims "as a brother, as a neighbour." "When you look at someone with eyes of love, you see a reality different from that of someone who looks at the same person without love, with hatred or even just indifference."[109]

So it is: "passing to the victims' side" (Luke 10:34), that is, seeing the victims' point of view (their epistemic or hermeneutical privilege), emerges as a touchstone of the legitimacy of our prevailing institutional arrangements. Indeed, the irony is doubled, for to "go and do likewise" (Luke 10:37) the lawyer must learn the meaning of the law from the despised "other," the Samaritan who alone sees and has compassion (Luke 10:33). In Tutu's liberation theology "seeing and having compassion," illumine the occasion of acting and inspire appropriate institutional redress where the victim is legion—in Jon Sobrino's words, "a whole suffering people on the way."[110] For Tutu or King a heritage of nonviolent resistance and the rituals of social reconciliation are thus at play, not only in declaration (ratification) and conjecture (revision) but in modeling (specifying) culturally fitting schematizations of basic rights.

Considerable variations may, of course, be wrung on these themes: the American civil rights movement inspired civil resistance against apartheid in South Africa, just as Mahatma Ghandi's *ahimsa* inspired King. But the culturally integrated embodiment of a rights regime precludes simple emulation. The grammar of rights is not self-interpreting (as warrants, rights justify but do not fully explain or rationalize action). We must discern how, in a particular setting, imperfect duties of provision and protection are fittingly *specified*—how the *habitus* of rights is nurtured in a religiously pluralist polity. Here, too, religiously affiliated institutions of civil society play a notable role, both in promoting a culturally fitting ethos of rights and in generating the social capital expended in their defense (e.g., the political mobilization of the Black churches and mosques).[111] In neither case is religion merely epiphenomenal to public reason—as Walzer might say, public reason is thick (in invoking religious wisdom, such as the parable of the Good Samaritan) before it is thin (redeeming proper political values).

Ethical Reciprocity

Familiar tales in other religious traditions, of course, serve no less to schematize basic rights rhetoric, so that Christian, Muslim, or Jew "do likewise" (Luke 10:37)—the family resemblance or overlapping consensus of their stories supports an integral and comprehensive culture of rights as civic *paideia,* or what Martha Nussbaum calls our "civic imagination."[112] In public reasoning we do not merely ratify regnant political values; for these are not given a priori as a final "metavocabulary" of rights. Our reading of the law may itself be revised, even as rights talk is embodied in going and doing likewise as in the nonviolent mobilization of the Black churches.

We may speak, then, of a religious/moral dialectic of *ethical reciprocity* in which distinctive religious and secular traditions support the discursive finality (telos) of the common good and the set of fitting civic virtues and institutional arrangements best suited to redeem agents' basic human rights.[113] Religious, like other narrative traditions, are not simply relegated to the background culture as private or nonpublic preferences.[114] Nor, as Rorty insists, is the price of religious liberty religion's privatization in a disenchanted public sphere.[115] For only with religious literacy, which includes what Rawls calls declaration, conjecture, and even witness, do we fully ratify, revise, and apply the grammar of the common good—or, more precisely, realize the *ideal* of public reason.[116] Yet, precisely so, the reverse moral/religious dialectic tempers the *telei* of our particular narrative traditions so that the learning is mutual and ongoing—an exercise of what David Hollenbach felicitously terms "intellectual solidarity."[117] The burden of such mutual learning is, pace Habermas, symmetrically borne: secular humanists, too, must translate or be prepared to translate the comprehensive doctrines tacitly at play in their deliberations.[118] For, as King reminds us, we cannot presume that religion is merely a grace note added to the obligato of secular reasoning. Worthy persuasion remains a function of ethical *reciprocity*—and discursive solidarity.

Nurturing such solidarity, deliberative tolerance unsettles our undogmatic slumbers, as in Rawls's (early) or Rorty's dismissal of Ignatius of Loyola as "fanatical." In later writings, to be sure, Rawls himself acknowledges John Courtney Murray's role in revising Catholic doctrine, for example, in *Dignitatis humanae*'s upholding the right of religious liberty. Yet Murray's ethical/political critique is no less an expression of his Ignatian spirituality. In extending Ignatius's "presupposition"—a foreshadowing of Davidson's principle of charity—to the American "proposition," Murray shows that the modern "politics of [human] rights" is implied by religious affirmations of the common good (the restricted province of government in promoting public order).[119] But so, too, in applying Ignatius's presupposition reciprocally to Catholic doctrine, Murray reveals to the civic polity the latent wisdom of his religious heritage as a complex web of belief that is raveled and rewoven anew.[120]

Maxims of Religious Reasoning in the Public Realm: Catholic Social Teaching Revisited

Let me say a word, then, about the implications of such wisdom for our public political reasoning. The promise of her social teaching is only imperfectly realized in the Church's politics. In religiously pluralist polities, worthy persuasion cannot be restricted to a single comprehensive doctrine. Yet where philosophical liberalism favors the politics of rights over those of the common good, our threefold hermeneutic refigures rights in a discursive common good: a grammar narratively embodied or schematized in a family of reasonable traditions such as Ujamaa or Ubuntu. Drawing on our threefold hermeneutic, then, let me propose three maxims for prophetic public engagement generally and Catholic social *teaching* in particular: of critical recognition, of constructive redemption, and of reconstructive redress.

The Maxim of Critical Recognition: Catholic Social Teaching

The sense of rights, as I argue in chapter 1, rests in rights' rhetorical force as tokens of worthy persuasion. In pluralist societies, says Murray, "no minority has the right to impose its own religious or moral views on other groups, through the use of methods of force, coercion, or violence."[121] Yet, just so, minority groups enjoy "the right to work toward the elevation of standards of public morality in a pluralist society, through the use of methods of persuasion and pacific argument." Persuasion is worthy, then, when, in accordance with the critical/deconstructive role of rights, we seek public consensus by translating our distinctive religious claims into persuasive political rhetoric—grounded not in secular metanarrative but in the family resemblance of well-formed narrative traditions. (It was thus that Nyerere, himself a devout Catholic, urged the Church to practice its rhetoric of rights—*haki za binadamu*—in supporting political liberation.[122]) By the same token, in supporting fundamental political positions regarding society's basic structure, citizens of faith, says the Catholic Church's *Dignitatis humanae,* must refrain from any "hint of coercion or of a kind of persuasion that would be dishonorable or unworthy."[123]

Appealing to worthy persuasion in realizing the mundane common good, the Second Vatican Council recalls Rawls's view that the exercise of coercive political power is proper "only when we sincerely believe that the reasons we offer for our political action may reasonably be accepted by other citizens as a justification of those actions."[124] Foremost among such reasons is the protection and provision of basic rights, including religious liberty. Yet, where for Rawls the burden of translation falls on individual citizens as "ideal legislators," we look rather to the critical working of tradition, such as in the Catholic Church's social teaching. Neither ecclesial declaration nor conjecture or witness, to be sure, are limited to rights rhetoric, as we shall see in part III. Yet the grammar of rights configures (or refigures) the Church's public reasoning. The Church can neither deny rights internally nor, in the public sphere, impose norms that cannot be reasonably be accepted by other citizens as a justification. For public morality, realizing a *common* good, is never merely personal morality writ large on the body politic.

We may invoke "intrinsic evil" in public reasoning but precisely inasmuch as rights rhetoric fixes certain action-descriptions, for example, genocide, atrocity, or rape, such that no further redescription in terms of intentions or circumstances is permissible.[125] Adopting John Paul II's gambit of appealing to basic human rights, we may speak of "deliberately subjecting workers or the poor to subhuman living conditions" and "racist behavior" as *intrinsece malum*.[126] In promoting such behavior we would be guilty of formal cooperation in grave evil. Yet not all gravely wrong acts entail such a perspicuous denial of rights. As we shall see in chapter 4, mass incarceration and anti-immigration legislation are rightly condemned, but not *ex objecto*—the mere action-description will not suffice.

Neither can we say that all acts once regarded as intrinsically evil on the basis of perfectionist teleology (e.g., masturbation, artificial contraception, or "redefining marriage") perspicuously violate basic human rights. This, too, must be shown. Indeed, the mere impermissibility of an act tells us little of its comparative moral gravity. *This* must be established on other persuasive moral grounds. Lying, for Augustine, is always impermissible, but not all lies are equally grave. Acts, moreover, may be judged to be intrinsically evil for *nonpublic* reasons, such as one's fidelity to traditional magisterial teaching.[127] Under our "first, most cherished liberty" such reasons are grounds for legal exemption. Yet the very religious liberty warranting legal exemption precludes imposing religious beliefs (i.e., insisting upon a single comprehensive doctrine of the good).[128] Belief that an act or practice is intrinsically evil does not, then, dictate a specific legislative remedy. Not all acts regarded by the Church as intrinsically evil are fit subjects of legal proscription; nor, as Murray reminds us, does the secular state enjoy the competence to pronounce on distinctively religious matters (e.g., the full, religious meaning of marriage).

Worthy persuasion, moreover, is not exhausted by declaration, conjecture, or witness. The charitable interpretation sought—that *our* distinctively religious beliefs be taken as tokens of human rights—must be offered in turn (Matt. 7:12). Citizens, that is, must exercise a hermeneutics of charity in interpreting others' public reasons.[129] At times explicit translation of such reasons is not necessary; a *fides implicita* in human rights suffices. Yet, in the give-and-take of public reasoning, when the interpretation or application of rights is itself contested (as in controversies regarding same-sex marriage) the maxim of critical recognition requires more. For as we saw in chapter 2, citizens are equally worthy of representation—each owed "an effort at identification" in public political reasoning.[130] That is, we must ask what it would mean to "save the proposition of the neighbor" from the perspective of our shared political grammar—the basic rights we hold in common in accordance with the maxim of recognition.[131]

The Maxim of Constructive Redemption: Catholic Social Teaching

The Church then, must seek to interpret its neighbors—Protestants, Jews, Muslims, Buddhists, secular humanists—aright, avoiding any "hint of coercion." Worthy persuasion demands such a dialectic of mutual recognition or deliberative tolerance, a tolerance informed by religious literacy. Yet even with such a charitable hermeneutics, differences will persist. Agreed-on public reasons such as basic rights do not exhaust the fund of public reasoning; nor is the implementation of a rights regime always obvious. Indeed, if in pluralist polities the "grammar" of rights makes public reasoning possible, the interpretation and application of rights makes such reasoning necessary. Rights are not self-interpreting, and public reasoning may invoke differing rights of differing weight and scope. And the same right may be fulfilled in differing ways. The maxim of recognition does not eo ipso guarantee agreement. Rather, in Murray's words, our public reasoning presumes the "reasonable disposition to argue our many disagreements in an intelligent and temperate fashion."[132]

Yet how do we adjudicate amid our "many disagreements" in exercising legitimate coercive power? A prudential (consequentially sensitive) note is sounded.[133] For policies are governed by basic rights as deontic side-constraints in terms of negative duties of avoiding deprivation and are subject to consequential evaluation in terms of positive duties of protection and provision. Since, consistent with the discursive ideal of the common good, satisfying these latter duties will be relative to prevailing political, economic, social, and cultural circumstances, we may ask, Of the set of policies deemed feasible, which will best satisfy persons' mutually implicative rights—and, in particular, the rights of the most vulnerable?[134] Let us call this the maxim of constructive redemption.

The basic rights of those "cruelly silenced for so long" become, in Weber's terms, "exemplary or binding" in public reasoning. If the maxim of recognition enjoins a charitable interpretation of proposed policies, the maxim of constructive redemption favors that policy which, all things considered, best fulfills the telos of a rights regime: the discursive common good. Here, too, the "ideal legislator's" public reasoning presumes the ethical reciprocity of free and equal citizens. Deliberative consensus will be halting, incremental at best, and subject to constant revision. As Aquinas realized, law remains an imperfect instrument. Counsels of prudence (Aristotelian phronēsis) must prevail as we aim, albeit imperfectly, at the mundane common good. As John Paul II acknowledges, the limited province of law in pluralist polities will inevitably embrace reasonable compromises.

Prudence must guide us in determining when "an elected official, whose absolute personal opposition to procured abortion was well known, could licitly support proposals aimed at limiting the harm done by [a pro-abortion] law and at lessening its negative consequences at the level of general opinion and public morality."[135] Laws *permitting* same-sex marriage or abortion are not, for that reason, themselves intrinsically evil. John Paul concludes that under the appropriate caveats, supporting such laws "does not in fact represent an illicit cooperation" with intrinsic evil but rather constitutes a "legitimate and proper attempt" to realize the political common good.[136]

The Maxim of Reconstructive Redress: Catholic Social Teaching

Law's paradise is imperfect, and invariably some will suffer or fail to be protected under its writ. And it is precisely because our maxims of recognition and redemption fail us that the reconstructive motif of redress retains its force. Still, there are victims, claims not fully recognized or redeemed, but also a place for prophecy. For Pope Francis, Martin Luther King Jr., Mother Teresa, Archbishop Tutu, and Dorothy Day the religious "option for the poor" or most vulnerable plays a critical role in redressing the moral myopia that invariably besets our mundane politics—in Dr. King's words, "the appalling silence" of the good.

The Church, too, must draw on its latent wisdom, in particular the wisdom of women, not only in receiving but in interpreting doctrine. For only by recognizing the hermeneutical privilege of those consigned to the ecclesial margins can the magisterium utter a truly prophetic word. Doctrine is but the final step of the tireless efforts and persistent work of those whose lives, like Dorothy Day's or Mother Teresa's, translate the Gospel "in our hearing" (Luke 4: 21). For traditio remains vital, not as a quasi-axiomatic system of inference but as a complex web of beliefs woven anew in each generation. Again and again certain doctrinal strands, once "taken as dispositive," are revised in light of other beliefs "already part of Christian teaching."[137] As I argued earlier, creedal affirmation bears fruit in a way of life woven of many complex strands of belief, including what Gadamer called the "infinity of the not said": the taken-for-granted background prejudgments or patterns of belief embedded in our latent wisdom.[138] The belated recognition of religious liberty or condemnation of slavery does not so much strike a discordant note as resolve a prevailing disharmony.

Our three maxims draw upon the latent wisdom of our tradition, in particular the Aristotelian/Thomistic conception of prudence (prudentia/phronēsis) ordered "naturally" to the common good. If in the public realm we cannot keep our metaphysics warm, we may still draw from its wisdom. For rights are best conceived as neither communitarian narrative nor liberal metanarrative, but as the deep grammar of well-formed narratives; rights, that is, as embodied or schematized in our differing narrative traditions. We need not, then, peg our discursive interpretation of the common political good to a particular, comprehensive doctrine. Neither need we relegate expressions of such doctrines to the vestibule of public reasoning. Rather, in ratifying our discursive consensus we leave a place (locus/topos) for prophecy. For in a disenchanted world, "When God speaks who can but prophesy?" We look, then, to the surplus of religious meaning.

III. THE SURPLUS OF RELIGIOUS MEANING: THE THEOLOGICAL VIRTUES

In the preceding parts I argued that the narrative schematization of rights illumines the complex role played by religious belief in modern pluralist societies. In grounding, explaining, and interpreting public reason—indeed, to the degree it does so—religion reveals itself to be both public and reasonable. In ethical reciprocity a consequentially sensitive embodiment of rights permits citizens of faith to recognize the *ethical* force of victims' claims in the "imperfect paradise" of law.[139] Yet there is, invariably, a moral remainder of legitimate claims that cannot be legitimately (legally) adjudicated. Wole Soyinka's eloquent plea for "evidence of mitigation—or remorse" was not justiciable in the TRC's amnesty hearings, yet the ritualized character of the hearings orchestrated a social drama in which such demands were made and perhaps honored. Though forgiveness fell beyond the purview of the judges, I recall one mother saying to the killer of her son, who begged in tears, "I can never forgive you, for what you have done," while another, immediately following, said, "It is my Christian duty to forgive you."

In the former case the legal provision of amnesty implies the institutional recognition of the victim's *right* to forgive—or a fortiori to withhold forgiveness. But the latter case raises a further question: What shall we say of such a Christian duty? The dictates of morality may reveal the command of the face.

Yet such recognition does not entail forgiveness nor does the rule of law provide for the love of enemies. How, then, shall we understand the "surplus" of religious meaning?[140] Not, I think, in the overdetermination of public reasons (where a religious rationale is superimposed upon a secular one) but rather in the distinctively religious sublation of the communicative virtues. Just as when I considered the implications of religious belief for public reasoning, so in this final part I turn to the distinctively religious implications of public reasoning: how citizens of faith interpret or "refigure" human rights practice. (I confine my reflections here to Christian faith, e.g., how the Pauline "*theological virtues*" sublate the discursive virtues, although fitting analogies may be drawn for other religious traditions.)[141]

Faith

Memory itself is no stay against atrocity. Rather, as discussed in chapter 1, stories become testimony only in anamnestic solidarity, invoking the grammar of basic rights. Only then can testimony be woven into a greater story that unites. Yet how, in the face of genocide, apartheid, or ethnic cleansing, are we to speak of godly things? Here victims raise the perennial question of theodicy, a question that resolves itself less as a metaphysical conundrum than as a lived lament. The psalms of lament give voice to the *morally* tragic character of unjust suffering for *all* victims, not only those officially recognized or commemorated.

In what Emmanuel Katongole calls the "valley of lament," evil is *recognized* ("O Lord, how long shall the wicked, how long shall the wicked exult. They crush your people, O Lord, and afflict your heritage" [Ps. 94:3, 5]) but goodness is remembered—one might even say proleptically, in the promise of *redemption* ("For the Lord will not forsake his people; he will not abandon his heritage; for justice will return to the righteous and all the upright in heart will follow it" [Ps. 94:14–15]).[142] Unlike Mother Courage's silence in Brecht's play, lament brings to word the transgressed command. In Gershom Scholem's words, lament defines the "border between the linguistic realms of speech and silence," between wretchedness and tragedy. Language "partakes of lament as its truly tragic point."[143] There is thus a performative aspect to lament, inscribing the victim's cry into the biblical litany of cries, the suffering and passion of the world. Telling the story becomes part of the greater story of divine vindication or *redress* ("If the Lord had not been *my* help, my soul would soon have lived in the land of silence" [Ps. 94:17]). In the Gospels lament becomes God's cry; the cry of the world is gathered in Jesus' cry (Mark 15:37), the Word uttered in the silence of Calvary.[144]

Interpreted thus, lament encodes the threefold elements of rights: recognition, redemption, and redress, albeit in a distinctively religious key.[145] "The cry of lament," says Katongole, "is not only a prayer but a social ethic—a passionate, pastoral, and practical engagement on behalf of the crucified of history."[146] Yet lament is but one inflection of the Gospel story that "today, in our hearing," speaks in the tongues of rights. For not only is "the struggle for human rights . . . an inescapable imperative" for "anyone who believes in God." "The struggle for human rights," says Sobrino, is an *in actu* concretization of our *faith* in God."[147] In Saint Paul's encomium of the theological virtues in 1 Corinthians 13:13, such faith "implies the recognition of the lordship of Jesus." In Pauline theology, "confession on the lips" that "Jesus Christ is Lord" entails not merely notional assent to "the proposition that 'Jesus is Lord,'" but the "obedience of faith" (Rom. 1:5; 10:8–10); in Joseph Fitzmyer's words, it is "a vital, personal commitment, engaging the whole person to Christ in all his or her relations with God, other human beings, and the world."[148] For Paul the "obedience of faith" (*hypakōe pisteōs*) is the fruition of "hearing" (*akoē*) the Gospel, the firstfruits of Christ's Lordship (Rom. 8:23). Such kerygmatic assent (in both its locutionary and its illocutionary aspects) is revelatory: the lordship of Jesus is revealed in the disciple's self-disposition in agapē—as "faith working itself out in love" (Gal. 5:6)—which, as for King, Tutu, and the Catholic bishops, entails the practice of basic human rights. Denying these rights, conversely, is "veritably blasphemous."

Yet to heed Jesus' command to "Go and do likewise" as the summary of the law is not merely to comply with our neighbors' rights in answer to the lawyer's question (what Karl Rahner terms the "essentialist" requirements of morality).[149] For to the lawyer's question in the parable, "Who is my neighbor?" (Luke 10:29)—seeking a precise delimitation of rights and duties—Jesus replies with a question of His own (Luke 10:36).[150] In Tutu's words, "Jesus summons the disciple not merely to love her neighbor, but to become a neighbor to the man in need." Tutu then proceeds to offer his political-theological exegesis:

> It is interesting that Jesus was asked the question, "who is my neighbour": and the questioner hoped that Jesus would say, "Your neighbour is so and so and not so and so," boundaries for the exercise of neighbourly concern. Note the answer Jesus gave—He described someone in need and someone who gave help to the one in need and two people who didn't. And then He asked a question in return in true Socratic fashion, so that the person addressed would discover the

> truth for himself. Now the radical point about Jesus' question is that He asks who proved a *neighbour* to the man in need.

To the women "gathered here," says Tutu, you are "not going round to discover who your neighbour is. . . . No you are meant to be asking 'To whom am I going to be a neighbour?—Who is in need and whose need must I meet as a neighbor with this privilege and this responsibility?'"[151]

So it is: the distinctively Christian theological virtue of *faith* defines the disciple's horizon of *recognition as discernment;* for "to be a Christian," says Gustavo Gutiérrez, "is to draw near, to make oneself a neighbor, not the one I encounter in my journey but the one in whose journey I place myself."[152] Christianly, one must incarnate Jesus' compassion in anamnestic solidarity with the *anāwîm.*[153] For if love "justices," as in the familiar Lukan parable, so "acting justly" is tempered by love (agapē) (Mic. 6:8). We must not merely take the victim's side (the "essential" requirement of ethics) but, finally, take the victim's side *as* our ownmost truth (in Rahner's words, the "formal, existential" demand of love).[154] The "law" of love cannot, then, simply be subsumed in the class of essential moral rules (e.g., human rights) or action-guiding principles (e.g., the "golden rule").[155] Rather, the parable, in evoking the disciple's "obedience of faith," reveals "simply what I do" as neighbor.[156] In the Christ of Luke's Gospel, one is always, already in communion with the anāwîm.

If for Rahner essential ethics defines the sphere of universal norms (e.g., human rights subsuming the *casus*), then a formal, existential ethics pertains to one as "*individuum ineffabile*" whom God has called by name, a name that is and can only be unique."[157] What is morally supererogatory (e.g., forgiveness, love of enemy, or even martyrdom) may in faith's obedience be demanded. Yet my becoming neighbor in fulfilling the divine command is never *in abstracto*; one discerns from within the world/word of the parable in which the *individuum ineffabile* of the *other* appears. The Samaritan sees the man fallen among thieves, not in respect of the man's social titles (the "socius," in Paul Ricoeur's terms), nor indeed as his generalized "other-I," but as one who appears in compassion as "the first-Thou."[158]

So it is: the disciple of the "Samaritan Church" who would walk humbly with her God (Mic. 6:8) must "see and have compassion," even as compassion (*esplanchnisthē;* being moved in one's inmost heart) itself becomes a "way" of seeing—in Tutu's words, "with eyes of love." In times of uncivil strife, civic rapprochement and compliance with a regime of rights may indeed depend upon such supererogatory evangelical inspiration. In *No Future without Forgiveness,* Tutu writes of the "magnanimity" of victims "who were made to suffer so grievously, yet despite this are ready to forgive"—a magnanimity, says Tutu, upon which the future of a stable democratic regime itself rests.[159] In a religious sublation of morality (*Aufhebung*), we are "standing on holy ground."[160]

Hope

In the preceding section I argued that the "obedience of faith" extends the bonds of obligation for the believer, that is, in *semantic recognition* of distinctive Christian duties that constitute the debt of love ("loving compassionately"). In compassion, in taking the victims' side *as* one's own, the disciple "justices"—acts for the sake of the "rights of the poor"—even when such *praxis* (e.g., martyrdom or forgiveness) remains morally supererogatory. The work of love, says T. S. Eliot, "costs not less than everything."[161] And yet, with Reinhold Niebuhr, we may be tempted to dismiss such distinctively Christian demands as "impossible ideals."[162] In a sometimes vile and violent world, anamnestic solidarity with victims may well seem but vain expectation.

Just so, with Saint Paul we "hope against hope" (Rom. 4:18). For Paul, hope is the theological virtue that looks to the coming of the kingdom in eschatological fulfillment. As Paul says, "In this hope we were saved" (Rom. 8:23–24). If the theological virtue of faith lets us "see" the formal-existential demands of agapē, then the cognate virtue of hope inspires us to prove them true in the obedience of faith (*epistemic recognition*). While faith affirms the *revelation* of truth (distinctively Christian obligations), "hoping against hope" enacts the *truth* of revelation. As Karl Barth tells us, command becomes permission.[163]

In her eloquent testimony Imaculée Ilibagiza describes the ordeal of hiding from the Interahamwe: "*Why do You expect the impossible from me?* I asked God. *How can I forgive people who are trying to kill me, people who may have already slaughtered my family and friends?*" She then speaks of a moment of grace, of divine compassion:

> In God's eyes, the killers were part of His family, deserving of love and forgiveness. I knew that I couldn't ask God to love me if I were unwilling to love his children. At that moment, I prayed for the killers, for their sins to be forgiven. . . . I held on to my father's rosary and asked God to help me, and again I heard His voice: Forgive them; they know not what they do.[164]

In part II we saw how Christian narrative inspires compliance with a rights regime. In fulfillment of the parable's admonition disciples recognize the epistemic validity of basic human claim-rights—even when fulfilling such "ordinary" demands requires moral heroism.[165] But to "go and do likewise" demands more than merely recognizing the deontic force of rights. The bonds of love are tighter, woven more firmly, in discerning the formal-existential commands of discipleship: forgiveness, love of enemies, martyrdom. Faith is the content; hope, even against hope, is the reason for fulfilling the commands. "Hope," says Pumla Gobodo-Madikizela, "is where transformation begins."[166]

Love

Faith and hope are the work of love (agapē). "Love," says Saint Paul, "believes all things, hopes all things" (1 Cor. 13:7). It is not the lawyer—or the reader of the parable—who sets the limits of love ("Who is my neighbor?"), even if the limits of *respect* are extended universally. One must rather answer Jesus' question and *become* neighbor to the anāwîm, that is, "what *I* do." In King's words one must, as the Samaritan, "project the 'I' into the 'thou.'"[167] Such is the deontic form of love (agapē): the disciple is not the still point from which love radiates. Rather, what is commanded is one's very self, "oneself demanded," says Rahner, "in the concreteness of one's heart."[168] In this "selving" disciples form the "beloved community"—beloved in the Beloved who, as Augustine says, becomes neighbor to our wounded humanity.[169]

So Jesus, in salvific irony, answers the lawyer's first question, "What must I do to live," by reversing the second. The command to love the Lord with *all* your heart, with *all* your soul, with *all* your strength, and with *all* your mind, and your neighbor as yourself (Luke 10:27) is fulfilled not merely in this or that deed of love but rather in one's "selving" *as* neighbor.[170] The irony is thus complete: what must I do to *live* is "turn" to the world of the poor, of the half-dead stranger—"becoming," in martyred Archbishop Óscar Romero's words, "incarnate in their world, . . . proclaiming the good news to them" even to the point of "sharing their fate"—a hard grace, indeed! But grace nonetheless.

In selving as neighbor (*metanoia*) the disciple is revealed as beloved in the Beloved. The command of love, exigent and costly, is *Love's* command: it is love commanding. So the impossible beatitudes of Jesus turn us to the One who speaks them: Jesus, God's Word of Blessing. Finally, this lordship is revealed in the disciple's "obedience of faith." In the obedience of faith the disciple's anamnestic solidarity bears a distinctively Christian imprimatur. Sobrino speaks thus of the "divine element" in human rights: "Instead of functioning as a mere thesaurus of citations to be invoked in support of a particular teaching—on human rights or anything else—scripture becomes a demand and a challenge, yes, but then lucidity, inspiration, and beatitude."[171]

Beatitude, yes, even for the slain: this is the final eschatological testimony of Christianity. It is not some other, but the Crucified who is risen. Love suffers because it is love, and nothing but love. In this crucified love, disciples believe the crucified people are redeemed. Resurrection is an eschatological hermeneutic, the truth of the love revealed at Calvary; to know that love, as in the Gospels of Matthew, Mark, and John, is to be placed once again at the beginning: to know it as if for the first time. To confess with the centurion at the end of Mark's Gospel, when Jesus breathes His last, "Truly, this is the Son of God," brings us to the first words of the Gospel, "The beginning of the Gospel of Jesus Christ, the Son of God." In Jesus' Spirit the Gospel becomes the disciple's story: remembrance redeemed, eschatological *anamnesis*.[172]

IV. ON FORGIVENESS AFTER MASS ATROCITY

We have done the needed "spadework" and can return to the original question: how Soyinka's plea for "evidence of mitigation—or remorse" can be reconciled with Tutu's appeal to the magnanimity of victims, a future resting on forgiveness. Forgiveness itself is a vexed notion, and many variations, religious and secular, are worked on the theme. The literature is vast and increasingly interdisciplinary; but given the constraints of our inquiry, I will touch primarily on controversies emerging in Christian theology.[173] In part I it was noted that du Toit's fears that religiously inspired redress (e.g., Tutu's appeal to forgiveness) might "supplant political and human rights concerns."[174] Others have argued in a similar vein. Thomas Brudholm criticizes Bishop Tutu, Mark Amstutz, and Lewis Smedes for eliding forgiveness and reconciliation, so that forgiveness becomes "the only viable" alternative "to revenge, retribution and reprisal."[175] Following Jean Améry, Brudholm decries "cheap forgetting" that would deny "the moral legitimacy of anger and resentment" after atrocity. For Améry, social reconciliation itself rests on moral *ressentiment* against the unreconciled past.

Such criticisms recall Dietrich Bonhoeffer's denunciation of "cheap grace"; certainly, vigilance in advocating for forgiveness is necessary.[176] Yet much turns on how we parse forgiveness. We may think of forgiveness as a tensive symbol at play in differing legal/juridical, ethical, and religious registers.[177] Although Tutu's account of the TRC bears the title *No Future without Forgiveness,* the TRC itself was grounded in the ethical rhetoric of human rights and centered upon victims' testimony. Indeed, forgiveness lay beyond the committees' writ, even if it figured informally in the broader drama orchestrated in the victim-centered hearings. In the quasi-juridical amnesty proceedings only conditional amnesty could be adjudicated; mitigation and remorse were not justiciable.[178]

Yet the registers (legal/juridical, ethical, and religious), though distinct, are not separate. I argued in part II that a religious schematization of rights permits us to distinguish a victim's *religious duty* to forgive as supervening upon her *moral/legal right* to forgive—and hence to withhold forgiveness. Within a comprehensive schema of social reconciliation, then, forgiveness presumes rather than supplants rights.

Let me elaborate. In our threefold hermeneutic of rights, critical or deconstructive and constructive uses combine into a reconstructive hermeneutic of redress. Testimony discloses (performatively) the systemic violation of victims' rights, warranting our outrage. Indeed, Hannah Arendt's ira figures constitutively in our critical/deconstructive recognition of transgression. And such recognition generates imperatives of redress for victim and perpetrator alike. In anamnestic solidarity with victims, wrong must be righted in redeeming victims' ancillary rights and fulfilling perpetrators' correlative duties. For the violation of human rights, though legion, remains ineluctably particular: testimony reveals *this* victim as subject of rights, *this* perpetrator as morally responsible and blameworthy.

Victims are accordingly owed expressions of repentance—not merely perpetrators' backward-looking remorse or regret but their forward-looking resolution to redress the systemic origins of wrongdoing. Merely acknowledging personal culpability in collective wrongdoing will not suffice. In repenting the wrongdoer must likewise acknowledge the nature, scope, and gravity of the collective wrong itself, that is, one's relative share in absolute, radical evil. Only in renouncing "the story that kills" can génocidaires truly repent of genocide. We must recognize both systemic violations of generalized respect in repenting of collective wrong and honor the debt to concrete victims—their ineluctably particular suffering.

Yet even the most authentic expression of repentance fails to pay the price of pain. The repentant perpetrator has no right to be forgiven. Rather, in the *reconstructive* hermeneutic of redress, "those who were cruelly silenced for so long, turned into anonymous, marginalised victims" gain voice.[179] Victims, that is, exercise autonomy (second-order volition in determining which desires/emotions are desired) in the disposition of redress, or whether to express or forswear anger, resentment, and satisfaction at the wrongdoer's suffering his/her just deserts.[180] Victims, we may say, possess not only a right to repentance but a further right: a positive liberty to forgive or eo ipso not to forgive. The object/substance of my right, then, is not merely the reactive desire or disposition—whether anger, resentment, or mercy—but the desire or disposition *as* desired. The right to forgive valorizes my positive liberty to desire just these desires *as* standing dispositions. Yet only with effort, and not only then, do occurrent desires become standing dispositions. Just as the path from desiring to acquiring virtue is arduous, so too is forgiving; the forswearing of resentment, anger, and so forth is less a punctual event than an incremental process played out over time, even over a life.

In forswearing anger or resentment, moreover, I presume their "moral legitimacy," that they are rightful or justified (proportioned, in the exercise of positive liberty, not only to the gravity of the wrong but to the culpability of the wrongdoer). Forgiving, of course, may also imply overcoming unbridled anger, a desire for vengeance, a yearning for reprisal, and so on; but under the rubrics of rights, revenge or vindictive reprisal cannot be rightfully entertained. Liberty is not license. Neither can we conflate the religious, ethical, and legal/juridical registers of reconciliation so that revenge and reprisal become the sole "viable alternatives" to forgiving.[181] The *right* to forgive turns, rather, on remitting "just deserts," on rightful anger, resentment, and punitive satisfaction.

Yet what are "just deserts" in the face of mass atrocity? As Arendt reminds us, legal/juridical retribution is necessarily limited; in the wake of the enormity of Nazi atrocities, "no punishment is severe enough."[182] Perhaps in the always imperfect paradise of law, what Arendt says is true: that we cannot pardon what we cannot punish. Yet the right to forgive differs from state-administered pardon. Victims' *moral* rights persist even if the wrongdoers' correlative duties cannot be fulfilled or the debt cannot be fully remitted in the legal/juridical realm. (For this very reason it is incumbent on juridical or quasi-juridical transitional processes to protect the victims' moral right to forgive lest she be doubly victimized, first by the wrongdoer and then by the expectation of forgiveness.)[183]

In redress of systemic rights violations, wrongdoers, too, incur correlative duties; not only of repentance but of seeking forgiveness, reparation, and, through the mediation of the state, of accepting proportionate punitive redress (retributive and/or consequential/instrumental punishment).[184] In modern complex polities, punishment, subject to the constraints of retributive proportionality, typically remains within the province of the state.[185] While victims cannot rightfully (legally/juridically) exact punitive retribution, they may take satisfaction in the wrongdoer suffering punishment, the kind or degree of suffering that punishment entails as his or her "just deserts." In forgiving I forbear from taking such satisfaction (for Christians, in the name of mercy) even as I may recognize the legitimacy of certain punitive legal/juridical measures such as censure, incapacitation, and deterrence.

Forgiveness, then, supervenes on the rhetoric of victims' rights and correlative duties borne by perpetrators. Yet just here the questions posed by Soyinka and du Toit recur, for the very rhetoric of rights might seem to militate against forgiving. Are there are times when forgiveness would be tantamount to "cheap forgetting"? Much depends upon our parsing of forgiveness. Katharina von Kellenbach questions Jürgen Moltmann's belief that redemption entails lifting the burden of memory or that the "final act of redemption," in Miroslav Volf's words, is "the grace of non-remembering."[186] Neither can we assume that forgiveness here and now implies a restoration to the *status quo ante,* treating the act as not having been. Memory is integral to forgiveness. In anamnestic solidarity memory is redeemed, not erased; what is forgiven is remembered *as* forgiven.

In such solidarity the grace of memory refigures the life story of both the one forgiving and the one forgiven. Yet grace can be rejected, as in Matthew's tale of the unforgiving servant (Matt. 18:21ff.): the servant is condemned for failing to remember the compassion he received. Indeed, remitting a perpetrator's debt makes sense only in a moral world in which such debts are recognized, even if not fully requited—where *recognition* of atrocity (the critical or deconstructive use of rights) underwrites not only *systemic* (the constructive use) but *interpersonal* redress (the reconstructive use). In forgiving, then, the wrong is remembered *as* wrong—in Christian nomenclature, as sin—even as the wrong/sin ceases to define my relation to the wrongdoer. In forswearing anger and resentment at the wrongdoer I cease to hold her guilt against her; but I do not exculpate nor excuse. Neither do I renounce my morally legitimate anger and resentment at the wrong done. Having suffered twenty-seven years of brutal incarceration, Mandela could write, "I knew that people expected me to harbor anger towards whites. But I had none. In prison, my anger towards whites decreased, but my hatred for the system grew. I wanted South Africa to see that I loved even my enemies, while I hated the system that turned us against one another."[187]

Within interpersonal redress forgiveness alters not my attitude to the deed but to the doer. Yet there is no simple separation of sin and sinner; the signature of the offender/sinner remains. As Augustine famously wrote, "*cum dilectione hominum et odio vitiorum.*"[188] Yet "hating the sin" while "loving the sinner" implies that it is the sinner one loves. I do not treat the wrong/sin as if it did not exist; but in forgiving I no longer relate to the one forgiven as simply offender/sinner. Altered, then, is not the history of offense but the narrative in which it figures—interpersonal redress is refigured so that, in accordance with the divine command of agapē, the sinner/offender is beloved. Neither need we assume, therapeutically, a mitigation of culpability.[189] The trace of transgression remains, but as the sign of Cain.

In forswearing anger, resentment, and retaliation, moreover, I remit the wrongdoer's moral debt to *me*; but, even so, the scope of forgiveness is necessarily limited. I cannot forgive offenses against another (e.g., mass atrocity) though I may forgive, inasmuch as these offenses affect me (e.g., a mother forgiving her child's murderer). Nor in forswearing anger, resentment, or retributive satisfaction do I thereby renounce all other ancillary rights and correlative duties deriving from rights violations (e.g., reparative claims, especially where others are affected). In forgiving I forgo satisfaction in punitive reparation enforced by the state, but reparation need not be intended as punitive. Indeed, under the teleological rubrics of restorative justice, reparation looks less to repaying the punctual debt incurred than to rectifying the resultant harm. Restorative reparation, as we shall see in the next chapter, seeks the social reintegration and well-being of both victim and wrongdoer. And seeking such reparation is fully consistent with forgiveness.[190]

Neither need the penitent wrongdoer perceive such reparative claims *as* punitive. In the Roman Catholic sacrament of Reconciliation, for instance, penance is imposed not under the rubrics of retributive punishment but rather as a sign of the penitent's resolve (metanoia) to amend his or her life and make fitting satisfaction. In imposing penance we acknowledge that inflicting pain cannot be the price of pain. Limited reparation to victims of mass atrocity figures prominently in regimes of restorative justice: in the TRC not only limited monetary compensation but knowledge of where a family member had been buried. In Rwanda, where atrocity was accompanied by grave material loss, victims who forgave still justly claimed a measure of indemnification for themselves and their families in the Gacaca courts. The victim may, to be sure, forgo reparation when it would impose too onerous a burden, but forgiveness itself does not preclude such restorative claims even if it is not strictly dependent upon them.[191]

Similar restrictions obtain in the legal/juridical realm. As seen in the TRC, forgiveness in the religious/moral sphere remains distinct if not separate from the exigencies of legal/juridical redress, both systemic and interpersonal. The state, that is, retains its legitimate interest in preserving the commonweal, for example, by censuring supremacist narratives or denying impunity to perpetrators. One may forgive, as in the hearings of the TRC, yet still recognize that the conditions of political amnesty are not fulfilled. Just as conferring legal amnesty does not entail forgiveness, so forgiveness itself does not imply amnesty. Indeed, unconditional amnesty or impunity—cheap forgetting—betrays the very logic of forgiveness as vindicating victims' rights. What is altered in forgiving, then, is not the possibility of the wrongdoer suffering just legal punishment—that remains the prerogative of the state—but my attitude toward it. In forgiving I renounce retributive satisfaction in punishment justly served. In mercy I regret the suffering that suffering punishment entails.[192] Whereas regimes of retributive justice often ignore victims in redressing offenses against the state, victims' sentiments play a significant role in restorative regimes (see chapter 4). Mercy and expressions of forgiveness favor mitigation inasmuch as it comports with the state's legitimate legal/juridical interests. Where retributive justice determines punctual just deserts, so restorative regimes recognize the possibility of reform and consequent diminution of desert. Mercy in moral redress may thus underwrite clemency in the legal/juridical realm.

Forgiveness need not, then, signify "cheap forgetting." Indeed, in interpreting forgiveness as a right we privilege the victim—not merely as a limited beneficiary of retributive justice administered by the state but as a rights bearer/subject entitled to determine the terms of interpersonal redress, that is, whether to forgive or to demand reparation. Forgoing justified anger, resentment, or retributive satisfaction at the wrongdoer pace Volf is not tantamount to forgoing a claim of justice, whether systemic or interpersonal. Rather, forgiveness "enthrones justice" in redeeming rights.[193] Mercy is not less than just.

And yet if forgiving is morally permissible, even supererogatory, as in the case of Imaculée Ilibagiza, we may still wonder if a religious *duty* to forgive is not too costly a grace. In the wake of mass atrocity, is this not to command the impossible? Our preceding reflections on the theological virtues are, I believe, illuminating. For forgiveness, as the quintessential expression of neighbor-love, transcends even as it presupposes the exacting rhetoric of rights. Forgiving cannot reinscribe victimhood. The Tutsi mother or the mother of Soweto who forgives her child's executioner acts in utter gratuity. Although morally she too must recognize the divine command upon her enemy's face, "Thou shalt not kill," still the dictates of *morality* do not entail the further command "Thou shalt love thy enemy." Here the "thou" uttered is utterly particular and the command divine. Only she can forgive, and her forgiveness is unexacted. The executioner has no moral, much less legal/juridical, claim to her forgiveness.

Yet what is morally permissible may be mandated by our distinctive religious traditions.[194] As I argued earlier, the divine command of agapē is fulfilled not in this or that deed of love but, Christianly, in one's "selving" as neighbor (metanoia), one's living into blessing, beatitude. Indeed, for Rahner every exercise of neighbor-love, as in forgiveness, is implicitly a graced response to grace.[195] Forgiving need not, then, be justified in *explicitly* Christian terms. Neither does the advocacy of forgiveness in the public realm depend upon "distinctively and irreducibly religious" belief.[196] The "obedience of faith" (Rom. 1:5; 16:26) underlying the disciple's confession of faith is finally the deed of a life, irreducible to a mere sectarian action-guide but one duty among others.

The Christian duty to forgive is often interpreted in such reductive terms. Arendt follows many a Christian apologist in interpreting Christ's command to forgive (Matt. 6:9–15; Luke 11:1–4) as just such a *do ut des* transaction (we forgive so that God will forgive). But the Gospel logic is otherwise: for the disciple, Christ is the divine utterance of mercy and forgiveness.[197] To receive mercy is to be conformed to the Word, to *be* merciful—Christlike (2 Cor. 3:17–18; Col. 1:14–15).[198] Our mercy is not a token exchanged for God's mercy; rather, mercy begets mercy. We are, says John, beloved, and to *be* beloved is to love *as* we are loved, conformed little by little to the Beloved (1 John 3:7–12). Metanoia is thus *self*-implicating: the graced labor of a life, even as it is made explicit in certain self-defining acts such as forgiveness.

Intertwining process and event, forgiveness is commanded in love and *as* love. Forgiving Christianly waits on grace, cannot outstrip grace; and for many who have suffered grievous offense it may indeed be the work of a life. At times, as Saint Ignatius tells us, in salvific humility we can but desire, the desire being already the work of mercy.[199] If still in the thralls of trauma, still "defined" by the wrong suffered, forgiveness may indeed be impossible. Only when memory, in Krog's words, ceases to "haunt you, push you around, bewilder you," only when "you have taken control of it" can you "move it wherever you want to." Only then is the substance of the right (to forgive or not to forgive) enjoyed; and only then, supervening on the right, can one speak of a religious duty.

God, says Augustine, does not command the impossible but, little by little, makes possible: grace does not annul, but perfects our willing (second-order volition).[200] For Aquinas, too, fulfilling the "new" or "evangelical law" rests primarily not in a forensic, legal transaction but in "the grace of the Holy Spirit which is given through faith in Christ."[201] The new law or Christian is inscribed in the heart as infused theological virtue (*caritas forma virtutum*). The Christian *duty* to forgive, then, must be understood not as an "essentialist" action-guide (spiritual or moral) but rather precisely as a formal-existential response to grace, mediated in the practice of the beloved community. "Strive for the greater gifts," says Saint Paul (1 Cor. 12:31): this is love as grace *and* command.

Advocacy for forgiveness in the wake of mass atrocity must accordingly be tempered. Disciples cannot judge others for not forgiving or not forgiving fully; all are "on the way" to mercy. So, too, we must be wary of what Jacques Derrida calls the institutional "globalization [*mondialisation*] of forgiveness."[202] As in the TRC, though the state can administer legal/juridical judgment, it cannot dispense forgiveness in the name of victims. States or kindred institutions such as churches can apologize for their roles in perpetuating systematic distortions (e.g., apartheid, anti-Semitism, white supremacy). Such apologies serve as promissory notes for institutional, systemic redress, but they do not supplant interpersonal redress. There can be no collective absolution, no legal/juridical remission of personal guilt for complicity.

I have spoken, thus far, of the nature, scope, and limits of forgiveness—of victims' religious duty to forgive supervening on their antecedent moral right. But what, we may ask, of the one forgiven? Must forgiveness wait, not only on grace but on "evidence of mitigation and remorse"? In his magisterial *Justice in Love,* Nicholas Wolterstorff holds that forgiveness presumes the latter: "Forgiveness, in the normal sense, is a response by the victim to indications of repentance on the part of the wrongdoer." For Wolterstorff, forgiving the unrepentant wrongdoer is not only "unacceptably arbitrary" but effectively "insult[s] him and . . . demean[s] oneself."[203] As Richard Swinburne argues, where the offense is not trivial, it is simply wrong for the victim "in the absence of some atonement, at least in the form of apology, to treat the [act] as not having been."[204] Though forgiveness may benefit the victim therapeutically, such benefits must defer to repentance; the "unrepentant wrongdoer," says Wolterstorff, continues to have a certain "moral control over his victim."[205]

Now, certainly, both interpersonal and social *reconciliation* depend upon ethical reciprocity; a rights-based solidarity implies fitting recognition and reparation for the wrong done. Yet Wolterstorff errs, I believe, in so conceiving forgiveness. For forgiveness, in the exercise of neighbor-love, implies a forgoing of resentment and anger at the wrongdoer and restoring the wrongdoer to the sphere of those one loves, whose good one seeks (*bene-volence*). Wolterstorff, too, understands forgiveness as "the enacted resolution of the victim no longer to hold against the wrongdoer what he did to one—or to use biblical language, no longer to count the sin against him."[206] In forgiving I do not excuse or exculpate the wrongdoer or hold her not blameworthy, wanting intention or knowledge. On the contrary: forgiveness presumes my believing that the wrongdoer *is* blameworthy but also resolving, here and now, not to hold the wrong/sin against her.

Such an "enacted resolution," however, need not imply the wrongdoer's repentance or reparation (in our rights-based schema, forgiveness presumes the victims' *right* to repentance yet does not depend upon its prior redemption). Divine mercy is gratuitous; we are beloved, says Saint Paul, even and precisely as sinners (Rom. 5:6–11). In Luke's Gospel, Christ and Saint Stephen, following Christ, forgive the unrepentant sinner (Luke 23:34; Acts 7:60: "Do not hold this sin against them"). But precisely because such forgiveness seeks to restore the sinner, seeks his or her good, forgiveness invites repentance and, where fitting, reparation. Indeed, forgiveness may itself incite repentance, softening the heart.

Being forgiven is a state graciously bestowed; to receive or accept forgiveness is no less an enacted resolution: love is freely given. But precisely *as* love it is costly, demanding. Which is precisely why forgiveness, divine and human, can be rejected, as by the religious elders of the Gospel. In the enacted parable of the sinful woman (Luke 7:36ff.), Jesus underscores the atoning fruit of divine love: "The one to whom little is forgiven, loves little" (Luke 7:47). We may say, then, that forgiveness completes itself in repentance and reparation but also deny that repentance is its sine qua non. After all, how difficult it is to read the heart: is the sinner truly repentant, or even psychologically capable, here and now, of recognizing the gravity of the harm done? What of those offenders who remain distant from me—the architects of genocide, whose very impersonality exacerbates the offense? Or what of those who have died? It is too great a burden, I think, to render forgiveness a function of finely calculated repentance, much less reparation. For some offenses, Levi reminds us, remain "forever irreparable."[207] Wolterstorff's concern to preserve the victims' self-respect is laudable. But in making forgiveness dependent on the perpetrator's choice to repent (rather than on recognizing repentance as a victim's right), Wolterstorff's gambit risks perpetuating the perpetrator's "moral control over his victim."

Certainly, "forgiving unconditionally" may, in Anthony Bash's words, yield "to the abusive power of the wrongdoer," such as when my "forgiving" is suborned or coerced or where I fail, cognitively or psychologically, to recognize the nature, scope, or gravity of the harm inflicted.[208] An "enacted resolution" to forgive represents an exercise of second-order volition, of positive liberty to determine our dispositions, thereby expressing—and indeed, deepening and ratifying—our moral self-knowledge as "dignified objects of respect, both in [our] own eyes and in the view of others."[209] Inasmuch as my liberty is impaired by ignorance or by direct or indirect intimidation or coercion, then, my "forgiving" is systemically distorted. Yielding to the abusive power of the wrongdoer is thus less a consequence of *unconditional* forgiveness than of an impaired capacity to forgive: to say "I forgive" under the conditions of ignorance or coercion represents a performative contradiction. Yet neither does repentance itself suffice to guarantee the ethical reciprocity presumed in reconciliation. For the repentant wrongdoer's power or privilege may generate an expectation of forgiveness, especially in the public forum. Having fulfilled what Wolterstorff and others regard as a necessary condition of forgiveness, the repentant perpetrator may come to view it as also sufficient—that forgiveness is his or her due. (Though forgiveness was not legally/juridically at issue in the TRC, some victims reported being pressured to forgive.)

In sum, I may, as Saint Stephen, forgive the unrepentant sinner and forgo my anger and resentment (Acts 7:54–60). But in forgiving I bind my enemy in love. I seek her good in reconciliation, in healing the breaches; a hard and patient grace. Memory is not suspended—I do not, as in a juridical or forensic model of forgiveness, treat the "act as not having been"; nor is the grace, in Volf's words, finally that of "non-remembering." Rather, in Easter's eschatological hermeneutic, memory is transformed and refigured in the beloved community. In the Resurrection appearances in John's Gospel, Christ's wounds remain. Just so: to receive forgiveness (as in the Catholic Sacrament of Reconciliation) implies repentance and fitting reparation; it is not a forgetting but rather a deepening responsibility for victims.

Divine forgiveness is utterly gratuitous but infinitely costly. And it is just this counterpoint of love (of grace as command, and command as grace) that Derrida fails to see in conceiving the "debt of love" in transactional terms, as a *do ut des* relationship. To be forgiven, to *receive* forgiveness, is to know a costly love, to be bound in anamnestic solidarity. The penitent is restored to covenant fidelity—absolved of guilt but not of responsibility: "If your brother or sister has something against you, leave your gift there before the altar and go; first be reconciled," we read in Matthew 5:24.

I argued that forgiveness implies the remission of debt—a renouncing of legitimate moral anger, resentment, and retributive satisfaction. But the "debt of love," says Paul in Romans 13:8, remains. The perpetrator's duties of repentance and reparation persist but as refigured precisely under the topos of the victim's gift of forgiveness: as duties of the *penitent* to his or her victim. Even at the limits—where, in the case of mass murder, the victims are silent and only God absolves—this holds; the perpetrator remains responsible, penitent. The remission of infinite guilt is infinite responsibility.[210] Both forgiving and receiving forgiveness are demanding, then, a life's work that is nourished in the beloved community's practice of anamnestic solidarity. For the Christian they turn on that first act of atoning love: forgiveness as what God has to offer in Christ.

The enacted resolution of forgiveness, I have argued, privileges the victim in the decision of whether to forgive. Perhaps we may say even more, extending such liberty to the very terms of forgiveness—whether the narrative embodiment or schematizing of forgiveness will entail remorse, repentance, reparation, and so on. For forgiveness is a tensive symbol at play in differing registers: the *moral* grammar of forgiving in forswearing legitimate anger, resentment, and punitive satisfaction may be schematized in differing narrative practices.[211] We need not adopt an "essentialist" conception of forgiveness, deciding morally, once for all, whether or which conditions obtain in forgiving. Christianly, I have argued, forgiveness seeks but does not necessarily presuppose repentance or reparation. Yet victims may freely draw on other religious or secular traditions in schematizing forgiveness. Maimonides, for instance, insists upon both fitting repentance and reparation. Since dignity always appears in local garb in religious and secular interpretations, we may acknowledge morally a family of legitimate, victim-centered interpretations, none of which "supplant political and human rights concerns."

V. CONCLUSIONS

In bidding us to "go and do likewise," the Gospel story reveals how the interpretative, explanatory, and justificatory roles of religion are internally related in "the obedience of faith." The divine command of agapē is the bedrock on which the disciples' spade is turned: the mutual respect of agents defining, in Kant's terms, a "kingdom of ends" that is transformed (sublated) into communion as firstfruits of the divine reign (Rom. 8:23). Our koinōnia with Christ is shown forth in communion and marked by our reverence for one another as "beloved" in Christ (Rom. 9:25). In Tutu's words, "Human beings must not just by rights be respected, but they must be held in awe and reverence." Indeed, to "treat a child of God as if he or she were less than this is not just wrong, which it is; is not just evil, as it often is; not just painful, as it often must be for the victim: it is veritably blasphemous."[212]

In anamnestic solidarity (schematizing the Gospel) the disciple must not merely take the victim's side (the "essential" requirement of ethics) but must also take the victim's side as her own (the "formal, existential" demand of love). So it is: the "truth for us" of "*Kyrios Iēsous*" (*fides quae*) is redeemed in the obedience of faith (*fides qua*), bringing our distinctive forms of life "under Christ's headship" (Eph. 1:10). Yet the disciple who in "loving compassionately" would "walk humbly" with her God must first "act justly" (Mic. 6:8). There is finally a place in our pantheon for both Tutu and Soyinka.

Where we await the Sabbath of the Word, where the world's passion is not yet spent, basic rights, as I showed in parts I and II, remain the grammar of dissent. Yet, as I argued in part III, they are finally no less a grammar of assent, charged with a surplus of religious meaning. As the "form of revelation (*caritas forma revelationis*)," love does not suspend but sublates the communicative virtues (*caritas forma virtutum*), a love, for Christians, defined supremely in the *kenosis* of Christ's redeeming, forgiving love.[213]

Sublating the communicative virtues, moreover, recalls Aquinas's account of the infused theological virtues wherein *by Christ* we are made "partakers of the Divine nature."[214] We might, indeed, speak of a "Thomistic constructivism" inasmuch as the maxim of practical reason becomes Love's command.[215] Here, too, subjective fulfilment (selving) rests in neighbor-love. In the disciples' gracious response to divine Love, the koinōnia teleios/communitas perfecta is transfigured in Christ as "the beloved community."[216] In Christ, love of God is incarnate in neighbor-love, in selving of the Word. Just as patristic allegory "identified the Samaritan with Christ coming to the aid of wounded humanity," so Jesus is the parable of God's "selving" (in the kenotic exaltation of Phil. 2:1–11).[217] His Word, the disciple avers, is love's word, His command of love, love's command, unveiling the "way" of crucified love.[218] For in becoming neighbor to the anāwîm the disciple loves *as* she is loved, forgiving those in our debt. Here, truly, we reach bedrock: for Jesus suffers, the Gospels tell us, because He is Love, because in a fallen world to "see and have compassion" is to be one with the Beloved—even, in Goethe's words, "to be nailed to the cross in the thirtieth year."[219]

NOTES

Epigraph: King, "Journey of Conscience," 337. See also Cone, "Martin Luther King, Jr. and the Third World," 353.

1. Weber, "Science as a Vocation," 148–55. See Berger, "Secularism in Retreat."
2. See Kant, "What Is Enlightenment," 385–88. For Kant, "public reason" is principally that of the "scholar rationally addressing his public" (386). For Rawls, public reason represents our "shared and public political reason." See Rawls, *Political Liberalism*, 9–11, 212–54; and Rawls, "The Idea of Public Reason Revisited," in Rawls, *The Law of Peoples*, 129–80.
3. See Sandel, "Introduction," 4, 6, 10. Where we can no longer appeal to "Objective Spirit," customary norms remain local, if not ethnocentric.
4. Gadamer, *Truth and Method*, 270. As Louis Dupré observes, "The Enlightenment's fight against [prejudices] stemmed itself from a prejudice and followed the Cartesian methodical rule that no position ought to be considered intellectually 'justified' before it was proven." Dupré, *The Enlightenment*, 10.
5. Wiesel, "A Tribute to Human Rights," 3.
6. Habermas, *Between Facts and Norms*, 97.
7. Rawls, *Political Liberalism*, 136.
8. Rawls, *A Theory of Justice*, 484–86. Poor Ignatius of Loyola does not fare well here, being taken with Nietzsche as exemplifying moral fanaticism.

9. Rawls, *Political Liberalism*, 9–10. See Dworkin, "Liberalism."
10. Rawls, *Political Liberalism*, 378.
11. Habermas, "To Seek to Salvage an Unconditional Meaning," 136. In Habermas's words, "from religious truths, after the religious world views have collapsed, nothing more and nothing other than the secular principles of a universalist ethics of responsibility can be salvaged" (*Die neue Unübersichlichkeit*, 52). Habermas subsequently qualifies this subscription of religion to the pastness of the past. See Habermas, *Religion and Rationality*, 67–94; Habermas, *An Awareness of What Is Missing*; Habermas and Ratzinger, *The Dialectics of Secularization*; and Habermas, "Vorpolitische Grundlagen des demokratischen Rechtsstaats?," in Habermas, *Zwischen Naturalismus und Religion*, 106–18. Cf. Junker-Kenny, "The Pre-Political Foundations of the State"; Junker-Kenny, *Habermas and Theology*; Browning and Fiorenza, *Habermas, Modernity, and Public Theology*.
12. Audi, *Religious Commitment and Secular Reason*, 86–100. In Audi's words, "One has a (prima facie) obligation to abstain from advocacy or support of a law or public policy that restricts human conduct, unless in advocating or supporting it one is sufficiently *motivated* by (normatively) adequate secular reason" (96).
13. Rorty, *Contingency, Irony and Solidarity*, 45.
14. Weber, *From Max Weber*, 148ff.
15. Sandel, *Liberalism and the Limits of Justice*, 192–93.
16. See Tillich, *Systematic Theology*, 11–15.
17. Bentham, *Works*, 523. See MacIntyre, *After Virtue*, 69.
18. Hauerwas, *The Peaceable Kingdom*, 60–61.
19. See Milbank, *Theology and Social Theory*, 13–18, 327–33; Milbank, Pickstock, and Ward, *Radical Orthodoxy*; and Bell, *Liberation Theology after the End of History*. For a critical assessment, see Doak, "The Politics of Radical Orthodoxy."
20. Perry, *The Idea of Human Rights*, 11–41; Stackhouse, "Human Rights and Public Theology," 13.
21. Walzer, *Thick and Thin*, 7, 4.
22. Tierney, *The Idea of Natural Rights*, 347.
23. See Third Global Conference on World Religions, "Universal Declaration of Human Rights by World Religions"; and Küng, *Yes to a Global Ethic*. See Little and Twiss, *Comparative Religious Ethics*; Twiss, "Comparative Ethics and Intercultural Human-Rights Dialogue." See Traer, *Faith in Human Rights*, in support of an ecumenical and interreligious consensus on the rhetoric of dignity and human rights.
24. See Kierkegaard, *Fear and Trembling*, 54–67.
25. For complicity of the Afrikaans Church, see Gobodo-Madikizela, *A Human Being Died That Night*, 52–54, 69, 72, 154–56.
26. Tutu, *No Future without Forgiveness*, 72.
27. See Gallagher, *Truth and Reconciliation*, 42–45.
28. Villa-Vicencio, "The Burden of Moral Guilt."
29. De Gruchy, "The Dialectic of Reconciliation."
30. Nelson Mandela, speech delivered to the Free Ethiopian Church of Southern Africa, Potchefstroom, December 14, 1992, as cited in de Gruchy, "The Dialectic of Reconciliation," 23.
31. Krog, *Country of My Skull*, 153.
32. Tutu, *No Future without Forgiveness*, 72.

33. See Charles Villa-Vicencio, "Ubuntu," in Villa-Vicencio, *Walk with Us and Listen*, 112–28.
34. Tutu, as quoted in Gallagher, *Truth and Reconciliation*, 118.
35. Tutu, *No Future without Forgiveness*, 72.
36. Du Toit, "Basic Purposes and Justifications," 20.
37. See Wheelwright, *Metaphor and Reality*, 130. Tensive symbols bear complex multiple referents.
38. Du Toit, "Basic Purposes and Justifications," 20.
39. See Carney, *Rwanda before the Genocide.*
40. See Karegeye and Rutembesa, *L'Eglise Catholique à l'épreuve du génocide*; Longman, "Church Politics and the Genocide in Rwanda."
41. Pope Francis, press communiqué: Audience with the President of the Republic of Rwanda, 20.03.2017, http://press.vatican.va/content/salastampa/en/bollettino/pubblico/2017/03/20/170320c.html.
42. Rorty, *Contingency, Irony and Solidarity*, 45.
43. See Hollenbach, "A Communitarian Reconstruction of Human Rights," 127–50.
44. UN, preamble to the Universal Declaration of Human Rights.
45. Shue, *Basic Rights*, 5–87. See Gewirth, *Human Rights*, 41–78, and *The Community of Rights*, 31–70.
46. Wittgenstein, *Philosophical Investigations*, pt. 1, pars. 497, 664.
47. See Rawls, *Political Liberalism*, 88–129; MacIntyre, *Whose Justice? Which Rationality?*, 88–145, 326–403; and Ricoeur, *Time and Narrative*, 52–87.
48. Wittgenstein, *Philosophical Investigations*, pt. 1, pars. 68, 179.
49. Public reasoning's telos rests in the discursive (rights-based) common good.
50. The schematization of a rights regime, we may say, is integral if it reflects the relative priority or weight of rights claims in relation both to other rights and to nonrights claims and it is comprehensive if it honors all pertinent claim-rights (negative and positive) and duty-bearers.
51. Rawls, "The Idea of an Overlapping Consensus," 12–13, and *Political Liberalism*, 9–11, 150–54.
52. Rawls, *Political Liberalism*, xlix–lx. The ideal of public reason and the duty of civility it implies is realized whenever judges, legislators, chief executives, or other government officials, as well as citizens are viewed as "ideal legislators" and explain to other citizens "their reasons for supporting fundamental political positions in terms of the political conception of justice they regard as the most reasonable." Political conceptions are reasonable only if they satisfy the criterion of reciprocity: our exercise of political power is proper "only when we sincerely believe that the reasons we offer for our political action may reasonably be accepted by other citizens as a justification of those actions." Rawls, *Political Liberalism*, xlviff., 217ff., and *The Law of Peoples*, 135–37.
53. Rawls, *Political Liberalism*, li–lii, and *The Law of Peoples*, 144, 146. For an analogous argument, see Greenawalt, *Religious Conviction and Political Choice*. Although critical of Rawls's proviso, Habermas, too, seeks "a universally accessible language without having to restrict the polyphonic diversity of voices at its very source." Habermas, "The Political," 26.
54. See Stout, *Democracy and Tradition*, 65–77.
55. Rawls, *The Law of Peoples*, 155–56.
56. Rorty, "Human Rights, Rationality and Sentimentality," 78, 71.
57. Rorty, "The Priority of Democracy to Philosophy," 268–69.

58. Rorty, "From Logic to Language to Play" and "Truth and Freedom," 279–89; W. H. Auden, "September 1, 1939," in Auden, *The Collected Poetry*, 57.
59. Even Rorty, who cites "Elizabeth Anscombe's famous argument that atheists are not entitled to the term 'moral obligation,'" would seem to concede the theists' "ought." See G. E. M. Anscombe, "Modern Moral Philosophy," in Anscombe, *Ethics, Religion and Politics*, 26–42.
60. See Dombrowski, *Rawls and Religion*, 114–16; Weithman, *Religion and the Obligations of Citizenship*, 148–79.
61. King, "Journey of Conscience," 337.
62. Rawls, *Political Liberalism*, lvn30, and *The Law of Peoples*, 153.
63. See Rawls, *Political Liberalism*, xlviiff., and *The Law of Peoples*, 179–80. In his "Letter from Birmingham City Jail" King appeals to an overlapping consensus of the Scriptures; of the writings of Augustine, Aquinas, Martin Luther, John Bunyan, Paul Tillich, and Reinhold Niebuhr; of the Jewish theologian Martin Buber; as well as of Thomas Jefferson and Abraham Lincoln. King, *A Testament of Hope*, 293.
64. Habermas, *Between Facts and Norms*, xli.
65. Jürgen Habermas, "Reflections on a Remark of Max Horkheimer," in Habermas, *Justification and Application*, 137.
66. Rorty, *Contingency, Irony and Solidarity*, 45.
67. Outka and Reeder, "Introduction," 5.
68. Habermas, *Religion and Rationality*, 74–78, 160.
69. See Habermas, "Discourse Ethics: Notes on a Program of Philosophical Justification," in Habermas, *Justification and Application*, 43–115. See also Habermas, *Between Facts and Norms*, 82–131.
70. Wittgenstein, *Philosophical Investigations*, pt. 1, par. 217.
71. See Wolterstorff, *Justice*, 323–61. As I have argued here, divine bestowal of dignity need not preclude a proximate, rational justification.
72. Tutu, *No Future without Forgiveness*, 11.
73. Nyerere, *Man and Development*, 119.
74. Rahner's transcendental epistemology permits him to affirm the ontological determination of experience by grace (the *supernatural* existential) while retaining a conception of pure, ungraced nature as a "remainder concept" (*Restbegriff*). Hans Urs von Balthasar, following Karl Barth, objects that Rahner's transcendental turn goes behind the back of God's gracious self-revelation in Scripture. Now our pragmatic turn offers a *via media*. For the apperception of rational autonomy (dignity) is simply given—and for the Christian it is given *as* sheer gift (what God *does*). Neither deducing the conditions of experience in general nor positing a *Restbegriff* is necessary to affirm our *experiencing* grace as grace. See my *The Ethics of Our Climate* for further elaboration.
75. King, *A Testament of Hope*, 293.
76. Wittgenstein, *Philosophical Investigations*, pt. 1, par. 217.
77. As Rawls observes, public reasons are thin, neither simply sacred nor secular. See *The Law of Peoples*, 143–44.
78. It would be more in keeping with the tenor of Audi's argument to say the grounding of dignity is not "specifically religious or theological" rather than to insist upon it being secular. See Audi, *Religious Commitment and Secular Reason*, 43.
79. For Habermas, too, the unschematized, or in his words "unsaturated," character of modern moral rights requires positive, interpretative specification, but there seems to be no

compelling reason to restrict our ethical (sittlich) inheritance to the dogmatically secular. A formal-pragmatic vindication of rights—one that renounces a transcendental foundation—cannot deny a priori the "logical force" of religion. See Habermas, *Between Facts and Norms*, 82–131. In later writings Habermas, like Rawls, recognizes that citizens, "in their role as democratic co-legislators," require a "costlier expenditure of motivation" that "cannot be legally enforced." Articulation of comprehensive religious doctrines in public reasoning is admitted; indeed, Habermas criticizes the Rawlsian proviso as "a tall order" (*unzumutbar*). Habermas, *Zwischen Naturalismus und Religion*, 109, 135ff.

80. Tutu, *No Future without Forgiveness*, 72.
81. Habermas, "A Reply to My Critics," 348, and *Zwischen Naturalismus und Religion*, 9.
82. Tutu, *No Future without Forgiveness*, 43.
83. See Audi, *Religious Commitment and Secular Reason*, 86–100.
84. Simone Weil, "Reflections on the Right Use of School Studies with a View to the Love of God," in Weil, *Waiting for God*, 115.
85. Gadamer, *Reason in the Age of Science*, 135.
86. See An-Na'im An-Na'im, "The Synergy and Interdependence of Human Rights." In An-Na'im's words, "the most serious objection to secularism as the foundation of the universality of human rights is its inability to inspire or motivate believers, who are the vast majority of the world population" (34).
87. Tutu, *No Future without Forgiveness*, 11.
88. Schrage, *The Ethics of the New Testament*, 74, 76 (emphasis added).
89. See Outka, "Universal Love and Impartiality," 10–11.
90. Rawls, *The Law of Peoples*, 153–54, 157; *Political Liberalism*, xlvi–li; and "The Idea of an Overlapping Consensus," 17.
91. USCCB, "Economic Justice for All," nos. 43, 68, 79.
92. King, *A Testament of Hope*, 301. In King's words, "One day the South will know that when these disinherited children of God sat down at lunch counters, they were in reality standing up for what is best in the American dream and for the most sacred values in our Judaeo-Christian heritage, thereby bringing our nation back to those great wells of democracy which were dug deep by the founding fathers in their formulation of the Constitution and the Declaration of Independence." Martin Luther King Jr., "A Time to Break Silence," in King, *A Testament of Hope*, 241.
93. For legal instruments guaranteeing religious liberty, see Witte and Green, *Religion and Human Rights*, 6–7, 13. These instruments comprise Articles 2 and 18 of the Universal Declaration of Human Rights; the International Covenant on Civil and Political Rights (1966); the United Nations Declaration of the Elimination of All Forms of Intolerance and Discrimination Based on Religion or Belief (1987); the Cairo Declaration on Human Rights (1990); the Concluding Document of the Vienna Follow-up Meeting of Representatives of the Participating States of the Conference on Security and Co-operation in Europe (the "Vienna Concluding Document"), (1991); and the Declaration on the Rights of Persons Belonging to National or Ethnic, Religious, and Linguistic Minorities (1992).
94. Rawls, *The Law of Peoples*, 155. See Wolterstorff, "The Role of Religion in Decision and Discussion of Political Issues," in Wolterstorff, *Religion in the Public Square*, 94.
95. Rawls, *The Law of Peoples*, 154–55.
96. Tutu, *God Has a Dream*, 63.
97. See Davidson, *Inquiries into Truth and Interpretation*, 155–70.
98. Rawls, *The Law of Peoples*, 154.

99. King, *A Testament of Hope*, 297–98.
100. Tutu, "The First Word," 1.
101. Rawls, *Political Liberalism*, liii.
102. Schrage, *The Ethics of the New Testament*, 74; King, *A Testament of Hope*, 298.
103. Rawls, *Political Liberalism*, 251n41 (emphasis added).
104. The phrase "moral squint" is drawn from Bolt, *A Man for All Seasons*, 19.
105. See Rawls's appeal to the Gospel parable as supporting "a special concern for the poor, as in the Catholic social doctrine" (*The Law of Peoples*, 155n55).
106. Tutu, *God Has a Dream*, 66.
107. Chenu, "*Les masses pauvres*," 169; Schrage, *The Ethics of the New Testament*, 78, 81.
108. See Outka, *Agape*, 20. See Dworkin, *Taking Rights Seriously*, 227. Camus, *The Plague*, 230.
109. Tutu, *Hope and Suffering*, 150, 152.
110. Jon Sobrino, "Companions of Jesus," in Sobrino, *Companions of Jesus*, 13.
111. See Putnam, "The Prosperous Community" and "Bowling Alone."
112. Nussbaum, *Cultivating Humanity*, 88.
113. An-Na'im, "The Synergy and Interdependence of Human Rights," 32, 35–38.
114. See Perry, *Morality, Politics, and Law*, and *The Role of Religion in American Politics*. See also Lovin, "Perry, Naturalism, and Religion in Public."
115. Rorty, "Religion as a Conversation-Stopper," 3.
116. Rawls, *The Law of Peoples*, 155–56. The consensual reciprocity of civility entails our interpretation of comprehensive religious doctrines, e.g., the witness of Christian nonviolence, which need not themselves be reciprocally justified. Here, too, the general hermeneutical maxim holds of interpreting the part (schematized rights) in terms of the whole (comprehensive doctrine). See Lovin, "Perry, Naturalism, and Religion in Public," 1528–32.
117. See Hollenbach's *The Common Good and Christian Ethics*, 168. What Rawls calls "the reasonable," says Hollenbach, is "forged in the interaction that forms the rich give-and-take among the diverse communities that form culture and civil society, including religious communities." Hollenbach cites the civil rights leadership of Rev. King as illustrating the "constant symbiosis and mutual influence" of faith and public reason (168–69). See also Hollenbach, *The Global Face of Public Faith*; and Sandel, *Liberalism and the Limits of Justice*, 216ff.
118. See Charles Taylor, "What Does Secularism Mean?," in Taylor, *Dilemmas and Connections*, 321.
119. See the affinity of the principle of charity with the "*Presupposition* of the Exercises," which as Pedro Arrupe notes, "demands a basic disposition at the outset of the retreat which is of immense value in inculturation: to be ready to 'save the proposition of the neighbor' (22). This is where authentic dialogue begins." Arrupe, "On Inculturation, to the Whole Society," 175. See Ignatius of Loyola, *The Spiritual Exercises of St. Ignatius*, par. 22.
120. Today saving truth—the evangelical imperative of *sĕdāqāh*—is "saved" with the hermeneutic turn to dignity and rights.
121. Murray, *We Hold These Truths*, 168.
122. No less than his contemporary Gutiérrez, Nyerere, I believe, may be regarded as a pioneering liberation theologian.
123. *Dignitatis humanae*, no. 4.
124. Rawls, *Political Liberalism*, xlviff., 217ff., and *The Law of Peoples*, 135–37.

125. The notion of "object" comprises, then, not only the brute empirical description but, as for Aquinas, morally relevant circumstances and intentions. See Aquinas, *Summa Theologiae* I–II, Q. 18. See Kaveny, *Law's Virtues*, 226–27, and "Appropriation of Evil"; and Dedek, "Moral Absolutes in the Predecessors of St. Thomas," "Premarital Sex," and "Intrinsically Evil Acts."
126. USCCB, "Forming Consciences for Faithful Citizenship," pars. 23, 34, 42.
127. In *Humanae vitae* Pope Paul VI admonishes his priests to heed "the pastors of the Church" who "enjoy a special light of the Holy Spirit in teaching the truth. And this, rather than the arguments they put forward, is why you are bound to such obedience" (par. 28).
128. USCCB, "Our First Most Cherished Liberty."
129. See Davidson, *Inquiries into Truth and Interpretation*, 168.
130. Williams, *Problems of the Self*, 236–37. "This injunction will be based on, though not of course fully explained by, the notion that men are conscious beings who necessarily have intentions and purposes and see what they are doing in a certain light." See Bernard Williams, "Saint-Just's Illusion," in Williams, *Making Sense of Humanity*, 135–50.
131. Rights play a critical role precisely as the "deep grammar" of our public, political reasoning: rights, that is, figure not only as deontic "side constraints" on political discourse (no reasonable consensus can violate citizens' basic rights) but also as constitutive conditions of public validity claims in pluralist polities like our own.
132. Murray, "The Bad Arguments Intelligent Men Make," 120.
133. See Sen, "Rights and Agency," and *On Ethics and Economics*, 74–78.
134. Nozick, *Anarchy, State, and Utopia*, 28–35. Sen favors "incorporating the value of right fulfillment and the disvalue of right violation in the assessment of resulting states of affairs"; yet I believe that policies that directly deny basic rights must be treated as limit cases. Even if certain rights violations are subject to a "consequence-sensitive deontological assessment," directly abetting torture or forced sterilization would never be permissible. See Sen, *On Ethics and Economics*, 73, as well as 47–51, 70–78.
135. In *Evangelium vitae* John Paul asserts, "Even scientific and philosophical discussions about the precise moment of the infusion of the spiritual soul have never given rise to any hesitation about the moral condemnation of abortion" (par. 61). For the Magisterium the value imputed to personhood is such that even the remote possibility of "hominization" suffices to warrant protection. Such casuistry is certainly reasonable, yet not uniquely so; no "meta-casuistry" compels other traditions, e.g., Jewish or Muslim, to adopt such a tutiorist position. I consider the implications of reconciling casuistic differences in public policy in "The Wisdom of Serpents."
136. John Paul II, *Evangelium vitae*, par. 73.
137. Noonan, "Development in Moral Doctrine," 669. See also Noonan, *A Church That Can and Cannot Change*, 17–123.
138. Gadamer, *Truth and Method*, 469.
139. Stevens, "The Poems of Our Climate," in Stevens, *The Palm at the End of the Mind*, 158.
140. See inter alia Schreiter, *Reconciliation* and *The Ministry of Reconciliation*; Jones, *Embodying Forgiveness*; Battle, *Reconciliation*; de Gruchy, *Reconciliation*; Daye, *Political Forgiveness*; Bole, Christiansen, and Hennemeyer, *Forgiveness in International Politics*.
141. My intent is not to explicate the theological virtues per se, a vast inquiry, but rather to consider their implications for the interpretation, motivation, and justification of public reasoning.

142. Katongole, *Born from Lament*, xvii. Katongole offers a profound interpretation of biblical lament in the context of contemporary Africa. I am indebted to his wisdom.
143. Scholem, "On Lament and Lamentation," 315, 314.
144. For Scholem, "God himself laments over the Temple." Scholem, "On Lament and Lamentation," 319.
145. John Endres observes that the "language of lament bespeaks a bond, a personal relationship between the one who prays and the God of the covenant. Such language rests on faith, relies on memories—both personal and communal—of a God hearing the cry of the oppressed, of the lamenter, of the lowly . . . and God answering that cry." Endres, "Cry Out to God in Our Need," 41. See Brueggemann, "From Hurt to Joy, From Death to Life"; Brueggemann, "The Formfulness of Grief"; Westermann, "The Role of the Lament in the Theology of the Old Testament."
146. Katongole, *Born from Lament*, 120.
147. Sobrino, *The Spirituality of Liberation*, 104 (emphasis added).
148. Fitzmyer, "Pauline Theology," 1407.
149. See Rahner, *Theological Investigations 2*, 217–34. Essential ethics refers to the set of universal action-guiding moral norms ascertained by natural reason (e.g., respect for persons' basic rights); we need not assume that such norms rest upon a foundationalist or essentialist metaphysics. "Existential ethics" refers to the (person, time, place) specific demands of a form or way of life.
150. See Donahue, "Who Is My Enemy?"
151. Desmond Tutu, "Love Reveals My Neighbour," in Tutu, *Hope and Suffering*, 149–52.
152. Gutiérrez, "Toward a Theology of Liberation," 74.
153. Gustavo Gutiérrez writes that "commitment to the poor means entering, and in some cases remaining in that universe with a much clearer awareness." Such solidarity "can therefore only follow an asymptotic curve," i.e., an ever-richer "seeing and having compassion." Gutiérrez, *We Drink from Our Own Wells*, 125–26.
154. Rahner, *Theological Investigations 2*, 217–34.
155. In his hermeneutical criticism, James Gustafson distinguishes moral (prescriptive) and theological (illuminative) uses of Scripture in Christian ethics. In these pages I argue, rather, that the "law" or command of agapē may itself function illuminatively by revealing a form of life, i.e., the way (*hodos*) of discipleship. See Gustafson, *Theology and Christian Ethics*, 129–38.
156. Wittgenstein, *Philosophical Investigations*, pt. 1, par. 217. While indebted to Rahner's analysis of the "fundamental option," I favor a Wittgensteinian construal: rather than assuming a transcendental ordination of the individual's pre-thematic consciousness to Absolute Being, I interpret my option as fundamental inasmuch as it expresses "what *I* do" when, in loving, "I have exhausted the justifications." "I" (one's ownmost self) is exhibited in the process of rationalizing action (what I *do*) rather than as logically independent of it, i.e., as a transcendental ordination expressed categorically. Such an interpretation, moreover, permits us to emphasize the intrinsically social aspect of putting on "the mind of Christ" (Phil. 2:5–11) in the beloved community.
157. Rahner, *Theological Investigations 2*, 226–27. The distinctively Christian character of the privilege of the poor rests in its ultimate theocentric grounding in agapē, the suasive force of such grounding, the illumination of the context of "acting justly," and the generation of formal, existential imperatives that, though ethically supererogatory, may be perceived as

love's demand. For a more detailed exposition, see my "The Distinctiveness of Christian Morality."

158. Paul Ricoeur, "The *Socius* and the Neighbor," in Ricoeur, *History and Truth*, 105; Kierkegaard, *Works of Love*, 69.
159. Tutu, *No Future without Forgiveness*, 43. Tutu notes that the "commitment to reconciliation" of "nearly all the leaders in the black community" was "due to the influence and witness of the Christian Churches." Theology prevents us from demonizing our enemies; thereby holding them "responsible for their deeds": "Theology says they still, despite the awfulness of their deeds, remain children of God with the capacity to repent" (73–74).
160. Desmond Tutu in Wiesenthal, *The Sunflower*, 267.
161. T. S. Eliot, "Four Quartets," in Eliot, *The Complete Poems and Plays*, 145.
162. See Niebuhr, *Interpretation of Christian Ethics*, 103–35.
163. See Karl Barth, "The Doctrine of God," in Barth, *Church Dogmatics*, II/2.
164. Ilibagiza, *Left to Tell*, 92–94.
165. In times of moral anomie, e.g., where supremacist narratives prevail, the distinction between what is morally obligatory and what is supererogatory seems blurred; but the deontic force of basic rights (especially correlative perfect duties of forbearance) persists.
166. Gobodo-Madikizela, *A Human Being Died That Night*, 126.
167. King, "I See the Promised Land," in King, *A Testament of Hope*, 284.
168. Karl Rahner, "The 'Commandment' of Love in Relation to the Other Commandments," in Rahner, *Theological Investigations* 5, 453; and Rahner, "The Theology of Freedom," in *Theological Investigations* 6, 178–96.
169. See Gerard Manley Hopkins, "As Kingfishers Catch Fire," in Hopkins, *The Poems of Gerard Manley Hopkins*, 90; Augustine, *Quaestiones Evangeliorum* 2:19.
170. See Rahner's observation that "freedom is not simply the capacity to do this or that but (formally) a self-disposing into finality." Karl Rahner, "Reflections on the Unity of the Love of Neighbour and the Love of God," in Rahner, *Theological Investigations* 6, 240. See Hopkins, "God's Grandeur," in Hopkins, *The Poems of Gerard Manley Hopkins*, 66.
171. Sobrino, *The Spirituality of Liberation*, 104.
172. My argument here recalls Johann-Baptist Metz's appeal to anamnestic reasoning in his critique of Habermas's postmetaphysical ethics. For Metz, "every rebellion against suffering is fed by the subversive power of remembered suffering" (*Faith in History and Society*, 190). Our differences, to the degree we differ, rest in my attempt to show just how practical reason *is* anamnestic. For as the deep grammar of discursive solidarity, rights configure memory, *anamnesis*. Grounding anamnestic reasoning in the communicative virtues permits us to distinguish, without separating differing ethical and religious registers: transcendence is from within, as the theological virtues sublate the communicative virtues. The *memoria passionis* at the heart of anamnestic solidarity is ineluctably human; only thus does it become divine.
173. See Murphy and Hampton, *Forgiveness and Mercy*; Murphy, *Getting Even*; and McCullough, Pargament, and Thoresen, *Forgiveness*. For differing religious perspectives, see Rye et al., "Religious Perspectives on Forgiveness."
174. Du Toit, "Human Rights Program."
175. Brudholm, "On the Advocacy of Forgiveness after Mass Atrocities," 131. See Améry, *At the Mind's Limits*; Amstutz, *The Healing of Nations*; Smeeds, *The Art of Forgiving*.

176. Bonhoeffer, *The Cost of Discipleship*; Ricoeur, *Memory, History, Forgetting*.
177. Recent studies address the psychological and therapeutic dimensions of forgiveness, e.g., the Human Development Study Group (HDSG) model. Such studies are promising yet exceed the bounds of our present inquiry. For a critique of the moral lacunae of prevailing psychological models, see Bash, *Forgiveness and Christian Ethics*, 36–56.
178. For a comparative assessment of forgiveness and amnesty in the TRC, see Lang, *Philosophical Witnessing*, chap. 12.
179. Tutu, *No Future without Forgiveness*, 32–33.
180. In sermons 8 and 9 Bishop Joseph Butler defines forgiveness as "forswearing resentment." Butler, *The Works of Joseph Butler*, 136–67.
181. See Minow, *Between Vengeance and Forgiveness*, 12. Vengeance, unlike just retribution, fails to recognize the perpetrator's dignity and basic human rights.
182. Arendt, *Hannah Arendt and Karl Jaspers—Correspondence*, 54.
183. The moral right to forgive, as all rights generally, entails the duties of forbearance, of protection, and of provision, e.g., therapeutic support.
184. In the legal/juridical realm, retributive justice imposes punishment proportionate to the crime's gravity and the perpetrators' culpability (intention/*mens rea*). For "positive" retributivists punishment, e.g., censure or rights deprivation through incarceration and reparation is warranted, wholly or in part, to repay a moral/legal debt as "just deserts." Instrumental (consequentialist) accounts, by contrast, justify punishment inasmuch as it serves to redress the social harm resulting from an offense, e.g., through censure, incapacitation, deterrence, reparation, and rehabilitation. For "negative retributivists" such instrumental punishment must also be imposed justly, i.e., proportionately.
185. While Arendt upholds the complementarity of forgiveness and punishment, Derrida separates them. See Derrida, "*Foi et Savoir suivi de le Siècle et le Pardon*"; Derrida, "Pardonneer"; and Perrone-Moisés, "Forgiveness and Crimes against Humanity."
186. Von Kellenbach, *The Mark of Cain*, 198; Volf, *Exclusion and Embrace*, 131, 138.
187. Mandela, *Long Walk to Freedom*, 494.
188. Augustine, *The Works of St. Augustine*, letter 211, par. 11.
189. Psychological "reframing" may deepen understanding of the wrongdoer's action yet need not diminish culpability. See Bash, *Forgiveness and Christian Ethics*, 39–47.
190. For the place of punishment in restorative justice, see Bash, *Forgiveness and Christian Ethics*, 141–58; Duff, *Punishment, Communication, and Community*; Wright, "Is it Time to Question the Concept of Punishment?"; Willemsens, "Restorative Justice"; Bennett, "Personal and Redemptive Forgiveness"; Gavrielides, "Some Meta-Theoretical Questions for Restorative Justice."
191. In restorative programs, what is intended by the victim as restorative may be perceived by the perpetrator as punitive. Much will depend upon the extent of the perpetrators' remorse and desire to repair the bonds broken by the offense. See Zehr, *Changing Lenses*, 80–81.
192. Viewed theologically, intentional heinous acts, atrocities, et al. estrange the sinner from God and neighbor. As self-implicating they entail a refusal of saving grace—which refusal is itself tantamount to willing harm or punishment. In *Summa Contra Gentiles* Aquinas writes, "God is not offended by us except by what we do against our own good" (*Summa Contra Gentiles*, pt. 2, chap. 122). Here punishment is not extrinsically imposed in juridical redress, e.g., in a *do ut des* transaction, but rather appears as the inherent consequence of the act itself, i.e., sin freely willed. Deriving from the very nature of the act,

such retributive punishment is "naturally" justified. Forgiveness, then, does not dispute the "just deserts" of such estrangement (anger, resentment, retribution) but rather seeks that the sinner be converted, repent, and live. Punishment remains, says Ernst Käsemann, "in the service of grace." Ernst Käsemann, "Sentence of Holy Law in the New Testament," in Käsemann, *New Testament Questions of Today*, 66–81.

193. Volf, *Exclusion and Embrace*, 123.
194. Forgiveness, of course, may be justified in secular terms, but it is the controverted role of forgiveness in Christian theology that concerns us here. See Philpott, "The Surprise of Forgiveness."
195. See Rahner, *Theological Investigations 5*, 439–59, and *Theological Investigations 6*, 231–49.
196. Brudholm, *The Religious in Responses to Mass Atrocity*, 142. Brudholm is responding to Allan J. Torrance's appeal to "deeply religious and sectarian theological beliefs" in Torrance, "The Theological Grounds for Advocating Forgiveness," 142.
197. See Anthony Bash's conclusion, that in the New Testament "forgiving others does not earn or merit God's forgiveness." Bash, *Forgiveness and Christian Ethics*, 99.
198. *Eleao* and cognate terms in Christian Scripture appear seventy-eight times, *aphiemi* (release, remit) sixty-four times, and, on several memorable occasions, *splanchnizomai* (to have compassion), e.g., in Luke 10:33, 37 and 15:20. See Rye et al., "Religious Perspectives on Forgiveness," 20–21, 24–25.
199. Ignatius of Loyola, *The Spiritual Exercises of St. Ignatius*, nos. 48, 55, 65, etc.
200. See John Mahoney's incisive reading of Augustine in *The Making of Moral Theology*, 48–57.
201. Aquinas, "De lege Evangelii, quod dicitur lex nova," in *Summa Theologiae* I–II, Q. 106, a. 1.
202. Derrida, *Foi et Savoir*, 104.
203. Wolterstorff, *Justice in Love*, 173, 174.
204. Swinburne, *Responsibility and Atonement*, 85–86.
205. Wolterstorff, *Justice in Love*, 175.
206. Wolterstorff, 169.
207. Levi in Wiesenthal, *The Sunflower*, 191.
208. Such ignorance may be cognitive, e.g., when the harm is misrepresented; or psychological, e.g., when the effects of trauma or long suffering limit the victim's reaction. Here, too, we may speak of "false consciousness" or "systematic distortion."
209. Feinberg, *Social Philosophy*, 58–59.
210. Perhaps divine judgment (retribution) rests in this: in refusing to accept responsibility, I refuse mercy. Judgment is not extrinsic to the act, i.e., of choosing curse or woe over blessing/beatitude, but rather its inherent consequence (Deut. 30:15–20; Luke 6:20–26).
211. How we parse forgiveness will in part determine the place of repentance. If we assume that forgiving entails a "bracketing" of memory—treating the act as not having been—self-respect would require repentance. But such an erasure of memory is misplaced.
212. Tutu, *God Has a Dream*, 63.
213. Balthasar, *Love Alone*, 49, 90.
214. Aquinas, *Summa Theologiae* I–II, Q. 62, a. 1.
215. Autonomy is thus not negated but rather is *sublated* as theonomy. For *eudaimonia/beatitudo* signifies not merely a realized subjective state but friendship with God as a "common final cause" (*Summa Theologiae* I–II, Q. 90, a. 2).
216. Saint Thomas understands the common good analogically; indeed, God is par excellence the *bonum commune* (*Summa Contra Gentiles* III, chap. 17). For the implications of an

analogical interpretation for the good of the *civitas,* see Dupré, "The Common Good and the Open Society."

217. Donahue, *The Gospel in Parable,* 133–34. See Augustine, *Quaestiones Evangeliorum,* 2:19. "Samaritan means 'guardian', and therefore the Lord Himself is signified by this name" (C. H. Dodd's translation in *The Parables of the Kingdom,* 11–12). See also Augustine, *De Natura et Gratia,* 43, 50.

218. For the theological significance of the "way" in Luke, see Fitzmyer, *The Gospel according to Luke I–X* (AB 28), 169–71.

219. Johann Wolfgang von Goethe, as quoted in Barth, *Church Dogmatics* IV/2, 391.

CHAPTER FOUR

Applying Human Rights

I say more: the just man justices;
Keeps grace: that keeps all his goings graces.
—Gerard Manley Hopkins

In chapter 1 I argued that basic human rights play a threefold hermeneutic role in the theater of testimony. In "telling the story" victims' cries are heard, their rights embodied (schematized) in narrative. Such embodiment entails both general, systemic redress in enshrining the rule of law after genocide and mass atrocity, and specific redress in honoring the rights of victims, such as the right to reparation. In chapter 2 I explored the implications of hearing the story, a hermeneutics of reception. Basic rights are neither a grand metanarrative nor the petit récit of the postmodern liberal bourgeoisie; rather, they constitute the deep grammar of anamnestic solidarity—a primordial solidarity with victims.[1] Such solidarity, considered in chapter 3, is inspired by our religious conviction: interpreting, motivating, and grounding our rights talk. Weaving these strands into a coherent moral schema resolves the seeming antinomies of (1) the politics of rights and the politics of the common good, (2) the thin metanarrative of abstract right (Moralität) and thick narrative ethics (Sittlichkeit), and (3) secular and sacred interpretations. We must, moreover, distinguish not only this threefold hermeneutic role of rights but differing registers of interpretation (legal/juridical, ethical, and religious). Ethical discourse generates systemic imperatives for legal/juridical protection, while religious discourse, such as of forgiveness, presumes even as it sublates rights rhetoric. A precis of our schema follows (see table 1).

In part I of this chapter I will briefly consider the implications of our schema for a theory of justice by comparing our Aristotelian constructivism with the Kantian constructivism of John Rawls, Jürgen Habermas's discourse ethics, and rival communitarian theories. I will test in part II what William James calls the "cash value" of our schema by applying it (1) nationally, to a restorative critique of race and mass incarceration in the United States;

Table 1. Rights as the Grammar of Anamnestic Solidarity

Registers of interpretation	A Threefold Hermeneutic: Critical recognition	Constructive redemption	Reconstructive redress
Legal/Juridical Discourse	Discovery process: victims' testimony, truth commissions, reporting of nongovernmental organizations, etc.	Incremental realization of a basic rights regime: implementing, preserving, or protecting a constitutional order, an impartial judiciary, etc.	Recognition/ redemption of ancillary rights and duties to victims: international tribunals, local tribunals, (selective) prosecution, granting of conditional amnesty, reparation, restitution, etc.
Ethical Discourse	Recognition of mutually implicative rights claims. Narrative deconstruction: interpretative rendering of effaced "other" (*Alter*).	Redemption of primary rights claims (duties of forbearance, systemic protection, and provision). Narrative embodiment: taking the victims' side.	Recognition and redemption of ancillary rights claims (duties of redress). Narrative embodiment: "shared memory" in anamnestic solidarity.
Religious (Christian) Discourse	Theology of repentance: biblical ideal of justice (sĕdāqāh) and peace (šālôm) in Christian narrative; victim as icon of the Crucified.	Theology of redemption: biblical understanding of reconciliation as eschatological anamnesis in narrative *of* discipleship; taking victims' side as one's own.	Theology of judgment: forgiveness and reparation in (enacted) narrative *as* discipleship.

(2) internationally, to migration and refugee policy; and (3) globally, to the religious integration of what Pope Francis recently called the "cry of the poor" and the "cry of the earth" in a "new humanism."[2]

I. COMPARATIVE ASSESSMENTS

One may, of course, object that our schema of basic rights is too thin to be considered a full theory of justice or, conversely, too thick for differing legal/ juridical, ethical, and religious discourses. However, the virtue of our theory of communicative virtue is, after all, precisely its limited scope. Our concern throughout has not been to provide a full theory of justice, much less of moral virtue; rather, justice emerges in a family of reasonable interpretations. Once basic rights are embodied or schematized within our specific traditions under the rubrics of the common good (i.e., the regulative ideal of a well-formed narrative), other justicizing criteria invariably come into play—merit, achievement, need, and so on. These in turn configure our particular comprehensive interpretations of the good, including how rights themselves are best circumstantially realized (e.g., in allocating duties of restitution or reparation). We ascribe rights, that is, not to sovereign selves squatting outside history, as Karl Marx would have it, but rather to concrete historical subjects. Yet, as we have seen, family resemblance is not infinitely malleable. The grammar of rights preserves anamnestic solidarity across our distinctive interpretations.

If, then, our Aristotelian constructivism thins the ontotheology of the medieval common good, so too it thickens the regnant liberal discourse of rights by introducing a restorative motif. A well-formed narrative will embody (schematize) a rights regime by recognizing what Gustavo Gutiérrez calls the "rights of the poor" and most vulnerable. We begin, that is, not by hypothesizing an ideal speech situation or putative social contract but with the concrete demands of anamnestic solidarity.

Rawls's Kantian Constructivism

For Rawls, anamnestic solidarity, as all ethical invocations of the common good, must be effectively bracketed within the original position. In Rawls's *A Theory of Justice* the parties' rational choice of liberty, modeled upon Kantian hypothetical, technical imperatives, is mutually disinterested, since persons in the original position "take no interest in one another's interests" (Rawls even assumes their "deep opposition of interests").[3] Yet what, one wonders, would such mutually disinterested agents say of genocide or apartheid? Must one's right not to be their victim be ascribed simply to the outcome of objective, rational choice under the veil of ignorance?

Presumably, genocide or apartheid would be described in the original position as an element of the nondiscriminating knowledge or general information that might affect the contracting parties' choice of the principles of justice. Yet such description "sine ira" is hardly, in Rawls's words, "natural and plausible."[4] For Hannah Arendt, to forgo indignation at genocide is to rob the phenomenon in question of "part of its nature" or "inherent qualities."[5] What the Convention on the Prevention and Punishment of the Crime of Genocide condemns as "an odious scourge" is not merely the frustration of a representative individual's interest (or, in other versions of liberal theory, a benefit due). Genocide and apartheid systemically deny the victims' very status as "free and equal moral persons"—what Rawls himself tacitly acknowledges as their "right to equal respect and consideration" presumed in the very design of the original position.[6]

In later writings Rawls turns explicitly to a richer conception of citizens whose "rational choice" is "subject to reasonable conditions," characterizing "the deliberation of the parties as representatives of free and equal persons."[7] Even so, in ascribing rights to a generalized other, liberal rights rhetoric remains essentially unencumbered.[8] My interest in forbearance does not perspicuously extend to recognizing the thicker bonds of solidarity—what Jean-François Lyotard calls the "human community present" in you.[9] And while *The Law of Peoples* may permit humanitarian intervention in extremis, peoples' motivation to protect citizens of outlaw states from systemic deprivation remains dubious.[10] Neither do there appear to be compelling grounds for specific redress of victims like the survivors of genocide. Indeed, while the difference principle regulates inequalities among liberal citizens, the conditions of restoring equality—solidaristic bonds of both general and specific redress—remain largely veiled.

Habermas's Discourse Ethics

For Habermas, too, anamnestic solidarity remains problematic: the formal requirements of universalizability proper to discourse (Habermas's intersubjective rendering of Kant's formal interpretation of the categorical imperative) must necessarily problematize any given solidarity (Sittlichkeit).[11] Habermas, more than Rawls, though, seeks to bring the semantic potential of anamnestic solidarity back into the universe of grounding speech. For Habermas, "anamnesis and storytelling can provide reasons and so drive philosophical discourse forward, even though they cannot be decisive for it."[12] "Compassionate solidarity with the despair of the tormented who have suffered what cannot be made good again" remains, perforce, "a limit concept of the discourse ethic."[13]

Habermas's polemics against a historicist forgetting of forgetting, alas, still do not permit him to take the final step of remembering fully—of seeing that anamnestic solidarity is the condition and not merely the consequence of discursive reason. The very meaning of rights depends upon the history of their use (e.g., in what Wiesel called the new literature of testimony[14])—grammar without narrative is empty. Anamnestic solidarity preserves transcendence from within. Elucidated in the threefold hermeneutic of rights, this transcendence rests not in abstract universalizability but in the concrete universality of recognition and respect—our pragmatic rendering of the material interpretation of the categorical imperative in the communicative virtues. Recognition and respect (prudence and morality) are finally inseparable.

We begin, then, with anamnestic solidarity, the first, seminal rapprochement of rights and the common good. Responsibility for history's victims bids us ask, here and now: Who are the most vulnerable, consigned to history's margins? Who is denied a place at the table of discourse? After all, the discursive construction of valid (universal) norms, such as nonbasic human rights, presumes the noncoercive inclusion of those most affected in applying Habermas's principle of discourse ethics: "Only those norms can claim to be valid that meet (or could meet) with the approval of all affected in their capacity as participants in practical discourse."[15] The modal "could" here is critical, for often the suffering and passion of the world—gendered violence, chronic hunger, preventable illness—silence the victims and render their cries unpronounceable.

Stories are told, to be sure; but stories become testimony only if we see the victim's face, hear her command. Even for Habermas discursive consensus is already implicitly governed (regulatively and constitutively) by the grammar of basic rights. As I argue in chapter 2, the formal universality of discursive will-formation presupposes the concrete universality of basic rights (recognizing and redressing evil). Only in taking the victims' side, in unlocking the discursive potential of "telling the story," can we enter "the universe of grounding speech." Only thus, in anamnestic solidarity, is the discursive "we" exhibited. And in that universe more comprehensive accounts of justice will emerge in what Seyla Benhabib calls "democratic iterations."[16] Ethics begins by seeing the face and hearing the transgressed command: "You were harmed and it was wrong."

Communitarian Solidarities

Our restorative appeal to anamnestic *solidarity* thickens the distributive theories of Rawls and Habermas. Narratively embedded, as in the US civil rights movement and South Africa's anti-apartheid struggle, rights and correlative duties configure our particular polities and constitute bonds of civic responsibility—Aristotle's "civic friendship" in late or postmodern guise. The breach of these bonds, conversely, undermines the civic common good and *in extremis* the very possibility of political legitimation. Particular solidarities thus become privileged *loci* of redeeming universal claims, of speaking grammatically. But if grammar without narrative is empty, so narrative (solidarity) without grammar is blind.

In South Africa, appeals to the latent wisdom of tradition failed to redress the systematic distortions of the supremacist narrative. On the contrary, the selfsame scriptural texts were used to justify and condemn apartheid.[17] If virtues sustain "the institutional forms" abetting our practices, as Alasdair MacIntyre asserts, criticism of supremacist practices will seem (to the practitioner) not virtuous but rather "an effect of the vices," portending "the corruption of institutions."[18] No longer anchored in the dialectical unfolding of Objective Spirit, ethics (Sittlichkeit), says Richard Rorty, becomes "something relatively 'local and ethnocentric.'"[19]

For Rorty, ethical substance is fragmented in our myriad traditions and the mute opacity of prejudice. In Rorty's "light-minded aestheticism" there is no "locus of human dignity," no self, but "centerless . . . a historical contingency all the way through." There is, indeed, "no such thing as *inner* freedom, no such thing as an 'autonomous individual'"; "there is nothing deep inside each of us, no common human nature, no built-in human solidarity."[20] We have nothing to say to the torturers of the innocent "of the form 'there is something within you which you are betraying.'"[21]

Metaphysically bereft, human rights become but "sad and sentimental stories"—even while other stories may be told, wherein "Hitler may be seen as in the right and the Jews in the wrong."[22] Such stories are indeed told. In the words of Emmanuel Katongole, "Rwanda's social history reveals to us how stories can kill. Yes, people did the killing in Rwanda. Yes, they needed weapons to do it. But apart from the story that taught Rwandans to understand themselves as Hutu and Tutsi, eternally at odds with one another, the genocide could not have happened."[23] *Our* distaste, if not outrage, for such "stories," though genuine, is of limited province. Cruelty, after all, is in the eyes of the beholder.

The rapprochement of rights and the common good belies Rorty's "light-minded aestheticism." In testimony, dignity appears under the sign of its negation—rights let us "get the memory right," fixing in words the transgressed command. Our theoretical perspective, in Amartya Sen's words, is thus a "realization-focused comparison" in which recognizing injustice (imagining evil) occurs prior to the transcendental idealization of a just institution, such as is found in Rawlsian contract theory.[24] "Justice," says Rawls, "is the first virtue of social institutions"; but under the rubrics of the common good the *virtue* of justice, as virtues generally, admits of degree. In a lifeworld still dominated by Hume's circumstances of justice (scarcity and limited altruism), the common good remains a regulative ideal that is only partially realized in any legal/juridical regime. The narrative schematization of rights, especially of the most vulnerable, is always incremental, always displayed not in the heuristic ideal of a social contract but in the discursive praxis of ethical reciprocity and critique—a praxis tempered by the voices of those whom, like Lucas Baba Sikwepere or Nomonde Calata, the dominant powers had silenced.

If our Aristotelian constructivism is in this respect "realization-focused," so, too, is it comparative. For if our Aristotelian constructivism resists closure, neither does it dictate a univocal, comprehensive theory of justice. The regulative ideal of the common good ranges over a family of well-formed narratives—or, better, narratives that incrementally realize the virtues of respect and recognition in a regime of rights. For the grammar of rights does not determine so much what we say as the manner of our saying. We can identify moral solecisms in realization-based comparisons even if our full, complex theories of justice differ. The grammar of basic rights, that is, constrains our deliberation (regulatively) and configures our "telling the story" (constitutively). But telling the story remains open-textured and leavened with the give-and-take of discourse (ethical reciprocity).

The hermeneutical flow, we might say, is from rights to incremental realizations and not pace Rawls from transcendental idealization to the construction of lexical norms. Indeed, the very imperfections of systemic redemption—dignity never fully respected—underscore the importance of specific redress in honoring the rights of victims. Taking the victim's side, even where the victims are legion, will always demand the telling of this ineluctably unique story. Adopting a realization-focused comparison thus restores restorative justice to its rightful place: the place (*locus*) where cries are heard.

II. REALIZATIONS: CONCRETE APPLICATIONS

Let us turn, then, to concrete applications. Other cases might, of course, be offered, but these draw on my own pastoral experience and illustrate the scope and, I hope, promise, of our reimagining human rights.

Race and Mass Incarceration in the United States

According to recently published figures from the US Bureau of Justice, inmates incarcerated in prison or jail number 2.2 million, a 500 percent increase over the last forty years. This is the highest official rate of incarceration in the world

(731 per 100,000 population).[25] Including those on probation or parole, the total number of citizens under the aegis of corrections departments now reaches 7.1 million, an increase of almost 300 percent since 1980. Today one out of every 137 Americans is incarcerated, an increase due less to changes in crime rates than to changes in sentencing law and policy.[26] Disaggregating for race and ethnicity, "Black men are nearly six times as likely to be incarcerated as white men and Hispanic men are 2.3 times as likely. For black men in their thirties, 1 in every 10 is in prison or jail on any given day." One in four, "born since the late 1970s has spent time in prison." Though only 37 percent of the US population, minorities constitute 67 percent of those incarcerated. "Overall, African Americans are more likely than white Americans to be arrested; once arrested, they are more likely to be convicted; and once convicted, they are more likely to face stiff sentences."[27] As Bryan Stevenson observes, "Racial disparities in sentencing are found in almost every crime category. Children as young as 13, almost all black, are sentenced to life imprisonment for nonhomicide offenses."[28]

Such racial and ethnic disparities in incarceration stem from a witches' brew of compounded social disadvantage, discriminatory policing practices, biased prosecutorial discretion, and sentencing.[29] And the stigmatization of felons and their families persists after incarceration, limiting access to employment, social welfare, and housing. Felony disenfranchisement deprives "1 of every 13 African Americans" of the right to vote.[30] Such systemic inequities, writes Michelle Alexander, perpetuate the New Jim Crow of "racial caste" and "racialized social control."[31] In Adam Gopnik's words, "mass incarceration on a scale almost unexampled in human history is a fundamental fact of our country today . . . as slavery was the fundamental fact of 1850. In truth, there are more black men in the grip of the criminal-justice system . . . than were in slavery then."[32]

The dramatic increase in prison populations over the past half century differs markedly from other Western democracies with comparable crime rates. Amnesty International reports that the "USA stands virtually alone in the world in incarcerating thousands of prisoners in longer-term or indefinite solitary confinement."[33] Racial and ethnic minorities disproportionately suffer the ultimate sanction—capital punishment—and poor and marginalized groups have less access to the legal resources needed to defend themselves. "Black defendants are 22 times more likely to receive the death penalty for crimes whose victims are white, rather than black."[34] Since the reinstitution of capital punishment in 1973, "150 US prisoners sent to death row have later been exonerated. Others have been executed despite serious doubts about their guilt."[35]

Despite evidence of other mitigating factors underlying a decrease in violent crime, punitive attitudes prevail in what William Stuntz calls the "harshest" judicial system "in the history of democratic government."[36] Repaying the offender's "debt to society" favors neither reparations for victims (recognizing victims' positive rights) nor reintegration of the offender into community. Indeed, as Ta-Nehisi Coates observes, with hyperincarceration of minorities "rehabilitation was largely abandoned in favor of retribution"—a policy of "penal harm . . . to make offenders suffer."[37] Social bonds are further attenuated as punishment is officially privatized. Crime may not pay, but punishment increasingly does, creating incentives for higher incarceration rates.[38] Yet several recent studies confirm that massive long-term incarceration fails to deter crime or recidivism. The US Justice Department itself acknowledges the failure of reintegration. Indeed, as John Tierney observes, "Some social scientists argue that the incarceration rate is now so high that the net effect is 'crimogenic': creating more crime over the long term by harming the social fabric in communities and permanently damaging the economic prospects of prisoners as well as their families. Nationally about one in forty children have a parent in prison. Among black children, one in fifteen have a parent in prison."[39]

A similar punitive stance favors summary apprehension, detention, and deportation of the some 10.5 million undocumented migrants—"illegal aliens"—in the United States.[40] Under the draconian policies of the Trump administration, immigration arrests have increased by 40 percent since 2016.[41] In my ministry at the Federal Women's Prison (FCI) in Dublin, California, the majority of the women I serve are poor migrants, some of whom will be summarily deported after completing their sentence. Federally mandated minimum sentences forcibly separate mothers from their children for years, their punishment exacerbated terribly by the punishment thus inflicted on their children. It is not surprising to hear a woman pray for her child who is now also incarcerated. Yet the crimes for which the women stand convicted are typically nonviolent drug offenses.[42]

A Punitive Rationale

Rehearsing the complex genealogy of retributive practices would exceed the limits of this discussion. My aim here is more modest; I wish only to touch on several salient themes emerging from our comparative critique in section I. We begin with crime, for crime and punishment are a hendiadys—punishment is determined by what we say of crime.

In modern liberal polities, constituted through the legal fiction of a social contract, crime typically appears as a voluntaristic legal construction, as an offense against the collective will of the body politic. For early contract theorists, meting and doling punishment were among the raisons d'être of the original contract. For Hobbes crime is principally an offense against the sovereign's rights and should be punished accordingly. In the Lockean tradition the powers to enforce and punish are no longer diffused through intermediate associations of the medieval *civitas*; citizens cede their natural right of punishment to the state. For Kant, legal punishment is just deserts for violating the social contract; justice is entirely retributive. Even where other strands of liberalism temper retribution, the rubrics of "just deserts" prevail: the adversarial adjudication of guilt and punishment vindicates the formal (procedural) rule of abstract right. Reaffirming the coercive prerogatives of the bureaucratic state in the name of freedom, punishment restores "the reciprocal contractual relationship between obedience to the law and benefits received from living under the law."[43]

Yet from the beginning the reciprocal contractual relationship was vitiated by systemic exclusion—most notably by the "peculiar institution" of slavery and the heritage of Jim Crow and white supremacy in its aftermath. From the beginning the appeal to self-evident rights masked systematic distortions in the collective will to punish in determining the crime, the criminal, and the debt to be repaid. Neither is the masking incidental: if the exchange of natural liberties underwrites the social contract, their unnatural denial must be explained. So the exclusionary logic of the contract is rationalized, first by a divinely sanctioned belief in the natural inferiority of slaves and second, with the demise of chattel slavery, the continued criminalization of Black bodies. In Coates's trenchant words, "Nearly a century and a half before the infamy of Willie Horton, a portrait emerged of blacks as highly prone to criminality, and generally beyond the scope of rehabilitation. In this fashion, black villainy justified white oppression—which was seen not as oppression but as 'the corner-stone of our republican edifice.'" Indeed, writes Stevenson, "anything that challenged the racial hierarchy could be seen as a crime, punished either by the law or by the lynchings that stretched from Mississippi to Minnesota."[44] Here is our country's "original sin": the perduring myth of what Coates calls, citing the white supremacist Hinton Rowan Helper, "the crime-stained blackness of the negro."[45]

The systematic distortions of our will to punish go further. For if the state's bureaucratic prerogatives are meant to discipline citizens, no less so do they penalize "aliens," whose bodies (and not mere behavior) become "illegal." The economy of exclusion signified by the social contract proceeds apace as "criminals" or "illegal aliens" are denied the very right to have rights. What Arendt says of forced migrants pertains no less to all those suffering the "loss of home and political status" (e.g., through mass, or perhaps better, hyperincarceration and felony disenfranchisement). Such loss, says Arendt, is tantamount to "expulsion from humanity altogether." The alien is not the exemplar of humanity in general (the generalized other) but, like the criminal, "a frightening symbol of difference as such."[46]

Such symbols, then, are naturally stigmatized, divested of moral standing, as the punitive regime constructs its own object: the alien becomes "illegal" and the young Black man becomes the "criminalblackman."[47] As Alexander argues, our ostensibly impartial, colorblind criminal justice system thus rationalizes and effectively erases its racial and ethnic partiality or bias.[48] In constructing criminal bodies, the state absolves itself. So, too, in our punitive regime: the symbolization/stigmatization of difference, whether of illegal aliens or criminals, blurs the lines between retribution and vengeance or scapegoating (the sublimation of vengeance). The will to punish, independent of consequential considerations, remains a potent force in polities wherein social bonds are already frayed and violence is naturalized. In a perverse dialectic, vindictive resentment, especially against frightening symbols of difference, seems to have its own cathartic rationale: difference is feared and punished, reproducing (essentializing) the very differences we fear and consequently punish.[49]

A Restorative Riposte

How, then, do we respond to the moral myopia of our carceral regime? Its distortions, as I have shown, are rooted in a systemic exclusion—a history hidden in the originary contract and subsequently silenced and rendered unpronounceable in iterations of Jim Crow. Systemic racial bias is masked and thereby perpetuated, criminalizing Black and Brown bodies in the name of legal/juridical impartiality. The women I serve in the federal prison would not be incarcerated if they were white.

We must, then, imagine otherwise. In recent years, restorative justice has emerged as an alternative rationale. One of its leading theorists, Mennonite theologian Howard Zehr, describes restorative justice as "a process to involve, to the extent possible, those who have a stake in a specific offense and to collectively identify and address harms, needs, and obligations, in order to heal and put things as right as possible."[50] For proponents of restorative justice, victim-offender reconciliation programs (VORPs), sentencing circles, and family group conferences (FGCs) represent an effective alternative to prevailing regimes of retributive justice.[51] Yet, as Zehr has recognized, the distinction fails to do full justice to what is entailed by putting things as right as possible in restorative practices, programs, and rationales. Neither retributive nor restorative justice is, after all, a rigidly limited conception.[52] Some interpretations of retributive justice include restorative elements, and some restorative practices do not exclude retributive sanctions. Indeed, proponents of restorative justice differ as to their proper balance, such as whether restorative practices should replace, complement, or be integrated within criminal justice systems.

Perhaps the crucial question, then, is just what is being restored. Advocates of transformative justice seek not only amelioration of correctional practices (victim-offender reconciliation) but also redress of the structural violence of racism in criminal justice. As discussed in chapter 1, such structural criticism overlaps with non-Western uses of restorative justice such as the South African TRC, where massive crimes against humanity precluded a strict juridical adjudication of individual guilt and punishment. Yet despite these considerable differences, a family resemblance holds among conceptions of restorative justice. While punitive practice in the United States views crime primarily as a legal offense against the body politic, restorative justice sees crime as a breach of Ubuntu—our natural sociality. In the words of Archbishop Tutu, chair of the TRC,

> Retributive justice—in which an impersonal state hands down punishment with little consideration for victims and hardly any for the perpetrator—is not the only form of justice. I contend that there is another kind of justice, restorative justice.... The central concern is not retribution or punishment but, in the spirit of ubuntu, the healing of breaches, the redressing of imbalances, the restoration of broken relationships. This kind of justice seeks to rehabilitate both the victim and the perpetrator, who should be given the opportunity to be reintegrated into the community he or she has injured by his or her offence.[53]

What might such restorative practices entail for American criminal justice, not only juridically but ethically and theologically? How might such non-Western wisdom, as in Tutu's appeal to Ubuntu, inflect both ethical and theological interpretations? Suffice to say, for the moment, that we turn from the hendiadys of "crime and punishment" to "crime and community." For if crime represents primarily a breach of natural social bonds, what must be restored are precisely the "broken relationships."[54]

RECOGNITION

As Alexander, Coates, Stevenson, and others argue, the first, critical hermeneutical task is the unmasking of the systemic racial and ethnic bias of our carceral regime. To take rights seriously is to see their play in our history—a history, Ralph Ellison reminds us, that is always also Black.[55] We must, then, begin with the civic bonds that constitute *our* polity or, more precisely, recognize such bonds under the sign of their negation—the breaches and broken relationships typified in mass incarceration. But it is not simply wreckage we see. If the original sin of slavery is our besetting sin as Americans, then the original blessing is resistance to white supremacy, such as of the historically Black churches. We do not begin *ab ovo*.

In anamnestic solidarity *we* must get the memory right; and this, as Martin Luther King Jr. foresaw, entails deploying rights integrally and comprehensively. The schematization of rights must be *integral* (recognizing the relative priority of basic human rights, including positive liberties of participation and correlative duties, both positive and negative) and *comprehensive* (recognizing all right- and duty-bearers). Where liberal forbearance restricts responsibility to personal choice, schematizing duties of protection and provision/redress unveils the systematic distortions of white privilege and extends the bonds of solidarity. We are not absolved of history but always, already implicated in besetting sin and blessing.

Rights thus configure memory, letting us see the nature, scope, and gravity of systemic racial/ethnic bias in discriminatory policing practices, in prosecutorial discretion, and in sentencing. As in the TRC, the liberties of effective participation must privilege those most affected in "telling the story" of the new Jim Crow—a hallmark of restorative justice. Compounded social disadvantage is only further compounded in silencing the voices of the internal exiles of our carceral regime. A comprehensive account, moreover, must recognize the rights of those most affected. The principal victims of incarcerating mothers for nonviolent drug offenses are their children; yet the state's victimizing is veiled in the sentences it metes and doles.

REDEMPTION (GENERAL REDRESS)

So, too, does redressing systemic racial bias and deprivation presume the effective participation of those most affected; rights are not self-interpreting. "Telling the story" of mass incarceration is critical if we are to tell a "greater story that unites"—our second hermeneutical task. Indeed, as in the TRC, telling the story is part of the story of constructing, in Alexander's words, "a thriving, multiracial, multiethnic democracy free from racial hierarchy."[56] Stories recounted by Alexander, Coates, Stevenson, and Greg Boyle, and the stories of the women I see at the Dublin FCI, become testimony, cries that are heard.[57] And as testimony is woven into collective memory, we may discern the lineaments of general redress.

Such general redress is parsed in terms of duties, the first being forbearance (*primum non nocere*). Again and again at the FCI I find myself wondering what conceivable social good is being served by incarcerating grandmothers or by the punitive segregation of mothers from their children during their most formative years.[58] Neither is there a place in a restorative regime for the inequities of capital punishment, in long-term or indefinite solitary confinement, in felony disenfranchisement, or in life sentences for juveniles. General redress of such systemic inequity is required; indeed, fulfilling the negative duty of forbearance finally presumes positive duties of protection and provision in implementing (schematizing) a rights regime. Systemic redress of discriminatory policing practices, biased prosecutorial discretion, and harsh sentencing follows suit. For bias in policing begins in early schooling (the "school-to-prison-pipeline") and far too often culminates in the extrajudicial killing of Black and Brown men. So, too, redressing bias in extensive prosecutorial discretion (e.g., in plea bargaining and jury selection) demands provision of judicial review, due process, and equitable legal representation. Under a statutory directive, the United States Sentencing Commission itself has recommended that mandatory minimum penalties should "(1) not be excessively severe, (2) be narrowly tailored to apply only to those offenders who warrant such punishment, and (3) be applied consistently."[59] From a restorative perspective, equity in juridical discretion must be restored to its rightful place in lieu of lengthy mandated sentences, especially for those accused of nonviolent crime.

SPECIFIC REDRESS

Such incremental systemic redress of our criminal justice system, of course, is but a beginning. Constructing "a thriving, multiracial, multiethnic democracy free from racial hierarchy" will require far more, such as restorative measures of reparation for the intergenerational consequences of racism. Where retributive measures of interpersonal reparation seek to apportion blame and indemnification across generations, restorative measures address the systemic inequities perpetuated by the heritage of slavery, Jim Crow, and mass incarceration—reparation as an exercise of anamnestic solidarity. As Tutu linked the final success of the TRC's narrative project to the fitting redress of the vast economic "disparities between the rich, mainly the whites, and the poor, mainly the blacks," so must we. "The huge gap between the haves and the have-nots, which was largely created and maintained by racism," poses a like "threat to reconciliation and stability in *our* country."[60]

In a restorative vein, reparation would thus redress the enduring consequences of systemic rights deprivation by acknowledging the cause—the legacy of racist bias. General redress, that is, would be schematized critically or deconstructively in specific redress, in redeeming general rights precisely *as* reparation to victims. So, too, for redressing the inequities of mass incarceration. Redressing the systematic distortions of our criminal justice system (schematizing general rights) implies specific redress for its victims.

Their effective participation will be critical, yet we may adumbrate elements of a reconstructive hermeneutic. Victims, not only of criminal behavior but those suffering state-sponsored violence like the women at the Dublin FCI, acquire ancillary positive rights: of legal/juridical recognition (that they were harmed and it was wrong), of provision (e.g., counseling and health care), and of reparation (retroactive sentence mitigation and restitution where feasible). Offenders, conversely, acquire ancillary positive duties: of confessing to the harm done, of rehabilitation, and of reparation through, for example, victim-offender reconciliation programs, sentencing circles, or family group conferences.[61] Where the state itself proves offender, corporate redress would entail legal/juridical recognition (e.g., apology, victim-centered testimony, and memorialization); legal/juridical reforms (including incorporation of restorative practices); and reparation, including restitution (e.g., of voting rights and indemnification for losses suffered).

In a similar vein, the ethical exigencies of specific redress—victims' rights and offenders' duties—qualify the systemic aims of deterrence. Assessments of deterrence must themselves be rights-based, integrating both forward- and backward-looking considerations. Where less coercive measures than protracted incarceration serve the purposes of deterrence and reparation (e.g., VORPs, FGCs), they would necessarily be preferred. Yet neither general redress of the systemic inequities of our carceral regime nor specific redress for its victims dictates a univocal practice. Rather, differing practices of restorative justice turn in part on the respective emphases placed upon general and specific redress and the nature of the harm or the crime itself. Informal victim-offender programs may be unsuitable for crimes of sexual or spousal abuse. General and specific redress must be taken together in a dynamic and fluid deliberative praxis.

A Religious Gloss

In integrating general and specific redress, restorative justice looks beyond the rubrics of commutative justice, to which it is often assimilated on the analogy of retributive justice.[62] Indeed, in recognizing systemic racial/ethnic bias and in redressing both general and specific inequities, such a "realization-focused" critique seeks to *restore* the social bonds at the heart of a distributively just social order. What must be restored is neither the legal status quo ante nor the pastness of the past (a repristinated *Gemeinshaft*); but rather the bonds of anamnestic solidarity.

These bonds are, for many, grounded in religious conviction, as in Tutu's appeal to traditional restorative justice in the TRC. So, too, traditional Maori and Mennonite beliefs inspire contemporary restorative practices and supply a rich moral repertory for imagining otherwise. The US bishops argue in a similar vein, drawing on the heritage of Catholic social teaching.

In their pastoral letter "Responsibility, Rehabilitation, and Restoration: A Catholic Perspective on Crime and Criminal Justice," the bishops write,

> An increasingly widespread and positive development in many communities is often referred to as restorative justice. Restorative justice focuses first on the victim and the community harmed by the crime, rather than on the dominant state-against-the-perpetrator model. This shift in focus affirms the hurt and loss of the victim, as well as the harm and fear of the community, and insists that offenders come to grips with the consequences of their actions. . . . Restorative justice also reflects our values and tradition. Our faith calls us to hold people accountable, to forgive, and to heal.[63]

This accountability must begin at home. As Brian Massingale has trenchantly observed, the Catholic hierarchy has yet to heed fully the wisdom of the Black Catholic Church in integrating racial and restorative justice.[64] As for the women I serve at the federal women's prison, such wisdom is born of long suffering in "the valley of lament."[65] Many find words in Scripture to tell their story. Consider the enacted parable of Luke 7:36–50:

> Now, one of the Pharisees invited Jesus to have dinner with him, so he went to the Pharisee's house and reclined at the table. When a woman who had lived a sinful life in that town learned that Jesus was eating at the Pharisee's house, she brought an alabaster jar of perfume, and as she stood behind him at his feet weeping, she began to wet his feet with her tears. Then she wiped them with her hair, kissed them and poured perfume on them. When the Pharisee who had invited him saw this, he said to himself, "If this man were a prophet, he would know who is touching him, and what kind of woman she is—that she is a sinner." Jesus answered him, "Simon, I have something to tell you." "Tell me, teacher," he said. "Two men owed money to a certain moneylender. One owed him five hundred denarii, and the other fifty. Neither of them had the money to pay him back, so he canceled

> the debts of both. Now which of them would love him more? Simon replied, "I suppose the one who had the bigger debt canceled." "You have judged correctly," Jesus said. Then he turned toward the women and said to Simon, "Do you see this woman? I came into your house. You did not give me any water for my feet, but she wet my feet with her tears and wiped them with her hair. You did not give me a kiss, but this woman, from the time I entered, has not stopped kissing my feet. You did not put oil on my head, but she has poured perfume on my feet. Therefore, I tell you, her many sins have been forgiven, for she loved much. But he who has been forgiven little loves little. Then Jesus said to her, "Your sins are forgiven." The other guests began to say among themselves, "Who is this who even forgives sins?" Jesus said to the woman, "Your faith has saved you; go in peace."

"Do you see this woman?" Jesus' question to Simon betrays the Pharisee's retributive moral squint: "If this man were a prophet, he would know who is touching him, and what kind of woman she is—that she is a sinner," thereby rendering Him ritually unclean, even as she washes His feet. Judgment precedes mercy in an economy of exclusion, doubled here because the sinner is a woman. At the federal prison the women incarcerated fall under Simon's gaze: sinners, unclean, who must be set aside; they are, in Gutiérrez's words, "nonpersons" in our regnant social narrative. But Jesus' question inverts the moral order and invites Simon to do the same: "Do you see this woman?" She is not a figure or cipher of transgression in this house of murmuring men, but *this* woman, who loves so richly, whose faith is saving, who leaves with the blessing of divine šālôm, "peace."

The restorative squint tutors our imagination, as what Jean-Marc Éla calls a "pedagogy of seeing": the ineluctably unique, concrete other, my neighbor.[66] Here we see not a "frightening symbol of difference" but one, in all her truth, says Simone Weil, "exactly like me," albeit "stamped with a special mark by affliction."[67] For Luke what we see, finally, is not merely a beloved sinner but the very model of disciple. Indeed, we see just how profoundly the moral order is inverted as the despised other, the sinful woman, proves true host. Her washing Jesus' feet is, in John's Gospel, the paradigmatic act of discipleship—for John it is the enacted parable of the Eucharist. This is precisely the way of discipleship, of metanoia: of doing what Jesus does as the "guest" of mercy becomes host. To see "this woman" is finally to see ourselves, beloved sinners blest in Jesus' ministry of blessing.

Saint Ignatius places us before the Crucified Jesus and in Him, as Ignacio Ellacuría reminds us, before the crucified people: discerning presumes even as it transcends moral deliberation.[68] In Christ we are always, already in communion with the ānāwîm; our solidarity implies not merely taking the victim's side (the essential requirement of ethics) but taking the victim's side as our own (in Rahner's terms, the formal, existential demand of love). As we saw in chapter 3, such a response entails discerning the *particular* call of God to the disciple as "*individuum ineffabile,* whom God has called by name, a name which is and can only be unique."[69] In the formal existential ethics of discernment we are summoned by name in the fullness of Christ's crucified love, summoned to discern how, here and now, in our concrete circumstances, to respond to Christ in the crucified people.[70]

The distinctively Christian virtue of solidarity with the ānāwîm thus defines the disciple's horizon of discernment. Living such election may seem to outstrip our capabilities. The kind of seeing that does not despair can only, I think, be born in love: in the crucified love of the Crucified. In putting ourselves in the sinful woman's place we must come to see as she sees. Why has she shown such great love? Surely it is because she has been greatly loved—the parable within the parable shows this, that one who is forgiven much, loves much, loves enough to brave the censoring gaze, the murmuring: loves enough to see only Jesus. At the end of our Mass at the prison, when we say a charismatic prayer for those about to be released, we sometimes sing a song, "*Mujer Libre,*" free woman. I wonder, in awe at such faith: Can I sing? For were my life so blighted, my resources so limited, my life still imprisoned, could I sing for another, in gratitude, in eucharist, "free woman"? No, they have taught me more of love, of justice, and of hospitality than I could have imagined.

Migration and Refugee Policy

We have seen how systemic racial and ethnic bias beget internal exiles—a bias by no means confined to the US carceral regime. Indeed, the crisis of forced migration exposes what Arendt calls the "perplexities" of liberal rights rhetoric. Let us, then, briefly take note of the nature, scope, and gravity of the crisis and then turn to the perplexities it poses for the politics of rights.[71]

The UNHCR reports current levels of displacement are the highest ever recorded. An unprecedented 70.8 million people have been forced from home, including nearly 25.9 million refugees, over half of whom are under the age of 18.[72] At least 41.3 million have been internally displaced; by the end of 2018, 3.5 million were seeking asylum. Millions of stateless people have likewise been denied nationality and access to basic rights such as education, healthcare, employment, and freedom of movement. Children are "particularly vulnerable to threats to their safety and well being," including "separation from families, sexual exploitation, HIV/AIDS infection, forced labour or slavery, abuse and violence, forcible recruitment into armed groups, trafficking, lack of access to education and basic assistance, detention and denial of access to asylum or family-reunification programs."[73]

Already victims of ethnic cleansing and mass expulsion, the majority of those fleeing persecution, 78 percent of all refugees (15.9 million), subsist in protracted refugee situations,[74] where "basic rights and essential economic, social and psychological needs remain unfulfilled after years in exile."[75] Living in camps "without any prospect of a durable solution to their plight," such refugees are increasingly perceived "not as victims but as perpetrators of insecurity."[76] Similar fears beset the domestic migration policies of the United States. As the tragedy that occurred at Lampedusa amply demonstrates, barriers against migration lead to borders being, in the words of Gloria Anzaldúa, "*una herida abierta* [an open wound] where the third world grates against the first and bleeds."[77] As in the European Union and Australia, closing borders to deter or relegating responsibility to poorer countries renders the migrant's journey even more perilous.[78]

Since the militarization of the US-Mexico border in the mid-1990s, "deaths of border crossers have occurred at a rate of at least one every twenty-four hours."[79] Kristin Heyer reports that "almost half of total unauthorized migrants to the United States are female, and women are nearly three times more likely to die from exposure" in our southern deserts "than men, with the vast majority falling victim to sexual assault." Endemic violence in the Northern Triangle of Central America (El Salvador, Honduras, and Guatemala) has spurred families and unaccompanied children to seek asylum at the US southern border. In response the Trump administration "has engaged in an unprecedented assault on asylum seekers and refugees seeking protection at the southern border. From criminally prosecuting asylum seekers to orchestrating delays and turn-backs at the ports of entry to family separation, the administration is pursuing an anti-immigrant agenda, including an attempt to send thousands of asylum seekers back to the violence and persecution that they fled."[80] Exacerbating the trauma that asylum seekers face, families and young children are illegally incarcerated in overcrowded immigration centers, where they are subjected to "inhuman treatment, jail-like conditions, sexual assault, insufficient medical care, and a total lack of the due process to which they are entitled."[81] As I noted in the discussion of mass incarceration, the threat of further displacement persists for those who succeed in crossing but remain subject to summary apprehension, detention, and deportation.

Here too we must single out the enduring tragedy of trafficking and forced labor in our midst, a modern form of slavery.[82] Trafficking "has claimed an estimated 20 million-plus victims worldwide—with more than 800,000 victims enslaved each year."[83] According to the International Labour Organization (ILO), "1 in 4 victims of modern slavery are children. Women and girls are disproportionately affected by forced labor, accounting for 99% of victims in the commercial sex industry, and 58% in other sectors."[84]

Economies of Exclusion

The world is at our door, yet its "suffering and passion" are never simply given. For how we see the displaced, especially the forcibly displaced, is itself a function of place with rival rhetorical loci (topoi) constituting our common sense. If partisans of liberal rights parse the social world in terms of citizens and aliens, communitarian critics look to the rhetorical commonplace (*locus communis*) of members and strangers. Let us briefly recall the arguments of chapter 1.

For communitarians, ethics begins at home and rests on what Burke called the "latent wisdom" or "prejudice" of a particular narrative tradition.[85] Our cherished liberty, says Burke, "has a pedigree and illustrating ancestors" that sharply distinguish members of the body politic.[86] So it is: rights become the patrimony of positive law—an "entailed inheritance" resting on the "politics of the common good"—the common good, that is, of particular narrative communities.[87] Recognizing the bonds of membership in our particular polity or subgroup is thus decisive. In Michael Walzer's words, "The primary good that we distribute to one another is membership in some human community. And what we do with regard to membership structures all our other distributive choices: it determines with whom we make those choices, from whom we require obedience and collect taxes, to whom we allocate goods and services."[88] The rhetorically circumscribed "we" need not, of course, be xenophobic or racist, although such "prejudices" cannot be ruled out.[89]

Liberal polities, conversely, appeal to the rhetoric of rights but through a mirror darkly. The claims of dignity are veiled in mutually disinterested choice. With the eclipse of traditional teleology, contractual legitimation rests in the formal, impartial constraint of prudence (rational self-love), not in thicker bonds of solidarity (Ujamaa and Ubuntu). Indeed, rights (negative liberties and immunities) are ascribed to sovereign selves, emancipated, says Arendt, from "all tutelage" of traditional mores and "natural" social relations.[90] Social bonds once derived from the ethical ideal of the common good must be constructed through exercise of individual will. Positive obligations extend primarily to fellow citizens privy to the social contract underlying the moral legitimacy of the state.

In such closed social systems, noncitizens are owed the duty of forbearance; but as "aliens" they lack legal title to the primary good of citizenship and its attendant claim-rights.[91] The liberal *jus cosmopoliticum* thus remains highly restricted.[92] In the absence of generally recognized positive duties of provision, protection, and redress (such as rescue, restitution, and reparation), claims of forbearance are all too often nugatory.[93] As Gil Loescher observes, "There is no mandate [generally recognized by states] to provide protection and assistance to refugees; almost all aid is voluntary and discretionary."[94] "Cross-border processes" are regarded "as a 'private matter' concerning only those immediately affected."[95]

We see, here, the "perplexities" of modern rights in political liberalism. As Hannah Arendy says, the "conception of human rights, based upon the assumed existence of a human being as such, broke down at the very moment when those who professed to believe in it were for the first time confronted with people who had indeed lost all other qualities and specific relationships—except that they were still human."[96] In the wake of global displacement, the world "found nothing sacred in the abstract nakedness of being human." Even with the subsequent ratification of the major instruments of modern refugee law, Arendt's critique remains germane. Refugees, to be sure, are no longer nominally "rightless" in international law. Yet a refugee is "still not considered to be a subject of international law, capable of enforcing his or her rights on the international plane."[97]

As the plight of refugees and international displaced persons (IDPs) in Syria, Yemen, and South Sudan attests, in the new millennium, as in the old, our very "right to have rights" typically depends upon membership in a particular national, ethnic, racial, or religious community.[98] Enjoying, asserting, or enforcing claim-rights—even with the partial eclipse of the "classical Westphalian regime of sovereignty"—seems ineluctably bound to citizenship, so that the "loss of home and political status" is tantamount to "expulsion from humanity altogether."[99] The "alien" becomes not the exemplar of the "generalized other" but, says Arendt, "a frightening symbol of difference as such."[100]

Is it surprising, then, that we speak of "illegal aliens," whose very bodies, rather than their behavior, become "illegal"? Deprived of their place in the world, such migrants are rhetorically effaced, divested of legal and even moral standing. The legal/juridical distinction between citizen and alien is now ethically "essentialized": citizenship is no longer a privileged means of redeeming rights but the very ground of their ascription and hence of their denial. The migrant women I meet at the prison are not like you and me—they are of a different race and ethnicity, they speak a different language, they are failed mothers (for we have deprived them of their children); in a word, they are "nonpersons" whose lives are not important failures.

But the story does not end here. A perverse dialectic plays out: as in the US carceral regime, in detaining forced migrants and asylees, we fear and then punish difference, and in so doing we reproduce (essentialize) the very differences we fear, criminalizing not only migrants' behavior but their bodies. Confronted with their "naked humanity," the source of the very rights we prize, we rationalize their exclusion, hiding their humanity and rendering their stories unpronounceable. Citizenship is inflected and becomes a signifier of exclusion, indeed a token of fixed *communitarian* membership in revanchist appeals to a lost or threatened civic identity. By essentializing "difference" as grounds for denying rights, we implicitly invoke "sameness" in their ascription and thereby reify or essentialize the collective "we" of the polity.

We come, then, full circle. In legally/juridically restricting rights to citizens we betray the ethical grammar of the very rights invoked—the closure of liberal citizenship as a performative contradiction.[101] By imagining the other we imagine ourselves: citizens become members and aliens become strangers. The "thickening" of membership proceeds in a dialectic of exclusion: what T. S. Eliot once called our liberal polity, "a people without history," invents one; imagined communities become real and beget internal exiles. Far from being merely manifestations of *illiberal* bias, white privilege and ethnonationalism are homegrown maladies; the betrayal is intimate.

A Restorative Riposte

The crisis of migration thus becomes a crisis of liberalism itself—what Habermas calls a "legitimation crisis."[102] Mere forbearance cannot sustain a regime of equal liberty, because even the most negative rights presuppose recognition of positive duties of protection and provision/redress. Indeed, we recognize claim-rights to liberty (and cognate basic rights)—we give them "special weight," in Rawls's words—just because they are threatened. Preserving liberty, even the most negative of liberties, finally rests in a thickening of membership, a recognition of richer social bonds, so that liberty itself compels us to choose: will citizenship be vindicated by the rights of the human community present in each "other" in anamnestic solidarity?[103] Or, conversely, will lesser local and ethnocentric solidarities prevail and will rights, now an entailed inheritance, be vindicated by closed citizenship, the patrimony of a particular imagined community?

RECOGNITION

The antinomy of rights and the common good is finally illusory. We are not faced with a Hobson's choice between a thick, hermetic ethnocentrism over the thin cosmopolitanism of an abstract "generalized other." Indeed, liberalism must be more than liberalism if it is to remain liberal and not succumb to a truncated, hermetic notion of citizenship. But what would such an "embedded cosmopolitanism integrating particular relationships" with "solidarity across borders" entail?[104] Anamnestic solidarity, as we intimated earlier, recognizes the bonds linking concrete others while respecting the "human community present in each." What Walzer calls the "primary good" of membership in a particular community remains vital to civic identity; it is never idly relinquished. Citizenship accordingly becomes a *concrete* universal, a privileged legal/juridical means of redeeming basic ethical rights through democratic iterations of constitutional regimes—in Rawls's words, "a people's political culture and its constitutional principles."[105]

We speak, then, not of abstract rights but of the family resemblance of well-formed civic narratives whose boundaries are porous and permeable. It is this very concrete ethical *universality* that relativizes the legal/juridical "place" of sovereignty: when states fail to protect vulnerable citizens or are themselves complicit in egregious human rights violations—notable push factors in forced migration.[106] Indeed, the first right of a forcibly displaced refugee, migrant, or stateless person is *not* to become one. As Arendt foresaw, the contemporary refugee crisis is *sensu emenenti* a crisis of human rights, with the very title "refugee" signifying systemic rights deprivation. Yet the crisis of rights extends beyond such official legal recognition.

IDPs, stateless persons, and migrants fleeing famine, generalized violence, or systemic deprivation, though excluded in varying degrees from the strict formal protections afforded to refugees under the Geneva Accords: these too are victims of rights violations; and, as we shall see, they are subject to fitting general and specific redress. Neither do the criteria stipulated in the 1951 Refugee Convention reflect the gender-specific persecution that women and girl children endure, such as rape, genital mutilation, domestic abuse, or forced marriage, or the particular vulnerabilities experienced by LGBTI persons. The critical or deconstructive use of rights thus unmasks the economies of exclusion and the proscribing of "illegal" bodies as "frightening symbols of difference." A critical hermeneutics likewise becomes a pedagogy of seeing the imagined "other," in Weil's words, "exactly like me," albeit "stamped with a special mark by affliction," whether affliction is due to a "well-founded fear of persecution" or other systemic rights violations.[107]

An integral account of rights would accordingly amend the restrictive definition of a refugee within international law (the Convention Relating to the Status of Refugees [1951] and the Protocol Relating to the Status of Refugees

[1967]), to include victims of general insecurity or famine.[108] More-inclusive definitions are already accepted by the OAU Convention Governing the Specific Aspects of Refugee Problems in Africa (1969), the Cartagena Declaration on Refugees (1984) endorsed by the Organization of American States (OAS), and in the operational practice of the UNHCR.[109] In accordance with the graduated urgency of their claims (i.e., the severity and imminence of harm), other victims of forced migration, for example, migrants fleeing the systemic denial of basic subsistence rights or ecological catastrophe, would likewise be owed fitting protection and provision.

REDEMPTION (GENERAL REDRESS)

Anamnestic solidarity generates systemic imperatives of both general and specific redress. Indeed, schematizing rights exhibits the complex interrelation of our threefold hermeneutic of recognition, redemption (general redress), and specific redress. As in the case of restorative reparation for the systemic inequities of racism, specific redress may be the occasion of recognizing and redeeming general rights. Or, as in the case of forced migration, recognizing victims' specific rights may constitute a condition sine qua non for their redemption: securing their "right to have rights." But a word first about the rights themselves, for *forced* migration is a tale of systemic rights denial.

Legitimated themselves by rights, democratic polities bear correlative duties to forbear from abetting rights violations in other states. By the same token, states must support the instruments of international human rights law and diplomacy and in extremis honor the responsibility to protect in the face of genocide or ethnic cleansing. Duties migrate before persons do. Where intrastate protections fail and lead to forced displacement, duties correlative to basic human rights persist and fall upon the community of states. The concrete *universality* of citizenship binds us in anamnestic solidarity—a family of solidarities privileging precisely those most vulnerable.

As in our consideration of mass incarceration, the constructive redemption of rights must be integral and comprehensive. Basic rights hang together *integrally* so that denying one right implicitly threatens all rights. The systemic violation of security rights underlying forced migration threatens subsistence and curtails liberty. But so, too, does systemic deprivation of adequate nutrition, health care, and education impel families to migrate. An integral rights regime, then, must address the complex "push" factors of forced migration—not only the well-founded fear of persecution but, as in Syria and Yemen, generalized violence, famine, and disease.

In a similar vein, refugees and IDPs, especially those in protracted refugee situations, are often systematically deprived of basic subsistence rights.

Here, too, denying such rights to adequate nutrition, potable water, education, health care, and so on, or rendering their satisfaction dependent upon charity, threatens both refugees' security and their civil liberty. When seeking firewood for sustenance outside of the refugee camps, women are put at risk of rape or other forms of gender and sexually based violence. This vulnerability is only exacerbated by a denial of their civil-political rights to participate effectively in the design and implementation of policies affecting them and their dependents.[110]

An integral rights regime must also be *comprehensive*. In a world ever more interdependent, citizens must seek a continual revision of programs, systems, and regimes so as to guarantee the full and effective implementation of the rights of the most vulnerable, including those condemned to stateless existence in camps of first asylum and, of these in particular, women and children. Such guarantees must provide effective legal-juridical redress of gender-specific forms of violence, including rape and genital mutilation. Correlative duties of protection and provision, moreover, must be allocated (schematized) equitably through systematic responsibility-sharing, for example, "through resettlement quotas and humanitarian visa programs."[111] Wealthier states must bear a fair share of the burden disproportionately borne by the poorer countries of first asylum.[112] Today nearly four of every five refugees live in a country neighboring their home. Countries in developed regions hosted 16 percent of refugees, while one third of the global refugee population (6.7 million people) were in the Least Developed Countries.[113]

SPECIFIC REDRESS

What Walzer calls "the primary good" of membership typically confers legal and political status on citizens, not only to enjoy but to assert and enforce basic claim-rights. The forcibly displaced, conversely, suffer not only the loss of home but also the legal and political benefits of citizenship—in Arendt's words, their "right to have rights." Yet forced migrants are not exiled from humanity. Similar to the cases of genocide, apartheid, or mass incarceration, victims of forced displacement acquire ancillary rights of specific redress for the rights violations impelling them to flee (e.g., restitution, reparation, public apologies). Perpetrators of forcible displacement, conversely, bear correlative duties of making restitution, reparation, apologizing, and so on.

Being denied the primary good of membership, however, is both a consequence of and a further cause of rights violations. Citizens have a right *not* to be forcibly displaced, an immunity from coercion; denying this right generates the ancillary rights and duties constituting the refugee regime. The forcibly displaced, that is, claim *specific* rights of redress just because they are forcibly displaced. These ancillary rights and correlative duties typically become the very conditions of constructively redeeming their *general* rights to security, welfare, and civil-political liberties.

Although restricted to those formally designated as refugees or asylees, foremost among such rights in international refugee law is the right of nonrefoulement.[114] Refugees or asylees cannot be forcibly repatriated to a country where there is a reasonable expectation of persecution. The Universal Declaration of Human Rights acknowledges that refugees have the right "to seek and to enjoy asylum": yet neither the 1951 Refugee Convention nor the 1967 Protocol imposes a correlative obligation upon states to grant it. In a similar vein, as Michael Dummet observes, the "Convention Relating to the Status of Stateless persons forbade any contracting state to expel stateless people lawfully resident on its territory, and required it to 'facilitate' their naturalisation; but it laid no obligation on any state to admit stateless people expelled from the country in which they were living."[115]

Indeed, as primary respondents of basic claim-rights, states often summarily dismiss asylum claims even though nonrefoulement remains a nonderogative right in international law. Interdiction in international waters, extraterritorial processing, and indefinite detention further erode potential asylees' basic security. Moreover, an integral and comprehensive rights regime likewise extends the refugee regime to encompass victims of generalized violence or famine. The graduated urgency of basic rights and correlative duties serves to indicate the lineaments of an equitable policy of specific redress: where borders remain porous, international and domestic law should take due cognizance of the moral priority of relative need (the gravity and imminence of harm), of the particular vulnerabilities of women and children, of familial relationships, of the complicity of the host country in generating refugee flows, of the relative capability to integrate forced migrants, of the historical or cultural affiliations such as historic patters of migration, and of a fair distribution of burdens among countries offering asylum.[116] The last consideration applies domestically as well: the burdens of local integration and resettlement should not fall disproportionately upon the most vulnerable citizens. Indeed, where humanitarian "charitable" assistance may pit refugee against citizen or engender dependency, an integral and comprehensive account of rights locates a refugee's claims within the systemic imperatives of equitable development and regional security.[117]

Even the granting of asylum is no guarantee of basic rights. "Barred from engaging in political activities," refugees confined to camps are often likewise denied rights to "engage in agricultural, wage-earning and income-generating opportunities."[118] Lacking access to land and having no prospect for gaining long-term residency rights or naturalization, they are not permitted to enter "the labour market, they cannot take out loans, and restrictions on their freedom of movement make it difficult for them to engage in trade." Furthermore, with the loss of traditional means of protection, women and children in camps, especially those unaccompanied, remain vulnerable to exploitation in the form of domestic abuse, rape, sexual exploitation, and other crimes. Such protracted refugee circumstances, moreover, may engender regional insecurity as camps become sites of armed resistance, as with the Hutu Interahamwe.[119] Forfeiting even limited legal protection in the camps, urban refugees similarly suffer discrimination in education, housing, employment, access to financial services, and other matters.[120]

Finally, an integral and comprehensive rights regime would enjoin equitable policies of voluntary repatriation, reintegration, rehabilitation, resettlement, and reconstruction (with particular attention to legal rights of widows, unaccompanied women, and children); hospitable treatment of those seeking to change nationality, whether through local integration in the host country or resettlement in a third country; assistance in their integration to a new homeland; respect for their cultural heritage; and recognition of the benefits of hosting and the contribution of migrants. Above all there is no "place" for warehousing refugees or incarcerating those seeking asylum, the criminalization of displacement.

Our threefold hermeneutic of rights thus integrates critical (deconstructive), constructive, and reconstructive uses of rights. An integral and comprehensive rights regime will protect the most vulnerable and, where protection fails, as in the case of the forcibly displaced, will honor victims' general human rights through a regime of specific redress, such as through the legal provision of nonrefoulement, integration, or, where appropriate, resettlement or voluntary repatriation. Indeed, their well-being will be a touchstone of legitimacy, and hence of citizenship—a state's democratic self-constitution warranted precisely inasmuch as rights render its borders porous.[121]

A Religious Gloss

Differing faith traditions reveal a similar displacement of identity—a rhetorical locus where stories of religious identity are configured by hospitality to the "other."[122] Time, and my own limitations, though, limit my treatment here to the Christian Scriptures and Catholic social teaching.

Leviticus's solemn words admonish us to remember the stranger or resident alien in our midst: "When an alien resides with you in your land, you shall not oppress the alien. The alien who resides with you shall be to you as the citizen among you; you shall love the alien as yourself; for you were aliens in the land of Egypt: I am the Lord your God" (Lev. 19:33ff.).[123] Save for worship of the one God, no command is repeated more often in the Hebrew Bible.[124] Yet for the children of Exile, the "golden rule" of Leviticus 19:18, "You shall love your neighbor as yourself," is no mere abstraction.[125] For Leviticus, love of neighbor bids us respect not a "generalized other" but the "concrete other" in need, epitomized by the migrant. Only in *remembering* her blessing as a sojourner in a strange land will Israel fulfill this "canon within the canon."[126]

In such lived remembrance, moreover, Israel proves her covenant fidelity (*sĕdāqāh*) in deeds of justice (*mišpāt*).[127] For a people born of exile, freedom is always "bonded," in Walzer's words, always proved true in the redemption of the ānāwîm. [128] In times of prosperity Israel is thus summoned to effective remembrance that the land "was a gift not a birthright."[129] So it is in gracious hospitality to the widow, orphan, or stranger—to those most vulnerable in kinship societies—that Israel realizes her distinctive covenant identity.[130] To oppress the alien, conversely, is no less than apostasy. Israel, says the Deuteronomist, must ever cherish "the heart of an alien, for you were aliens in the land of Egypt" (Exod. 23:9). Cultivating the virtue of hospitality to the stranger or alien is thus no mere supererogatory act of "charity," as hospitality is often seen today.[131] It is the measure of righteousness, *our* token of belonging.

For Christians, too, memory speaks. In Luke's gospel Jesus inaugurates His prophetic ministry in His exodus to Jerusalem by recalling the words of Isaiah: "The Spirit of the Lord is upon me, because he has anointed me to bring good news to the poor. He has sent me to proclaim release to the captives and recovery of sight to the blind, to let the oppressed go free, to proclaim the year of the Lord's favour" (Luke 4:18–19). Here the divine reign, the "good news" for the widow, orphan, and migrant, takes flesh. "Today," says Jesus, "this scripture has been fulfilled in your hearing" (Luke 4:21). Luke's Greek speaks of a fulfillment that persists in history, at once invitation and demand.[132] At the heart of Christian ethics is the law of love (Luke 10:27; see Lev. 19:18, 33; Deut. 6:4ff.; Mark 12:30ff.; Matt. 22:37ff.); and for Jesus' disciple in Luke's gospel it is the stranger, and not the scribe or religious expert, who reveals its meaning.

The parable of the Good Samaritan unfolds as a hortatory midrash (example story) of the great Levitical injunction (Luke 10:29–37). Jesus' disciples are called to "go and do likewise," to love the nameless, half-dead stranger as themselves. In anamnestic solidarity with the stranger—like the man fallen among thieves, stripped of title, status, and role—disciples thus "prove themselves" faithful to the covenantal demands of agapē (Luke 10:36). Citizens of faith "see and have compassion" (*esplanchnisthē* signifies being moved in one's inmost heart), even as compassion (literally, a "suffering with") becomes a way of seeing the stranger "in all her truth."[133] In what is described in chapter 3 as a surplus of Christian meaning, such seeing entails "crossing over"—the disciple must herself become neighbor. For the question posed in Jesus' reading of the law is not finally "Whom shall I love?" but rather "Who shall I become (prove myself to be) in loving?" In Kierkegaard's words, "Christ does not speak about recognizing one's neighbor but about being a neighbor oneself, about proving oneself to be a neighbor, something the Samaritan showed by his compassion."[134] This makes all the difference.

Not surprisingly, then, Christian hospitality to "strangers and aliens" (*xenoi kai parokioi*) shaped the earliest understanding of disciples as fellow "citizens with the saints" in the "household of God" (*oikeioi tou theou*) (Eph. 2:19). Indeed, hospitality (*philoxenia,* or love of the stranger) is at the very heart of Christian discipleship. In Donald Senior's words, "Jesus begins his earthly journey as a migrant and a displaced person—Jesus who in this same gospel would radically identify with the 'least' and make hospitality to the stranger a criterion of judgment (Matt. 25:35)."[135] For Luke, with salvific irony, "seeing and having compassion" for these least, the naked, the half-dead stranger, marks the "way" of eternal life. Luke's narrative reveals the boundless universal scope of love precisely in demanding a moral solidarity with those who suffer—my "neighbor, the masses."[136] The trope "neighbor" in Luke's parable thus serves as a metaphorical "bridge" between identity and difference (*xenos* came to signify both guest and host): a hermeneutics of hospitality enjoins anamnestic *solidarity* where care is offered, not to the alien or stranger but rather to my neighbor "stamped with a special mark by affliction."[137]

In "passing over" to the world of the migrant as neighbor, the metaphor is "proved true" by Jesus' disciple. Christian imaginary attests to this decentering of self—this "selving" in utter dependence on God—in imaging disciples themselves *as* "beloved aliens and exiles" (1 Pet. 2:11–12). Christians, the "strangers and foreigners on earth," says Senior, seek "a better homeland," the world-affirming reign of God (Heb. 11:12–15; see Rom. 15:7).[138] For disciples of the *way* (Acts 18:25ff.; 19:23; 22:4; 24:14), such displacement becomes the place (rhetorical locus) of revelation. Hebrews recalls the revelatory hospitality of Sarah and Abraham at Mamre in Genesis 18: "Do not neglect to show hospitality to strangers, for by doing that some have entertained angels without knowing it" (Heb. 13:2). In the Synoptic Gospels the image of a feast "for all peoples" (Isa. 25:6) reveals God "powerfully and eschatologically as Israel's host"—a fundamental motif recalled in the eschatological *anamnasis* of the Eucharist. Again and again, in the image of the eschatological feast (Amos 9:13–15; Joel 3:18; Isa. 25:6–8), hospitality is offered, not to kin and kind but to those whose only claim is vulnerability and need (Matt. 8:11; 22:1–14; Luke 14:12–24). For Matthew, as for Luke, that becomes the sine qua non of salvation: "I was a stranger (*xenos*)" unrecognized, "and you welcomed me" (Matt. 25:35; see John 20:11ff.; 21:1–14). In the parable of the final judgment (Matt. 25:31–46) the disciple passes over from being "host" to "guest" of Christ at the eschatological fiesta. In hospitality the Christian, says Gregory Nazianzen, welcomes Christ, who "for your sake was a stranger."[139] For, as at Emmaus (Luke 24:13–35), only in welcoming the stranger on the way is there revelation "in the breaking of the bread" (of Christ, and in Christ, of the disciples who "set out at once" to proclaim the Good News)—hospitality lets Easter in.

As Pope Francis eloquently reminds us, such hospitality becomes the moral squint of modern Catholic social teaching: the theological virtues underwrite our generalized respect for the concrete other.[140] For Francis the Gospel is fulfilled, "in our hearing," as the great biblical injunctions of covenant fidelity (sĕdāqāh) and agapē are translated in the threefold hermeneutic of rights.[141] Catholic social teaching thus integrates the civic virtues of liberal respect and communitarian recognition in an ethics of anamnestic solidarity, of becoming neighbor to those "stamped with a special mark by affliction." The Church accordingly recognizes not open but porous borders, respecting persons' right to change nationality for social or economic or political reasons. For in view of the "common purpose of created things" (and the mutually implicative character of basic rights), "where a state which suffers from poverty combined with great population cannot supply such use of goods to its inhabitants . . . people possess a right to emigrate, to select a new home in foreign lands and to seek conditions of life worthy" of their common humanity.[142]

Pope Paul VI and his successors urge acceptance of "a charter which will assure [persons'] right to emigrate, favor their integration, facilitate their professional advancement and give them access to decent housing where, if such is the case, their families can join them."[143] Among the most exigent duties enshrined in such a charter is the preservation and protection of families and of these the most vulnerable (e.g., victims of human trafficking). Citizens of faith, conversely, can never accept detention of undocumented children or threats of massive deportation separating families, many of whom are of "mixed status." Such policies, as immigrants' stories attest, undermine the rule of law and imperil the very raison d'être of citizenship.

In conjunction with the bishops of Mexico, the US bishops favor comprehensive and equitable immigration reform—reforms that seek to redress the massive poverty, the global inequities, and the systemic violence spurring migration. So, too, the bishops support expanded family reunification opportunities; a restoration of due process for migrants and asylum seekers; earned legalization; an equitable temporary work program, including a path to permanent residency that is achievable and verifiable; job portability that allows workers to change employers; the same labor protections that apply to US workers; mechanisms and resources to enforce workers' rights; wages and benefits that do not undercut the livelihoods of domestic workers; and mobility, both between the United States and homeland and within the United States.[144]

In anamnestic solidarity, then, the migrant is never the object of a policy of assimilation but rather is a source of blessing. Indeed, both guest and host are transformed when the "alien who resides with you" is treated "as the citizen among you" (Lev. 19:33). Like Israel of exile, the Church must "become what it has never been before"—a "new creation."[145] The command of love is love's command: in loving one comes to see oneself—one is revealed—as beloved in the beloved community. We "pass over" to the Crucified and Risen One who, Christians believe, first passed over to us: Christ who is our Good Samaritan, coming to the aid of our wounded humanity.

Ecological Responsibility

"Generations have trod, have trod, have trod; And all is seared with trade; bleared, smeared with toil."[146] Gerard Manley Hopkins's lament of 1877 strikes a prophetic note, for generations have indeed trod, and trade and toil have bleared our moral landscape. Unsustainable climate change, loss of biodiversity, endemic pollution: all these are, in large part, anthropogenic, as is the increasing phenomenon of "climate refugees"—those fleeing their homelands due to environmental degradation. Yet still "the soil is bare" and political will is wanting.[147] Let me first touch briefly on the immediate ethical implications of global warming and then consider two particularly vexing questions for an ethics of rights: what we owe (a) to future generations and (b) to nonhuman nature.

The Global Commons

Drawing upon the latest scientific studies, the United Nations Environment Programme "Emissions Gap Report 2018" compares current and estimated future greenhouse emissions with "the emission levels permissible for the world to progress on a least-cost pathway to achieve the goals of the Paris Agreement." This "emissions gap" signifies the "difference between 'where we are likely to be and where we need to be.'" The report concludes,

> Current commitments expressed in the NDCs [nationally determined contributions] are inadequate to bridge the emissions gap [by] 2030. Technically, it is still possible to bridge the gap to ensure global warming stays well below 2°C and 1.5°C, but if NDC ambitions are not increased before 2030, exceeding the 1.5°C goal can no longer be avoided. Now more than ever, unprecedented and urgent action is required by all nations. The assessment of actions by the G20 countries indicates that this is yet to happen; in fact, global CO2 emissions increased in 2017 after three years of stagnation.[148]

The global commons is threatened. Yet not all have trod equally; life's natural lottery seems rigged against those least responsible or able to adapt. As the Intergovernmental Panel on Climate Change reports, climate change is expected to "exacerbate poverty in most developing countries and create new poverty pockets in countries with increasing inequality, in both developed and developing countries."[149] Those "who are socially, economically, culturally, politically, institutionally, or otherwise marginalized are especially vulnerable to climate change. . . . This heightened vulnerability is rarely due to a single cause. Rather, it is the product of intersecting social processes that result in inequalities in socioeconomic status and income, as well as in exposure. Such social processes include, for example, discrimination on the basis of gender, class, ethnicity, age, and (dis)ability."

My earlier arguments are telling here, for in embodying (schematizing) a rights regime, a realization-focused critique *recognizes* just such systemically interrelated distortions. Our threefold hermeneutic of rights privileges those whose equal dignity and rights are unequally denied or threatened. Indeed, a distributively just order will necessarily be restorative, *redeeming* what Gutiérrez calls the "rights of the poor" or most vulnerable. Those already concentrated in high-risk areas have just claims of *redress* in preserving and protecting already threatened climate-sensitive resources such as local water and food supplies.

Intergenerational Responsibility

Yet the irony persists, as failure to take "unprecedented and urgent action" burdens not only poor communities but future generations. What say have they in preserving our common home? If rights claims justify duties in our regnant liberal tradition, how can *future* claims oblige? Can we redress future ills? Indeed, the moral landscape is itself blurred, for it seems odd to say that future persons bind us if their very existence is contingent upon our present choices. What, then, do we owe to future generations? Our hermeneutical critique offers the promise, I believe, of an initial response. Let me briefly recall, in summary form, the arguments of chapters 1 and 2, as they bear on the question:

(1) The communicative virtues, as standing dispositions, underwrite the redemption of basic rights in well-formed narratives. And the telos of redeeming such rights (the discursive common good) can be formulated as a maxim: *Claim-rights are to be redeemed.* In fulfilling the maxim the virtuous community thus seeks to preserve, protect, and enhance the narratively embodied (schematized) practice of rights (anamnestic solidarity). Just as "getting the memory right" binds us here and now, so the practice is open and temporally extended for $S_{1,2,3,\ldots n.}$

(2) The maxim, in turn, grounds threefold duties. Because rights are to be redeemed (goods of agency realized), members of the virtuous community must *forbear* from denying agential goods of security, liberty, subsistence; *protect* agential goods, typically through systemic safeguards; and *provide* the substance of agential goods, where fitting. Narratively redeeming (schematizing) basic claim-rights *specifies* the threefold duties. $S_{1,2,3,\ldots n.}$, that is, rightly assert and enforce correlative duties of forbearance, protection, and provision through legal/juridical protections of a constitutional regime. But where neither subject/claimant nor claims can be specified, as in the case of future subjects, the maxim pertains to the rhetorical *practice* of claim-making itself, and a fortiori to the agential goods it presumes—the basic conditions or capabilities of agency. Thus, forbear now from impeding subjects' agency in the future; protect against systemic deprivation; provide for the realization of future agential goods.

(3) The telos of redeeming rights is thus realized, rhetorically, not only in what we say (redeeming $S_{1,2,3,\ldots n.}$'s specific claims) but in what we show (the communicative virtues underwriting the practice of claim-making). As such, we must distinguish the set of possible persons whose existence is contingent in part upon present decisions from the finite yet still unspecified set of persons who *will* exist (and can suffer harm) in the future, that is, prospective agents/subjects of claim-rights. Here, too, the threefold hermeneutic of rights applies. Rights' rhetoric permits us to *recognize pro tanto* the nature, scope, and gravity of future harm like predictable loss of habitat or biodiversity. In a similar vein, preserving and protecting the practice of *redeeming* rights generates duties of forbearance, protection, and provision. We rightly say "never again" to atrocity or destruction of indigenous

> habitats. Indeed, pledging now to forbear, protect, and provide is just "what *we* do" as virtuous agents; the *ethos* of respect and recognition as standing dispositions marks our character (*ēthos*). Finally, we might speak of proleptic *redress,* for though we cannot repair future ills, subjects in the future may justly claim reparation (e.g., from corporate bodies for causing foreseeable harm).

Appealing to the rhetorical practice of claim-making thus resolves our initial conundrum. Rights, I argue, are less properties or powers of sovereign selves abstracted from the ensemble of social/historical relations than they are warranted claims—claims, that is, that "make sense" precisely as schematized rhetorical practice. Under the rubrics of the common good, we do not implement basic rights seriatim but integrally and comprehensively: how can the rights of all, and especially of the most vulnerable, be fittingly recognized and redeemed, not only now but in the foreseeable future? Intergenerational responsibility is thus not added to but rather is constitutive of our initial schematization, so that duties to present and prospective subjects are mutually implicative. Not only the immediate but longer-term consequences must be assessed in a consequentially sensitive embodiment (schematization) of a rights regime. We must, in a Lockean vein, leave as good and enough for future generations.

The Ethics of Enchantment

The foregoing arguments, to be sure, remain anthropocentric; yet in enjoining *intergenerational* responsibility for the most vulnerable, our restorative critique underscores the exigency of closing the "emissions gap." As Pope Francis reminds us, the "cry of the poor" resonates in the "cry of the earth."[150] Indeed, for Francis the earth too is charged with God's grandeur, bearing the divine *imago*. Yet how do we say this in our "godless and prophetless" time? Why, after all, should religious claims be staked in the public realm? Can the spiritual wisdom of *Laudato Si'*, or comparable spiritual traditions, be translated into the rhetoric of public political reasoning, such as in respect for the intrinsic value of nonhuman nature?

A biocentric ethics need not, of course, appeal to religion. Yet the modern disenchantment of the lifeworld leaves our soil bare, and it is here we must begin. Let me then briefly set the stage by recalling the arguments of the previous chapter. For Max Weber the eclipse of the "ultimate and most sublime" values in modernity left in its wake a demystified world—in Habermas's words, the "secular sublation (*Aufhebung*) of ontotheology by the philosophy of history."[151] Divested of formal and final causality, the book of nature (the ontotheological cosmology of the medievals) ceases to tell a moral tale. In "the new cosmology developed by Galileo, Descartes, and Newton, the operative principle of causality," writes Louis Dupré, "was the so-called efficient one. Soon modern philosophy with few exceptions (Leibniz) reduced all forms of causality to the efficient one conceived on the model of the mechanist theory of motion. Creation had always been interpreted in a causal way, but never as the exclusive effect of an efficient cause."[152]

In such a mechanistic worldview God becomes ever more a supernumerary of creation. Indeed, religion is confined to the private sphere, assimilated at best to the realm of personal taste or predilection. Our conception of justice, writes Rawls, "should be, as far as possible, independent of the opposing and conflicting philosophical and religious doctrines that citizens affirm."[153] Under the veil of ignorance, Rawls's Kantian constructivism confines "nonpublic" religious belief to the vestibule of such an inquiry, while Habermas's more comprehensive liberalism divests "higher or deeper" doctrines of any logical force on their own."[154] And Rorty's "postmodernist bourgeois liberalism" abjures every "trace of divinity," either "in the form of a divinized world or a divinized self."[155]

Practical reasoning follows suit. As Michael Sandel observes, "For the empiricist philosophers, including the utilitarians, reason is wholly instrumental. It enables us to identify means for the pursuit of certain ends—ends that reason itself does not provide."[156] Construing felicity in terms amenable to empirical methodology, Hobbes assumes that the victorious desire terminating deliberation (as the transmission of motions) explains the transmission of practical obligation. With the attenuation of Aristotelian *boulesis* to mere appetite (*epithumia*), prudence is reduced to technical expertise. Reason is but the servant of interest as "the Thoughts, are to the Desires, as Scouts and Spies, to range abroad, and find the way to the things Desired."[157]

"Prudent" thus becomes a commendation of Hume's "sensible knave," whose cleverness is devoted to the pursuit of "self-love and private interest." For if the realm of value emerges as a purely subjective constitution that is explicable in terms of the mere incidence of pain or pleasure, then, as Hume says, there can be "no eternal rational measures of right and wrong."[158] Multiple variations are wrung upon this technical reduction of prudence, but modern moral theorists typically follow Kant in assuming that the perfection of prudence (*Klugheit*) is not "practical wisdom" in the service of the perfect community but rather sagacity in pursuing one's own lasting advantage. For moderns like Rawls, Habermas, and R. M. Hare, the boundaries between prudential self-love and morality become distinct and sharp.

In a disenchanted world that is governed by technical reasoning (*Zweckrationalität*), morality must, then, be sui generis: for Kant the invention of morality rests not in natural teleology but in the deliverances of pure reason alone.[159] In Kantian Moralität the apodictic force of moral prescription derives from the "mere Idea of the qualification of a maxim for the universality of a practical law."[160] Only a categorically prescribed action is "good in itself and therefore . . . necessary, in virtue of its principle, for a will which of itself accords with reason." If the dignity of such a rational will survives, it does so precisely in its separation (diremption) from nonhuman nature, which possesses but instrumental value that is contingent upon human purposes. The mechanism of the world is there to be exploited. Here land cannot be "sacred," and indigenous spiritual beliefs are lost to secular sublation.[161]

Visions and Revisions

Public reasoning, then, bears the mark of our modern or postmodern prejudices, that is, the disenchantment of the world, the technical reduction of prudence, and the invention of morality. Let us turn to the latter prejudices, since what we say about them will offer a "clearing" for reenchantment. First, a word about prudence, for the technical reduction of Aristotelian phronēnis is far less perspicuous than Hume or Kant imagined. Indeed, the general formula for technical (problematical) imperatives cannot suffice for the objective determination of action. Let me briefly recall our argument: Since technical imperatives do not justify an action per se, but only as relative to a contingent "merely possible purpose," my intention to perform an action would be justified even though my end may fail to enjoy deliberative priority. As the modal conclusion "one ought to perform 'A' under the description 'd'" is detached from the ensemble of beliefs and attitudes comprising one's best reason(s) for acting, even the incontinent agent might be said to deliberate in this "technical" sense.

Inasmuch as the semantic opacity of intentional action descriptions implies that an action may be variously characterized with respect to the reasons that rationalize it, it may be that I ought to perform action A under one description yet ought to refrain from performing A under another. After all, there is nothing inconsistent about the attribution of implicitly conflicting desires. Clearly we must look beyond the merely analytical relation of willing an end and willing its necessary means. For the practically exclusive sense of ought (*Sollen*) implies that it cannot be the case that under one description I ought to do A but under another I ought not. Rather, the conclusion of the apodosis (that I ought to perform A) presumes that no further pertinent reasons tell decisively against my performing A. In short, we must say that an agent acts rationally only if she acts in accordance with her *best* reasons, all things considered.

Prudence thus introduces a formal deliberative maxim not immediately derivable from instrumental reasoning (the analyticity of hypothetical imperatives). For just as for Carl Gustav Hempel the "requirement of 'total evidence'" is not a postulate of a theory of inductive logic, but in Davidson's words, a "maxim" for its application, so reason is applied in the practical realm as the intentions of a practically rational agent are conformed to her best judgment.[162] Prudence cannot be reduced instrumentally; neither is it the slave of atomistic passions or interests, "producing" value in a mechanistic construal of nature. Rather, for prudential agents the lifeworld is given as always, already interpreted; custom (*nomos*) emerges as "second nature" in providing an interpretative repertory of our best judgments—the streams of life and thought in which not only words but desires have meaning.[163]

The soil, it seems, is not so barren, and we may say more. For if satisfying the formal maxim (acting in accordance with one's best reasons) is, in Wittgenstein's words, "simply what I do" as a practically rational agent, it is not without ethical significance. If here "explanations run out," it is not that I act without reason but rather that no further reasons are necessary.[164] Satisfying the formal maxim suffices to determine my will *tout court:* this is simply what I (as a practically rational agent) do. And if the formal maxim suffices to determine the will, then we may say not only that practically rational agents will act in accordance with their best reasons but that they *ought* to do so if tempted otherwise. When we play the language game of practical reason we commend prudential action and exhibit a pro-attitude or interest in agents satisfying the formal maxim. To say you "ought" to do A implies my practical interest in your acting in accordance with your best reasons, all things considered.

Again, these reasons remain formally indeterminate, but it follows that the interpretation of reasons proper to me must be consistent with the (higher-order) interest exhibited in my practical legislation: my particular interests, that is, must be consistent with my interest in agents acting rationally or eo ipso my respect for practically rational agents. This is, I recognize, no more than sketching the lineaments of an argument more fully developed in the second chapter, but it suffices to show that a modest reconstruction of Aristotelian prudence (phronēsis) underwrites a precept of respect for persons—a precept calling us to the things of this world, not to the noumenal realm separating us from nature.

Reenchantment?

The foregoing summary offers a "clearing" for demystifying our "agnostic" pieties, not only of the technical reduction of prudence or of the invention of morality (postulating a noumenal realm) but of the lifeworld itself. A pragmatic and not transcendental "deduction" grounded in the reflective apperception of "what we do" suffices to establish our entitlement to respect and recognition. But what of the lifeworld? Here, hermeneutical understanding must yield to explanation. If we conceive prudence non-instrumentally and forgo an appeal to noumenal causation, how is agential causation in the lifeworld possible?

Aristotle, again, offers a clue. For if the emergence of a maxim *limiting* interests or passions so as to generate the *possibility* of rationally autonomous action can be rendered in terms of formal causality, then acting in accordance with the maxim exhibits the form of rational agency, that is, "what I do" when no further explanations are necessary. The emergent form cannot be reduced atomistically to the interests it governs; rather, we must recognize the emergence of a higher-order interest in realizing the form so that our arguments regarding formal causality might likewise be understood with Aristotle to adumbrate a final causality. Acting in accordance with the maxim is just "what I do" when explanations run out; reflectively valorizing form suffices. In prescribing "$S_{1.2.3...}$ *ought* to do A," then, formal and final causality are generalized for S in what we have called the communicative virtues of recognition (semantic and epistemic *recognition* of $S_{1.2.3...}$'s best reasons/judgment) and respect.

The lifeworld is, to this limited extent, reenchanted; formal and final causality are liminally at play in interpreting our best reasons.[165] We cannot divest the lifeworld of the very conditions (formal and final causality) by which we as agents interpret it.[166] Intrinsic value (dignity), we may say, is thus self-implicating: exhibited *as* we interpret the lifeworld or "produce" value, dignity grounds the family resemblance of our interpretations (anamnestic solidarity). As such, dignity appears in "local garb" and is figured in our complex cultural systems. Our repertory of attitudes (values), including dignity, is internally related to our system of beliefs. The lifeworld is "given," not as a mélange of brute interests or passions but rather as preinterpreted complex cultural systems. Prudence is always, already at play in the world we interpret.

Indeed, the technical reduction of "nature" in the cognitive sciences makes sense only as a methodological abstraction *of* prudence. But such a methodological *epochē* (i.e., a bracketing of formal and final causality) cannot explain itself, much less explain the value-laden prejudgments (truth-telling, impartiality, transparency, et al.) that inform "what we *do*" in normal science.[167] Such values, exhibited in interpreting nature, we might well call natural; for we cease to do science if we falsify or fall prey to bias or otherwise betray the nature of our inquiry. But of course not all values given in our cultural systems are perspicuously field-encompassing or practically self-implicating. Some may be proper to culture (pushpin or poetry?); others may be dependent upon metaphysical beliefs that for many remain methodologically undecidable (e.g., belief in a Creator God or the sacredness of ancestral lands).

How, then, to assess our differing value-laden cultural schemas? Clearly we must reject the notion that *all* value is instrumentally produced or constructed; prudence belies such a technical reduction. Neither a fortiori can the methodological epochē be uncritically extended to the practical realm in assuming the commensurability of value, for example, in a calculus of utilities. Indeed, the epochē entailed by *theoria* is compatible with differing complex systems of belief (e.g., in a divine creator, an elegant universe, or the sacredness of ancestral lands). In assessing such systems we must look rather to the distinctive *practical* criteria adumbrated earlier: coherence of evaluative premises, including the evaluative prejudgments of *theoria* and adequacy in schematizing the communicative virtues.

Consider, then, a case in which a governmental development project would displace an indigenous community from its ancestral land. Enlightenment "prejudices" would dismiss belief in the land's sacredness as quaint, a trace of the ontotheological synthesis long sublated in modernity. Indigenous interests are considered, but in the crucible of utility all interests are commensurable (measured by quantity, intensity, and duration)—land is a fungible commodity and adequate compensation may be given. For the community, however, everything is lost in translation: the currency of utility does not so much disprove its claims as deprive its claims of meaning—they are rendered unpronounceable.

These "modern" gambits are by no means warranted. Utility has no privileged standing; indeed, utilitarians are hard-pressed to account for our noncommensurable "interest" in dignity. As Rawls objects, criteria of personal choice are transposed to social choice so that *my* best reasons, those that express my personal autonomy, are subsumed in a suprapersonal calculus of interests. Dignity and rights, even if acknowledged, are subordinated to collective aims. Rawls accordingly imposes the formal constraints of universalizability upon hypothetical "prudential" choice, while Habermas looks to the formal universalizability of discourse ethics. In either case the form of Kantian morality (Moralität) is imposed on the realm of prudential ethics (Sittlichkeit), preserving personal autonomy.

And yet dignity, I argue, appears in local garb, schematized in local cultural systems: universality is *ab ovo* concrete, expressed not in traces of Moralität's abstract formalism but rather in the deliberative determination of ethical reciprocity. For many indigenous people *my* best reasons are expressed in a richer "*we,*" that is, myself as a member of this people.[168] Respect for persons—that each, in Bernard Williams's words, "should be regarded from the human point of view"—thus entails respect for peoples and a demand to see the world from *their* perspective. Deeply held values such as belief in the sacredness of ancestral land must then be respected, all the more so if the *substance* of belief is linked to the very bases of self-respect. As Williams observes, merely honoring another's "consciousness of his own activities" will not suffice; for "we evidently need something more," such as the precept "that one may not suppress or destroy that consciousness" or sense of worth.[169] Where belief in the sacredness of persons is intimately related to the sacredness of land, despoiling the land is tantamount to despoiling persons' dignity.

Claims to cultural rights to land are thus basic inasmuch as they preserve and protect the conditions of cultural agency and hence the schematization of dignity. Where cultural values conflict such rights, even if not absolute, must be accorded a threshold weight against collective, utilitarian aims that, after all, do remain commensurable. The alternative costs of rerouting a pipeline pale in comparison to desecrating ancestral land. The former can be measured and duly compensated; the latter not. Even the agnostic, then, has good reason to respect religious belief in the intrinsic value of nonhuman nature and the sacredness of land.

III. CONCLUSIONS

We have, then, good religious warrants for respecting nonhuman nature just because we have good general warrants for respecting persons. Indeed, in resolving one dichotomy, of morality and prudence, we have, implicitly, resolved another. It turns out that an anthropocentric hermeneutics (a phronetic reconstruction) yields a biocentric ethics, or better, a cosmotheandric ethics, by which a generalized respect for the concrete other warrants respect of the intrinsic value of nonhuman nature.[170] A reconstruction of prudence in elaborating a prudential ethics belies the world's disenchantment, for in respecting persons as sacred we cannot bracket the grounds they invoke for that respect, such as the sacredness of creation, of nature itself.

"Believing in one God who is Trinitarian communion," writes Francis, "suggests that the Trinity has left its mark on all creation . . . St. Bonaventure . . .

teaches us that each creature bears in itself a specifically Trinitarian structure, so real that it could be contemplated if only the human gaze were not so partial, dark and fragile."[171] Created in the imago Dei, our dignity for Francis rests precisely in exercising providential care for all creation: transcendence is in and of but never opposed to nature. We need not, of course, agree with *Laudato Si'* or its cosmotheandric defense of indigenous rights; but we cannot deny its place (locus) in public reasoning. As Hopkins reminds us, "Generations have trod, have trod, have trod; And all is seared with trade; bleared, smeared with toil," but "for all this, nature is never spent."[172] There is still a brief for poetry.

NOTES

Epigraph: Hopkins, "As Kingfishers Catch Fire," *The Poems of Gerard Manley Hopkins*, 90.

1. Perelman, *The Realm of Rhetoric*, 5; see also 17–18. For the relation of Aristotelian rhetoric and hermeneutics as phronetic disciplines, see Gadamer, *Truth and Method*, 71–72, 567.
2. James, *Pragmatism*.
3. Rawls, *A Theory of Justice*, 109–12, 457.
4. Rawls, 142, 16.
5. Arendt, "A Reply," 78–79.
6. Rawls, "Fairness to Goodness," 539.
7. Rawls, *Political Liberalism*, 290, 370–71. See Habermas, *Justification and Application*, 27–28.
8. See Benhabib, "The Generalized and the Concrete Other," 87.
9. Jean-François Lyotard, "The Other's Rights," in Lyotard, *The Politics of Human Rights*, 81.
10. See Hoogvliet, "Preventing Rwanda in a Rawlsian World," article 5; and Müller, "Rawls's Relational Conception of Human Rights," 61–70. See Rawls, *The Law of Peoples*, 80–81, 90, 93–94.
11. Habermas now rejects his earlier claim that justice "conceived deontologically requires solidarity as its reverse side" inasmuch as such a formal discursive account "leads to a moralization and depoliticization of the concept of solidarity." See Habermas, "Plea for a Constitutionalization of International Law," 12n8.
12. Jürgen Habermas, "Israel or Athens," in Habermas, *Religion and Rationality*, 133–34.
13. Habermas, "A Reply to My Critics," 246–47. See Peukert, *Science, Action, and Fundamental Theology*.
14. Wiesel, "The Holocaust as Literary Inspiration," 9.
15. Habermas, *Moral Consciousness and Communicative Action*, 66.
16. Benhabib, *Dignity in Adversity*, 15–17, 75–76, 88–89, 112–13, 129–31, 151–53.
17. See Tutu, *No Future without Forgiveness*, 61–63.
18. MacIntyre, *After Virtue*, 195.
19. Rorty, "The Priority of Democracy to Philosophy," 259.
20. Rorty, *Contingency, Irony and Solidarity*, 177.
21. Rorty, *Consequences of Pragmatism*, xlii.

22. Rorty, "Truth and Freedom," 284.
23. Katongole and Wilson-Hertgrove, *Mirror to the Church*, 67.
24. Sen, *The Idea of Justice*, 1–27.
25. US Bureau of Justice Statistics information, summarized by the Sentencing Project, "Fact Sheet."
26. US Bureau of Justice Statistics information, summarized by the Sentencing Project, "Facts about Prisons and Prisoners."
27. The Sentencing Project, "Fact Sheet."
28. Stevenson, "Mass Incarceration," 81.
29. Hadar Aviram attributes such disparities to "racialized assumptions and practices that precede the incarceration stage: social disadvantage that produces violent crime; discriminatory policing practices; extensive prosecutorial discretion which is very resistant to judicial review; the everyday realities of lower courtroom practices; and the impact of race, and other demographic factors that intersect with it, on sentencing." Aviram, "Why Are Racial Minorities Overrepresented in the Prison Population?", 27.
30. The Sentencing Project, "Felony Disenfranchisement." The Sentencing Project reports that there were an estimated 1.17 million people disenfranchised in 1976, 3.34 million in 1996, and more than 5.85 million in 2010. The rate of felony disenfranchisement for Black Americans of voting age is more than four times greater than for non-African Americans. See Uggen, Shannon, and Manza, "State-Level Estimates of Felon Disenfranchisement."
31. Alexander, *The New Jim Crow*, 258. See Cassidy and Mikulich, *Interrupting White Privilege*.
32. Gopnik, "The Caging of America," 73. Gopnik notes that in the last two decades, "the money that states spend on prisons has risen at six times the rate of spending on higher education" (73).
33. Amnesty International, "Entombed," 2.
34. Stevenson, "Mass Incarceration," 81.
35. Amnesty International, "Death Penalty."
36. Stuntz, *The Collapse of American Criminal Justice*, 3.
37. Coates, "The Black Family in the Age of Mass Incarceration."
38. "Private prisons in the United States incarcerated 126,272 people in 2015, representing 8% of the total state and federal prison population. Since 2000, the number of people housed in private prisons has increased 45%." The Sentencing Project, "Private Prisons in the United States."
39. John Tierney, "For Lesser Crimes, Rethinking Life behind Bars," *New York Times*, December 11, 2012, A24.
40. Pew Research Center, Hispanic Trends.
41. "Blocking a Bad Immigration Law," *New York Times*, September 1, 2017, A20.
42. Meda Chesney-Lind notes that "nearly half the women in the nation's prisons are women of color: notably 27 percent are African American and 17 percent are Hispanic. The number of Latinas incarcerated increased by 65 percent in the first decade of this century, a figure that reflects a general population increase, but also the increasing involvement of the criminal justice system in the criminalization of immigration, as well as policies and practices relating to the war on drugs." Chesney-Lind, "'Remember the Ladies,'" 42.
43. In his analysis of Kant's views on crime and punishment, Roger Sullivan writes that "justice may be mitigated by benevolence, but the criminal still owes *society* a strict debt to restore the reciprocal contractual relationship between obedience to the law and benefits received from living under the law." See Sullivan, *Immanuel Kant's Moral Theory*, 243.

44. Stevenson, "Mass Incarceration," 81.
45. Coates, "The Black Family in the Age of Mass Incarceration," 30, 32.
46. Arendt, "The Perplexities of the Rights of Man," 290, 297, 299, 301.
47. Kathryn Russell, *The Color of Crime*, cited in Alexander, *The New Jim Crow,* 107. Coates writes, "Postbellum Alabama solved this problem by manufacturing criminals. Blacks who could not find work were labeled vagrants and sent to jail, where they were leased as labor to the very people who had once enslaved them." Coates, "The Black Family in the Age of Mass Incarceration," 31.
48. Alexander, *The New Jim Crow*, 236–44. Shawn Copeland writes from a womanist perspective: "A white, racially bias–induced horizon defines, censors, controls and segregates different, other, non-white bodies." Copeland, *Enfleshing Freedom*, 15. See also Ada Maria Isasi-Díaz's analogous *mujerista* critique in Isasi-Díaz, *En la Lucha / In the Struggle.*
49. Joel Feinberg writes that "punishment generally expresses more than judgment of disapproval; it is also a symbolic way of getting back at the criminal, of expressing vindictive resentment." "The Expressive Function of Punishment" in Feinberg, *Doing and Deserving*, 100.
50. Zehr, *The Little Book of Restorative Justice*, 37.
51. See Johnstone and Van Ness, *Handbook of Restorative Justice*; Von Hirsch et al., *Restorative Justice and Criminal Justice*; Johnstone, *A Restorative Justice Reader*; Van Ness and Heetderks Strong, *Restoring Justice*; Zehr, *Changing Lenses*; and Llewellyn and Philpott, *Restorative Justice, Reconciliation, and Peacebuilding.*
52. For differing rationales, processes, and programs, see Johnstone, *Restorative Justice,* 10–35, 161–71.
53. Tutu, *No Future without Forgiveness*, 51.
54. Amnesty International (www.amnestyusa.org) and Human Rights Watch (www.hrw.org) condemn the systemic abuse of human rights in the US criminal justice system.
55. See Ralph Ellison, "What America Would Be like without Blacks," in Ellison, *The Collected Essays of Ralph Ellison*, 583.
56. Alexander, *The New Jim Crow,* 259.
57. See Boyle, *Tattoos on the Heart.*
58. See Moberly, *The Ethics of Punishment*, 97–98.
59. US Sentencing Commission, "2011 Report to Congress: Mandatory Minimum Penalties in the Federal Criminal Justice System," 368. The Sentencing Commission prepared this report pursuant to a congressional directive contained in section 4713 of the Matthew Shepard and James Byrd, Jr., Hate Crimes Prevention Act of 2009, Pub L. No. 111–84, and to the commission's general authority under 28 U.S.C. §§ 994–995 as well as its specific authority under 28 U.S.C. § 995(a)(20) to "make recommendations to Congress concerning modification or enactment of statutes relating to sentencing, penal, and correctional matters that the Commission finds to be necessary and advisable to carry out an effective, humane, and rational sentencing policy." https://www.ussc.gov/research/congressional-reports/2011-report-congress-mandatory-minimum-penalties-federal-criminal-justice-system.
60. Tutu, *No Future without Forgiveness*, 221 (emphasis added). Pumla Gobodo-Madikizela writes in a similar vein: "True social transformation—and healing of victims—will come about only if the issues of economic justice and the myriad problems that post-apartheid South Africa faces are addressed" (*A Human Being Died That Night*, 126).
61. See Zehr, *Changing Lenses*, 197.

62. Commutative justice rectifies the transactions of legal individuals, whether voluntary (e.g., through contracts) or involuntary (e.g., through crime).
63. USCCB, *Responsibility, Rehabilitation, and Restoration*, 11.
64. Massingale, *Racial Justice and the Catholic Church.*
65. Katongole, *Born from Lament*, xvii.
66. Éla, "Christianity and Liberation in Africa," 143.
67. Simone Weil, "Reflections on the Right Use of School Studies with a View to the Love of God," in Weil, *Waiting for God*, 115.
68. See my "What San Salvador Says to Nairobi: The Liberation Ethics of Ignacio Ellacuría," in Tarimo and O'Neill, "What San Salvador Says to Nairobi."
69. Rahner, *Theological Investigations*, 217–34.
70. See Sobrino, *Companions of Jesus*, 3–56.
71. See Castles, de Hass, and Miller, *The Age of Migration.*
72. UNHCR, "Global Trends," https://www.unhcr.org/dach/wp-content/uploads/sites/27/2019/06/2019-06-07-Global-Trends-2018.pdf.
73. UNHCR, *The State of the World's Refugees 2006*, 47–48.
74. UNHCR, "Global Trends," 22. The UNHCR reports that in 2018, 10.1 million refugees lived in protracted displacement situations of less than twenty years, more than half of whom were Syrians in Egypt, Iraq, Jordan, Lebanon, and Turkey. Another 5.8 million lived in a situation lasting twenty years or more, dominated especially by the 2.4 million Afghan refugees in the Islamic Republic of Iran and Pakistan, where the displacement situation has lasted for forty years.
75. Loescher and Milner, *Protracted Refugee Situations*, 7. In identifying such situations the UNHCR applies the "crude measure of refugee populations of 25,000 persons or more who have been in exile for five or more years in developing countries" (13).
76. UNHCR, *The State of the World's Refugees 2006*, 64. See Loescher and Milner, *Protracted Refugee Situations*, 23–34.
77. Anzaldúa, *Borderlands La Frontera*, 25.
78. See Gammeltoft-Hansen and Tan, "The End of the Deterrence Paradigm?" "Last year more than 5,000 migrants and refugees were registered dead or missing in the Mediterranean (IOM 2016). A record number, this makes the Mediterranean account for more than two-thirds of all registered migrant fatalities worldwide (IOM 2016). Many more asylum seekers are subjected to various forms of violence and abuse during the migratory process as a result of their inherently vulnerable and clandestine position" (28). See IOM, Missing Migrants Project.
79. Heyer, *Kinship across Borders*, 9.
80. Human Rights First, "O.A. v. Trump." Gammeltoft-Hansen and Tan observe that "current deterrence policies may be seen to fall into five main categories: 1) non-admission policies limiting access to asylum procedures, 2) non-arrival measures preventing access to the territory of asylum states through migration control, 3) offshore asylum processing and relocation of refugees to third countries, 4) criminalization of irregular migration and human smuggling, and 5) indirect deterrence measures intended to make the asylum country less attractive" ("The End of the Deterrence Paradigm?" 34).
81. Human Rights First, Freedom for Detained Refugees Project and "Immigration Detention."
82. See van den Anker and van Liempt, *Human Rights and Migration.*

83. Human Rights First, "Human Trafficking," https://www.humanrightsfirst.org/topics/human-trafficking.
84. International Labour Organization, "Forced Labour, Modern Slavery and Human Trafficking" https://www.ilo.org/global/topics/forced-labour/lang-en/index.htm.
85. Burke, *Reflections on the Revolution in France*, 138.
86. Burke, 83, 85.
87. See Sandel, "Introduction," 4, 6, 10.
88. Walzer, *Spheres of Justice*, 31. See also Walzer, "The Moral Standing of States" and "Nation and Universe." For a comparative analysis of Rawls and Walzer on admissions policy, see Gibney, *Strangers or Friends*, 3–34.
89. Peter Brimelow, for instance, contends that Americans "have a right to insist that their government stop shifting" the country's racial balance from its "specific ethnic core" that "has been white." See Brimelow, *Alien Nation*, 264.
90. Arendt, "The Perplexities of the Rights of Man," 290.
91. Rawls, *Political Liberalism*, 41. See the more cosmopolitan liberalism of Joseph H. Carens in Carens, "Aliens and Citizens"; "Who Belongs?," 415; and "Immigration and the Welfare State," 215. See also Ackerman, *Social Justice in the Liberal State*; and Beitz, "Cosmopolitan Ideals and National Sentiment" and *Political Theory and International Relations*.
92. See Benhabib's analysis of Kant's "cosmopolitan right" in Benhabib, *The Rights of Others*, 25–48; Kant, *Perpetual Peace*.
93. The assistance given "burdened societies" in Rawls's law of peoples does not extend to burdened citizens forced to migrate because of generalized violence or famine. See Benhabib, "The Law of Peoples, Distributive Justice, and Migrations," 1761–87.
94. Loescher, *Beyond Charity*, 139.
95. Held, "Law of States, Law of Peoples," 4. See Benhabib, *The Rights of Others*, 41.
96. Arendt, "The Perplexities of the Rights of Man," 295.
97. Godwin-Gil, *The Refugee in International Law*, 134.
98. Arendt, "The Perplexities of the Rights of Man," 299.
99. Benhabib, *The Rights of Others*, 40ff.
100. Arendt, "The Perplexities of the Rights of Man," 297, 301.
101. Gammeltoft-Hansen and Tan underscore "the growing schism between the liberal values and self-protective stance of the developed world in regard to refugee protection" ("The End of the Deterrence Paradigm?," 32). "Restrictive migration control policies are today the primary, some might say only, response of the developed world to rising numbers of asylum seekers and refugees. This has produced a distorted refugee regime in Europe and globally—a regime fundamentally based on the principle of deterrence rather than human rights protection. While the vast majority of European states still formally laud the international legal framework to protect refugees, most of these countries simultaneously do everything in their power to exclude those fleeing international protection and offer only a minimalist engagement to assist those countries hosting the largest number of refugees" (28).
102. Habermas, *Legitimation Crisis*.
103. See Belic, "When the Practice Gets Complicated," 181–203.
104. Van den Anker, "A Cosmopolitan Approach to Human Rights," 214.
105. Rawls, *The Law of Peoples*, 39.
106. Rawls's later emphasis upon the solidarities of peoples undercuts the concrete universality of basic rights schematized in anamnestic solidarity.

107. Weil, *Waiting for God,* 115.
108. See Hathaway, *The Rights of Refugees in International Law*; and Musalo et al., *Refugee Law and Policy*.
109. See UNHCR, *The State of the World's Refugees,* 57–94.
110. See Nowrojee, "Sexual Violence, Gender Roles, and Displacement"; and Martin, "Justice, Women's Rights, and Forced Migration."
111. Gammeltoft-Hansen and Tan, "The End of the Deterrence Paradigm?," 47.
112. On December 17, 2018, the UN General Assembly affirmed the Global Compact on Refugees, including the Comprehensive Refugee Response Framework providing for more predictable and equitable responsibility-sharing. See UNHCR, "The Global Compact on Refugees," https://www.unhcr.org/the-global-compact-on-refugees.html.
113. UNHCR, "Global Trends," 17–18.
114. Other rights enumerated by international convention, though often overridden or infringed upon, include entitlements to freedom of religion, education, social security, public assistance, work, and limited travel documents. See Godwin-Gil, *The Refugee in International Law*.
115. Dummett, *On Immigration and Refugees,* 29.
116. For an illuminating assessment of states' ethical responsibilities and major humanitarian initiatives, see Hollenbach, *Humanity in Crisis*.
117. See Loescher and Milner, *Protracted Refugee Situations,* 67–84.
118. UNHCR, *The State of the World's Refugees 2006,* 47–48.
119. Loescher and Milner, *Protracted Refugee Situations,* 35–65.
120. UNHCR, *The State of the World's Refugees 2006,* 50. See Abebe Feyissa's eloquent testimony in Feyissa and Horn, "There Is More than One Way of Dying"; and Wagacha and Guiney, "The Plight of Urban Refugees in Nairobi, Kenya."
121. See Benhabib, *The Rights of Others,* 120, 211, 221. See Seyla Benhabib, "Hospitality, Sovereignty, and Democratic Iterations," in Benhabib, *Another Cosmopolitanism*.
122. For differing religious interpretations of migration, see Collier and Strain, *Religious and Ethical Perspectives on Global Migration*.
123. For a consideration of Israel's Sabbath obligation to treat the landless poor as "brothers and sisters," see Brueggemann, *The Land,* 56–65.
124. See Plaut, "Jewish Ethics and International Migrations," 20–21. Plaut distinguishes the differing legal statuses accorded temporary vs. permanent migrants in the Hebrew Bible and Talmud.
125. See Schuller, "The Debate on the Specific Character of a Christian Ethics," 210.
126. Schrage, *The Ethics of the New Testament,* 71.
127. For an interpretation of biblical conceptions of justice, see Donahue, "The Bible and Catholic Social Teaching."
128. Walzer, *Exodus and Revolution,* 53, 73–90.
129. Senior, "Beloved Aliens and Exiles," 21.
130. "The word most often associated with hospitality in the LXX and the NT is *xenos,* which literally means foreigner, stranger, or even enemy. In its derived sense, however, the term comes to denote both guest and host alike. Typically, the verb used to describe the extending of hospitality is *xenizein* (Sir. 29:25; 1 Macc. 9:6; Acts 10:23; Heb. 12:2)." In the New Testament one who receives visitors is said to be *philoxenos,* i.e., a lover of strangers, or to be practicing the virtue of *philoxenia* (1 Tim. 3:2); 1 Pet. 4:9; Rom. 12:13; Heb. 13:2). Koenig, "Hospitality." See Brueggemann, *The Land*.

131. See Pohl, *Making Room*.
132. Karris, "The Gospel according to Luke," 690.
133. Weil, *Waiting for God*, 115.
134. Kierkegaard, *Works of Love*, 38.
135. Senior, "Beloved Aliens and Exiles," 23.
136. Chenu, "Les masses pauvres," 169.
137. As Koenig observes, "The Jesus movement was itself both guest and host of the kingdom" ("Hospitality," 301). I am especially grateful to Victor Adangba, SJ, for his wisdom in developing this insight.
138. See Senior, "Beloved Aliens and Exiles," 28.
139. Nazianzen, *Oration on Holy Baptism*, 327. See Pohl, *Making Room*, 33.
140. Heyer's *Kinship across Borders* offers an incisive critical account of Catholic social teaching on migration.
141. See Pope Francis, "Pope on Lampedusa."
142. Sacred Congregation of Bishops, "Instruction on the Pastoral Care of People," par. 351.
143. Paul VI, *Octogesima adveniens*, note 17.
144. United States Conference of Catholic Bishops and Conferencia del Episcopado Mexicano, *Strangers No Longer*.
145. Brueggemann, *The Land*, 42. With the crossing of the Jordan, "Israel does indeed become a new creation, a slave becomes an heir, a helpless child becomes a mature inheritor (see Ezek. 16:1–14)."
146. Hopkins, "God's Grandeur," in Hopkins, *The Poems of Gerard Manley Hopkins*, 66.
147. Hopkins, 66.
148. United Nations Environment Programme, "Emissions Gap Report 2018."
149. International Panel on Climate Change, "Climate Change 2014," 12, 20.
150. Pope Francis, *Laudato Si'*.
151. Habermas, "To Seek to Salvage an Unconditional Meaning," 136.
152. Dupré, "On the Intellectual Sources of Modern Atheism."
153. Rawls, *Political Liberalism*, 9–10. "In formulating such a conception," concludes Rawls, "political liberalism applies the principle of toleration to philosophy itself."
154. Rawls, *A Theory of Justice*, 118–23. In later writings Rawls departs from such an "exclusive" conception in favor of an "inclusive" and finally "wide" view of public reason.
155. Rorty, *Contingency, Irony and Solidarity*, 45.
156. Sandel, *Justice*, 118.
157. Hobbes, *Leviathan*, chap. 8, 57, 139.
158. Hume, *An Inquiry concerning the Principles of Morals*, 95n6, 102.
159. Williams, *Ethics and the Limits of Philosophy*, 174–96.
160. Kant, *Groundwork of the Metaphysics of Morals*, 414.
161. Even anthropocentric ethics if adequately elaborated supports an ecological ethics, inasmuch as respect for an intergenerational "kingdom of ends" enjoins care for the environment.
162. Davidson, "Reply to Essays I–X," 206.
163. Wittgenstein, *Philosophical Investigations*, par. 173.
164. Wittgenstein, par. 210.
165. Prudence, conceived as practical wisdom in the phronetic tradition of Aristotle and Aquinas, provides "a means through which relationships, attitudes and motivations can be assessed." See Deane-Drummond, *The Ethics of Nature*, 92.

166. The arguments adumbrated here (the formal constraints posed by the maxim for prudential reasoning) are supported by Terrence Deacon's analysis of emergent formal and final causality in natural processes. See Deacon, *Incomplete Nature.*
167. Celia Deane-Drummond writes, "To suppose so-called objective truth claims, themselves subject of human interpretation and revision, are superior to other forms of truth, including religious truth, demonstrates not so much insight as hubris" ("Experience Wonder and Seeking Wisdom," 587).
168. Celia Deane-Drummond offers an eloquent defense of the place of such wisdom (and wonder) in an evolutionary perspective. Citing Jeffrey Schloss, Deane-Drummond notes that wisdom is "not mere knowledge, . . . but involves deep insight into the functioning, meaning and purpose of existence along with the ability to discern how to live correspondingly, that is, in accord with the way things are" (*Wonder and Wisdom,* 10–11). See Schloss, "Wisdom Traditions as Mechanism for Organismal Integration," 156.
169. Williams, *Problems of the Self,* 236–37.
170. See Mveng, "Black African Art," 137–42; Magesa, *African Religion*; Bujo, *African Theology in Its Social Context*; and Panikkar, *The Cosmotheandric Experience.*
171. Pope Francis, *Laudato Si',* 239.
172. Hopkins, "God's Grandeur," in *The Poems of Gerard Manley Hopkins,* 66.

Conclusion

In his *Lyrical and Critical Essays,* Albert Camus writes, "It is the failing of a certain literature to believe that life is tragic because it is wretched."[1] Wretchedness, certainly, surrounds us—cries that fall like rain in summer. Yet we must say more. For in telling the story, cries are heard. In the new literature of testimony, the transgressed command reveals the face: beauty under the sign of its negation.

This is the work of rights, the grammar of remembrance, of anamnestic solidarity. History, I have argued, bears the mark of Cain, and rights are revelatory, even a form of prophetism, in Levinas's words: prophetism that imagines evil and reveals what is effaced.[2] This is the critical or deconstructive use of rights. So, too, memory commands that we redeem in our own time and place the cri de coeur of "Never again." Again, and yet again. We must tell the story; that is the constructive use. Still, there is the burden of specific reconstructive redress—the cries of victims that are finally irreparable, of "Rachel, weeping for her children, refusing to be comforted, because they are no more" (Jer. 31:15).

Yet the cry does not cease because we have no balm, no comfort or redress. Indeed, it runs through history, making of each life a theodicy. For religion can speak in the tongues of rights, yet it must also say more, hoping against hope in the silence of each Calvary—for we cannot *know* that "all will be well." This is not knowledge but the wager of a life.[3] Somehow ethics, theological ethics, must *say* this. And others, certainly, will say better than I. This work is a flawed, humble beginning, more abandoned, as Paul Valéry would say, than finished—but abandoned into a future with hope (Jer. 29:11).

NOTES

1. Camus, *Lyrical and Critical Essays,* 201.
2. Lévinas, *Ethics and Infinity,* 113.

3. See T. S. Eliot, "Little Gidding" and "Four Quartets," in Eliot, *The Complete Poems and Plays,* 145. Eliot is referencing Julian of Norwich, from her *Book of Showings* (long text chap. 31, short text chap. 14); see Raitt, *Christian Spirituality,* 203.

BIBLIOGRAPHY

Achebe, Chinua. *Things Fall Apart*. New York: Ballantine, 1959.

Ackerman, Bruce. *Social Justice in the Liberal State*. New Haven, CT: Yale University Press, 1980.

Africa Rights. *Rwanda: Death, Despair and Defiance*. Rev. ed. London: Africa Rights, 1998.

Alexander, Michelle. *The New Jim Crow: Mass Incarceration in the Age of Colorblindness*. Rev. ed. New York: New Press, 2012.

Alwin, Diemer. *Philosophical Foundations of Human Rights*. Paris: UNESCO, 1986.

Améry, Jean. *At the Mind's Limits: Contemplations by a Survivor on Auschwitz and Its Realities*. Translated by S. Rosenfeld and S. P. Rosenfeld. London: Granta, 1999.

Amnesty International. "Death Penalty." www.amnesty.org/en/what-we-do/death-penalty, accessed March 2, 2016.

———. "Entombed: Isolation in the US Federal Prison System." London: Amnesty International, 2014.

Amstutz, Mark, *The Healing of Nations: The Promise and Limits of Political Forgiveness*. Lanham, MD: Rowman & Littlefield, 2005.

An-Na'im, Abdullahi A. "The Synergy and Interdependence of Human Rights, Religion, and Secularism." In *The Library of Global Ethics and Religion*, vol. 4, *Human Rights and Responsibilities in the World Religions*, edited by Joseph Runzo, Nancy M. Martin, and Arvind Sharma, 27–50. Oxford: Oneworld, 2002.

Anscombe, G. E. M. *Ethics, Religion and Politics: The Collected Philosophical Papers of G. E. M. Anscombe*. Vol. 3. Oxford: Blackwell, 1981.

Anzaldúa, Gloria. *Borderlands La Frontera: The New Mestiza*. 3rd. ed. San Francisco: Aunt Lute, 2007.

Appiah-Kubi, Kofi, and Sergio Torres, eds. *African Theology en Route: Papers from the Pan-African Conference of Third World Theologians, December 17–23, 1977, Accra, Ghana*. Maryknoll, NY: Orbis, 1977.

Aquinas, Thomas. *Political Writings*. Edited by R. W. Dyson. Cambridge: Cambridge University Press, 2002.

———. *Summa Contra Gentiles*, book 3, *Providence*. Translated by Vernon J. Bourke. New York: Hanover House, 1955–57. Notre Dame, IN: University of Notre Dame Press, 1975.

———. *Summa Theologiae*. Translated by Thomas Gilby. New York: McGraw-Hill, 1965.

Arendt, Hannah. *Hannah Arendt and Karl Jaspers—Correspondence, 1926–1969*. New York: HBJ, 1992.

———. *The Human Condition*. Chicago: University of Chicago Press, 1958.

———. "The Perplexities of the Rights of Man." In *The Origins of Totalitarianism*. New York: Harcourt, Brace & World, 1966.

———. "A Reply." *Review of Politics* 15, no. 1 (January 1953): 76–84.

Aristotle. *Nicomachean Ethics.* Translated by J. A. K. Thomson. Revised by Hugh Tredennick. Harmondsworth, UK: Penguin, 1976.

———. *The Politics.* Translated by T. A. Sinclair. New York: Penguin, 1962.

Arrupe, Pedro. "On Inculturation, to the Whole Society." In *Other Apostolates Today: Selected Letters and Addresses III*, edited by Jerome Aixala, 171–81. St. Louis: Institute of Jesuit Sources, 1981.

Arthur, Paige. "How 'Transitions' Reshaped Human Rights: A Conceptual History of Transitional Justice." *Human Rights Quarterly* 3 (2009): 321–67.

Asmal, Kader, Louise Asmal, and Ronald Suresh Roberts. *Reconciliation through Truth: A Reckoning of Apartheid's Criminal Governance*. Cape Town, South Africa: David Philip, 1996.

Auden, W. H. *The Collected Poetry of W. H. Auden*. New York: Random House, 1945.

Audi, Robert. *Religious Commitment and Secular Reason.* Cambridge: Cambridge University Press, 2000.

Augustine of Hippo. *De Natura et Gratia*. In *Patrologiae Cursus Completus* series of Jacques-Paul Migne (1844–49) *Latina* 44: 247–90.

———. *Quaestiones Evangeliorum*, 2:19. In *Patrologiae Cursus Completus* series of Jacques-Paul Migne (1844–49) *Latina* 35: 1340.

———. *The Works of St. Augustine: A Translation for the 21st Century, part 2, Letters, vol. 4, Letters 211–270.* Edited by Boniface Ramsey. Translated by Roland Teske. Hyde Park, NY: New City, 2005.

Aviram, Hadar. "Why Are Racial Minorities Overrepresented in the Prison Population? A Systemic Institutional Inquiry." In *"Today I Give Myself Permission to Dream": Race and Incarceration in America*, edited by Erin Brigham and Connor Rae Kimberly, 17–30. San Francisco: Lane Center, 2018.

Balthasar, Hans Urs von. *Love Alone.* Translated by Alexander Dru. New York: Herder & Herder, 1969.

Barker, Ernest. *Social Contract: Essays by Locke, Hume, Rousseau.* Oxford: Oxford University Press, 1947.

Barth, Karl. *Church Dogmatics*. Edited by G. W. Bromiley and T. F. Torrance. Translated by G. W. Bromiley et al. Edinburgh: T & T Clark, 1957.

Bash, Anthony. *Forgiveness and Christian Ethics: New Studies in Christian Ethics.* Cambridge: Cambridge University Press, 2007.

Battle, Michael. *Reconciliation: The Ubuntu Theology of Desmond Tutu.* Cleveland, OH: Pilgrim, 1997.

Baxi, Upendra. *The Future of Human Rights.* 3rd ed. Oxford: Oxford University Press, 2008.

———. *Human Rights in a Posthuman World: Critical Essays.* Oxford: Oxford University Press, 2007.

Beck, Lewis White. *A Commentary on Kant's Critique of Practical Reason.* Chicago: University of Chicago Press, 1960.

Bediako, Kwame. *Christianity in Africa: The Renewal of a Non-Western Religion*. Maryknoll, NY: Orbis, 1995.

Beitz, Charles R. "Cosmopolitan Ideals and National Sentiment." *Journal of Philosophy* 80, no. 10 (1983): 591–600.

———. *The Idea of Human Rights.* New York: Oxford University Press, 2009.

———. *Political Theory and International Relations.* Rev. ed. Princeton, NJ: Princeton University Press, 1999.

Belic, Jelena. "When the Practice Gets Complicated: Human Rights, Migrants and Political Institutions." In *Moral and Political Conceptions of Human Rights: Implications for Theory and Practice*, edited by Reidar Maliks and Johan Karlsson Schaffer, 181–203. Cambridge: Cambridge University Press, 2017.

Bell, Daniel M. *Liberation Theology after the End of History: The Refusal to Cease Suffering*. New York: Routledge, 2001.

Benhabib, Seyla. *Another Cosmopolitanism (The Berkeley Tanner Lectures)*. Oxford: Oxford University Press, 2004.

———. *Dignity in Adversity: Human Rights in Troubled Times*. Cambridge: Polity, 2011.

———. "The Generalized and the Concrete Other: The Kohlberg-Gilligan Controversy and Feminist Theory." In *Feminism as Critique*, edited by Seyla Benhabib and Drucilla Cornell, 77–95. Minneapolis: University of Minnesota Press, 1987.

———. "The Law of Peoples, Distributive Justice, and Migrations." *Fordham Law Review* 72, no. 5 (2004): 1761–87.

———. *The Rights of Others: Aliens, Residents, and Citizens*. Cambridge: Cambridge University Press, 2004.

———. *Situating the Self: Gender, Community and Postmodernism in Contemporary Ethics*. New York: Routledge, 1992.

Benjamin, Walter. *The Arcades Project*. Cambridge, MA: Harvard University Press, 2000.

———. *Illuminations*. Edited by Hannah Arendt. Translated by Harry Zohn. New York: Schocken, 2007.

———. "N [Theoretics of Knowledge; Theory of Progress]." Translation of *Konvolut N* of the *Passagenwerk*. *The Philosophical Forum* 15, nos. 1–2 (Winter 1983–84): 18–19.

———. *The Origin of German Tragic Drama*. London: Verso, 1977.

Bennett, Christopher. "Personal and Redemptive Forgiveness." *European Journal of Philosophy* 11 (2003): 127–44.

Bentham, Jeremy. *The Works of Jeremy Bentham*, vol. 2. Edinburgh: William Tait, 1843.

Berger, Peter. "Secularism in Retreat." In *Islam and Secularism in the Middle East*, edited by John L. Esposito and Assam Tamini, 38–51. New York: New York University, 2000.

Berlin, Isaiah. *Four Essays on Liberty*. London: Oxford University Press, 1969.

Bernasconi, Robert. "'You Don't Know What I'm Talking About': Alterity and the Hermeneutic Ideal." In *The Specter of Relativism: Truth, Dialogue, and Phronēsis in Philosophical Hermeneutics*, edited by Lawrence K. Schmidt, 178–94. Evanston, IL: Northwestern University Press, 1995.

Berstein, Richard. *Beyond Objectivism and Relativism: Science, Hermeneutics, and Praxis*. Philadelphia: University of Pennsylvania Press, 1983.

Beverley, John. "The Margin at the Center: On *Testimonio*." In *The Real Thing: Testimonial Discourse and Latin America*, edited by Georg M. Gugelberger, 23–41. Durham, NC: Duke University Press, 1996.

Biggar, Nigel, ed. *Burying the Past: Making Peace and Doing Justice after Civil Conflict*. Washington, DC: Georgetown University Press, 2003.

Bohman, James. "Two Versions of the Linguistic Turn: Habermas and Poststructuralism." In *Habermas and the Unfinished Project of Modernity: Critical Essays on the Philosophical Discourse of Modernity*, edited by Maurizio Passerin d'Entrèves and Seyla Benhabib, 197–220. Cambridge, MA: MIT Press, 1997.

Bole, William, Drew Christiansen, and Robert T. Hennemeyer. *Forgiveness in International Politics: An Alternative Road to Peace*. Washington, DC: US Conference of Catholic Bishops, 2004.

Bolt, Robert. *A Man for All Seasons*. New York: Random House, 1990.

Bonhoeffer, Dietrich. *The Cost of Discipleship*. Translated by R. H. Fuller. New York: Macmillan, 1963.

Boraine, Alex. "Truth and Reconciliation in South Africa: The Third Way." In *Truth v. Justice: The Morality of Truth Commissions*, edited by Robert Rotberg and Dennis Thompson, 141–57. Princeton, NJ: Princeton University Press, 2000.

Boyle, Gregory. *Tattoos on the Heart: The Power of Boundless Compassion*. New York: Free Press, 2010.

Brecht, Bertolt. *Bertolt Brecht Poems, 1913–1956*. Translated by John Willett. New York: Methuen, 1976.

Brett, Annabel S. *Liberty, Right and Nature: Individual Rights in Later Scholastic Thought*. Cambridge: Cambridge University Press, 1997.

Brimelow, Peter. *Alien Nation*. New York: Random House, 1995.

Browning, Don S., and Francis Schüssler Fiorenza, eds. *Habermas, Modernity, and Public Theology*. New York: Crossroad, 1992.

Brudholm, Thomas. "On the Advocacy of Forgiveness after Mass Atrocities." In *The Religious in Responses to Mass Atrocity: Interdisciplinary Perspectives*, edited by Thomas Brudholm, 124–56. Cambridge: Cambridge University Press, 2009.

Brueggemann, Walter. "The Formfulness of Grief." *Interpretation* 31 (1977): 263–75.

———. "From Hurt to Joy, from Death to Life." *Interpretation* 28 (1974): 3–19.

———. *The Land*. 2nd. ed. Minneapolis: Fortress, 1977.

Buchanan, Allen. *The Heart of Human Rights*. Oxford: Oxford University Press, 2013.

Bujo, Bénézet. *African Theology in Its Social Context*. Translated by John O'Donohue. Nairobi, Kenya: St. Paul, 1986.

———. *The Ethical Dimension of Community: The African Model and the Dialogue between North and South*. Translated by Cecilia Namulondo Nganda. Nairobi, Kenya: St. Paul, 1997.

Burke, Edmund. *Reflections on the Revolution in France*. Oxford: MDB Oxford, 1854.

———. "Speech on Moving His Resolutions for Conciliation with America." In *The Works of the Right Honourable Edmund Burke*. Vol. 2. London: J. C. Nimmo, 1887.

Burnet, Jennie E. "The Injustice of Local Justice: Truth, Reconciliation, and Revenge in Rwanda." *Genocide Studies and Prevention* 3, no. 2 (August 2008): 173–93.

Butler, Joseph. *The Works of Joseph Butler*, vol. 2, *Sermons*. Edited by William Ewart Gladstone. Bristol, UK: Thoemmes, 1995.

Cahill, Lisa Sowle. "Embodying God's Image: Created, Broken, and Redeemed." In *Humanity before God: Contemporary Faces of Jewish, Christian, and Islamic Ethics*, edited by William Schweiker et al., 55–77. Minneapolis: Fortress, 2006.

Camus, Albert. *Lyrical and Critical Essays*. Translated by Ellen Conroy Kennedy. New York: Alfred A. Knopf, 1968.

———. *The Plague*. Translated by Stuart Gilbert. New York: Alfred A. Knopf, 1960.

Carens, Joseph H. "Aliens and Citizens: The Case for Open Borders." In *Theorizing Citizenship*, edited by Ronald Beiner, 229–55. New York: SUNY Press, 1995.

———. "Immigration and the Welfare State." In *Democracy and the Welfare State*, edited by Amy Gutmann, 207–30. Princeton, NJ: Princeton University Press, 1988.

———. "Who Belongs? Theoretical and Legal Questions about Birthright Citizenship in the United States." *University of Toronto Law Journal* 37, no. 4 (1987): 413–43.

Carney, J. J. *Rwanda before the Genocide: Catholic Politics and Ethnic Discourse in the Late Colonial Era*. Oxford: Oxford University Press, 2014.

Carroll, Lewis. *The Complete Works of Lewis Carroll*. London: Nonesuch, 1939.

Cassidy, Laurie M., and Alex Mikulich, eds. *Interrupting White Privilege*. Maryknoll, NY: Orbis, 2007.

Cassirer, Ernst. *Rousseau, Kant, Goethe: Two Essays*. Translated by James Gutman, Paul Oskar Kristeller, and John Herman Randall Jr. Princeton, NJ: Princeton University Press, 1945.

Castles, Stephen, Hein de Hass, and Mark J. Miller. *The Age of Migration: International Population Movements in the Modern World*. 5th ed. New York: Guilford, 2014.

Catullus. *The Poems of Catullus*. Translated by Peter Whigham. Baltimore: Penguin, 1966.

Chenu, M. D. "Les masses pauvres." In *Eglise et pauvreté*, edited by G. Cottier et al., 169–76. Paris: Cerf, 1965.

Chesney-Lind, Meda. "'Remember the Ladies': The Problem with Gender-Neutral Reform." In *To Build a Better Criminal Justice System: 25 Experts Envision the Next 25 Years of Reform*, edited by Marc Mauer and Kate Epstein, 42–43. Washington, DC: The Sentencing Project, 2012.

Clark, Phil, and Zacharay D. Kaufman, eds. *After Genocide: Transitional Justice, Post-Conflict Reconstruction and Reconciliation in Rwanda and Beyond*. New York: Columbia University Press, 2009.

Coates, Ta-Nehisi. "The Black Family in the Age of Mass Incarceration." *The Atlantic* (October 2015): 19. https://www.theatlantic.com/magazine/archive/2015/10/the-black-family-in-the-age-of-mass-incarceration/403246/.

Cobbah, Josiah A. M. "African Values and the Human Rights Debate: An African Perspective." *Human Rights Quarterly* 9, no. 3 (August 1987): 309–31.

Collier, Elizabeth W., and Charles R. Strain, eds. *Religious and Ethical Perspectives on Global Migration*. Lanham, MD: Lexington, 2014.

Cone, James. "Martin Luther King, Jr., and the Third World." In *The Future of Liberation Theology: Essays in Honor of Gustavo Gutiérrez*, edited by Marc H. Ellis and Otto Maduro, 346–57. Maryknoll, NY: Orbis, 1989.

Constant, Benjamin. "De la liberté des anciens comparée a celle des modernes." In *Oeuvres politiques de Benjamin Constant*, edited by C. Louandre, 258–86. Paris: Charpentier et cie, 1874.

Copeland, M. Shawn. *Enfleshing Freedom: Body, Race, and Being*. Minneapolis: Fortress, 2010.

Cornell, Drucilla. "The Ethical Affirmation of Human Rights: Gayatri Spivak's Intervention." In *Can the Subaltern Speak? Reflections on the History of an Idea*, edited by Rosalind C. Morris, 100–116. New York: Columbia University Press, 2010.

Cranston, Maurice. *What Are Human Rights?* New York: Basic, 1962.

Crocker, David A. "Truth Commissions, Transitional Justice, and Civil Society." In *Truth v. Justice: The Morality of Truth Commissions*, edited by Robert Rotberg and Dennis Thompson, 99–121. Princeton, NJ: Princeton University Press, 2000.

Curran, Charles. *Catholic Social Teaching: A Historical, Theological, and Ethical Analysis*. Washington, DC: Georgetown University Press, 2002.

———. *The Development of Moral Theology: Five Strands*. Washington, DC: Georgetown University Press, 2013.

———. *Tradition and Church Reform: Perspectives on Catholic Moral Teaching*. Maryknoll, NY: Orbis, 2015.

Davidson, Donald. *Essays on Actions and Events*. Oxford: Clarendon, 1980.

———. *Inquiries into Truth and Interpretation*. Oxford: Clarendon, 1984.

———. "Reply to Essays I–X." In *Essays on Davidson: Actions and Events,* edited by Bruce Vermazen and Merrill B. Hintikka, 195–229. Oxford: Oxford University Press, 1985.

Daye, Russell. *Political Forgiveness: Lessons from South Africa.* Maryknoll, NY: Orbis, 2004.

Deacon, Terrence. *Incomplete Nature: How Mind Emerged from Matter.* New York: W. W. Norton, 2011.

Deane-Drummond, Celia. *The Ethics of Nature.* Malden, MA: Blackwell, 2004.

———. "Experience Wonder and Seeking Wisdom." *Zygon* 42, no. 3 (2007): 587–90.

———. *Wonder and Wisdom: Conversations in Science, Spirituality, and Theology.* West Conshohocken, PA: Templeton Foundation, 2006.

DeBerri, Edward P., James E. Hug, Peter J. Henriot, and Michael J. Schultheis. *Catholic Social Teaching: Our Best Kept Secret.* 4th rev. ed. Maryknoll, NY: Orbis, 2003.

Dedek, John F. "Intrinsically Evil Acts: An Historical Study of the Mind of St. Thomas." *The Thomist* 43 (1979): 385–413.

———. "Moral Absolutes in the Predecessors of St. Thomas." *Theological Studies* 38 (1977): 654–80.

———. "Premarital Sex: The Theological Argument from Peter Lombard to Durand." *Theological Studies* 41 (1980): 643–67.

de Gruchy, John W. *Christianity, Art and Transformation: Theological Aesthetics in the Struggle for Justice.* Cambridge: Cambridge University Press, 2001.

———. "The Dialectic of Reconciliation." In *The Reconciliation of Peoples: Challenge to the Churches,* edited by Harold Wells and Gregory Baum, 16–29. Eugene, OR: Wipf & Stock, 1997.

———. *Reconciliation: Restoring Justice.* Minneapolis: Fortress, 2002.

d'Entrèves, A. P. *Natural Law.* London: Hutchinson, 1951.

Derrida, Jacques. *Adieu to Emmanuel Lévinas.* Translated by Pascale-Anne Brault and Michael Naas. Stanford, CA: Stanford University Press, 1999.

———. *Demeure: Maurice Blanchot.* Paris: Galilée, 1988.

———. "Des Tours de Babel." In *Difference in Translation,* edited by Joseph F. Graham, 165–207. Ithaca, NY: Cornell University Press, 1985.

———. *Foi et Savoir suivi de le Siècle et le Pardon.* Interviews with Michel Wieviorka. Paris: Suil, 2000.

———. "Force of Law: The Mystical Foundation of Authority." In *Deconstruction and the Possibility of Justice,* edited by Drucilla Cornell et al., 3–67. New York: Routledge, 1992.

———. "Pardonneer: l'impardonable et l'imprescritible." *Cahier de L'Herne Derrida.* Paris: Éditions de L'Herne, 2004.

Derrida, Jacques, and Maurizio Ferraris. *A Taste for the Secret.* Edited by Giacomo Donis and David Webb. Translated by Giacomo Donis. London: Polity, 2001.

Destexhe, Alain. *Rwanda and Genocide in the Twentieth Century.* Translated by Alison Marschner. New York: New York University Press, 1995.

Doak, Mary. "The Politics of Radical Orthodoxy." *Theological Studies* 63, no. 2 (2007): 368–93.

Dodd, Charles Harold. *The Parables of the Kingdom.* London: Religious Book Club, 1942.

Dombrowski, Daniel A. *Rawls and Religion: The Case for Political Liberalism.* New York: SUNY Press, 2001.

Donahue, John. "The Bible and Catholic Social Teaching: Will This Engagement Lead to Marriage?" In *Modern Catholic Social Teaching: Commentaries and Interpretations,* edited by Kenneth R. Himes, 9–40. Washington, DC: Georgetown University Press, 2004.

———. *The Gospel in Parable: Metaphor, Narrative, and Theology in the Synoptic Gospels.* Philadelphia: Fortress, 1988.

———. "Who Is My Enemy? The Parable of the Good Samaritan and the Love of Enemies." In *The Love of Enemy and Nonretaliation in the New Testament,* edited by Willard M. Swartley, 137–56. Louisville, KY: Westminster/John Knox, 1992.

Donne, John. *John Donne: The Complete English Poems.* Edited by A. J. Smith. New York: Penguin, 1976.

Donnelly, Jack. *Universal Human Rights in Theory and Practice.* 3rd. ed. Ithaca, NY: Cornell University Press, 2001.

Drèze, Jean, and Amartya Sen. *Hunger and Public Action.* Oxford: Clarendon, 1989.

Duff, Anthony R. *Punishment, Communication, and Community.* New York: Oxford University Press, 2001.

Dummett, Michael. *On Immigration and Refugees.* London: Routledge, 2001.

Dupré, Louis. "The Common Good and the Open Society." *Review of Politics* 55, no. 4 (Fall 1993): 687–712.

———. *The Enlightenment and the Intellectual Foundations of Modern Culture.* New Haven, CT: Yale University Press, 2004.

———. *Marx's Social Critique of Culture.* New Haven, CT: Yale University Press, 1983.

———. "On the Intellectual Sources of Modern Atheism." *International Journal for Philosophy of Religion* 45, no. 1 (1999): 1–11.

du Toit, André. "Basic Purposes and Justifications." In *Truth Commissions: A Comparative Assessment,* edited by Henry J. Steiner, 20–21. Cambridge, MA: Harvard Law School Human Rights Program and World Peace Foundation, 1997.

———. "Human Rights Program." In *Truth Commissions: A Comparative Assessment,* edited by Henry J. Steiner, 7–13 . Cambridge, MA: Harvard Law School Human Rights Program and World Peace Foundation, 1997.

———. "The Moral Foundations of the South African TRC: Truth as Acknowledgment and Justice as Recognition." In *Truth v. Justice: The Morality of Truth Commissions,* edited by Robert Rothberg and Dennis Thompson, 122–40. Princeton, NJ: Princeton University Press, 2000.

Dworkin, Ronald. "Liberalism." In *Liberalism and Its Critics,* edited by Michael Sandel, 60–79. New York: New York University Press, 1984.

———. *Taking Rights Seriously.* Cambridge, MA: Harvard University Press, 1978.

Eagleson, John, and Philip Scharper, eds. *Puebla and Beyond: Documentation and Commentary.* Maryknoll, NY: Orbis, 1979.

Eaglestone, Robert. *The Holocaust and the Postmodern.* Oxford: Oxford University Press, 2004.

———. "Identification and the Genre of Testimony, Immigrants, and Minorities." *Immigrants and Minorities: Historical Studies in Ethnicity, Migration and Diaspora* 21, no. 1–2 (2002): 117–40. DOI: 10.1080/02619288.2002.9975035.

Éla, Jean-Marc. "Christianity and Liberation in Africa." In *Paths of African Theology,* edited by Rosino Gibellini, 136–53. Maryknoll, NY: Orbis, 1994.

———. "*La Foi des pauvres en acte.*" *Telema* 35 (July–September 1983): 45–72.

———. *Le Cri de l'homme africain.* Paris: Harmattan, 1980.

Eliot, T. S. *The Complete Poems and Plays: 1909–1950.* New York: Harcourt, Brace & World, 1962.

———. *Criticism: The Major Texts.* Edited by Walter Jackson Bate. New York: Harcourt, Brace and World, 1952.

Ellison, Ralph. *The Collected Essays of Ralph Ellison*. Edited by John F. Callahan. New York: Modern Library, 1994.

———. *Invisible Man*. New York: Random House, 1992.

Endres, John. "Cry Out to God in Our Need: Psalms of Lament." *The Way Supplement* 87 (Autumn 1996): 34–44.

Feinberg, Joel. *Doing and Deserving*. Princeton, NJ: Princeton University Press, 1970.

———. *Social Philosophy*. Upper Saddle River, NJ: Prentice Hall, 1973.

Feyissa, Abebe, with Rebecca Horn. "There Is More than One Way of Dying: An Ethiopian Perspective on the Effects of Long-Term Stays in Refugee Camps." In *Refugee Rights, Ethics Advocacy, and Africa,* edited by David Hollenbach, SJ, 13–26. Washington, DC: Georgetown University Press, 2008.

Finlayson, James Gordon, and Fabian Freyenhagen, *Habermas and Rawls: Disputing the Political*. New York: Routledge, 2011.

Fitzmyer, Joseph A. *The Gospel according to Luke I–X*. Garden City, NY: Doubleday, 1981.

———. "Pauline Theology." In *The New Jerome Biblical Commentary,* edited by Raymond Brown et al., 1382–1416. Englewood Cliffs, NJ: Prentice Hall, 1990.

Foot, Philippa. *Virtues and Vices*. Oxford: Basil Blackwell, 1978.

Frankfurt, Harry. *The Importance of What We Care About*. Cambridge: Cambridge University Press, 1988.

Freeman, Michael. *Human Rights: An Interdisciplinary Approach*. 2nd ed. Cambridge, UK: Polity, 2011.

Friedlander, Saul. "Trauma, Memory, and Transference." In *Holocaust Remembrance: The Shapes of Memory,* edited by Geoffrey H. Hartman, 252–63. Oxford: Blackwell, 1994.

Friedman, Milton. "Good Ends, Bad Means." In *The Catholic Challenge to the American Economy,* edited by Thomas M. Gannon, SJ, 99–106. New York: Macmillan, 1987.

Gadamer, Hans-Georg. *Philosophical Hermeneutics*. Translated by David E. Linge. Berkeley: University of California Press, 1976.

———. *Reason in the Age of Science*. Translated by Frederick G. Lawrence. Cambridge, MA: MIT Press, 1981.

———. "Text and Interpretation." In *Dialogue and Deconstruction: The Gadamer-Derrida Encounter,* edited by Diane P. Michelfelder and Richard E. Palmer, 21–51. Albany: State University of New York, 1989.

———. *Truth and Method*. 2nd rev. ed. Translated by Joel Weinsheimer and Donald G. Marshall. New York: Crossroad, 1989.

Gallagher, Susan Van Zanten. *Truth and Reconciliation: The Confessional Mode in South African Literature*. Portsmouth, NH: Heinemann, 2002.

Galloy, Martine, ed. *Women's Bodies as a Battleground: Sexual Violence against Women and Girls in the Democratic Republic of the Congo—South Kivu (1996–2003)*. London: International Alert, 2005. https://repositories.lib.utexas.edu/bitstream/handle/2152/4949/4053.pdf, accessed August 31, 2017.

Gammeltoft-Hansen, Thomas, and Nikolas F. Tan. "The End of the Deterrence Paradigm? Future Directions for Global Refugee Policy." *Journal on Migration and Human Security* 5, no. 1 (2017): 28–56.

Gavrielides, Theo. "Some Meta-Theoretical Questions for Restorative Justice." *Ratio Juris* 18 (2005): 82–106.

Geertz, Clifford. *The Interpretation of Cultures*. New York: Basic, 1973.

———. *Islam Observed: Religious Development in Morocco and Indonesia.* Chicago: University of Chicago, 1973.

Gewirth, Alan. *The Community of Rights.* Chicago: University of Chicago Press, 1996.

———. *Human Rights: Essays on Justification and Application.* Chicago: University of Chicago Press, 1982.

———. *Reason and Morality.* Chicago: University of Chicago Press, 1978.

Gibellini, Rosino, ed. *Paths of African Theology.* Maryknoll, NY: Orbis, 1994.

Gibney, Mark. *Strangers or Friends: Principles for a New Alien Admission Policy.* New York: Greenwood, 1986.

Giddens, Anthony. *New Rules of Sociological Method.* London: Hutchinson, 1976.

Glendon, Mary Ann. *Rights Talk: The Impoverishment of Political Discourse.* New York: Simon & Schuster, 1991.

———. *A World Made New: Eleanor Roosevelt and the Universal Declaration of Human Rights.* New York: Random House, 2001.

Gobodo-Madikizela, Pumla. *A Human Being Died That Night: A South African Woman Confronts the Legacy of Apartheid.* Boston: Houghton Mifflin, 2003.

Godwin-Gil, Guy S. *The Refugee in International Law.* 2nd ed. Oxford: Clarendon, 1966.

Gopnik, Adam. "The Caging of America." *New Yorker* 87, no. 46 (January 30, 2012): 73.

Gourevitch, Philip. *We Wish to Inform You That Tomorrow We Will Be Killed with Our Families: Stories from Rwanda.* New York: Farrar, Straus and Giroux, 1998.

Grabe, Shelly, ed. *Women's Human Rights: A Social Psychological Perspective on Resistance, Liberation, and Justice.* New York: Oxford University Press, 2018.

Gramsci, Antonio. *Selections from the Prison Notebooks.* Translated by Quentin Hoare and Geoffrey Nowell Smith. New York: International Publishers, 1971.

Gray, John. *Enlightenment's Wake.* London: Routledge, 1995.

Greenawalt, Kent. *Religious Conviction and Political Choice.* New York: Oxford University, 1988.

Greene, Graham. *The Portable Graham Greene.* Edited by Philip Stratford. New York: Viking, 1973.

Griffin, James. *On Human Rights.* Oxford: Oxford University Press, 2008.

Grotius, Hugo. *Prolegomena to the Law of War and Peace.* Translated by Francis W. Kelsey. Indianapolis, IN: Bobbs-Merrill Company, 1955.

Guichaoua, André. *From War to Genocide: Criminal Politics in Rwanda, 1990–1994.* Translated by Don E. Webster. Madison: University of Wisconsin Press, 2015.

Gustafson, James. *Theology and Christian Ethics.* Philadelphia: United Church, 1974.

Gutiérrez, Gustavo. *A Theology of Liberation: 15th Anniversary Edition.* Translated by Sister Caridad Inda and John Eagleson. Maryknoll, NY: Orbis, 1988.

———. "Toward a Theology of Liberation." In *Liberation Theology: A Documentary History,* edited and translated by Alfred T. Hennelly, 62–76. Maryknoll, NY: Orbis, 1990.

———. *We Drink from Our Own Wells: The Spiritual Journey of a People.* Translated by Matthew J. O'Connell. Maryknoll, NY: Orbis, 1984.

Habermas, Jürgen. *An Awareness of What Is Missing: Faith and Reason in a Post-Secular Age.* Translated by Ciaran Cronin. Cambridge: Polity, 2010.

———. *Between Facts and Norms: Contributions to a Discourse Theory of Law and Democracy.* Translated by William Rehg. Cambridge, MA: MIT Press, 1996.

———. "The Concept of Human Dignity and the Realistic Utopia of Human Rights." *Metaphilosophy* 41, no. 4 (July 2010): 464–80.

———. *Die neue Unübersichlichkeit.* Frankfurt am Main: Suhrkamp, 1985.

———. *Eine Art Schadensabwicklung.* Frankfurt: Suhrkamp, 1987.

———. "The Hermeneutic Claim to Universality." In *Contemporary Hermeneutics: Hermeneutics as Method, Philosophy, and* Critique, edited by Josef Bleicher, 181–211. London: Routledge and Kegan Paul, 1980.

———. "Israel or Athens: Where Does Anamnestic Reason Belong?" Translated by Peter Davis. In *Religion and Rationality: Essays on Reason, God, and Modernity,* edited by Roberto Mendieta, 129–38. Cornwall, UK: Polity, 2002.

———. *Justification and Application: Remarks on Discourse Ethics.* Translated by Ciaran Cronin. Cambridge, MA: MIT Press, 1993.

———. *Legitimation Crisis.* Translated by Thomas McCarthy. Boston: Beacon, 1975.

———. *Moral Consciousness and Communicative Action.* Translated by Christian Lenhardt and Shierry Weber Nicholsen. Cambridge: MIT Press, 1990.

———. *The New Conservatism: Cultural Criticism and the Historians' Debate.* Edited by Shierry Weber Nicholsen. Cambridge, MA: MIT Press, 1991.

———. "Plea for a Constitutionalization of International Law." *Philosophy and Social Criticism* 40 (2014): 5–12.

———. "The Political: The Rational Meaning of a Questionable Inheritance of Political Theology." In *The Power of Religion in the Public Sphere,* edited by Eduardo Mendieta and Jonathan VanAntwerpen, 15–33. New York: Colombia University Press, 2011.

———. *The Postnational Constellation: Political Essays.* Translated by Max Pensky. Cambridge, MA: MIT Press, 2001.

———. *Religion and Rationality: Essays on Reason, God, and Modernity.* Cambridge, MA: MIT Press, 2002.

———. "A Reply to My Critics." In *Habermas: Critical Debates,* edited by John B. Thompson and David Held, 219–83. Cambridge: MIT Press, 1982.

———. "Reply to My Critics." Translated by Ciarin Cronin. In *Habermas and Religion,* edited by Craig Calhoun, Eduardo Mendieta, and Jonathan VanAntwerpen, 347–90. London: Polity, 2013.

———. "A Review of Gadamer's *Truth and Method.*" In *Understanding and Social Inquiry,* edited by Fred R. Dallmayr and Thomas A. McCarthy, 335–63. Notre Dame, IN: University of Notre Dame Press, 1977.

———. *The Theory of Communicative Action,* vol. 1, *Reason and the Rationalization of Society.* Translated by Thomas McCarthy. Boston: Beacon, 1984.

———. *The Theory of Communicative Action,* vol. 2, *Lifeworld and System: A Critique of Functionalist Reason.* Translated by Thomas McCarthy. Boston: Beacon, 1987.

———. *Zwischen Naturalismus und Religion.* Frankfurt: Suhrkamp, 2005.

Habermas, Jürgen, and Joseph Ratzinger. *The Dialectics of Secularization: On Reason and Religion.* Translated by Brian McNeil. San Francisco: Ignatius, 2006.

Hacking, Ian. *Rationality and Relativism.* Cambridge, MA: MIT Press, 1982.

Hare, R. M. *Moral Thinking.* Oxford: Oxford University Press, 1963.

———. "Rawls' Theory of Justice." In *Reading Rawls: Critical Studies on Rawls' "A Theory of Justice,"* edited by Norman Daniels, 81–107. New York: Basic, 1975.

Hart, H. L. A. "Are There Any Natural Rights?" *Philosophical Review* 64, no. 2 (April 1955): 175–91.

Hathaway, James C. *The Rights of Refugees in International Law.* Cambridge: Cambridge University Press, 2005.

Hatzfeld, Jean. *Life Laid Bare: The Survivors in Rwanda Speak.* Translated by Linda Coverdale. New York: Other Press, 2000.

Hauerwas, Stanley. *The Peaceable Kingdom.* Notre Dame, IN: University of Notre Dame Press, 1983.

Hayner, Patricia B. *Unspeakable Truths: Transitional Justice and the Challenge of Truth Commissions.* 2nd ed. New York: Routledge, 2011.

Hegel, G. F. *Philosophy of Right (Hegel's Philosophy of Right).* Translated by T. M. Knox. Oxford: Oxford University Press, 1952.

Hehir, J. Brian. "The Modern Catholic Church and Human Rights: The Impact of the Second Vatican Council." In *Christianity and Human Rights,* edited by John Witte and Frank S. Alexander, 113–34. Cambridge: Cambridge University Press, 2010.

Held, David. "Law of States, Law of Peoples." *Legal Theory* 8 (2002): 1–44.

Hempel, Carl G. "Inductive Inconsistencies." *Synthese* 12, no. 4 (1960): 439–69.

Heyer, Kristin E. *Kinship across Borders: A Christian Ethic of Immigration.* Washington, DC: Georgetown University Press, 2012.

Hinga, Teresa M. "Jesus Christ and the Liberation of Women in Africa." In *Feminist Theology from the Third World,* edited by Ursula King, 261–70. Maryknoll, NY: Orbis, 1994.

Hobbes, Thomas. *Leviathan or The Matter, Forme, and Power of a Common-Wealth Ecclesiasticall and Civill.* London: Arthur Crooke, 1651.

Hochschild, Adam. *King Leopold's Ghost: A Story of Greed, Terror, and Heroism in Colonial Africa.* New York: Mariner, 1998.

Hogan, Linda. *Keeping Faith with Human Rights.* Washington, DC: Georgetown University Press, 2015.

Hohfeld, Wesley. *Fundamental Legal Conceptions.* New Haven, CT: Yale University Press, 1923.

Holkeboer, Mieke. "Out of the Crooked Timber of Humanity: Humanising Rights in South Africa." In *To Repair the Irreparable: Reparation and Reconstruction in South Africa,* edited by E. Doxtader and C. Villa-Vicencio, 149–65. Cape Town, South Africa: David Philip, 2004.

Hollenbach, David. *The Common Good and Christian Ethics.* Cambridge: Cambridge University Press, 2002.

———. "A Communitarian Reconstruction of Human Rights: Contributions from Catholic Tradition." In *Catholicism and Liberalism: Contributions to American Public Philosophy,* edited by R. Bruce Douglass and David Hollenbach, 127–50. Cambridge: Cambridge University Press, 1994.

———. *The Global Face of Public Faith: Politics, Human Rights, and Christian Ethics.* Washington, DC: Georgetown University Press, 2003.

———. *Humanity in Crisis: Ethical and Religious Response to Refugees.* Washington, DC: Georgetown University Press, 2019.

Hoogvliet, Gerbrand. "Preventing Rwanda in a Rawlsian World." *Macalester Journal of Philosophy* 19, no. 1 (2010).

Hopgood, Stephen. *The Endtimes of Human Rights.* Ithaca, NY: Cornell University Press, 2013.

Hopkins, Gerard Manley. *The Poems of Gerard Manley Hopkins.* 4th ed. Edited by W. H. Gardner and H. M. MacKenzie. New York: Oxford University Press, 1970.

Horkheimer, Max. *Critical Theory: Selected Essays.* New York: Seabury, 1972.

Hountondji, Paulin J. "The Master's Voice—Remarks on the Problem of Human Rights in Africa." In *Philosophical Foundations of Human Rights.* Introduced by Paul Ricoeur. Paris: UNESCO and International Institute of Philosophy, 1986.

Human Rights First. Freedom for Detained Refugees Project. https://www.humanrightsfirst.org/campaigns/freedom-for-detained-refugees-project, accessed July 17, 2019.

———. "Human Trafficking." https://www.humanrightsfirst.org/topics/human-trafficking, accessed July 24, 2019.

———. "Immigration Detention." https://www.humanrightsfirst.org/topics/immigration-detention, accessed July 17, 2019.

———. "O.A. v. Trump: Challenging the Asylum Ban." https://www.humanrightsfirst.org/resource/oa-v-trump-challenging-asylum-ban, accessed July 17, 2019.

Human Rights Watch. *Leave None to Tell the Story.* New York: Human Rights Watch, 1999.

Human Security Report 2009/2010. Oxford: Oxford University Press, 2010.

Hume, David. *An Inquiry concerning the Principles of Morals.* Edited by Charles W. Hendel. New York: Macmillan, 1957.

———. "A Treatise of Human Nature, Book 2, Part 3." In *British Moralists: 1650–1800*. Vol. 2. Edited by D. D. Raphael. Oxford: Clarendon, 1969.

Hunt, Lynn. *Inventing Human Rights: A History.* New York: W. W. Norton, 2007.

Ignatieff, Michael. *Human Rights as Politics and Idolatry.* Princeton, NJ: Princeton University Press, 2005.

Ignatius of Loyola. *The Spiritual Exercises of St. Ignatius*. Translated by George E. Ganss, SJ. St. Louis, MO: Institute of Jesuit Sources, 1992.

Ilesanmi, Simeon O. "Civil-Political Rights or Social Economic Rights for Africa? A Comparative Ethical Critique of a False Dichotomy." *Annual of the Society of Christian Ethics* 17 (1997): 191–212.

———. "Human Rights Discourse in Modern Africa: A Comparative Religious Ethical Perspective." *Journal of Religious Ethics* 23 (1995): 309–16.

Ingram, David. "Mediating the Theory and Practice of Human Rights in Morality and Law." In *Moral and Political Conceptions of Human Rights: Implications for Theory and Practice,* edited by Reidar Maliks and Johan Karlsson Schaffer, 97–124. Cambridge: Cambridge University Press, 2017.

International Organization for Migration (IOM). Missing Migrants Project. 2016. http://missingmigrants.iom.int.

International Panel on Climate Change. "Climate Change 2014: Impacts, Adaptation, and Vulnerability, Part A: Global and Sectoral Aspects. Contribution of Working Group II." In *Fifth Assessment Report of the Intergovernmental Panel on Climate Change,* edited by C. B. Field, V. R. Barros, D. J. Dokken, K. J. Mach, M. D. Mastrandrea, T. E. Bilir, M. Chatterjee, K. L. Ebi, Y. O. Estrada, R. C. Genova et al., 1–32. Cambridge: Cambridge University Press, 2014. https://www.ipcc.ch/site/assets/uploads/2018/02/ar5_wgII_spm_en.pdf.

Isasi-Díaz, Ada Maria. *En la Lucha / In the Struggle: A Hispanic Women's Liberation Theology.* Minneapolis: Fortress, 1993.

Ishay, Micheline R. *The History of Human Rights: From Ancient Times to the Globalization Era.* Berkeley: University of California Press, 2004.

James, William. *Pragmatism: A New Name for Some Old Ways of Thinking.* Edited by Fredson Bowers. Cambridge, MA: Harvard University Press, 1975.

Johnstone, Gerry. *Restorative Justice: Ideas, Values, Debates.* Portland, OR: Willan, 2002.

———, ed. *A Restorative Justice Reader*. 2nd. ed. New York: Routledge, 2013.

Johnstone, Gerry, and Daniel W. Van Ness, eds. *Handbook of Restorative Justice.* Portland, OR: Willan, 2007.

Jones, L. Gregory. *Embodying Forgiveness: A Theological Analysis*. Grand Rapids, MI: Eerdmans, 1995.

Junker-Kenny, Maureen. *Habermas and Theology*. New York: T & T Clark, 2011.

———. "The Pre-Political Foundations of the State." In *The New Pontificate: A Time for Change?* edited by Erik Borgman, Maureen Junker-Kenny, and Janet Martin Soskice, 106–17. London: SCM, 2006.

Kant, Immanuel. *Critique of Practical Reason*. Translated by Lewis White Beck. Indianapolis: Bobbs-Merrill, 1956.

———. "What Is Enlightenment." In *The Enlightenment: A Comprehensive Anthology*. Translated by Peter Gay. New York: Simon and Schuster, 1973.

———. *Groundwork of the Metaphysic of Morals*. Translated by H. J. Paton. New York: Harper & Row, 1964.

———. *The Metaphysical Elements of Justice: Part I of the Metaphysics of Morals*. Translated by John Ladd. Indianapolis: Bobbs-Merrill, 1965.

———. *Perpetual Peace, and Other Essays on Politics, History, and Morals*. Translated by Ted Humphrey. Indianapolis: Hackett, 1983.

———. *Religion within the Limits of Reason Alone*. Translated by Theodore M. Greene and Hoyt H. Hudson. New York: Harper & Row, 1960.

Karegeye, Jean-Pierre, and Faustin Rutembesa, eds. *L'Eglise Catholique à l'épreuve du génocide*. Montreal-Butare: Africana-Presses Universitaires du Rwanda, 2000.

Karekezi, Alice, Alphonse Nshimiyimana, and Beth Mutamba. "Localizing Justice: Gacaca Courts in Post-Genocide Rwanda." In *My Neighbor, My Enemy: Justice and Community in the Aftermath of Mass Atrocity*, edited by Eric Stover and Harvey M. Weinstein, 69–84. Cambridge: Cambridge University Press, 2004.

Karekezi, Augustin. "In Memory of the Victims of the Genocide in Rwanda." Mimeograph of address presented in Kigali, Rwanda, April 12, 1995.

Karris, Robert J. "The Gospel according to Luke." In *The New Jerome Biblical Commentary*, edited by Raymond Brown, Joseph Fitzmyer, and Roland Murphy, 675–72. Englewood Cliffs, NJ: Prentice Hall, 1990.

Käsemann, Ernst. *New Testament Questions of Today*. London: SCM, 1969.

Katongole, Emmanuel. *Born from Lament: The Theology and Politics of Hope in Africa*. Grand Rapids, MI: Eerdmans, 2017.

Katongole, Emmanuel, and Jonathan Wilson-Hertgrove. *Mirror to the Church: Resurrecting Faith after Genocide in Rwanda*. Grand Rapids, MI: Zondervan, 2009.

Kaveny, M. Cathleen. "Appropriation of Evil: Cooperation's Mirror Image." *Theological Studies* 61 (2000): 280–313.

———. *Law's Virtues: Fostering Autonomy and Solidarity in American Society*. Washington, DC: Georgetown University Press, 2012.

Keane, Fergal. *Season of Blood: A Rwandan Journey*. London: Penguin, 1995.

Kierkegaard, Søren. *Fear and Trembling*. Translated by Howard V. Hong and Edna H. Hong. Princeton, NJ: Princeton University Press, 1962.

———. *Works of Love*. Translated by Howard and Edna Hong. New York: Harper & Brothers, 1983.

Kigali Genocide Memorial. *We Survived Genocide in Rwanda*. Edited by Wendy Whitworth. Nottinghamshire, UK: Quill, 2006.

King, Martin Luther. "Journey of Conscience." Unpublished handwritten preliminary draft of "Beyond Vietnam" speech. In *The Autobiography of Martin Luther King, Jr.*, edited by Clayborne Carson. New York: Warner, 1998.

———. *A Testament of Hope: The Essential Writings of Martin Luther King, Jr.* Edited by James Melvin Washington. San Francisco: Harper & Row, 1986.

Kneale, Martha, and William Kneale. *The Development of Logic*. Oxford: Clarendon, 1962.

Koenig, John. "Hospitality." In *The Anchor Bible Dictionary*, vol. 3, edited by David Noel Freedman, 299–301. New York: Doubleday, 1992.

Körner, Stephan. *Kant*. Harmondsworth, UK: Penguin, 1955.

Kristeva, Julia. *Revolution in Poetic Language*. New York: Columbia University, 1984.

Krog, Antjie. *Country of My Skull*. Johannesburg, South Africa: Random House, 1998.

Küng, Hans, ed. *Yes to a Global Ethic*. New York: Continuum, 1996.

Lang, Berel. *Philosophical Witnessing: The Holocaust as Presence*. Waltham, MA: Brandeis University Press, 2009.

Langan, John. *Human Rights in the Americas: The Struggle for Consensus*. Washington, DC: Georgetown University Press, 1982.

Langer, Lawrence L. *Holocaust Testimonies: The Ruins of Memory*. New Haven, CT: Yale University Press, 1991.

Lemkin, Raphaël. *Axis Rule in Occupied Europe*. Washington, DC: Carnegie Endowment for International Peace, 1944.

Lenhardt, Christian. "Anamnestic Solidarity: The Proletariat and Its Manes." *Telos* 25 (September 21, 1975): 133–54.

Levi, Primo. *The Drowned and the Saved*. Translated by Raymond Rosenthal. London: Abacus, 1989.

Lévinas, Emmanuel. *Ethics and Infinity*. Translated by Richard A. Cohen. Pittsburgh, PA: Duquesne University Press, 1985.

Little, David, and Sumner B. Twiss. *Comparative Religious Ethics: A New Method*. San Francisco: Harper & Row, 1978.

Llewellyn, Jennifer, and Daniel Philpott, eds. *Restorative Justice, Reconciliation, and Peacebuilding*. Oxford: Oxford University Press, 2014.

Locke, John. *The Second Treatise of Government*. Edited by Thomas P. Peardon. Indianapolis: Bobbs-Merrill, 1952.

Loescher, Gil. *Beyond Charity: International Co-operation and the Global Refugee Crisis*. New York: Oxford University Press, 2003.

Loescher, Gil, and James Milner. *Protracted Refugee Situations: Domestic and International Security Implications*. London: International Institute for Strategic Studies, 2005.

Lonergan, Bernard. *A Third Collection*. Edited by F. E. Crowe. New York: Paulist, 1985.

Longman, Timothy. "Church Politics and the Genocide in Rwanda." *Journal of Religion in Africa* 31, no. 2 (2001): 163–86.

———. *Memory and Justice in Post-Genocide Rwanda*. Cambridge: Cambridge University Press, 2017.

Longman, Timothy, and Théoneste Rutagengwa. "Religion, Memory, and Violence in Rwanda." In *Religion, Violence, Memory, and Place*, edited by Oran Baruch Stier and J. Shawn Landres, 132–49. Bloomington: Indiana University Press, 2006.

Louw, Dirk. "The African Concept of *Ubuntu* and Restorative Justice." In *Handbook of Restorative Justice*, edited by D. Sullivan and L. Tifft, 161–73. New York: Routledge, 2006.

Lovin, Robin. "Perry, Naturalism, and Religion in Public." *Tulane Law Review* 63 (1989): 1517–39.

Lukes, Steven. "Relativism in Its Place." In *Rationality and Relativism*, edited by Martin Hollis and Steven Lukes, 261–305. Cambridge, MA: MIT Press, 1982.

Lyotard, Jean-François. *The Politics of Human Rights*. Edited by Obrad Savić. London: Verso, 1999.

———. *The Postmodern Condition: A Report on Knowledge*. Translated by G. Bennington and B. Massouri. Minneapolis: University of Minnesota Press, 1984.

MacIntyre, Alasdair. *After Virtue*. 2nd. ed. Notre Dame, IN: University of Notre Dame Press, 1984.

———. "Community, Law, and the Idiom and Rhetoric of Rights." *Listening: Journal of Religion and Culture* 26, no. 2 (Spring 1991): 96–110.

———. *Three Rival Versions of Moral Inquiry*. Notre Dame, IN: University of Notre Dame Press, 1990.

———. *Whose Justice? Which Rationality?* Notre Dame, IN: University of Notre Dame Press, 1988.

Mackie, J. L. *Ethics: Inventing Right and Wrong*. New York: Penguin, 1977.

Magesa, Laurenti. *African Religion*. Maryknoll, NY: Orbis, 1997.

———. "Christ the Liberator and Africa Today." In *Faces of Jesus in Africa*, edited by Robert J. Schreiter, 151–63. Maryknoll, NY: Orbis, 1991.

Mahoney, John. *The Making of Moral Theology: A Study of the Roman Catholic Tradition*. Oxford: Oxford University Press, 1987.

Maliks, Reidar, and Johan Karlsson Schaffer, eds. *Moral and Political Conceptions of Human Rights: Implications for Theory and Practice*. Cambridge: Cambridge University Press, 2017.

Mamdani, Mahmood. "Reconciliation without Justice." *South African Review of Books* 46 (November–December 1996): 3–5.

———. *When Victims Become Killers: Colonialism, Nativism, and the Genocide in Rwanda*. Princeton, NJ: Princeton University Press, 2001.

Mandela, Nelson. *Long Walk to Freedom: The Autobiography of Nelson Mandela*. Boston: Little, Brown, 1994.

Mandeville, Bernard. *The Fable of the Bees: or, Private Vices, Publick Benefits*. 2 vols. With a Commentary Critical, Historical, and Explanatory by F. B. Kaye. Indianapolis: Liberty Fund, 1988.

Maritain, Jacques. *Human Rights: Comments and Interpretations*. Edited by UNESCO. Paris: UNESCO, 1948.

———. *The Social and the Political Philosophy of Jacques Maritain*. Edited by Joseph W. Evans and Leo R. Ward. New York: Charles Scribner's Sons, 1955.

Martin, Susan. "Justice, Women's Rights, and Forced Migration." In *Refugee Rights, Ethics Advocacy, and Africa*, edited by David Hollenbach, SJ, 137–60. Washington, DC: Georgetown University Press, 2008.

Marx, Karl. *The Marx-Engels Reader*. Edited by Robert Tucker. New York: W. W. Norton, 1978.

———. "Preface to *A Contribution to the Critique of Political Economy*." Translated by Victor Schnittke. In *Karl Marx and Frederick Engels: Collected Works* 29, edited by Eric Hobsbawm, John Hoffman, Nicholas Jacobs, Monty Johnstone, Martin Milligan, Jeff Skelley, and Ernst Wangermann, 261–65. London: Lawrence and Wishart, 1987.

Massingale, Bryan. *Racial Justice and the Catholic Church*. Maryknoll, NY: Orbis, 2010.

McCarthy, Thomas. *Ideals and Illusions: On Reconstruction and Deconstruction in Contemporary Critical Theory*. Cambridge, MA: MIT Press, 1991.

McCullough, Michael E., Kenneth I. Pargament, and Carl E. Thoresen, eds. *Forgiveness: Theory, Research, and Practice*. New York: Guilford, 1999.

Mead, George Herbert. *Mind, Self, and Society from the Standpoint of a Social Behaviorist*. Edited by Charles W. Morris. Chicago: University of Chicago Press, 1962.

Melden, A. I. *Rights and Persons*. Berkeley: University of California Press, 1980.

Mendeloff, David. "Trauma and Vengeance: Assessing the Psychological and Emotional Effects of Post-Conflict Justice." *Human Rights Quarterly* 31 (2009): 592–623.

Metz, Johann-Baptist. *Faith in History and Society: Toward a Practical Fundamental Theology*. New York: Seabury, 1980.

———. *Memoria Passionis: Ein provozierendes Gedächnis in pluralistisher Gesellschaft*. Freiberg, Germany: Herder, 2006.

Milbank, John. *Theology and Social Theory: Beyond Secular Reason*. Malden, MA: Blackwell, 1990.

Milbank, John, Catherine Pickstock, and Graham Ward, eds. *Radical Orthodoxy: A New Theology*. New York: Routledge, 1999.

Minogue, K. R. "Natural Rights, Ideology and the Game of Life." In *Human Rights*, edited by Eugene Kamenka and Alice Ehr-Soon Tay, 13–35. New York: St. Martin's, 1978.

Minow, Martha. *Between Vengeance and Forgiveness: Facing History after Genocide and Mass Violence*. Boston: Beacon, 1998.

Moberly, Walter H. *The Ethics of Punishment*. London: Faber & Faber, 1968.

Morris, Rosalind C., ed. *Can the Subaltern Speak? Reflections on the History of an Idea*. New York: Columbia University Press, 2010.

Mulago, Vincent. "Vital Participation." In *Biblical Revelation and African Beliefs*, edited by K. A. Dickson and P. Ellingworth, 137–58. Maryknoll, NY: Orbis, 1969.

Müller, Luise Katharina. "Rawls's Relational Conception of Human Rights." In *Moral and Political Conceptions of Human Rights*, edited by Reidar Maliks and Johan Karlsson Schaffer, 58–76. Cambridge: Cambridge University Press, 2017.

Murphy, Jeffrie G. *Getting Even: Forgiveness and Its Limits*. New York: Oxford University Press, 2004.

Murphy, Jeffrie G., and Jean Hampton. *Forgiveness and Mercy*. Cambridge, MA: Cambridge University Press, 1988.

Murray, John Courtney. "The Bad Arguments Intelligent Men Make." *America* 96 (November 3, 1956): 120–23.

———. *Bridging the Sacred and the Secular: Selected Writings of John Courtney Murray, S.J.* Edited by Leon Hooper. Washington, DC: Georgetown University Press, 1994.

———. Memo to Cushing on Contraception Legislation, 1965. Murray Archives, file 1-43. Woodstock Theological Library, Georgetown University, Washington, DC.

———. *We Hold These Truths: Catholic Reflections on the American Proposition*. New York: Sheed and Ward, 1960.

Musalo, Karen, Jennifer Moore, Richard Boswell, and Annie Daher. *Refugee Law and Policy: A Comparative and International Approach*. 5th ed. Durham, NC: Carolina Academic Press, 2018.

Mutua, Makau. *Human Rights: A Political and Cultural Critique*. Philadelphia: University of Pennsylvania Press, 2002.

———. "Human Rights in Africa: The Limited Promise of Liberalism." *African Studies Review* 51, no. 1 (April 2008): 17–39.

Mveng, Engelbert. "Black African Art as Cosmic Liturgy and Religious Language." In *African Theology en Route: Papers from the Pan-African Conference of Third World Theologians, December 17–23, 1977, Accra, Ghana*, edited by Kofi Appiah-Kobi and Sergio Torres, 137–42. Maryknoll, NY: Orbis, 1977.

———. "Impoverishment and Liberation: A Theological Approach for Africa and the Third World." In *Paths of African Theology*, edited by Rosino Gibellini, 154–65. Maryknoll, NY: Orbis, 1994.

Nasimiyu-Wasike, Anne. "The Missing Voices of Women." In *Catholic Theological Ethics, Past, Present, and Future: The Trento Conference*, edited by James F. Keenan, 107–15. Maryknoll, NY: Orbis, 2011.

National Constituent Assembly of France. *Declaration of the Rights of Man and of the Citizen.* Translated by Thomas Paine. In David G. Richie, *Natural Rights: A Criticism of Some Political and Ethical Conceptions*, 290–94. London: George Allen and Unwin, 1916.

Nazianzen, Gregory. *Oration on Holy Baptism*, series 2, vol. 7 of *Nicene and Post Nicene Fathers*, 360–77. Grand Rapids, MI: Eerdmans, 1983.

Niebuhr, Reinhold. *Interpretation of Christian Ethics*. New York: Harper, 1935.

Noonan, John T. *A Church That Can and Cannot Change: The Development of Catholic Moral Teaching*. Notre Dame, IN: University of Notre Dame Press, 2005.

———. "Development in Moral Doctrine." *Theological Studies* 54 (December 1993): 662–67.

Nowrojee, Binaifer. "Sexual Violence, Gender Roles, and Displacement." In *Refugee Rights, Ethics Advocacy, and Africa*, edited by David Hollenbach, SJ, 125–36. Washington, DC: Georgetown University Press, 2008.

Nozick, Robert. *Anarchy, State, and Utopia*. Oxford: Basil Blackwell, 1974.

Nussbaum, Martha C. "Beyond the Social Contract: Toward Global Justice." The Tanner Lectures on Human Values. https://tannerlectures.utah.edu/_documents/a-to-z/n/nussbaum_2003.pdf.

———. *Cultivating Humanity: A Classical Defense of Reform in Liberal Education*. Cambridge, MA: Harvard University Press, 1997.

———. "Emotions and Women's Capabilities." In *Women, Culture, and Development: A Study of Human Capabilities*, edited by Martha C. Nussbaum and Jonathan Glover, 364–98. Oxford: Clarendon, 1995.

———. "Human Capabilities." In *Women, Culture, and Development: A Study of Human Capabilities*, edited by Martha C. Nussbaum and Jonathan Glover, 61–104. Oxford: Clarendon, 1995.

———. *Women and Human Development: The Capabilities Approach*. Cambridge: Cambridge University Press, 2000.

Nussbaum, Martha C., and Jonathan Glover, eds. *Women, Culture, and Development: A Study of Human Capabilities*. Oxford: Clarendon, 1995.

Nyerere, Julius. *Freedom and Development (Uhuru Na Maendeleo): A Selection from the Writings and Speeches, 1968–1973*. Oxford: Oxford University Press, 1974.

———. *Freedom and Socialism (Uhuru na Ujamaa): A Selection from Writings and Speeches, 1965–1967*. Oxford: Oxford University Press, 1968.

———. *Freedom and Unity (Uhuru na Umoja): A Selection from Writings and Speeches, 1952–1965*. Oxford: Oxford University Press, 1966.

———. *Man and Development (Binadamu na Maendeleo)*. Oxford: Oxford University Press, 1974.

———. *Ujamaa: Essays on Socialism*. Oxford: Oxford University Press, 1974.

O'Brien, David J., and Thomas A. Shannon, eds. *Catholic Social Thought: The Documentary Heritage*. Maryknoll, NY: Orbis, 2010.

Oduyoye, Mercy Amba. "Christian Feminism and African Culture: The 'Hearth' of the Matter." In *The Future of Liberation Theology: Essays in Honor of Gustavo Gutiérrez*, edited by Marc H. Ellis and Otto Maduro, 441–49. Maryknoll, NY: Orbis, 1989.

———. *Daughters of Anowa: African Women and Patriarchy*. Maryknoll, NY: Orbis, 1995.

———. "Feminist Theology in an African Perspective." In *Paths of African Theology*, edited by Rosino Gibellini, 166–81. Maryknoll, NY: Orbis, 1994.

———. "The Value of African Religious Beliefs and Practices for Christian Theology." In *African Theology en Route: Papers from the Pan-African Conference of Third World Theologians, December 17–23, 1977, Accra, Ghana,* edited by Kofi Appiah-Kobi and Sergio Torres, 109–16. Maryknoll, NY: Orbis, 1977.

Okoth-Ogendo, H. O. W. "Human and Peoples' Rights: What Point Is Africa Trying to Make?" In *Human Rights and Governance in Africa,* edited by Ronald Cohen, Göran S. Hydén, and Winston P. Nagan, 74–86. Gainesville: University Press of Florida, 1993.

Okure, Teresa. "The Will to Arise: Reflections on Luke 8:40–56." In *The Will to Arise: Women, Tradition, and the Church in Africa,* edited by Mercy Amba Oduyoye and Musimbi R. A. Kanyoro, 221–30. Maryknoll, NY: Orbis, 1992.

O'Neill, Onora. "Justice, Capabilities, and Vulnerabilities." In *Women, Culture, and Development: A Study of Human Capabilities,* edited by Martha C. Nussbaum and Jonathan Glover, 140–52. Oxford: Clarendon, 1995.

O'Neill, William, SJ. "'The Bond of Peace': A Hermeneutical Rapprochement?" *Journal of Ecumenical Studies* 51, no. 1 (Winter 2016): 114–27.

———. "The Distinctiveness of Christian Morality: A Dispute Revisited." *Philosophy and Theology* 7 (1993): 405–23.

———. *The Ethics of Our Climate: Hermeneutics and Ethical Theory.* Washington, DC: Georgetown University Press, 1994.

———. "Imagining Otherwise: The Ethics of Social Reconciliation." *Journal of the Society of Christian Ethics* 22 (Fall 2002): 183–99.

———. "No Amnesty for Sorrow: The Privilege of the Poor in Christian Social Ethics." *Theological Studies* 55, no. 4 (December 1994): 638–56.

———. "Rights as Rhetoric: Nonsense on Stilts." *Listening: Journal of Religion and Culture* 26, no. 2 (Spring 1991): 111.

———. "The Wisdom of Serpents: Conscience, Power, and Politics in the Abortion Controversy." In *Conscience and Catholicism: Rights, Responsibilities, and Institutional Responses,* edited by David E. DeCosse and Kristin E. Heyer, 183. Maryknoll, NY: Orbis, 2015.

Opongo, Elias O. "Between Violence, Reconciliation Rituals and Justice in Northern Uganda." In *Practicing Reconciliation, Doing Justice, and Building Peace,* edited by Agbonkhianmeghe E. Orobator, 23–29. Nairobi, Kenya: Paulines, 2013.

Organisation of African Unity (OAU). "Rwanda: The Preventable Genocide." OAU International Personalities, International Panel of Eminent, 2000.

Orobator, Agbonkhianmeghe E., ed. *Practicing Reconciliation, Doing Justice, Building Peace: Conversations on Catholic Theological Ethics in Africa.* Nairobi: Paulines, 2013.

Osiel, Mark. *Mass Atrocity, Collective Memory, and the Law.* New York: Routledge, 1997.

Outka, Gene. *Agape.* New Haven, CT: Yale University Press, 1972.

———. "Universal Love and Impartiality." In *The Love Commandments: Essays in Christian Ethics and Moral Philosophy,* edited by Edmund N. Santurri and William Werpehowski, 1–103. Washington, DC: Georgetown University Press, 1992.

Outka, Gene, and John P. Reeder, eds. "Introduction." In *Prospects for a Common Morality,* edited by Gene Outka and John P. Reeder, 3–28. Princeton, NJ: Princeton University Press, 1993.

Panikkar, Raimon. *The Cosmotheandric Experience: Emerging Religious Consciousness.* Edited by Scott Eastham. Maryknoll, NY: Orbis, 1993.

Paton, H. J. *The Categorical Imperative: A Study in Kant's Moral Philosophy.* Philadelphia: University of Pennsylvania Press, 1948.

p'Bitek, Okot. *African Religions in Western Scholarship*. Kampala, Uganda: East African Literature Bureau, 1970.

Pensky, Max. "On the Use and Abuse of Memory: Habermas, 'Anamnestic Solidarity,' and the Historikerstreit." *Philosophical and Social Criticism* 15, no. 4 (October 1989): 351–80.

———. "Solidarity with the Past and the Work of Translation: Reflections on Memory Politics and the Post-Secular." New York University Institute for Public Knowledge/Social Science Research Council Workshop, October 2009.

Perelman, Chaïm. *The Realm of Rhetoric*. Translated by William Kluback. Notre Dame, IN: University of Notre Dame Press, 1982.

Perelman, Chaïm, and L. Olbrechts-Tyteca. *The New Rhetoric: A Treatise on Argumentation*. Translated by John Wilkinson and Purcell Weaver. Notre Dame, IN: University of Notre Dame Press, 1969.

Pérez Esquivel, Adolfo. "Afterword." In *The International Bill of Rights*, edited by Paul Williams, 105–8. Glen Ellen, CA: Entwistle, 1981.

Perrone-Moisés, Cláudia. "Forgiveness and Crimes against Humanity: A Dialogue between Hannah Arendt and Jacques Derrida." In *Zeitschrift für politische Denken* 1, no. 2 (September 2006). http://www.hannaharendt.net/index.php/han/article/view/90/146.

Perry, Michael J. *The Idea of Human Rights: Four Inquiries*. New York: Oxford University Press, 1998.

———. *Morality, Politics, and Law: A Bicentennial Essay*. New York: Oxford University Press, 1988.

———. *The Role of Religion in American Politics*. New York: Oxford University Press, 1991.

Peukert, Helmut. *Science, Action and Fundamental Theology: Toward a Theology of Communicative Action*. Translated by James Bohman. Cambridge: Cambridge University Press, 1984.

Pew Research Center. Hispanic Trends. https://www.pewhispanic.org/interactives/unauthorized-trends/, accessed July 27, 2019.

Philpott, Daniel. "The Surprise of Forgiveness in Modern Catholic Teaching and Practice." In *The Surprise of Reconciliation in the Catholic Tradition*, edited by J. J. Carney and Laurie Johnston, 288–311. New York: Paulist, 2018.

Plaut, W. Gunther. "Jewish Ethics and International Migrations." *International Migration Review: Ethics, Migration and Global Stewardship* 30 (Spring 1996): 18–36.

Pohl, Christine D. *Making Room: Recovering Hospitality as a Christian Tradition*. Grand Rapids, MI: Eerdmans, 1999.

Pollis, Adamantia, and Peter Schwab. *Human Rights: Cultural and Ideological Perspectives*. New York: Praeger, 1979.

Pope Francis. "*Laudato Si'*: On Care for Our Common Home." http://w2.vatican.va/content/francesco/en/encyclicals/documents/papa-francesco_20150524_enciclica-laudato-si.html.

———. "The Pope on Lampedusa: 'The Globalization of Indifference.'" Homily of July 8, 2013. http://www.news.va/.

Pope Gregory XVI. *Mirari vos arbitramur*. 32nd ed. In *Enchiridion symbolorum*. Edited by H. Denzinger and A. Schönmetzer. Westminster, MD: Christian Classics, 1965.

Pope John XXIII. *Mater et magistra*. http://www.vatican.va/content/john-xxiii/en/encyclicals/documents/hf_j-xxiii_enc_15051961_mater.html.

———. *Pacem in terris*. http://www.vatican.va/content/john-xxiii/en/encyclicals/documents/hf_j-xxiii_enc_11041963_pacem.html.

Pope John Paul II. *Sollicitudo rei socialis*. http://www.vatican.va/content/john-paul-ii/en/encyclicals/documents/hf_jp-ii_enc_30121987_sollicitudo-rei-socialis.html.

———. *Veritatis splendor*. http://www.vatican.va/content/john-paul-ii/en/encyclicals/documents/hf_jp-ii_enc_06081993_veritatis-splendor.html.

Pope Paul VI. *Octogesima adveniens*. http://www.vatican.va/content/paul-vi/en/apost_letters/documents/hf_p-vi_apl_19710514_octogesima-adveniens.html.

———. *Populorum progressio*. http://www.vatican.va/content/paul-vi/en/encyclicals/documents/hf_p-vi_enc_26031967_populorum.html.

Pope Pius XII. Radio Message, Pentecost, June 1, 1941, AAS XX–XIII.

Power, Samantha. *A Problem from Hell: America and the Age of Genocide*. New York: Basic, 2002.

Prunier, Gérard. T. *Africa's World War: Congo, the Rwandan Genocide, and the Making of a Continental Catastrophe*. New York: Oxford University Press, 2008.

———. *The Rwanda Crisis: History of a Genocide*. New York: Columbia University Press, 1995.

Putnam, Hilary. "Pragmatism and Moral Objectivity." In *Women, Culture, and Development: A Study of Human Capabilities*, edited by Martha C. Nussbaum and Jonathan Glover, 99–224. Oxford: Clarendon, 1995.

———. "Why Reason Can't Be Naturalized." In *After Philosophy: End or Transformation?* edited by K. Baynes, J. Bohamn, and T. McCarthy, 217–44. Cambridge, MA: MIT Press, 1987.

Putnam, Robert. "Bowling Alone: America's Declining Social Capital." *Journal of Democracies* 6 (1995): 65–78.

———. "The Prosperous Community: Social Capital and Public Life." *American Prospect* 4 (1993): 35–42.

Quine, Willard Van Orman. *From a Logical Point of View*. 2nd. ed. Cambridge, MA: Harvard University Press, 1961.

———. *Word and Object*. Cambridge, MA: MIT Press, 1960.

Rahner, Karl. *Theological Investigations 2*. Translated by Karl H. Kruger. Baltimore: Helicon, 1963.

———. *Theological Investigations 5*. Translated by Karl H. Kruger. New York: Seabury, 1966.

———. *Theological Investigations 6*. Translated by Karl and Boniface Kruger. New York: Seabury, 1974.

Raitt, Jill, ed. *Christian Spirituality: High Middles Ages and Reformation*. New York: Crossroad, 1997.

Raphael, D. D. "Human Rights." *Aristotelian Society Supplements* 39 (1965): 205–18.

Rawls, John. "Fairness to Goodness." *Philosophical Review* 84, no. 4 (October 1975): 536–54.

———. "The Idea of an Overlapping Consensus." In *Oxford Journal of Legal Studies* 7, no. 1 (Spring 1987): 1–25.

———. *John Rawls: Collected Papers*. Edited by Samuel Freeman. Cambridge, MA: Harvard University Press, 1999.

———. "Kantian Constructivism in Moral Theory." *Journal of Philosophy* 77, no. 9 (1980): 515–72.

———. *The Law of Peoples, with "The Idea of Public Reason Revisited."* Cambridge, MA: Harvard University Press, 1999.

———. *Lectures on the History of Moral Philosophy*. Edited by Barbara Herman. Cambridge, MA: Harvard University Press, 2000.

———. *Political Liberalism*. New York: Columbia University Press, 1993.

———. "Social Unity and Primary Goods." In *Utilitarianism and Beyond*, edited by Bernard Williams and Amartya Sen, 159–86. Cambridge: Cambridge University Press, 1982.

———. *A Theory of Justice*. Rev. ed. Cambridge, MA: Belknap, 1999.

Raz, Joseph. "Human Rights without Foundations." In *The Philosophy of International Law*, edited by Samantha Besson and John Tasioulas, 321–31. New York: Oxford University Press, 2010.

———. *The Morality of Freedom*. Oxford: Clarendon, 1986.

Rehg, William. *Insight and Solidarity: A Study in the Discourse Ethics of Jürgen Habermas*. Berkeley: University of California Press, 1994.

———. "Solidarity and the Common Good: An Analytic Framework." *Journal of Social Philosophy*: 38, no. 1 (April 5, 2007): 7–21.

Ricoeur, Paul. *Hermeneutics and the Human Sciences*. Edited and translated by John B. Thompson. Cambridge: Cambridge University Press, 1981.

———. *History and Truth*. Translated by Charles A. Kelbley. Northwestern University Studies in Phenomenology and Existential Philosophy. Evanston, IL: Northwestern University Press, 1965.

———. *Memory, History, Forgetting*. Translated by Kathleen Blamey and David Pellauer. Chicago: University of Chicago Press, 2004.

———. *Time and Narrative*. Vol. 1. Translated by Kathleen McLaughlin and David Pellauer. Chicago: University of Chicago Press, 1984.

Rilke, Rainer Maria. *Selected Poems of Rainer Maria Rilke*. Translated by Robert Bly. New York: Harper & Row, 1981.

Rorty, Richard. *Consequences of Pragmatism*. Minneapolis: University of Minnesota Press, 1982.

———. *Contingency, Irony and Solidarity*. Cambridge: Cambridge: Cambridge University Press, 1989.

———. "From Logic to Language to Play." *Proceedings and Addresses of the American Philosophical Association* 59 (1986): 747–53.

———. "Human Rights, Rationality and Sentimentality." In *The Politics of Human Rights*, edited by Obrad Savić, 67–83. London: Verso, 1999.

———. *Philosophy and the Mirror of Nature*. Princeton, NJ: Princeton University Press, 1989.

———. "The Priority of Democracy to Philosophy." In *The Virginia Statute for Religious Freedom: Its Evolution and Consequences in American History*, edited by Merrill D. Peterson and Robert C. Vaughan, 257–82. New York: Cambridge University Press, 1988.

———. "Religion as a Conversation-Stopper." *Common Knowledge* 3, no. 1 (1994): 1–6.

———. "Truth and Freedom: A Reply to Thomas McCarthy." In *Prospects for a Common Morality*, edited by Gene Outka and John P. Reeder, 279–90. Princeton, NJ: Princeton University Press, 1993.

Rosen, Michael. *Dignity: Its History and Meaning*. Cambridge, MA: Harvard University Press, 2012.

Rosenfeld, Alvin H. *A Double Dying: Reflections on Holocaust Literature*. Bloomington: Indiana University Press, 1988.

Rotberg, Robert, and Dennis Thompson, eds. *Truth v. Justice: The Morality of Truth Commissions*. Princeton, NJ: Princeton University Press, 2000.

Rousseau, Jean-Jacques. *The Social Contract: Or, The Principles of Political Rights*. Translated by Maurice Cranston. New York: Penguin, 1968.

Rye, Mark S., Kenneth I. Pargament, M. Amir Ali, Guy L. Beck, Elliot N. Dorff, Charles Hallisey, Vasudha Narayanan, and James C. Williams. "Religious Perspectives on Forgiveness." In

Forgiveness: Theory, Research, and Practice, edited by Michael E. McCullough, Kenneth I. Pargament, and Carl E. Thoreson, 17–40. New York: Guilford, 1999.

Sachs, Albie. Untitled essay in "The Task for Civil Society." In *The Healing of a Nation*? edited by Alex Boraine, Janet Levy, and Kader Asmal, 106. Cape Town, South Africa: Rondebosch, 1995

———. *Spring Is Rebellious: Arguments about Cultural Freedom*. Cape Town, South Africa: Buchu, 1990.

Sacred Congregation of Bishops. "Instruction on the Pastoral Care of People Who Migrate." August 22, 1969. https://www.acmro.catholic.org.au/.../409-instruction-de-pastorali-migratorum-cura/file.

Said, Edward W. "Nationalism, Human Rights, and Interpretation." *Raritan* 12, no. 3 (Winter 1993): 26–51.

Sandel, Michael J. "Introduction." In *Liberalism and Its Critics*, edited by Michael Sandel, 1–12. New York: New York University Press, 1984.

———. *Justice: What's the Right Thing to Do?* New York: Farrar, Straus and Giroux, 2009.

———. *Liberalism and the Limits of Justice*. Cambridge: Cambridge University Press, 1982.

Savić, Obrad, ed. *The Politics of Rights*. London: Verso, 1999.

Scarry, Eileen. *The Body in Pain: The Making and Unmaking of the World*. New York: Oxford University Press, 1985.

Schloss, J. P. "Wisdom Traditions as Mechanism for Organismal Integration: Evolutionary Perspectives on Homeostatis 'Laws of Life.'" In *Understanding Wisdom: Sources, Science, & Society*, edited by Warren S. Brown, 151–91. Philadelphia: Temple University Press, 2000.

Scholem, Gershom. "On Lament and Lamentation." Translated by Lina Barouch and Paul Schwebel. In *Lament in Jewish Thought: Philosophical, Theological and Literary Perspectives*, edited by Ilit Ferber and Paul Schwebel, 313–19. Berlin: De Gruyter, 2014.

Schrage, Wolfgang. *The Ethics of the New Testament*. Translated by David E. Green. Philadelphia: Fortress, 1988.

Schreiter, Robert J. *The Ministry of Reconciliation: Spirituality and Strategies*. Maryknoll, NY: Orbis, 1998.

———. *Reconciliation: Mission and Ministry in a Changing Social Order*. Maryknoll, NY: Orbis, 1992.

Schuller, Bruno. "The Debate on the Specific Character of a Christian Ethics." In *Readings in Moral Theology*, vol. 2, *The Distinctiveness of Christian Ethics*, edited by Charles Curran and Richard McCormick, 207–33. New York: Paulist, 1980.

Second Vatican Council. *Dignitatis humanae*. In *Vatican Council II: Constitutions, Decrees, Declarations*. Translated by Laurence Ryan. Northport, NY: Costello, 1996.

Sells, Michael. *A Bridge Betrayed: Religion and Genocide in Bosnia*. Berkeley: University of California Press, 1996.

Sen, Amartya. *Development as Freedom*. New York: Anchor, 1999.

———. "Gender Inequality and Theories of Justice." In *Women, Culture, and Development: A Study of Human Capabilities*, edited by Martha C. Nussbaum and Jonathan Glover, 259–73. Oxford, UK: Clarendon, 1995.

———. *The Idea of Justice*. Cambridge, MA: Belknap, 2009.

———. *On Ethics and Economics*. Oxford, UK: Basil Blackwell, 1987.

———. *Poverty and Famines: An Essay on Entitlement and Deprivation*. Oxford, UK: Clarendon, 1981.

———. *Resources, Values and Development*. Oxford, UK: Blackwell, 1984.

———. "Rights and Agency." *Philosophy and Public Affairs* 11, no. 1 (1982): 3–39.

———. "Well-Being, Agency, and Freedom: The Dewey Lectures 1984." *Journal of Philosophy* 82, no. 4 (1985): 169–22.

Senior, Donald. "Beloved Aliens and Exiles." In *A Promised Land, a Perilous Journey: Theological Perspectives on Migration*, edited by Daniel G. Groody and Gioacchino Campese, 20–34. Notre Dame, IN: University of Notre Dame Press, 2009.

The Sentencing Project. "Facts about Prisons and Prisoners." www.sentencingproject.org, January 2012, accessed August 22, 2012.

———. "Fact Sheet: Trends in U.S. Corrections." www.sentencingproject.org/wp-content/uploads/2016/01/Trends-in-US-Corrections.pdf, accessed September 1, 2017.

———. "Felony Disenfranchisement." www.sentencingproject.org, accessed November 7, 2014.

———. "Private Prisons in the United States," August 28, 2017. http://www.sentencingproject.org/publications/private-prisons-united-states/, accessed November 4, 2017.

Shriver, Donald W. *An Ethic for Enemies: Forgiveness in Politics*. Oxford: Oxford University Press, 1995.

Shue, Henry. *Basic Rights: Subsistence, Affluence, and U.S. Foreign Policy*. Princeton, NJ: Princeton University Press, 1980.

Slaughter, Joseph R. *Human Rights, Inc.* New York: Fordham University Press, 2007.

Smeeds, Lewis. *The Art of Forgiving*. New York: Ballantine, 1996.

Sobrino, Jon. *Companions of Jesus: The Jesuit Martyrs of El Salvador*. Maryknoll, NY: Orbis, 1990.

———. *The Spirituality of Liberation: Toward Political Holiness*. Translated by Robert R. Barr. Maryknoll, NY: Orbis, 1988.

Soyinka, Wole. *The Burden of Memory, the Muse of Forgiveness*. New York: Oxford University Press, 1999.

Spivak, Gayatri Chakravorty. "In Response: Looking Back, Looking Forward." In *Can the Subaltern Speak? Reflections on the History of an Idea*, edited by Rosalind C. Morris, 272–36. New York: Columbia University Press, 2010.

———. "Righting Wrongs." In *Human Rights, Human Wrongs*, edited by Nicholas Owen, 164–227. Oxford: Oxford University Press, 2002.

Stackhouse, Max. "Human Rights and Public Theology." In *Religion and Human Rights*, edited by James Gustafson and Peter Juviler, 12–35. Armond, NY: M. E. Sharpe, 1999.

Stearns, Jason K. *Dancing in the Glory of Monsters: The Collapse of the Congo and the Great War of Africa*. New York: Public Affairs, 2011.

Stevens, Wallace. *The Palm at the End of the Mind*. New York: Random House, 1972.

Stevenson, Bryan. "Mass Incarceration." In The 1619 Project, *New York Times Magazine*, August 18, 2019.

Stone, Dan. "Holocaust Testimony and the Challenge to the Philosophy of History." In *Social Theory after the Holocaust*, edited by Robert Fine and Charles Turner, 219–34. Liverpool, UK: Liverpool University Press, 2000.

Stout, Jeffrey. *Democracy and Tradition*. Princeton, NJ: Princeton University Press, 2004.

Stover, Eric, and Harvey M. Weinstein, eds. *My Neighbor, My Enemy: Justice and Community in the Aftermath of Mass Atrocity*. Cambridge: Cambridge University Press, 2004.

Straus, Scott. *Fundamentals of Genocide and Mass Atrocity Prevention*. Washington, DC: United States Holocaust Memorial Museum, 2016.

Stuntz, William J. *The Collapse of American Criminal Justice.* Cambridge, MA: Harvard University Press, 2011.

Suárez, Francisco. *Selections from Three Works*, vol. 1, *A Treatise on the Laws and God the Lawgiver*. Indianapolis: Liberty Fund, 2015.

Sullivan, Roger. *Immanuel Kant's Moral Theory.* Cambridge: Cambridge University Press, 1989.

Sunder, Madhavi. "Keeping Faith: Reconciling Women's Human Rights and Religion." In *Religion and Human Rights: An Introduction*, edited by John Witte and M. Christian Green, 281–98. Oxford: Oxford University Press, 2012.

Swinburne, Richard. *Responsibility and Atonement.* Oxford: Oxford University Press, 1989.

Tarimo, Aquiline, SJ, and William O'Neill, SJ. "What San Salvador Says to Nairobi: The Liberation Ethics of Ignacio Ellacuría." In *Love That Produces Hope: The Thought of Ignacio Ellacuría*, edited by Kevin F. Burke, SJ, and Robert Lassalle-Klein, 237–49. Collegeville, MN: Liturgical Press, 2006.

Tavuchis, Nicholas. *Mea Culpa: A Sociology of Apology and Reconciliation.* Stanford, CA: Stanford University Press, 1991.

Taylor, Charles. *Dilemmas and Connections.* Cambridge, MA: Belknap, 2011.

———. *Sources of the Self: The Making of the Modern Identity.* Cambridge, MA: Harvard University Press, 1989.

Third Global Conference on World Religions. "The Universal Declaration of Human Rights by World Religions." In *Human Rights and Responsibilities in the World Religions, The Library of Global Ethics and Religion*, vol. 4, edited by Joseph Runzo, Nancy M. Martin, and Arvind Sharma, 141–48. Oxford: Oneworld, 2002.

Tierney, Brian. "Church Law and Alternative Structures: A Medieval Perspective." In *Governance, Accountability, and the Future of the Catholic Church*, edited by Francis Oakley and Bruce Russett, 49–61. New York: Bloomsbury Academic, 2004.

———. *The Idea of Natural Rights: Studies on Natural Rights, Natural Law, and Church Law, 1150–1625.* Emory University Studies in Law and Religion. Atlanta: Scholars, 1997.

———. "Natural Law and Natural Rights: Old Problems and Recent Approaches." *Review of Politics* 64, no. 3 (Summer 2002): 389–406.

Tillich, Paul. *Systematic Theology.* Vol. 1. Chicago: University of Chicago Press, 1951.

Torrance, Allan J. "The Theological Grounds for Advocating Forgiveness and Reconciliation in the Sociopolitical Realm." In *Politics of Past Evil: Religion, Reconciliation, and the Dilemmas of Transitional Justice*, edited by Daniel Philpott, 45–86. Notre Dame, IN: University of Notre Dame Press, 2006.

Traer, Robert. *Faith in Human Rights: Support in Religious Traditions for a Global Struggle.* Washington, DC: Georgetown University Press, 1991.

Truth and Reconciliation Commission of South Africa (TRC). *Truth and Reconciliation Commission of South Africa Report.* Cape Town, South Africa: TRC, 1998.

Tuck, Richard. *Natural Rights Theories: Their Origin and Development.* Cambridge: Cambridge University Press, 1979.

Tutu, Desmond M. "The First Word: To Be Human Is to Be Free." In *Christianity and Human Rights: An Introduction*, edited by John Witte and Frank S. Alexander, 1–7. Cambridge: Cambridge University Press, 2010.

———. *God Has a Dream: A Vision of Hope for Our Time.* New York: Doubleday, 2004.

———. *Hope and Suffering: Sermons and Speeches.* Compiled by Mothobi Mutloatse. Edited by John Webster. Grand Rapids, MI: Eerdmans, 1984.

———. *No Future without Forgiveness.* London: Rider, 1999.

———. *The Rainbow People of God: The Making of a Peaceful Revolution.* Edited by John Allen. New York: Doubleday, 1994.

———. "The Theology of Liberation in Africa." In *African Theology en Route,* edited by Kofi Appiah-Kubi and Sergio Torres, 162–68. Papers from the Pan-African Conference of Third World Theologians, December 17–23, 1977, Accra, Ghana. Maryknoll, NY: Orbis, 1977.

Twiss, Sumner B. "Can a Perpetrator Write a Testiminio? Moral Lessons from the Dark Side." *Journal of Religious Ethics* 38, no. 1 (March 2010): 5–42.

———. "Comparative Ethics and Intercultural Human-Rights Dialogues: A Programmatic Inquiry." In *Christian Ethics: Problems and Prospects,* edited by Lisa Sowle Cahill and James F. Childress, 357–78. Cleveland: Pilgrim, 1996.

Uggen, Christopher, Sarah Shannon, and Jeff Manza. "State-Level Estimates of Felon Disenfranchisement in the United States, 2010." www.sentencingproject.org/doc/publications/fd_State_Level_Estimates_of_Felon_Disen_2010, accessed July 2012.

United Nations (UN). Universal Declaration of Human Rights. U.N.G.A. Res. 217A (III), 3(1)U.N. GAOR Res. 71, UN Doc. A/810, 1948.

United Nations Environment Programme. "Emissions Gap Report 2018: Executive Summary." https://wedocs.unep.org/bitstream/handle/20.500.11822/26879/EGR2018_ESEN.pdf?sequence=10.

United Nations High Commissioner for Refugees (UNHCR). "Global Trends: Forced Displacement in 2018." https://www.unhcr.org/globaltrends2018, accessed July 23, 2019.

———. "Protracted Refugee Situations." Report of the Executive Committee of the High Commissioner's Programme, Standing Committee 30th Meeting, UN Doc. EC/54/SC/CRP.14, June 10, 2004.

———. *The State of the World's Refugees 2006: Human Displacement in the New Millennium.* Oxford: Oxford University Press, 2006.

United Nations International Criminal Tribunal for Rwanda (ICTR). "The Prosecutor versus Jean-Paul Akayesu." Case No. ICTR-96-4-T.

United Nations Women. "Beijing Declaration and Platform for Action: Beijing+5 Political Declaration and Outcome." 1995. https://www.unwomen.org/-/media/headquarters/attachments/sections/csw/pfa_e_final_web.pdf?la=en&vs=800.

United States Conference of Catholic Bishops (USCCB). "Economic Justice for All." http://www.usccb.org/upload/economic_justice_for_all.pdf.

———. "Forming Consciences for Faithful Citizenship." http://www.usccb.org/issues-and-action/faithful-citizenship/forming-consciences-for-faithful-citizenship-title.cfm.

———. "Our First Most Cherished Liberty: A Statement on Religious Liberty." Ad Hoc Committee for Religious Liberty. March 2012. http://www.usccb.org/issues-and-action/religious-liberty/our-first-most-cherished-liberty.cfm?ref=nf.

———. *Responsibility, Rehabilitation, and Restoration: A Catholic Perspective on Crime and Criminal Justice.* Washington, DC: USCCB, 2000.

United States Conference of Catholic Bishops and Conferencia del Episcopado Mexicano. *Strangers No Longer: Together on the Journey of Hope.* Washington, DC: USCCB, 2003.

van den Anker, Christien. "A Cosmopolitan Approach to Human Rights: Global Citizenship or Local Hospitality?" In *Human Rights and Migration: Trafficking for Forced Labour,* edited by Christien van den Anker and Ilse van Liempt, 208–23. New York: Palgrave Macmillan, 2012.

van den Anker, Christien, and Ilse van Liempt, eds. *Human Rights and Migration: Trafficking for Forced Labour.* New York: Palgrave Macmillan, 2012.

Van Ness, Daniel W., and Karen Heetderks Strong. *Restoring Justice*. 2nd ed. Cincinnati: Anderson, 2002.

Verwoerd, Wilhelm. "Continuing the Discussion: Reflections from within the Truth and Reconciliation Commission." *Current Writings* 8, no. 2 (1996): 66–85.

Villa-Vicencio, Charles. "The Burden of Moral Guilt: Its Theological and Political Implications." *Journal of Church and State* 39, no. 2 (Spring 1997): 237–52.

———. "Telling One Another Stories." In *The Reconciliation of Peoples*, edited by Harold Wells and Gregory Baum, 30–41. Eugene, OR: Wipf & Stock, 1997.

———. "Truth and Reconciliation: In Tension and Unity." Occasional Paper. Johannesburg: Truth and Reconciliation Commission, 1998.

———. *Walk with Us and Listen: Political Reconciliation in Africa*. Washington, DC: Georgetown University Press, 2009.

Villa-Vicencio, Charles, and William Verwoerd. "Constructing a Report: Writing Up the 'Truth.'" In *Truth v. Justice: The Morality of Truth Commissions*, edited by Robert Rotberg and Dennis Thompson, 279–94. Princeton, NJ: Princeton University Press, 2000.

Vincent, R. J. *Human Rights and International Relations*. Cambridge: Cambridge University Press, 1986.

Vlastos, Gregory. "Justice and Equality." In *Social Justice*, edited by Richard B Brandt, 31–72. Englewood Cliffs, NJ: Prentice-Hall, 1962.

Volf, Miroslav. *Exclusion and Embrace: A Theological Exploration of Identity, Otherness, and Reconciliation*. Nashville, TN: Abingdon, 1996.

von Hirsch, Andrew, Julian Roberts, Anthony E. Bottoms, Kent Roach, and Maria Schiff, eds. *Restorative Justice and Criminal Justice: Competing or Reconcilable Paradigm?* Portland, OR: Hart, 2003.

von Kellenbach, Katharina. *The Mark of Cain: Guilt and Denial in the Post-War Lives of Nazi Perpetrators*. Oxford: Oxford University Press, 2013.

Wagacha, John Burton, and John Guiney. "The Plight of Urban Refugees in Nairobi, Kenya." In *Refugee Rights, Ethics Advocacy, and Africa*, edited by David Hollenbach, SJ, 91–102. Washington, DC: Georgetown University Press, 2008.

Waldron, Jeremy. *Nonsense upon Stilts: Bentham, Burke and Marx on the Rights of Man*. New York: Methuen, 1987.

———. *The Right to Private Property*. Oxford: Clarendon, 1988.

Walzer, Michael. *Exodus and Revolution*. New York: Basic, 1985.

———. "The Moral Standing of States." *Philosophy and Public Affairs* 9 (1980): 209–29.

———. "Nation and Universe." *The Tanner Lectures on Human Values XI*, edited by G. B. Petersen, 509–56. Salt Lake City: University of Utah Press, 1990.

———. *Spheres of Justice: A Defense of Pluralism and Equality*. New York: Basic, 1983.

———. *Thick and Thin: Moral Argument at Home and Abroad*. Notre Dame, IN: University of Notre Dame Press, 1994.

Weber, Max. *Economy and Society*. 2 vols. Edited by G. Roth and C. Wittich. Berkeley: University of California Press, 1978.

———. *From Max Weber*. Translated and edited by H. H. Gerth and C. Wright Mills. New York: Oxford University Press, 1946.

Weil, Simone. *Waiting for God*. Translated by Emma Craufurd. New York: G. P. Putnam's Sons, 1951.

Weithman, Paul J. *Religion and the Obligations of Citizenship*. Cambridge: Cambridge University Press, 2002.

Wells, Harold, and Gregory Baum, eds. *The Reconciliation of Peoples: Challenge to the Churches.* Eugene, OR: Wipf & Stock, 1997.

West, Cornell. *Prophesy Deliverance: An Afro-American Revolutionary Christianity.* Philadelphia: Westminster, 1982.

Westermann, Claus. "The Role of the Lament in the Theology of the Old Testament." *Interpretation* 28 (1974): 20–38.

Weston, Burns H. "Human Rights." In *Human Rights in the World Community: Issues and Action,* edited by Richard Pierre Claude and Burns H. Weston, 12–28. Philadelphia: University of Pennsylvania Press, 1989.

Wheelwright, Philip. *Metaphor and Reality.* Bloomington: Indiana University Press, 1972.

Wiesel, Elie. "The Holocaust as Literary Inspiration." In *Dimensions of the Holocaust: Lectures at Northwestern University,* annotated by Elliot Lefkovitz, edited by Elie Wiesel et al., 5–19. Evanston, IL: Northwestern University Press, 1990.

———. "A Tribute to Human Rights." In *The Universal Declaration of Human Rights: Fifty Years and Beyond,* edited by Yael Danieli, Elsa Stamatopoulou, and Clarence J. Dias, 3–4. Amityville, NY: Baywood, 1999.

Wiesel, Elie, Lucy Dawidowicz, Dorothy Rabinowicz, Robert Brown, Lacy Baldin Smith. "Dimensions of the Holocaust: Lectures at Northwestern University." Annotated by Elliot Lefkovitz. Evanston, IL: Northwestern University Press, 1990.

Wiesenthal, Simon. *The Sunflower: On the Possibilities and Limits of Forgiveness.* Symposium on Simon Wiesenthal. Rev. ed. New York: Schocken, 1998.

Wilkins, Burleigh Taylor. *The Problem of Burke's Political Philosophy.* Oxford: Clarendon, 1967.

Willemsens, Jolien. "Restorative Justice: A Discussion of Punishment." In *Repositioning Restorative Justice,* edited by Lode Walgrave, 24–42. Cullompton, UK: Willan, 2003.

Williams, Bernard. *Ethics and the Limits of Philosophy.* Cambridge, MA: Harvard University Press, 1805.

———. "An Inconsistent Form of Relativism." In *Relativism: Cognitive and Moral,* edited by Michael Krausz and Jack W. Meiland, 171–74. Notre Dame, IN: Notre Dame University Press, 1982.

———. *Making Sense of Humanity: And Other Philosophical Papers, 1982–1993.* Cambridge: Cambridge University Press, 1995.

———. *Moral Luck: Philosophical Papers, 1973–1980.* New York: Cambridge University Press, 1981.

———. *Problems of the Self: Philosophical Papers, 1956–1972.* Cambridge: Cambridge University Press, 1973.

Wilson, Neil. "Substances without Substrata." *Review of Metaphysics* 12 (1959): 521–39.

Witte, John, and Frank S. Alexander, eds. *Christianity and Human Rights: An Introduction.* Cambridge: Cambridge University Press, 2010.

Witte, John, and M. Christian Green, eds. *Religion and Human Rights: An Introduction.* Oxford: Oxford University Press, 2012.

Wittgenstein, Ludwig. *On Certainty.* Translated by Denis Paul and G. E. M. Anscombe. New York: Harper & Row, 1969.

———. *Philosophical Investigations.* 3rd ed. Translated by G. E. M. Anscombe. New York: Macmillan, 1958.

———. *Tractatus Logico-Philosophicus.* Translated by C. K. Ogden. Mineola, NY: Dover, 1998.

Wolterstorff, Nicholas. *Justice: Rights and Wrongs.* Princeton, NJ: Princeton University Press, 2008.

———. *Justice in Love.* Grand Rapids, MI: Eerdmans, 2011.

———. "Modern Protestant Developments in Human Rights." In *Christianity and Human Rights: An Introduction,* edited by John Witte Jr. and Frank S. Alexander, 155–72. Cambridge: Cambridge University Press, 2010.

———. *Religion in the Public Square: The Place of Religious Conviction in Political Debate.* New York: Rowman & Littlefield, 1997.

Wright, Martin. "Is It Time to Question the Concept of Punishment?" In *Repositioning Restorative Justice,* edited by Walgrave Lode, 3–23. Cullompton, UK: Willan, 2003.

Yeats, W. B. *Collected Poems: W. B. Yeats.* London: Macmillan, 2010.

Young, Iris Marion. *Justice and the Politics of Difference.* Princeton, NJ: Princeton University Press, 1990.

Young, James E. *The Texture of Memory: Holocaust Memorials and Meaning.* New Haven, CT: Yale University Press, 1993.

Zalaquett, José. "Balancing Ethical Imperatives and Political Constraints: The Dilemma of New Democracies Confronting Past Human Rights Violations." *Hastings Law Journal* 43 (August 1992): 1425–38.

———. *Introduction to the English Edition of the Report of the Chilean National Commission of Truth and Reconciliation.* Translated by Philip E. Berryman. Notre Dame, IN: University of Notre Dame Press, 1993.

Zehr, Howard. *Changing Lenses: Restorative Justice for Our Times.* Harrisonburg, VA: Herald, 2015.

———. *The Little Book of Restorative Justice.* Intercourse, PA: Good Books, 2007.

INDEX

Notes and tables are indicated by n and t following the page number.

ABOUT THE AUTHOR

WILLIAM R. O'NEILL, SJ, is a member of the Society of Jesus and professor emeritus of social ethics at the Jesuit School of Theology of Santa Clara University. He held the Lo Schiavo Chair at USF's Lane Center from 2018 to 2019. He received his doctorate from Yale University in 1988. His writings include *The Ethics of Our Climate: Hermeneutics and Ethical Theory* and book chapters and journal articles addressing questions of human rights, social reconciliation, restorative justice, refugee and immigration policy, mass incarceration, and the Church and public reason. He has served as Catholic chaplain at the Federal Women's Prison in Dublin, California, and is currently serving with the Jesuit Refugee Service in Nairobi, Kenya.